Also by Daniel Mark Epstein

WHAT LIPS MY LIPS
HAVE KISSED

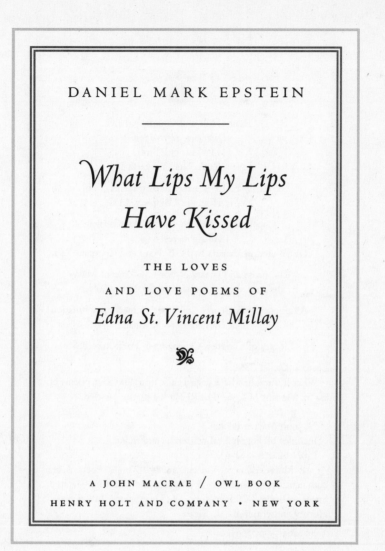

DANIEL MARK EPSTEIN

*What Lips My Lips
Have Kissed*

THE LOVES
AND LOVE POEMS OF
Edna St. Vincent Millay

A JOHN MACRAE / OWL BOOK
HENRY HOLT AND COMPANY · NEW YORK

Henry Holt and Company, LLC
Publishers since 1866
115 West 18th Street
New York, New York 10011

Henry Holt® is a registered trademark of
Henry Holt and Company, LLC.

The prose and poetry of Edna St. Vincent Millay
are quoted by permission of the Millay Society.

All quotes from George Dillon are printed by permission
of Nan Sherman Sussman.

Library of Congress Cataloging-in-Publication Data

Epstein, Daniel Mark.
What lips my lips have kissed : the loves and love poems of
Edna St. Vincent Millay / Daniel Mark Epstein.—1st ed.
    p. cm.
"A John Macrae book."
Includes bibliographical references and index.
ISBN 0-8050-7181-4
    1. Millay, Edna St. Vincent, 1892–1950. 2. Poets, American—
20th century—Biography. 3. Women and literature—United
States—History—20th century. 4. Love poetry, American—
History and criticism. I. Title.

PS3525.I495 Z636 2001
811'.52—dc21
[B]   2001024543

Henry Holt books are available for special promotions
and premiums. For details contact: Director, Special Markets.

First published in hardcover in 2001 by Henry Holt and Company

First Owl Books Edition 2002

A John Macrae / Owl Book

Designed by Victoria Hartman

Printed in the United States of America

1 3 5 7 9 10 8 6 4 2

For Rosemary Knower,

Vincenti dabo ei manna abscondium

—Revelation 2:17

CONTENTS

❧

PART 3

Marriage

PREFACE

❧

This book is based upon unpublished diaries, journals, and letters to and from Edna St. Vincent Millay that have been read by no more than four people since they were written more than half a century ago. These include the poet's sister, Norma Ellis, who jealously guarded the documents until her death in 1986, and possibly one other biographer whom she engaged to write a book in the 1970s.

When I discovered in 1999 that these documents had landed at the Library of Congress "unprocessed" but might nevertheless be made available to a biographer under certain conditions and constraints still dictated by the poet's estate, I lost no time in securing the necessary legal permissions. I arrived at the Library of Congress Reading Room in midsummer to find six tall filing cabinets stuffed with twenty thousand items: papers, books, and photographs, in no discernible order. The librarians were apologetic, resourceful, and tirelessly accommodating. I dived into that welter of twentieth-century history and Millay's private life and did not come up for air until autumn, when I had answered for myself certain questions that had haunted me since I was a boy and first read Millay's poetry. These were the exact riddles that troubled Edmund Wilson, her friend and one of her lovers, the same questions that had been raised, or avoided, by the six biographers whose books about Millay had been published, from Elizabeth Atkins in 1936 to Anne Cheney in 1975. (More recent biographers of Millay have been discouraged by the inaccessibility of the poet's papers.)

Who was the girl who wrote "Renascence," that precocious marvel of twentieth-century poetry? Out of what reflection, childhood trauma, or spiritual odyssey did it come? Who were Millay's lovers, the men and women who inspired the unforgettable sonnets? And after such a public career (she was one of the few American poets to become a celebrity), why did she disappear into seclusion after 1940?

The answers are there, in that slippery mountain of fading, crumbling literature, legal and medical records, and canceled checks. It was my privilege, during months of such excitement that often my hands trembled, to get a rare view of a poet's psyche.

❧

She was America's foremost love poet, a poet of the erotic impulse and erotic condition whose finest lyrics invite comparison with the sonnets of Sir Philip Sidney and Elizabeth Barrett Browning, and the amorous verses of Catullus and Horace. She saw herself in the tradition of English and European classicism, and those poets were her models, as she wrote:

> What lips my lips have kissed, and where, and why
> I have forgotten, and what arms have lain
> Under my head till morning; but the rain
> Is full of ghosts tonight, that tap and sigh
> Upon the glass and listen for reply,
> And in my heart there stirs a quiet pain
> For unremembered lads that not again
> Will turn to me at midnight with a cry.
> Thus in the winter stands the lonely tree,
> Nor knows what birds have vanished one by one,
> Yet knows its boughs more silent than before:
> I cannot say what loves have come and gone,
> I only know that summer sang in me
> A little while, that in me sings no more.
>
> (Sonnet XLII)

The American poets who followed her—her friends Elinor Wylie and Louise Bogan, and Bogan's friend Theodore Roethke—each wrote individual love poems of great beauty. But no one else managed to sustain an inspiration like Millay's, beginning with "Bluebeard," written in 1916, and culminating in the book-length sonnet sequence *Fatal Interview* in 1931.

Of the American poets who preceded her—Poe, Whitman, and Dickinson—the love poems of all three suffer from varying degrees of abstraction; only the Whitman of *Calamus* preserves the heat of the body in lovemaking. Yet some of his verse lacks lyric concentration. Such heat as his love poems generate is sometimes dissipated in a frame too loosely knocked together to hold them. In the case of Poe, on the other hand, or Dickinson, the most perfect architecture serves as no more than a haunted house for lovers who had less substance in life than in art.

Millay's lovers were flesh-and-blood men and women, and her sonnets preserve them in vivid detail:

Love me no more, now let the god depart,
If love be grown so bitter to your tongue!
Here is my hand; I bid you from my heart
Fare well, fare very well, be always young.
As for myself, mine was a deeper drouth:
I drank and thirsted still; but I surmise
My kisses now are sand against your mouth,
Teeth in your palm and pennies on your eyes.
(from *Fatal Interview*)

If she had written no poems but the love poems, Millay would nonetheless warrant our serious consideration. For after all, when we think of poetry do we not often think first of love poems? Of Sappho and Swinburne? Of Marlowe's "Come live with me and be my love," Shakespeare's "Shall I compare thee to a summer's day?" Of Dante's Beatrice and Petrarch's Laura and Yeats's fiery Maude Gonne? Cultures are distinguished and measured, and nations are characterized by their love poems, their approach to "this passion compared to which the rose seems crude and the perfume of violets like the sound of thunder" (Caid Ali). Compared to the French, Latin, English, Italian, and Spanish literatures, our American tradition offers very little love poetry. Our "major" poets of the twentieth century—T. S. Eliot, Marianne Moore, Robert Frost, and Wallace Stevens—together did not produce three love poems comparable to Millay's "Pity me not because the light of day," "Love Is Not All: It Is Not Meat Nor Drink," or this, from *Fatal Interview*:

Not in a silver casket cool with pearls
Or rich with red corundum or with blue,
Locked, and the key withheld, as other girls
Have given their loves, I give my love to you;
Not in a lovers' knot, not in a ring . . .
. . . Love in the open hand, no thing but that,
Ungemmed, unhidden, wishing not to hurt,
As one should bring you cowslips in a hat
Swung from the hand, or apples in her skirt . . .

The modernist temperament of Eliot, Moore, Frost, and Stevens shrank from such outpourings. We have to step down to the "minor" poets (minor by current academic consensus) such as e. e. cummings, John Crowe Ransom, William Carlos Williams, and H.D., to find love poetry of enduring value, almost as if the heat of their passion had made them unfit for the American

Pantheon of Major Poets. There is that much of the Puritan still weighing upon the arbiters of such matters.

But Edna St. Vincent Millay's contribution did not begin, nor did it end, with her love sonnets. In 1912, at the age of twenty, she published "Renascence," a 214-line poem, in a literary annual called *The Lyric Year*. It is a visionary narrative, a cosmic love poem, recounting a spiritual epiphany. The poem's impact was sensational and enduring. In America it has always been extremely difficult to cause a sensation by publishing a poem. William Cullen Bryant did it in 1817 when he was seventeen with "Thanatopsis," widely regarded as the first important poem written by an American. In 1845 Poe managed it with "The Raven," and in 1899 a now largely forgotten poet named Edwin Markham made a sensation with a sentimental celebration of the workingman called "The Man with the Hoe." After Millay's "Renascence" no individual poems of merit have registered as public events, excepting Eliot's "The Waste Land" and Allen Ginsberg's "Howl." With the exception of Markham's poem, all of these works are acknowledged classics, appreciated for their intrinsic value as well as their cultural influence. Each was proof of genius. Each spoke for its time. To have written any one of them guaranteed its author a place in literary history.

And then there was Millay's career in the theater. In December of 1919 her chamber verse-drama *Aria da Capo*, which she directed, opened at the Provincetown Playhouse on Macdougal Street in Greenwich Village. This was not her first play. She had written and acted in several of her own plays when she was a student at Vassar, being the veteran of nearly fifty roles in amateur and professional stage productions from the age of fifteen. In a season of dramas at the Provincetown that included pieces by Eugene O'Neill and Floyd Dell, Millay's poetic, poignant masque *Aria da Capo* with its antiwar theme was a resounding hit, lauded by critics and audiences alike. If she had not already made her name with "Renascence," then *Aria da Capo* would have made her famous. Within a year her play was seen in dozens of cities coast to coast in productions both authorized and pirated, as well as in England, France, and Germany. She was twenty-eight years old at the time, and most of the poetry upon which her literary reputation would rest had yet to be seen.

In short order she published *A Few Figs from Thistles* (1920), *Second April* (1921), and *The Harp-Weaver and Other Poems* (1923), winning the Pulitzer Prize in poetry that year, the first woman ever to garner that honor. If she had died then, she might have been canonized, embalmed in the eternal honey of youth and beauty that has preserved John Keats, Percy Shelley, Sylvia Plath,

Marilyn Monroe, and Dylan Thomas. It was not to be. In 1926 she composed
the libretto for *The King's Henchman*, an opera with music by Deems Taylor.
The world premiere at the Metropolitan Opera in New York City, February
17, 1927, was a resounding success, and music historians consider the work
to be the first important opera written by Americans. That winter it had a
profitable run in New York, and the touring company would take the show
to audiences in thirty U.S. cities in a year's time. Harper's edition of the
libretto entered its eighteenth printing in November of 1927, and Millay's
new book of verse, *The Buck in the Snow*, published in September of 1928,
sold forty thousand copies before Christmas.

So now Edna St. Vincent Millay was not only famous for writing poetry
of undeniable genius, she was also rich. Let it be said that there has never
been nearly enough fame or money to go around in the world of poetry. So
people whose enthusiasm for Millay's work had become, with her increasing
celebrity, pinched by envy, now were eaten alive by it. Also, she belonged
to a nineteenth-century tradition the modernists were laboring to dismantle.
The modernist critics had no just cause to disparage Millay's brand of classicism in the 1920s, so they ostentatiously ignored it, as one might avoid the
Forum in Rome, hoping eventually it might fall down.

Edna St. Vincent Millay was one of the last important American poets to
hold the devoted interest of the serious general reader—that is, the reader
who is not a professor, critic, or poet. Of the forty thousand who purchased
The Buck in the Snow before Christmas of 1928, and the one hundred thousand who read the book as it passed from hand to hand, the majority were
passionate common readers. They had no idea they were an endangered
species. Soon Eliot, Pound, and their followers would see to it that poems
not bristling with paradox, irony, ambiguity, and allusion would not be called
poems anymore. All versifying that appealed to an audience as large as Millay's would be regarded, prima facie, as sentimental fodder for the dull-
witted and unenlightened.

The poetry audience (never a thick-skinned lot) got the message. In the
1940s they went into hiding with their battered, gilt-edged volumes of Tennyson, Longfellow, and Millay, disappearing into private studies where the
modernists might not snicker at them. Just about this time Millay played into
the hands of her enemies by writing propaganda poems for the Allies. No
one had explained to her that a "serious" poet must not write poetry with
an "ulterior motive, such as, for instance, the winning of a world-war to keep
democracy alive," as she wrote to her editor. If anyone had posed the art-
for-art's-sake argument to this stubborn woman, she would have turned a

deaf ear. She had always gone her own way. Her husband was a Dutchman whose family and friends lived in terror of the Germans, and during the war Millay wrote little other than war poetry and patriotic articles. The poems that appeared in *Make Bright the Arrows* (1940) were shrill and rhetorical; she soon regretted having published these, as literary critics fell upon them triumphantly, citing the work as proof of what they had always suspected. This, they declared, was not a great artist, but rather a "personality" blown hither and thither by sentiment. Now the war had distracted her, as love did once, and the war had reduced her lines to hysteria and bathos.

Although Millay would write praiseworthy poetry again before her death in 1950, her reputation never recovered from the lapses of *Make Bright the Arrows* and the erosion of the general audience that had bought her books. These readers were dying off in the 1940s and 1950s, never to be replaced. Setting aside the fans of Allen Ginsberg and Lawrence Ferlinghetti (whom Millay would have enjoyed—*vide* her enthusiasm for Kenneth Patchen), by the last half of the twentieth century few were left to read poetry but "professionals" and bored, reluctant students. What had always been a rich and vital passion became a dreary science.

Now, I do not mean to discredit the poet-critics Eliot, Pound, and Moore, their poetry, or the cadre of brilliant scholar-critics such as William Empson and R. P. Blackmur who promoted avant-garde verse. These men and women rebelled against cliché, cant, rhetoric, and sentimentality that had clouded efficient expression. They revolutionized the medium of poetry, making it more responsive to the volatile emotions and chaotic perceptions of the twentieth century. But their victory came at the expense of some very fine poets. It could not have been foreseen, and it could scarcely have been desired, that the modernists, in burying the sentimental Sara Teasdale, Edgar Lee Masters, and Carl Sandburg, would also push deep into the shadows the superb E. A. Robinson, Robinson Jeffers, or a great rearguard poet and verse dramatist such as Edna St. Vincent Millay.

She had been a world celebrity, like Housman or Gide. She never needed anyone's help. She helped others. She had always been famous. Who could imagine her being forgotten? Fiercely intelligent, revolutionary in morals, blessed with beauty of line and the rare musical gift Auden calls the ability to enchant the ear, who could think Millay would ever go unread by lovers, by students on college campuses? Author of the mystical "Renascence," the magical *Aria da Capo*, and the triumphant *King's Henchman*, by fiat a major poet before her thirty-fifth birthday, who could predict that in 1976 her name would be left out of *The New Oxford Book of American Verse*?

How did it happen that the professors who made spacious rooms in the canon and in voluminous anthologies for poets who addressed every theme but romantic love could find no corner for the woman who sang so shamelessly and beautifully the delights and the torments of eros—our most illustrious love poet?

· PART I ·

Love o' Dreams

LOVE O' DREAMS

In the town of Camden, Maine, at midnight of October 3, 1911, in the lower tenement of a clapboard house on Chestnut Street overlooking the harbor, a girl was absorbed in a curious ritual. If a passerby had been tempted by the flicker of candlelight beneath a shade to peep into the sparely furnished bedroom, he might have thought the girl was mad, or the votary of some pagan cult.

She was writing in a small brown notebook, and saying aloud to herself and to invisible presences strange and passionate words:

"Be these my fairies: Strong-Heart, Clean-Hand, Clear-Eye, Brave-Soul, Sweet-Tongue, and Thou—my Robin Good-Fellow, who will come unseen, unheard, unqueried by all but me, and with thy shadowy flail thresh for me 'In one night, ere glimpse of morn . . . / What ten day-laborers could not end.' "

In her white nightgown, with her long braids of red hair brushing her thighs, she looked more like a girl than she actually was. The nightgown concealed the petite but perfectly formed figure of a nineteen-year-old woman.

"We have been betrothed just half a year tonight," she chanted. "I have been faithful to you. I have loved you more and better every day. It seems to me you might come before long. I am very lonely. I wish I might go to sleep tonight with my head on your arm. Or if I might only know just where you are this minute. You would seem very near to me even though you were way across the world. You have been everything to me for half a year. . . . I start in tomorrow on the second half and I am going to try and make it better than the first. I must keep always before my mind the thought of what you want me to be. I will try harder than ever before. But I am so tired! But when you come I shall rest."

There was no one in the candlelit room but Edna St. Vincent Millay. In the night sky over the town shone the constellation of the winged horse Pegasus, beloved of the Muses. The four-room flat included a sitting room with two more windows on the harbor side, the kitchen, and another bedroom looking out on the stained-glass front window of the Baptist Church. Millay's sisters Norma, eighteen, and Kathleen, sixteen, were sleeping in the other bedroom, and her mother, nurse Cora Buzzell Millay, was away in nearby Rockland working on a medical case. Cora Millay and her husband were divorced, and the girls' father lived far away.

Vincent, as she was called, rose from her writing table. She imagined her lover was seated in a mahogany-paneled room reading by the light of a study lamp. She parted imaginary curtains and coyly looked through them, pretending he could see her.

"How do you like my hair, sir? All you can see is my head now for I'm hiding. Wait just a minute, and I'll come out. I am wearing a fluffy lavendar thing over my nightdress. It is very soft and long and trails on the rug behind me. My bare feet sink into the rug. My hair is in two wavy red braids over my shoulders. My eyes are very sweet and serious. My mouth is wistful."

She imagined him watching her from his chair. She moved slowly over the rug toward him. She rested her head gently on his knee. Her braids curled in fiery coils on the floor.

With the grace of a trained actress the girl mimed the love scene. She looked into her imaginary lover's eyes. She felt him gather her into his arms. Her gowns fell softly about her feet as she kissed his face. . . .

On her ring finger she wore a tin ring she had found in a "fortune" cake. Her ghost ring, she called it, "a cheap little thing in imitation of a solitaire, just the sort of ring to link me to a 'Love-o'-Dreams'; I love it with a passion that is painful." Rising from the floor, she kissed the ring on her hand seven times.

The ritual had begun with the lighting of a wax candle from the drawer of the writing table, and the entertaining of her spirit lover would not end until the candle had burned out—that is, if no one interrupted her. This bizarre ceremony, which the girl had been practicing on the third of every month since April 3, 1911, when she formally "consecrated" her soul to this "love o' dreams," was not so much the evidence of madness as it was an elaborate defense against it.

She was a vulnerable, neurasthenic girl whom life had dealt a difficult hand. Born in Rockland, Maine, on February 22, 1892, the eldest of three sisters, she had seen her father for the last time early in 1901 when her mother threw him out (for "bitter abuse," according to the divorce testimony). In September of that same year, all three girls—ages nine, eight, and five—were stricken with typhoid fever and certainly would have died had it not been for their mother Cora's skill in nursing. After that early trauma, life proved to be one struggle after another, yet the women survived with stubborn determination and a kind of desperate humor. Vincent won amateur poetry prizes, starred in stage plays, and graduated with honors from Camden High School in June of 1909.

But since graduation the young poet and actress had suffered from a series of crises—physical, emotional, and spiritual—that led her periodically to the edge of despair.

Now it seemed that only a perfect love, or the raptures of poetry, could save her:

> My anguished spirit, like a bird,
> Beating against my lips I heard;
> Yet lay the weight so close about
> There was no room for it without.
> And so beneath the weight lay I
> And suffered death, but could not die.
> (from "Renascence")

This is the story of a girl locked in a room that was her life in Camden, Maine, in 1911, and how she used her pen like a magic key to unlock the door. In order to understand the sorcery that Millay worked to win her liberty, in that hard year when she began to write the great poem "Renascence," we must go back to an earlier beginning, the story of her mother, Cora Millay, recently divorced, and how she scratched out a living for her three daughters from the rocky Maine soil.

CORA

They had been poor, poor relations thrown upon the mercy and irregular charity of uncles and aunts and grandparents from Newburyport, Massachusetts, Cora's hometown, to Ring Island located just across the Merrimac River, and back again, finally washing up in Camden. From spare room to spare room in farmhouses and town houses, mother and daughters moved with their trunks of books and papers and homemade clothing and precious few other belongings dragging behind them.

First, during the winter of 1901 they stayed with Cora's brother Charles Buzzell and his wife, Jenny, on Ring Island while the girls went to school there. Cora worked in Newburyport until she could afford rent on a bungalow at 78 Lime Street. But they had not lived long in that little house before Cora went up to Maine to get her divorce, thinking that might guarantee her alimony. She left her daughters in the care of a Miss Kendall in Camden while she journeyed alone to the court in Rockland, where she received her divorce decree on January 11, 1904.

That winter was the coldest in memory, with temperatures plunging to forty degrees below, and Cora and her daughters returned to Newburyport in the throes of a coal shortage. Cora was too proud to take from the city supply of coal, although it was offered to them as it was to all the poor. Cora's younger sister Clem bought them half a ton, and with the coke from the gashouse, and using shingles ripped from a ramshackle house next door, they were able to keep one fire going in their tiny kitchen. Cora would throw the shingles over the fence, and after school the girls would pick them up to put on the fire.

But then Cora contracted influenza and was so sick she could not get out of bed. The doctor said her illness came from overwork and undernourishment. "Not a good combination," Cora later remarked with grim humor. "I was away down, subnormal, pulse and temperature, and nothing could seem to bring me up." Her brother Charlie fixed up her life insurance, that was how serious things looked. And her well-to-do sister Clem stopped by often, sweeping in wearing "a heavy cape of double-faced goods, which the girls will never forget," Cora wrote.

"For, with all the work there was to do here, with a sick mother, and all in school, Aunt Clem never took her cape off on any of these calls. Clem did bring in things for me to eat, which she had cooked at home, at Aunt Sue's. But there was no help for the little ones who might be left alone now, any minute." (These quotes, with their lilting Irish rhythms, are from Cora's writings. She frequently wrote about herself in the third-person maternal, as "the mother.") Cora hung on, while the girls went to school and did the housework. "Vincent had learned to make yeast bread, and it was excellent," Cora recalled. It was during her mother's near-fatal illness that her eldest daughter learned to take command of the household. "And many a night the mother went to bed when she did not have much idea of seeing the morning. But she did not tell them so." She did not have to tell them: children know these things instinctively.

Despite Cora's tendency to self-dramatize her life in her letters and memoirs, in this case she did not distort the truth. The forty-year-old mother of twelve-year-old Edna St. Vincent Millay nearly died during the winter of 1904. Her health rallied in the spring, just in time to take care of her youngest child, eight-year-old Kathleen. "Kathleen was sick, as if stricken. The little limbs unnaturally unruly, and the child sick, as they thought, unto death." Kathleen's fever marked the onset of the dread disease that one day would be known as infantile paralysis—polio.

That summer, having seen enough hard luck in Newburyport, "the mother picked up some things, and turned the key in the Lime Street House, and took the children to Maine." First they went to Union, where they stayed for a while with friends who were obliged to Cora, whose nursing had saved the life of their youngest boy. From there they went to the hill farm of Uncle Fred Millay, where there was milk and cream, horses, and a blueberry pasture where the girls loved to play.

"For the little one [Kathleen] to climb toward the blueberry pasture she needed help, and the queer pitiful limping hurried gait was sad to see. For the left leg would not do its part, nor would the left hand, for it shook and trembled so that the only way she could keep it still, when she was eating, using the right, was to hold it between her knees."

There at the farm Cora nursed Kathleen day and night, massaging her legs and arms several times a day with cocoa butter and giving the child infusions of skullcap "to quiet the little shattered nerves."

From there Uncle Austin Millay took them in during the time that his wife was away nursing. But Uncle Austin was drunk much of the time, and a mean drunk he was, too, so "the family of visitors moved on, and went for a short visit to Eva Fales, a cousin of mother's at Beech-Woods Street, Thomaston . . . then they went to Camden, and up to Aunt Clara's till some other arrangement could be made."

Aunt Clara Millay was a big, handsome woman, goodhearted and generous, who kept a boardinghouse on Washington Street just on the outskirts of town. Grandpa Buzzell was riding down from Searsmont to get Vincent and Norma, and frail Kathleen was going to stay with Aunt Clara while Cora took a nursing job for Professor John Tufts, a pianist who was to be operated on in Rockland before returning to Camden. Cora would attend him in his big house on Chestnut Street.

All summer long Cora took care of Mr. Tufts, walking a mile uphill and down each day to Aunt Clara's so she could give Kathleen her cocoa butter rubbings and skullcap infusions and doses of cod liver oil. Then in October she received a letter from Grandpa Buzzell's wife, Delia, saying that the old man was on the verge of a nervous breakdown with the racket of so many youngsters in his little house (they had three boys living there before Vincent and Norma arrived). "She did not know but that he might be going crazy or out of his mind, and she was uneasy about the girls and their being there."

❧

A man from Appleton who boarded at Aunt Clara's when he was staying in Camden owned a small rental house in the field downhill from Washington Street, between Aunt Clara's and the river that powered the mills. Across the Megunticook River was nothing but woodlands, and up the hill across the road rose the cemetery and the rocky height of Mount Battie.

The dilapidated house in the field had been empty for some time. The man from Appleton said that Cora could have the little house for her and her children to live in. If they would just clean it and make certain repairs for which he would provide the materials—like painting and papering—he would give them a month's rent free.

The doctors in Camden wanted Cora to work for them there and in the outlying towns. So she decided to return to Newburyport only long enough to close up the house on Lime Street and then make a new home for herself and her family in that house in the field in Camden.

On November 4, 1904, still in Newburyport packing the trunks, she wrote to Vincent and Norma at Grandpa Buzzell's in Searsmont. "Be a good lot of girls and mind Delia, and be good to Grandpa. Kiss each other for Mama who is so homesick for you she is crying while she is writing. I hope you are all well, and that Kathleen is gaining all the time. Don't get discouraged because Mama seems so long; she is doing a man's work; and you just plan how cosy we'll have our new little home, when once it is cleaned and settled and banked up snug and warm for the winter. Somehow I don't dread this winter as I did last . . ."

Between 1901 and 1904 they seem to have had no permanent home, but made do wherever they could be together for a few weeks or months. Cora traveled with a trunkload of classic books: Shakespeare, Milton, Burns, Scott, etc., and read aloud to her daughters with a dramatic voice, slightly inflected with an Irish brogue. As a girl she had acted in amateur theatricals. She sang beautifully in a mellow mezzo-soprano, and played Bach, Beethoven, and Mendelssohn on the piano, when one was handy. She firmly shaped her daughters in her own image, though with a sense of humor.

Soon they had their own language and pet names for one another. They had their own customs and legends, binding them each to each while separating them from the world of strangers and protecting them from those who would never understand their ways. Men often felt threatened by the women, as if they were a coven of witches.

After years of wandering, the prospect of having their first house together in this picturesque and welcoming suburb of Camden, a house at the edge of town but not entirely out of it, was a relief to them all. The house stood in an open field, with Cora's aunt's house on the town side, and a meadow on the other side sloping down to the Camden Mill. In back was another field, and below that was the Megunticook River, flowing from the lake of the same name through a valley and on down through the town to the harbor. This current turned the wheels of the five woolen mills that constituted the town's main industry.

In autumn, under the red maples and golden leaves of the oak trees, the fields were colorful with staghorn sumac, wild blue asters, wild pink orchids, fleabane, and goldenrod; in the spring there would be violets and arbutus, dandelions and trilliums. In the summer the sisters played hide-and-seek in the grasses that were never mown, and swam in the river on days when the water was not tinted from the dyes that colored the cloths in the mill vats, fashioning water-wings out of pillowcases blown up like bladders.

Cora recalled: "Another joy in the tall grasses was when it was raining hard. Then there was nothing the girls so much liked as stripping, and putting on thin print dresses and running out into the grass and leaping about in the rain, letting the summer showers soak them until it ran in little rivers from their hair and faces. Then they came in and stripped and I rubbed them down with a rough Turkish towel till they glowed and tingled amid their laughter."

But the house, neglected by the landlord, was brutally cold in the winter. When the rent was not paid up, Cora could not press too hard about repairs. "The snow outside made as good a winter playground as the grasses in summer, but there is need of warm cover within reach to make playing in the snow drifts enjoyable. This we had, but it did not cover the whole house."

Their dwelling was no more than four small rooms. On the ground floor was the kitchen, which had the only indoor plumbing, a cold water sink that had to trickle constantly so the pipe would not freeze. One day the water ran over the basin, and Cora returned home from work to find the girls merrily skating on the kitchen floor.

Next to the kitchen was the dining room, which in good weather also served as the library and music room. There was a cooking stove in the kitchen, but in the coldest part of winter these lower rooms could not be heated. The main coal stove stood in the living room upstairs (where Cora and Kathleen slept), next to the bedroom of the older girls. Everything in the house that had to be kept from freezing—milk, potatoes, onions, bread, and butter—had to be taken upstairs to the living room. "And this was a chore, and did not add to the order of the room," Cora remembered.

"Mother had a lot of work nursing, right away," Cora recalled, referring to herself, "and the doctors liked her. And after a little while she got more pay, but for a long time not more than ten dollars a week. And she took care of the sick folks all the time, night and day, unless at times when someone would give her a chance to go lie down," and when she insisted upon going home to check up on her girls.

As soon as she could afford it she had a telephone installed so she could keep in touch with Vincent from the patients' homes. The telephone, and Aunt Clara's boardinghouse a few hundred yards across the meadow, were Vincent's only lifelines on many cold days and nights.

Vincent was twelve then, Norma eleven, and Kathleen nine. The sisters had to grow up fast.

Later Vincent recalled: "To live alone like that, sleep alone in that house set back in the field on the very edge of Millville, the bad section of town where the itinerant mill-workers lived—this was the only way they could live at all. . . . But they were afraid of nothing—not afraid of the river which flowed behind the house, in which they taught themselves to swim; not afraid of that other river, which flowed past the front of the house and which on Saturday nights was often very quarrelsome and noisy, the restless stream of mill workers. . . . Once it took all three of the children, flinging themselves against the front door, to close it and bolt it, and just in time. And after that, for what seemed like hours, there was stumbling about outside, and soft cursing."

Their mother had a way with the girls, a subtle psychology that brought greater results in exacting obedience and labor than cruelty could ever have wrought. She constantly reminded them (with more or less wry humor) of her own valiant struggles and sufferings on their behalf, and how much they needed each other in order to survive the trials of poverty; at the same time she never let them forget they were, all of them, princesses, aristocrats of the spirit, in beauty and brains and talent second to none, equal only to each other.

By nursing the sick and weaving hairpieces for ladies, Cora made the money to feed and clothe them and pay the rent. The children took care of each other and their house and did the cooking and laundry. They never questioned this need. They loved Cora and they feared her, feared her displeasure, and they felt searing guilt and shame if ever they let her down. When she was rested she was full of songs and rhymes, stories and jokes; she baked sugar cookies in the shapes of birds that were the envy of all the town children. But weary—or out of sorts—she was a terror.

Cora made each of her departures an occasion to put the girls on their honor to do their best and be their best while she was away. "And to be put on your honor by a mother who did not say anything about it, and went away to work for you," Cora recalled, "was a lot heavier load to carry, a lot harder to throw off, than things that were said to you about what to do, and what not to do, when mother was right there to see. . . . For in the one case the responsibility was on mother who was used to it, and in the other case it was on you, who were not so used to responsibility but were getting used to it very fast."

Of course, the greatest burden fell to the eldest, Vincent, who was also her mother's favorite. The two were almost unnaturally close. Two themes dominate the early diaries of Edna Millay: how painfully she misses her mother, and how exhausted she becomes with the laundry, cooking, cleaning, schoolwork, and baby-sitting. That autumn, soon after they settled into the cottage and the girls had enrolled in the Elm Street School across from the Congregational Church, the eldest daughter found herself in charge of the household and her younger sisters. More than once she refers to herself humorously as Cinderella. She was small, with bones as frail and delicate as a bird's—not meant for heavy lifting.

Vincent missed her mother so much that in desperation she invented an imaginary black "mammy" to whom she could turn in her diary for strength and comfort in her loneliness:

> You'll have to take the place of Mama when she's gone, which is most of the time. It seems strange, doesn't it, that you, an old mammy, who are not my real Mama at all, should take the place of my real Mama when she is away. . . . It's so comfy when she's home to sit down in the kitchen—I keep the kitchen clean and shiny all the time, Mammy—to sit down near the stove when the wood is crackling and sending out little sparks . . . when you hear the wind outdoors and know it can't get in where you are and where the little girls are sleeping in the next room. I make two cups of tea in the blue china teapot, and we sit opposite each other and drink it nice and hot while we watch each other's faces in the firelight of the crackling stove. It makes up for all the time she's

gone. I forget all about the things that went wrong and she forgets all about the doctors and the patients and the surgery and the sleepless nights. . . .

I love my mama, more than I can ever think of loving you, and you mustn't be jealous a bit. You are very like her, so I love you in something of the way I love her, though not one-millionth part as much.

Throughout her childhood and youth she fell ill about once a month with a cold or the grippe—or with what could only be called nervous exhaustion—and she took to her bed. Nothing then would please her more than if her real mama, the practical nurse, would leave her paying job and journey home to the drafty house in "Millville" to comfort and care for her. And sometimes Cora did.

In this house in the field the adolescent Edna St. Vincent Millay wrote her first prize-winning poems.

Vincent had thick, wavy hair of a deep shade of red or auburn. Norma was blond, and Kathleen, who soon grew stronger and taller than her sisters, was a brunette.

When their mother stayed home on a Saturday or a summer afternoon in 1906, the family might be found in the music room, Mother ironing her white uniforms on the table, and the girls on short stools with chair-seats for tables drawn up to them, all busy at work.

"I'm going to write a novel," Vincent announced, "and it's going to be published, too."

Mother felt a twinge, because she had been writing all her life, poems and journals and stories, so many words that might never be published.

"I wish't I thought it," said Norma.

And mother asked what Norma was writing.

"A play," she replied.

Then the youngest looked up from a paper upon which she had drawn a blank musical staff, and now was commencing to write a score.

"Is there already a *Green* march?" Kathleen asked no one in particular, with an eye toward avoiding plagiarism.

Mother would rather see her children practicing musical instruments. She imagined them as a chamber group taking the music world by storm: Vincent at the piano, Norma playing the cornet (given her lovely plump pink arms and neck) in a low-necked and short-sleeved dress, and Kathleen, with her long, graceful fingers, plucking a harp.

When time came for the girls to be vaccinated for smallpox, Cora saw to it the serum was scratched into their legs, so as not to mar the perfect, smooth skin of their arms.

But even before music entered the girls' lives in the form of pianos, cornets, and harps, literature had another rival: painting and drawing. Crayons were never long out of their fingers; an artist visiting the cottage, the friend of a neighbor, was astonished by the children's drawings. As Cora put it, "The little girls were so enthralled with their new interest, that as a new box of crayons seemed always to come when either of them was shut up in the house with a bad cold, or anything, that they almost welcomed such days."

In that low room downstairs next to the kitchen, Cora somehow managed to assemble one of the best private libraries in Camden—or so she proudly insisted years later. In the same space they had a Mason and Hamlin pump organ, which served Vincent for her first keyboard lessons, and as soon as they could afford it they would install a small upright piano.

Cora's patient Mr. John Tufts, a composer and piano teacher retired from the New England Conservatory, heard Vincent play one of her own keyboard compositions in his living room in 1905, when she was thirteen. Impressed, he offered to give her piano lessons for free. The professor's sight was failing, and long after he had quit teaching her, after she had started taking lessons with Mrs. Leila Bucklin French, she regularly visited the blind man and read aloud to him.

For the next five years music rivaled poetry as Vincent's chief passion. While reading her way through Cora's library, including all of Shakespeare, Tennyson, Milton, Wordsworth, Keats, Shelley, and Coleridge (and in the summer of 1906 Caesar's *Gallic Wars* in the original Latin), the aspiring writer / pianist practiced piano daily in preparation for public recitals. Her hands were small, but she stretched them strenuously each day over the piano keys, praying that they might grow.

SCHOOL DAYS
AND STAGE LIGHTS

❧

The artistic hothouse of the Millay library *cum* music room did not breed flowers that were altogether welcome in the Camden public schools. The girls learned to be independent, proud, and forthright. And like their mother, none of them considered men, by being men, as worthy of any special consideration or deference in matters of business or social relations.

Although her manners were proper, Vincent's attitude often suggested a certain arrogance that men in particular found offensive. Miss Millay had been named after a hospital, St. Vincent's in New York, which had saved her uncle's life just before she was born. She preferred the triumphant-sounding title to plain "Edna" (Hebrew for "rejuvenation") and asked to be called "Vincent," which somehow rubbed the school principal, Frank Wilbur, the wrong way. He made sport of calling her by any woman's name beginning with a V: Vanessa, Viola, Vivian, anything but Vincent. "Yes, yes, Mr. Wilbur," she would answer, with weary patience, "but my name is *Vincent.*"

She had not attended the green-shingled Elm Street School for three months, as an eighth-grader, when her conflict with the principal came to a head. In the winter of 1905–1906, Mr. Wilbur, who also taught history, one afternoon found himself on the losing end of an argument with his most brilliant pupil. She would not be convinced and she would not be silenced. At last he shouted at her, "You have run this school long enough!" which may have come as a surprise to the other children, who fell to giggling and guffawing at his angry face, whereupon the schoolteacher threw a book at the red-haired girl.

Vincent, who loved books, picked this one up from the floor, dusted it off, and carried it to his desk. Then, without a word, she turned on her heel, walked out of the classroom and down the schoolhouse stairs, and went home.

It seems unlikely that Mr. Wilbur did not know that Vincent's father, Henry Tolman Millay, was the superintendent of schools in nearby Union, where the family had lived before the divorce. Eventually Cora would appeal to Henry, but not before marching to the square schoolhouse, with its old-fashioned peaked belfry, and storming up the wooden steps and into Mr. Wilbur's classroom. In her own words, "Before his whole class, she told him just what she thought of him. And he had taken her by the throat, and pushed her out the door . . . she saw some lawyers, and was going to have him arrested, but didn't." Instead she conferred with her ex-husband, and the principal of the Camden High School, a Mr. Mitchell, who agreed with Mr. Wilbur that Miss Millay was a good enough scholar to start right in with high school, thereby not wasting more of anyone's time in grade school on Elm Street.

So midway in the school year of 1905–1906, Vincent enrolled in the Camden High School class of 1909, and the school literary magazine *The Megunticook* soon published her first personal essay, "The Newest Freshman." Witty and generous, full of fun and high spirits, Vincent was enormously popular with the high school girls, but much less so with the boys, who found her haughty. One, Raymond Tibbetts (class of 1907), recalled, "I remember Vincent as a scrawny girl—not nearly so attractive as her pretty sister, Norma—and too smart for most of us. She hadn't learned, as many brilliant women do, to conceal her superior gifts from young male clods." Eventually the male clods' resentment would coalesce in a strategem to put the proud young woman in her place, a plot more effective by far than heaving books at her brainy little head.

But for the time being, the next two years found Vincent happier than she had ever been before, happier perhaps than most teenagers, despite her load of housework and responsibility for the younger girls, now fourteen and twelve. Cora remembers how Vincent made games out of housework. "They played 'corner.' When the room needed cleaning on all sides, each of the girls took a corner, but there were but three of them, and there were four corners. Taking their corners they worked toward the middle of the room. [Then] they made a concerted attack on the other corner and made short work of that, three on one corner!"

During the school year her schedule of studies, piano lessons, baking, marketing, Sunday school, laundry, and housekeeping would hardly seem to allow time for poetry and a diary. Yet she managed to juggle these activities gayly, until she dropped from exhaustion, on the average once a month, and "took to her bed."

By 1906 she was filling notebooks with verses, and she began to send poems to the popular children's magazine *St. Nicholas*. This monthly offered not only publication to budding writers but medals and cash awards as well.

In October of that year the magazine published her poem "Forest Trees," an eighteen-line ode that ends with this stanza:

> Around you all is change—where now is land
> Swift vessels plowed to foam the seething main;
> Kingdoms have risen, and the fire fiend's hand
> Has crushed them to their mother earth again;
> And through it all ye stand, and still will stand
> Till ages yet to come have owned your reign.

It was signed "by Vincent Millay (Age 14)." This slice of mysticism shows the influence of nineteenth-century Romantic masters: Keats, Shelley, and Wordsworth. Five months later a much longer, more ambitious narrative poem, "The Land of Romance," not only appeared in the pages of *St. Nicholas*, but it won the magazine's first prize, a gold badge.

> Show me the road to Romance! I cried, and he raised his head;
> I know not the road to Romance, child. 'Tis a warm, bright way,'
> he said.
> And I trod it once with one whom I loved—with one who is long
> since dead.

Here are echoes of Tennyson, Sir Walter Scott, and the long line of our own Henry Wadsworth Longfellow. The seeker of Romance, twice denied, is at last shown the way by a fairy child:

> In the hush of the dying day,
> The mossy walls and ivy towers of the land of Romance lay.
> The breath of dying lilies haunted the twilight air
> And the sob of a dreaming violin filled the silence everywhere.

Cora Millay showed the published poem to editors of the Camden *Herald*, who reprinted it. More significantly, the piece was anthologized in the April edition of *Current Literature*, where it appeared alongside works by well-known poets such as Edwin Markham and Witter Bynner, not to mention the famous Edwin Arlington Robinson, whose poem "Miniver Cheevy" was first published in the same issue.

The girl poet from Camden was fifteen.

In the back of her diary a few years later (1910), this obsessive chronicler of her own life, this collector and hoarder of badges, prizes, publications, and programs featuring her name, this diligent list maker, made a short list of "Things to Remember." These were the signal events, the red-letter days of her youth. At the top of her list is "Gold badge in St. Nicholas League for poem 'The Land of Romance,' March 1907," followed by "Silver badge for poem 'Young Mother Hubbard' in August 1909," and a performance she gave in a play in Fairfield in the autumn of that same year. Then she mentions a music concert in Rockland—not her own performance but rather a recital by soprano Madame Frieda Langendorff, which she swears is near the most thrilling experience of her life.

Although in her diary she mentions her own piano concerts, it is clear that as the girl became a woman her piano playing took a back seat to poetry and the theater. For all her passion for Bach, Mendelssohn, and Chopin, and her daily practice at the keyboard, her hands simply would not grow enough to stretch over an octave. Yet she was imposing in other ways. Not more than an inch over five feet tall, on August 24, 1909, the girl weighed a little more than a hundred pounds. Her shoe size was 4½, her glove size was 5¾, and her collar measurement was 12½. With her big green eyes and her spectacular floor-length, golden-red hair she looked like a lovely Celtic fairy. Folks on the corner would whisper as she passed, considering the wonder.

She would write in her journal: "My soul is too big for the rest of me," which was poignantly evident from her poetry, her deep-throated voice, and the impression made by her increasing appearances in local stage plays.

Vincent's genius for writing poetry and her natural talent for mimicry and playacting strengthened simultaneously. These powers bore her forward, now one, now the other, toward literary and dramatic triumphs that cannot be explained separately. Likewise her character—which eventually became so theatrical, so full of poses, tempests, and impostures that she resembled her idol Sarah Bernhardt more than she did the demure Elizabeth Browning, or the demonstrative Sara Teasdale—must be studied as the sum of many dramatic parts. Her friends and lovers, her public, and her biographers agree that Edna St. Vincent Millay was an enigma, sweetly intimate and available for a little while before becoming maddeningly remote, mysterious, unknowable. Her photographs capture a hundred different faces, the mood colorings of a chameleon. Which portrait is really Vincent? The child, the ingenue, the nun, the whore, the comedienne, the seductress, the librarian? Only when we have begun to understand Millay the actress can we come to know the lyric poet and the woman. Acting came as naturally to her as breathing; she created several different roles for herself in the private world of her imagination before she ever began to play roles for her friends, her lovers, and the public.

To her weekly routine of high school classes (a five-minute walk from home in good weather), church and Sunday school at the white, sharp-steepled Congregational Church on Elm and Free Streets, and piano lessons, Vincent soon added, in April of 1907, nightly play rehearsals at the Camden Opera House on the corner of Elm and Washington. Walking the mile and a half from home up Washington Street, the starry-eyed girl thrilled at the sight of the high, three-story opera house. The Federal-style, nineteenth-century brick theater, with its triple-arched windows above and its grand arched entrance on brownstone pilasters, lent a sense of grandeur and a promise of culture to the citizens of the mill town port, although it rode upon the humble back of civic duty: the police station and town hall took up the ground floor. Entering the heavy doors under the brick keystone, the teenage actress climbed a wide staircase with a mahogany rail. She passed the box offices and the red-carpeted lobby, and entered the opulent theater.

The stage curtain under the square gilt proscenium arch was decorated with a pagan sylvan scene of nymphs and satyrs in the hills of Pompeii. A gaslight chandelier in the center of the high ceiling illuminated the interior: hundreds of red-velvet seats, a sweeping balcony with plaster-swag moldings, and small upper and lower boxes on either side of the proscenium where rich folks lounged with their elbows upon the balustrades. It was large enough for the townspeople to feel the place was "grand," but small enough to be intimate and easy to fill.

Here in this theater in the heart of Camden, at the head of the street where she lived, Millay first acted in *Triss, or Beyond the Rockies*, a melo-drama with a sighing maiden and a villain in pursuit, twirling his mustache. On Friday evening, April 5, 1907, for twenty-five cents general admission (thirty-five cents reserved) you could have seen Millay in the role of Susie Smith, "all learning and books." She wrote in her diary on April 8: "*Triss* went off even better than I had expected, and we are going to Rockland as I had hoped. Everyone says that it is the best home talent performance ever given here, and a great many consider it better than the production of the traveling companies. I have received many congratulations on my acting of Susie Smith. My part isn't very large, but it is important and rather hard. I hope we will get as good a house in Rockland. . . ."

At fifteen she was stagestruck, infatuated with the makeup, costuming, the oversized make-believe passions of the theater, and she loved the applause. Fugitive playbills and fleeting references in her diaries make it impossible to know every role she played as a teenager. She acted in school plays, as well as amateur and professional productions. These include the lead in *Gypsy the Mountain Waif*, December 6, 1907; Cynisca, Pygmalion's wife in Shaw's *Pygmalion*, November 14, 1908; Kitty Peters in *The College Outcast*; Marion Brooks in *The Brookdale Mystery*, November 25, 1908—all at the Camden Opera House.

Just before playing Cynisca in *Pygmalion*, Vincent and her mother and sisters moved out of the cottage on Washington Street. "That fall," Cora wrote, "it grew colder and colder, and the little house needed repairs more and more . . . downstairs where the library was you could poke a broom-stick right out of doors through the wall." Cora chose rent day to move; a teamster came with his cart and horses to move their goods to a lower-story tenement on Chestnut Street, adjacent to the water and Bay View Street. The landlord's family lived over one part of them, another tenant over the other. Most of their windows faced the harbor, but they went in and out from a porch on the Chestnut Street side. Across Chestnut Street was the Baptist Church and the village green. Millay had only a short walk now, cutting across the corner of the village green and Elm Street, to get to her rehearsals at night.

On the stage, acting role after role, she developed the prodigious memory that was the envy of listeners lucky enough in later years to hear her recite her own poetry, Keats's "Eve of St. Agnes," or his odes, or the *Carmine* of Catullus in the original Latin, all by heart. Language to her was a kind of music; once she got the tune in her head it became hers forever. She developed her memory, and she learned the repertoire of gestures, facial expressions, and deportment that were an actress's stock-in-trade at the turn of the century, before Stanislavski's "Method" transformed the actor's craft from entertainment into personal catharsis.

She must have been very good at it. In October 1909 she played the leading role of Milly in the play *Willowdale* at the Opera House with a professional traveling repertory company that cast only a few of the parts locally. The next month, when the show moved to Fairfield, Maine, the director telephoned Vincent Millay in a panic because of the sudden illness of his new Milly. In a five-page unpublished 1909 memoir called "For One Night Only," Millay describes the experience of being called away as a professional actress:

Not that the paint-stick, and the rouge-paw, and the eyebrow-pencil and all the varied apparatus that bring about the theatre's nightly illusion were up to that time unknown to me. No indeed. I had not needed to be told more than once to "look up, dear," while the pencil was busy beneath my eyes, or how to hold my mouth when its Cupid's bow was being adjusted.

Hot, stuffy dressing rooms with paint-streaked tobacco-stained walls, and floors strewn with burnt matches, with low tables standing unsteadily on their scarred legs . . . little dim mirrors near which are always tied the long brown cords of specked electric light bulbs—oh, I knew them—and I loved them for the stories they could tell. The smell of the stage, that is like nothing else in the world, I knew, and loved.

But this was different. For while at home, I might pretend to myself as much and as long as I liked—until the deep-vibrant note I had discovered in my voice out-drowned in my mind's ear the tones of Marlowe; until, rendering with passionate reserve and hysterical calm Ibsen's inimitable lines, I had in my mind's eye out-Hedda'ed Nazimova—yet was my native village unthrilled and unconvinced; I was asked to serve ice cream at church socials, and the grocer-boy called me by name.

It was this desire to be lifted away above the church socials and grocery boys of Camden, that the theater world promised to satisfy; she hoped it might give her wings, a crown, or a halo.

The director met Vincent as she stepped off the train at Fairfield station, and he hurried her to the town's hotel. She thought she was too excited to eat, but took a cup of coffee and a few bites of a beefsteak in the hotel restaurant. He handed her a copy of the play, "But I had no time to run over my lines. I remember now that I was not in the least afraid of forgetting."

Arriving at the theater she had only twenty minutes to dress and get made up. Now she begins to get the sort of attention for which she has longed—the only sort, it appears, that satisfies her.

The other girls, who were quite ready and wandering about behind the scenes or looking through a hole in the curtains, rushed down to help me when they heard that I had come. One hooked me up the back and pinned me together in a dozen places, one knelt and put on my shoes while I balanced with my hand on her shoulder, one went to find the frilly sun-bonnet I was to carry on in the first act.

It is the Queen's royal toilet, or the privileged levee of the Sun King, a type of scene that will be reenacted again and again in her life. "They were all very much excited and very eager to do something for me. *I* was a professional, sent on to play the leading role. I knew just how thrilled I should have been to be in their places. As it was, I did my best to conceal the thrills that were surely mine."

These thrills included the sound of the rising curtain heard from the dressing room below, and the heart-pounding excitement of her entrance—the sudden hush descending upon the house as the strangers beheld "the girl who had been sent from out of town." Millay writes:

> How I enjoyed myself! There, away from home, I was under no restraint from loving friends in the orchestra seats or hated rivals whose talent and time had not been solicited. I did not hurry with my lines. I used continually my deep-vibrant note. I made my pauses tell. I felt that the audience liked me, and I did my best to make it love me. I did little wistful things, made little forlorn gestures, and once or twice smiled piteously. They laughed and cried with me all the way through. And at the end they gave me such a hand as I had never had before.

By the autumn of her senior year in high school, Vincent Millay had several real enemies in her hometown, "hated rivals" who would try to destroy her, at least that part of her that she had presented to the world as artistic and superior. These enemies were not girls. She had many close girl-friends including Abbie Evans, the preacher's daughter, with whom she taught Sunday school for years, and Corinne Sawyer, Ethel Knight, and Stella Derry, all members of both the Sunday school class at the Congregational Church and a reading group they called the "Huckleberry Finners." Jessie Hosmer, one of the reading group, told a journalist that Vincent was "the life of the party, wherever she went." The girls took nature walks on Mount Battie and around the harbor; in good weather they swam and went rowing and sailing in Penobscot Bay, and took picnic lunches to the nearby islands. Stella Derry remembered: "My mother used to ask me why I liked washing dishes and making potato stew at the Millays' when I hated doing those things at home. It was because Vincent made everything wonderful fun. She was always making up songs and games, and on walks she would make birds and plants and wild flowers as fascinating as people. . . . She could be a spit-fire if she thought something wasn't fair. No one ever heard a word of gossip from Vincent, or a swear word." (All her life she was known as an inviolable confidante.) Eleanor Gould added: "I think I'd have failed Latin if Vincent Millay, younger than I, hadn't explained sentence construction to me. She could read Latin as easily as English. She also taught me to waltz. She was a marvelous dancer, and would give up her recess to teach dance steps to us older girls (she was the youngest in her class) and help us with our lessons."

Her diaries of 1909 and 1910 are bright chronicles of work and study, piano lessons, picnics, and a great deal of sewing and embroidery, fashioning dresses to be worn to parties: high school parties, the Fireman's Ball, the ball at the University of Maine, and countless other hoedowns and fairs. The diaries before 1910 are sporadic, so sometimes it is necessary to look ahead for clues to events that occurred earlier. By 1910 it is all but certain the Millays' finances (though they remained in debt) were adequate for the three girls to enjoy the social life of Camden's middle class—even if they did have to make their own clothing and bake their own bread.

But the diaries also begin to capture the brooding side of Vincent's personality, as the girl copes with the unexpected emotions of womanhood. Her conflict with boys seems to begin with the confusion of falling in love with one or another of them, which she describes in humorous and sympathetic detail.

> Of course I'm not in love with him. It's ridiculous. But I think of him all of the time and it makes me nervous. I don't want to think of anyone all the time, just yet . . . If I'm in love it isn't with his beauty, for I can't remember his face—I've tried to so much that it has become a blur in my mind. Somehow I seem to see the look of his eyes, and then again the curve of his mouth when he smiled, but it's gone in a flash. I can remember and feel all over again, the way I felt when he looked at me— but I can't remember how he looked. It's very singular.
>
> I feel restless and hysterical and horrid, like going off somewhere and crying—miserably and luxuriously.

Nowhere in our literature is there a better account of an adolescent crush than in Millay's diary of April 1909, as she tells how it has rained day and night since she glimpsed the young Romeo, whom she does not name, at a dance. She decides she will have to stay in the house, for if she goes out, surely she will be rude to someone, or too gloriously unhappy for safety. She ambles around the house. If she starts to sweep, soon she forgets what she is doing; lost in her vision of the boy, she leaves the broom leaning against the kitchen table and drifts into the sitting room. The piano stool stops her. She sits and plays, listlessly and loosely, a nocturne; but soon, with an exasperated discord, she pushes the stool away and rises.

> Reading won't do. Love stories make me worse than ever and my head is too unsettled for anything else. Embroidery would drive me raving crazy. All I can do is sit at the window and watch the rain until I can hardly keep from screaming. Am I in love with him? Or am I simply in love with love? Whatever it is, I wish it would get either worse or better right off, for one thing is certain, I can't stand this long.

And at last she declares, "If this be love, I've had enough of it!" So says the budding lover and love poet at age eighteen.

Like many an attractive adolescent girl before and since 1909, Vincent developed a sophisticated approach / avoidance technique in order to handle her many and very persistent suitors. This "technique" arose out of a very real ambivalence. She loved boys, and was heartily in love with the idea of love, but she was also sensibly afraid of it. In the same entry she wrote, "I've always expected it to come but now that there seems a possibility of it, I'm beginning to be afraid." Along with her deep need to love and be loved, Millay possessed an overwhelming habit and need to be in control of things. And to fall in love is, by definition, to lose control.

"The boys don't like me," she reflects, "because I won't let them kiss me." The sentence contains volumes. The boys liked her a lot, otherwise she would never have known that they wanted to kiss her. The diaries abound in boys' names: Russell Avery, Charlie Swan, Winthrop Wilson, George Frohock, boys who take her canoeing, dancing, and hiking, boys who act in plays with her and go on picnics with her by the Megunticook, and boys who read poetry to her. But none is able to win her her heart, not even Russell Avery, who comes closest in the summer of 1910 by wooing her with verses from *The Rubaiyat* and Palgrave's *Golden Treasury*.

When she refers to boys in general, as on January 28, 1910, it is often with condescension. Stella Derry had come to dinner that night. When her boyfriend Fred Gregory came to pick her up, Vincent was busy embroidering a butterfly's wing on a dress, and Fred made fun of it. "Boys don't know anything anyway. Stella makes one exception but so far I don't." Doubtless this attitude, as stated in her diary, was hard to conceal from Fred and the other Camden fellows. On March 9 she writes that a Mrs. Pendleton has promised a luncheon to "the first girl of us who gets engaged. I don't know who it will be but I know mighty well who it won't be." It won't be Vincent, who will steer clear of the altar until the spinsterly age of thirty-one.

The beginning of the end of Vincent's innocence was the open feud between the haughty young beauty and the lusty swains of Camden. She had airs, affectations, and attitudes they could no longer abide. Under the leadership of their best and brightest, George Frohock, the Baptist preacher's son, they conspired to take Vincent down a peg. Frohock, a fine student who, with Vincent, played romantic roles at the Camden Opera House (the day before Thanksgiving 1908 he had played opposite her in *The Brookdale Mystery*), would have been the star of the class of 1909 had he not been outshone by the fiery poet. They stand out in the graduation picture of twenty students: Vincent, front row center, seated in full skirt and high-necked white blouse, hands folded demurely in her lap, hair swept back, her head tilted ever so dreamily; Frohock in suit and necktie, square-jawed, dark, and handsome, leaning slightly against the chair of the girl in front of him, his hand jauntily placed on his hip, the picture of swaggering male confidence. One can just imagine the sparks flying between them.

On cue, the boys began to giggle at Vincent during morning exercises, and mimic her as she read aloud from the psalms or the daily calendar. During class meetings the twelve boys would stamp their feet and make catcalls whenever she tried to speak. None of this seemed to bother her all that much. But when they plotted to deprive her of an honor that she deserved, Frohock and his gang at last scored mightily against her.

"The first big disappointment of my life," she wrote in her diary on April 17, 1909 (remarkably it was the first, considering all she had endured to date), "I graduate in June—without the class poem. You wouldn't have believed it, would you? But it's true, all too cruelly true." Poetry meant something precious in those days, and being the class poet was a high honor. "I'll tell you to whom they gave it. There is a boy in my class who, when we were juniors, used to amuse himself by writing to me." That boy was Henry Hall, whom Cora Millay described as "a sort of country moron under the wing of Fred Cassons, another of the same type." Cora believed that Cassons wrote the "minor poetry" that appeared in the high school magazine under the name of Hall, "or at least the influence was there." In any case the twelve boys decided to nominate the dullard Hall for class poet, thus humiliating Vincent; this was outrageous, because Vincent was known all over Knox County as the only native poet who had ever achieved national recognition.

With characteristic dignity, choking back tears, "Vincent at once took herself out of it entirely. There was no vote," Cora recalls. "But it hurt her. And she was young, and slight, and very tired with the work of the year. She left school for a time. She played for a bit in one of the motion-picture houses in Rockland, but that was not her kind of music ["a big fat vaudeville man whose acccompaniments I have to play from dirty manuscripts. It's awful," said Vincent] and it wore on her frightfully, so her mother had her give it up. And that was not all." Cora goes on to describe a depression in her eldest daughter that made Mother fear for the girl's life.

"Her mother made a stiff fight for the very life of the girl so run-down and frail and disheartened. She gave her all the strengthening foods possible, and more than that she went every day down to the shore and got sea-water which she heated and with which she gave the girl baths and rubbings. At the first seeming improvement she adopted different tactics." These included encouraging "the pride and sense of outrage of the frail girl." Cora knew that Vincent had written part of a beautiful poem called "La Joie de Vivre," and she discovered from the principal that the class-prize essays might be in prose *or* verse. "She asked Vincent why she did not finish up this poem for an essay, and 'show 'em'?" She did finish it, and the labor of writing the poem was part of her healing that spring.

"In time, when she was better, she went back to school. She graduated with her class, in June of 1909, in the little white lawn dress made for her by her Aunt Sue." At graduation exercises she stood on the stage of the Opera House where she had known so many triumphs, and in the voice of the trained actress recited her prize-winning "essay" in verse, "La Joie de Vivre":

> The world and I are young!
> Never on lips of man
> Never since time began
> Has gladder song been sung.

Much to the embarrassment of Henry Hall, class poet, whose poor doggerel verses no one would ever remember.

※

So if Edna St. Vincent Millay, in the spring of 1909, was not yet ready to die for love, she does seem to have been about ready to die for poetry.

Religion might have provided some consolation or solace. Many adolescent girls of Vincent's generation took to religion with zeal, as a refuge from or an outlet for animal energies otherwise thwarted. They could not go to war, get drunk, play football, *or* make love. Every Sunday morning the Millays entered the Congregational Church door, which opened beneath a graceful corner bell tower, the bustling, tardy women risking censure as they squeezed into the pine pew with the mahogany scrolled armrests. The spacious church was austere and colorless, with no stained glass or frescos, only a simple cross with candles on either side of the altar.

The Millays liked to sing, and Vincent loved the hymns of the *Bay Psalm Book* and *Genevan Psalters*, all the wealth of the "Free" Church traditions. Her mellow contralto could be heard above the other voices:

> Lord Jesus think on me
> And purge away my sin
> From earth-born passions set me free
> And make me pure within.

> Lord Jesus think on me
> That when my life is past
> I may the eternal brightness see
> And share thy joy at last.

These lines of Synesius of Cyrene and the sweet tunes of Hyfrydol and the prayers and liturgy of the reformed Church might once have soothed the nerves and healed the psychic wounds of the sensitive young woman. But her diary protests that the church, and Sunday school, which was central to her social life, only made her emotional existence more miserable in those years of 1909 and 1910.

Her best friend was Abbie Evans, the minister's daughter. A few years older than Vincent, Abbie was also an aspiring poet and served as a role model; the older girl was genuinely devout and led the teenagers in a small Sunday school class that met in a high-windowed northwest corner room over the choir loft. There the girls took turns preaching and teaching the class, which soon became, in the hands of these bright students, a no-holds-barred theology seminar in which the skeptics challenged the believers, and the believers gave as good as they got.

Vincent must have started as a believer, in order to serve as acolyte to Abbie; otherwise she would never have become so vehement later, when she turned heretic. The chief theme of her diary, the year after she graduated from Camden High, is not romance or poetry or even the fatigue of caring for her sisters in her mother's absence or her longing for Cora. It is the crisis of faith, brought on superficially by her exasperation with the Sunday school class, but more deeply and effectively by a genuine, finely articulated battle between reason and belief. Like Percy Shelley, one of Millay's first idols, Vincent had a rare, preternatural understanding of intellectual ideas at an age many thinkers are only beginning to grasp them. The woman who eventually would compartmentalize so much of her personal and artistic life kept two diaries after 1909: one a very complete, if sometimes commonplace record of events that is our chief source of her history; the other a series of private journals, meditations, and irregular notes that record her innermost thoughts, feelings, and impressions. The first diary might casually be left open on a table or armchair. The second had to be hidden from prying eyes, under a loose floorboard or a mattress; it is dark, tormented, and sometimes rather frightening.

"My diary is and is to be my confidante, and that *e* on the end makes it feminine. . . . It would be out of my power to tell all these things to a mere confidant," i.e., a *man*—so she writes on July 19, 1908, before her spiritual crisis. "She is the only one of my friends who can keep quiet long enough for me to talk, and talk I must or my boiler will burst." She was boiling over having to go to Sunday school. "It looks like rain, and I hope it will rain cats and dogs and hammers and pitchforks and silver sugar spoons and hay ricks and paper-covered novels and picture frames and rag carpets and tooth-picks and skating rinks and birds of paradise and roof gardens and burdocks and French grammars before Sunday school time. There! If it does I shan't have to go anyway. Besides I don't see how I could go if I wanted to, because I haven't anything to wear." Then she launches into several hundred words of colorful wardrobe and needlework details, about hemming a blue skirt or darning a green dress, before giving it up: "Guess I'll weep awhile. Guess I won't, I mean. Guess I'll dance a Highland fling on top of the ink bottle. There isn't enough in it to upset. That reminds me—I don't know why, I'm sure, but it does—that I didn't bake beans yesterday, thinking it was Friday, so I must do it today. Beans are cheap, and we must have them at least once a week or we will be bankrupt."

One way or the other the little comedienne meant to cut Sunday school class. But she ended up going, in her white muslin dress with the soiled hem, that Sunday, and every Sabbath for years, despite a growing disillu-sionment with the Congregational religion. Three weeks earlier, in a thought-ful diary entry that reveals the impact of the Free Church upon her, she had earnestly presumed to rewrite the Ten Commandments of Moses, to suit herself:

> I have laid down for myself two commandments:
> 1. Respect thyself.
> 2. Be worthy of thine own respect.
> If I live up to these two I shall need no Ten Commandments. For I shall not respect myself unless I am worthy of it, and if I respect myself I shall have no gods before the real God. I shall make unto him no graven images; I shall honor my father and my mother; I shall not kill, nor steal, nor covet, nor commit adultery—and as for remem-bering the Sabbath day and doing no work upon it, I work on Sunday as I see fit . . . for honest work is no desecration, and dishonest work I have no use for—though if I had it would be as bad one day as another.

Now here is a recipe to try the patience of the holiest of Saints and the most indulgent of Sunday schoolmarms, a creed that subverts the Decalogue

of Moses to the liberty and proud selfhood of a high school junior. But young
Vincent swears by it. Elements of this philosophy will survive long into her
adulthood and middle age, enabling her to shred all of the Mosaic laws save
two or three. One of her moral guides was Shelley (his picture hung in her
study) who said, "Poets are the unacknowledged legislators of the world."
Millay writes:

> I remember the Sabbath day and keep it as holy as I keep any day, for
> I do not believe in saving up all one's praise, prayer and song for Sun-
> day, and then, to make up for the unnatural goodness of one day, going
> to extremes of wickedness every other day of the week.

Her logic is unassailable, and the depth of her monotheistic passion remains
persuasive even as it manifests itself in curious, polytheistic ways:

> My God is all gods in one. When I see a beautiful sunset, I worship
> the god of Nature; when I see a hidden action brought to light, I wor-
> ship the god of Truth; when I see a bad man punished and a good man
> go free, I worship the god of Justice; when I see a penitent forgiven, I
> worship the god of Mercy. And never a day passes that I do not, for
> something beautiful, for something truthful, for something just, or for
> something merciful, give praise to my all-powerful Creator.

Her worship is spontaneous, unbidden, and sincere. She prefers her own to
all other religions, otherwise she would not practice it: "For I know that only
one's best is good enough for God. To Thee, God of my praise, I offer this
prayer:

> Help me to be worthy of my own respect . . . for each bad act in my life,
> help me to do a good act; and for each good act in my life let me do
> another good act, so that my soul's good may be stronger than the bad.

Then she launches into a long and eloquent prayer of praise and thanksgiving
that would be welcome in most Christian church services the world over.

If this diary entry of June 28, 1908, sounds like the musing and soul-
searching of an aspiring saint, it is because a saint's processes are similar to
the spiritual upheavals of a budding religious poet. To become a saint one
must first recognize that one is a hopeless sinner; to become a religious poet,
a poet of any religion at all, it is necessary to feel and understand the sufferings of a sinner as well as the potential exaltations of an angel. At sixteen
years of age the poet who would soon write the immortal lines

> All sin was of my sinning, all
> Atoning mine, and mine the gall
> Of all regret.

had firsthand, intimate knowledge of the pain of sin. What, one might ask, could this good-hearted, hardworking virgin have known about sin? The answer appears in her diary the next day:

> I guess I'm going to explode. I know just how a volcano feels before an eruption. Mama is so cross she can't look straight, Norma's got the only decent rocking chair in the house (which happens to be mine) and Kathleen is so unnaturally good that you keep thinking she must be sick. I suppose this is an awful tirade to deliver after the sermon I wrote yesterday. . . . But it is very hard to be sixteen and the oldest of three. It is such a relief to have a diary to run to. . . .

Vincent Millay is not supposed to get angry or sad or tired. She is supposed to cook daily, bake several times weekly, wash clothing for herself and her sisters until her hands literally bleed from the friction (more on this later), sew and embroider, shovel snow and coal, and between times practice piano, finish her schoolwork, and write poetry. All this is to be done with a smile on her face and a song in her heart. Her diary she may write in her spare time. The whole routine is spelled out on a schedule that mother has nailed to the kitchen wall. And it is clear to God and His children that mother Cora, with her nursing career and hair-weaving work, is a certified Saint, and that the cross her daughter St. Vincent has to bear is but a willow wand in comparison.

At seventeen she wrote this ode to Cora:

To My Mother

> You are my guardian angel. Year by year
> Up from the time that I can scarce recall
> Your dear gray eyes have watched me lest I fall,
> Your careful hand has ever hovered near.

The poem goes on to tell how her mother's sympathy has taught her to bear childish griefs and hard disappointments, and ends with the prayer, "Be with me all the time that I shall live . . . To every hurt of mine your healing give / Till all unhappiness for me is o'er"—a sentiment as pathetically unrealistic as most of Vincent and Cora's expectations of each other. Not until Cora's death twenty years later will it become apparent that Vincent never outgrew that childish need. Nor did Cora ever shed the notion that her eldest daughter should be perfect.

In short, Vincent's idea of sin was to be something less than perfect, and perfection was a virtual impossibility under her mother's eagle eye. Vincent's long list of moral and domestic resolutions in her diary during these years is ambitious to the point of being heartrending. No mortal could be so good, so industrious, so cheerful as she desires to be—for her mother, for her sisters, for God, and finally for her "husband-to-be." She has formed, by her late teens, a monstrously hyperactive conscience; she was what is now called an overachiever (notwithstanding her prodigious gifts) in spades, with superhuman expectations for herself. Failing to reach these goals she would, literally, regularly, fall ill from her exhaustion and disappointment, and take to her bed. Then Cora or Norma would nurse her to health and put her back in harness.

❧

During 1910, after graduating from Camden High, Vincent devoted herself to her family with the selflessness of a sister of charity. There was no question then of her going to college like Abbie Evans who had enrolled at Radcliffe (with scholarship aid). The Millays were too poor and needed Vincent at home.

By an unquestioned and seemingly inevitable division of labor, Vincent, now free from her high school routine, would do the housekeeping, sewing, baking, banking, marketing, and laundry full-time, allowing Cora to spend more time away on nursing jobs. The daughter's scattered prayers ask for strength to this noble end, to serve her family, and she asks no more of God than to make her perfect in that endeavor. Not that she is a humorless drudge. She greets 1910 at a fancy New Year's Ball. Her diary tells of her joy in Bach and Mendelssohn, as she continues her weekly piano lessons with Mrs. French. "Bach and I are getting acquainted," she notes on January 13, "and I find him very fascinating." On Sunday, January 16, she went to hear Pastor L. D. Evans preach his last sermon before leaving for Egypt, and asked him to please bring her a bit of sand from the Sphinx. Afterward in Sunday school she got "deathly sick." It was only her third turn as teacher of Sunday school since Abbie had left for Radcliffe. She had made Vincent promise she would keep things going even in her absence. On Monday she "stayed in bed and mother stayed home to nurse me," and on Tuesday she felt better but was still weak, as if recovering from a fever.

"If Church-going has such an effect on me I shall most certainly stay at home." But she didn't. So sick that she canceled her piano lesson that week, and "Mrs. French says she's going to find out what I do to get sick so often," still Vincent was back in that corner classroom over the choir loft on Sunday the twenty-third. Her friend Ethel Knight was there, too, having returned from college in Boston, and Vincent wrote, "Ethel and I had a heated discussion and nearly kicked over the pulpit." She did not describe the argument then, but on January 30, she recalled, "Went to Sunday school. Florence was there for a wonder and became highly enraged because I refused to believe the Jonah and the Whale yarn." So it appears that Vincent's "higher criticism" at this juncture was simply challenging the inconsistencies and improbabilities of the Bible stories, and teasing her literal-minded girlfriends who believed in them.

On her birthday, February 22, 1910, she "went to the Fireman's Ball as a birthday dissipation. I'm eighteen today." Her gifts included the sheet music for Mendelssohn's "Songs Without Words," some fancy stationery, a green hair ribbon, a ring, a handkerchief, and from her mother a copy of the *Rubaiyat of Omar Khayyam*. The winter passed by without incident, in a whirl of parties, dances, concerts, and Sunday school classes. And then, there was "Muffin." With several suitors at bay, Vincent fell madly in love with a kitten from the litter of Mrs. Frye's tabby next door. Thus, the first of March:"I am in love with that little yellow kitten. Must have it." And on the sixth: "I am to have the yellow kitten as soon as he is weaned, and am thinking of naming him 'Muffin.'" On the eleventh: "Mrs. Frye's cat was cross and wouldn't let me take Muffin. Cats don't know anything. Why do dear little kittens have to grow up?" She got her kitten, of course. But she would not be able to keep the kitten from becoming a cat, any more than she could remain a girl forever, although in a few months she would struggle desperately with a stratagem for putting off womanhood.

On March 15 she read Elizabeth Browning's amorous *Sonnets from the Portuguese*. The next day she wrote, "I got out my green check suit today. It is disgracefully short and gives me a tiny hope that I have grown since commencement. A sixteenth of an inch would be gratefully received." And a day later she complained that she was completely deaf in her right ear.

As Easter approached Vincent rejoiced that there would be no Sunday school that day, "my last, thank the fates." And on Easter, March 27, she congratulated herself on her perfect attendance: She had gone every Sunday for a full year. But the next week she reported, "A row in Sunday school today. I've decided not to go anymore.... It was all about

Fatalism which is a tommyrot idea. . . . There's no sense in my going any-more. I don't believe as they do, and we can't agree."

Vincent's Protestantism had graduated from criticizing the whales and wonders in the Bible to a profound and abiding protest against fatalism, which somehow had wormed its way into the loose body of tenets that shaped the Congregational Church on Elm Street. Bear in mind that the Congregational Church, or Free Church, then as now allowed a maximum of latitude for each parish to thrash out its own doctrine. So the brethren in Camden might believe that faith without works is dead, while the congregation in the church over the mountains believed the opposite. And just as likely in either church you might share a pew with some Christian whose notions of fate, sin, or salvation were as odd to you as a Buddhist's.

Anyway she found herself surrounded that day by disciples of fatalism, and of course she hated it, being the eldest daughter of Cora Millay, a living advertisement for the power of free will. Vincent was not about to listen to any claptrap suggesting that she, and her sisters, and their mother, were not the masters of their own fates. Though she still felt a deep loyalty to keep the school alive while her best friend was away at Radcliffe, not until Abbie returned in June did Vincent begin attending again regularly.

Meanwhile she continued to fill notebooks with poetry.

On April 16 she got a call from Ethel Knight, who had just read the May issue of *St. Nicholas*. Millay wrote in her diary: "Words cannot express my feelings when she told me I had been awarded a cash prize of $5 for the best verse on the subject of 'Friends.' " It was the last poem she had sent the editors before turning eighteen, after which she was ineligible to compete. "I had given up all hope of ever getting a cash prize, which is the hardest of all to get. Imagine my state of mind." The poem was printed at the head of the magazine, and half an editorial was spent in praising it. "Never before have I seen in the League [the magazine was officially known as *The St. Nicholas League*] an individual criticism of anything. I am simply crazed with delight. I think I shall get a beautifully bound 'Browning' with my prize." She meant, of course, Robert Browning and not his wife, whose poetry she had already read. On June 28 she reports, with understated pride, that the *New Bedford Evening Standard* has devoted two-thirds of a column to "an awful puff about my 'Friends,' " adding to her already considerable local fame as a poet.

LITTLE GIRL GROWN UP

❧

*I*n the spring and summer of 1910, Vincent experienced bewildering sexual stirrings and an outpouring of lyric poetry that began in her journals before taking shape in publishable verses.

On April 22 she attended the University of Maine's concert and ball in Orono. "The time of my life. Winthrop Wilson, a junior at the University of Maine, came home with me. Very nice and very interesting. I danced every dance—eight with the towns and eight with the gowns."

She now braided her long hair up in a fiery "cornet," and many of her diary entries are descriptions of sewing and embroidery for herself and others: "Finished my corset cover all but the eyelets for the ribbon. It is lovely. I'm going to give it to Mama." It is difficult to capture the Millays' passion for colorful detail, evident in their scrapbooks, homemade valentines and Christmas cards, pressed flower arrangements, letters, and sewing. It is hard to imagine most Americans today ever loving so well the language of colors, flowers, threads, and fabrics; these evoked the joy of their daily lives, in which almost nothing beautiful existed except what they made for themselves or witnessed in nature. Little was store-bought. The girls designed their own clothing and household ornaments as a poet creates poetry. The effect of this vanishing way of life on the writing of poetry, which is wedded to the naming of beloved details and finding a music for the beauty of things, is impossible to measure, but everywhere manifest in Millay's poetry.

Her mother was away on nursing cases more than she was home, so Vincent had to share the excitements of her life through vivid letters. She discovered the carnal hedonism of *The Rubaiyat*, and played at falling in love with any man or boy refined enough to read it aloud to her.

July 9, 1910

Dear Muvver,

. . . . . .

Where do you think I went last Sunday? We took our shade hats and bathing suits and went up to Charlie Swan's house and he paddled us up the river in his canoe. Oh, beautiful! He has the dearest little camp.

Swan's lodge was decorated, to Vincent's delight, with choice epigrams from the Bible, folklore, and *The Rubaiyat*. Over the table: "Stay me with flagons, comfort me with apples." Over the fireplace: "Tomorrow's tangles in the winds resign, nor heed the rumble of a distant drum." And in the guest room, where one would see it upon awakening, was Vincent's favorite:

> Awake! For morning in the bowl of night
> Has cast the stone that puts the stars to flight.
> > The hunter of the east has caught
> The Sultan's turret in the noose of light.

"Wasn't that great," she wrote Cora. "His nephew, Harvey Swan, did it and I am about as near in love as I ever was in my life—with another *Rubaiyat* friend way off somewhere."

Somewhere way off, beyond the hills of Camden, or beyond the Penobscot Bay, her true love awaits her. She may not know much about him, but she's certain the fellow must know and love the *Rubaiyat* and lots of other splendid poems. If Vincent can only find him, she is almost ready, with Omar, to "Come, fill the Cup, and in the fire of Spring" fling off that winter garment of Repentence.

Almost, but not quite. Though there are neighborhood boys like Russell Avery willing to read Omar Khayyam to the pretty, auburn-haired girl until they are hoarse, she has her eye on bigger, more exotic game: the perfect lover. Or perhaps no lover at all. She writes nun poems, such as: "I'll make of me a nunnery / And shut my heart inside. / There the passionate heart of me / Quiet and cold shall bide." Of course she did not really long for the convent—she just didn't want to be mastered by sex, which she already suspected had the power to rob a woman of autonomy. And both Vincent and her mother were fond of the story of Abelard and Héloïse, the notion of a love that is too good for this world of flesh.

The Vincent Millay of July 1910 was a roiling mass of contradictions, conflicting urges, erotic and chaste. She expressed the central conflict eloquently in her private "Journal of a Little Girl Grown Up," which she began on the evening of July 20, 1910, the week after an idyllic boating trip with her poetic admirer Russell Avery, and the day after she and Norma found "a letter torn up under the bridge on High Street. We pieced it together and it is a perfectly scandalous love-letter from a married woman. It is awful." Vincent is piecing together, scrap by scrap, the maculate fabric of adult life, and what the curious girl discovers is at once fascinating, irresistible, and revolting.

I'm tired of being grown up! Tired of dresses that kick around my feet, tired of high-heeled shoes; tired of conventions, and proprieties. . . . I want to be a little girl again. It seems to me, looking back over my jump-rope and hop-scotch days, that I never played half hard enough; I always came in a little too soon, lay abed a little too long. If I had only known, and had climbed enough trees and made enough mud-pies to last me through the awful days when I would want to and couldn't!

Millay is certainly, and sadly, a sensitive girl whose childhood was taken from her too soon. It is characteristic of this brave soul to blame no one but herself. In the coming weeks and months she will charge fate, the gods, and a corrupt society for her miserable servitude, but rarely will she point her finger at her sisters, and *never* at her mother, apart from wishing, plaintively, that the traveling nurse would come home and take care of her.

"Journal of a Little Girl Grown Up" covers nine pages of Vincent's private diary, Wednesday through Friday, July 20 to 22, 1910. Like the rest of the diaries, it has never before been published. After nearly a hundred years in darkness, it reveals a girl struggling to liberate her imagination, a budding philosopher who was about to become a master poet.

Vincent describes the rare phenomenon of eidetic memory, soon to become a major strength in her life as a writer, but for the present only a painful burden. "I can remember every thing I ever did, every place I was ever in, every face I ever saw. My mind is a labyrinthian picture gallery in which every painting is a scene from my life. . . ." The faintest sound or scent can evoke scenes. A little yellow flower growing in clusters on a bush, called clove or flowering currant—the smell of it always "took her back" into a playhouse she made once under such a bush, against the church-yard fence.

It is a hot summer afternoon. The air is drowsy with the sweetness of the tiny trumpet-shaped flowers above my head, and, save for the monotonous droning of many bees, there is no sound anywhere. I am painstakingly trimming a rhubarb-leaf hat with white clover and butter-cups. . . . Beside me are two long, slender white wands from which I have been peeling the bark for ribbons (with primitive implements of sharp teeth and nails). I taste again the sweetness of the smooth round stick in my mouth. I see again the moist, delicate green of the bark's lining.

So much sensual poetry she finds here in the lush, fragrant world of child-hood! She roams from picture to picture in the gallery of memory, "Through a meadow where at every step I had to pick the violets to clear a place for my feet," across the stubble of a field and up a "path to a secret spot where fox-berries grew bigger, sweeter and more plentifully than anywhere else in the world."

"If I could just go back," she yearns in the diary entry, "like a little girl and revisit each scene alone! Who would there be to say 'Go away, you can't come here for you are a little girl no longer.' "

She couldn't sleep for brooding over it. Wrestling with the blankets for a while ("they seemed to be nailed to the bed"), she then reached into the darkness by her bed for a match. Her groping hand knocked a tray to the floor. She slid out of bed and began to crawl about on her knees in search of the match, only to find one that had already been struck.

"From sheer vexation and discomfort, I began to cry, sitting back on my heels, my hands hanging limply beside me and my face disconsolately upthrust into the dark, cried until I had cried down into the tears of that strange, resentful grief which had grown bitter from lying in my heart so long."

At last, following an impulse from childhood, she pulled the sheets and blankets in armfuls from the bed into a mound on the floor. Then with a sigh she "wriggled down into their grateful warmth and went to sleep."

The catharsis of that tearful night yielded in dreams an answer, a thrilling epiphany. "The idea came so suddenly that I hardly dare trust it."

> All at once I sat straight up and stared out into the darkness, and the darkness rolled up like a curtain and left it there, clear and perfect in every detail like the setting of a play. The broad low house clung easily to the slope of the hill. It seemed to fit there somehow; as if under the measured hammering of the years it had relaxed unresistingly to become at last a part of the soil on which it stood.

She struggled to identify the brilliant white house and the green grass, and "I caught my breath in an ecstasy of recognition." It is the house of an aunt she knew only in childhood, the kind Auntie Bines who once took care of her, and where she once had been truly happy. "The-Little-Girl-I-Used-To-Be was standing on the step, her small face upthrust in the sunlight—silent and adoring.

"I am homesick for that little girl on the step. Perhaps she would let me play with her, for indeed I have not forgotten how. . . . Oh Auntie Bines, if I might just come back and be your little girl again! You would know me, you would love me just the same, Auntie Bines, and we would forget that I had ever been away. . . . Why not? Why not?"

※

She would learn to accept the loss of childhood, but it would not be by rushing into womanhood—at least, not by giving herself to a boy.

Three days later she went for a walk with Russell all the way down Chestnut Street, by the lily pond, and they had a "falling out," as she calls it in her diary—surely to him a lover's quarrel, given that he had cause to think she might never love him. And then she fell ill, recovering only in time for her solo piano recital on August 3. "Wore my green silk for the first time. Played Dvorak's 'Humoresque' and Neven's 'It Was a Lover and Her Lass,' " she wrote, and "I didn't make a single mistake." She would always take comfort in her own virtuosity, on the piano, in her verses, anywhere she might have absolute control.

During that summer of 1910, and in the same journal she decorated with Redon-like colored-pencil drawings of birds, flowers, and butterflies, the poet declared, "My soul is too big for the rest of me." And she began drafting the prophetic verses:

> Give her to me who was created mine!
> Just as she is; half pixy, half divine!
> Who, list'ning feels in her own throbbing throat
> The flutter of the nightingale's soft note;
> Whose fingers vibrate with intense desire
> Of vibrant life; who is made up of fire,
> And wind, and music, fashioned for delight . . .

This poem of thirty-two couplets, which was never included in Millay's books, proves that in the summer of 1910 the poet had established the main persona—created the leading role—that was to deliver her verses for decades to come: a vatic, magical, pantheistic muse.

> Shall I not know, when we at last shall meet
> The wanton, wistful tread of her small feet?
> Her April eyes? Her smile, whose strange caress
> Is radiant with some sacred tenderness?
> Her sweet nun-mouth behind its chastity
> Tense with the kisses that she keeps for me?
> Her voice? The autumn glory of her hair?
> Think you I would not know her anywhere?

In this self-portrait she is laying her claim to that muse, the persona that has been born of her native personality, the mountains and waterways of Maine, and the seeds of the goddesses Athena and Aphrodite. Now it begins to become evident what that crossbred background—genetic, geographic, and divine—has cost her, in daily toil and the nightly harrowing of her psyche.

On Halloween she and her girlfriends Martha, Corinne, Jesse, and Gladys gathered at Ethel Knight's for a Halloween party. "I have the dearest witch costume which I wore," she notes, adding cryptically, "I met my fate and everything is satisfactorily settled." There is a quaint photograph of the pretty red-haired witch, with her pointed, wide-brimmed hat, black robes, and broomstick, posing balefully in a cropped field against the backdrop of Mount Battie. She has met her fate, and we know more about that than the eighteen-year-old sorceress did; but because she has neglected her diary we cannot be sure what fate *she* thinks she has recently met, or what, exactly, has been satisfactorily settled. It is not a young beau, this fate, that much is certain. It is also certain that the girl-turned-woman has summoned a primeval and autochthonic power, a daemon "half pixy, half divine," and in this powerful daemon her fate is sealed. One book that she keeps constantly by her side in these years, and until the eve of her death, is Sir Walter Scott's classic *Demonology and Witchcraft*. Her mother might well have given it to her.

Now it would be as much of a mistake to dwell too long on the demonic, pagan impulses of this young New Englander as it would be to ignore them altogether. The fact is that Vincent Millay, like her mother with her healing herbs, potions, and chants, and like many strong-willed women since the Inquisition, was turning away from a Christianity that virtually disenfranchised her, and in its stead was embracing the untrammeled free instruments of the creative, individual will. Toward the close of 1910 Vincent would abandon Christian prayer, even the idiosyncratic prayers she had written to serve her purposes two years earlier. Henceforth she will continue to get what she wants and needs by an exercise of sheer will power and homemade, clay-pot sorcery. She will bring to her paganism a devotion and discipline that owes much to her Christian education.

She records this journey in her secret journals, which from 1911 until 1913 largely supplant the more commonplace diaries. They are a stunning record of her spiritual struggle, her yearning for love, and the power of her will. In July of 1908 she had explained that her diary must be her *confidante*, i.e., a female ear. Now in April of 1911 she addresses, with due dignity and solemnity, her new confessor, a man. Not just any man but the most perfect man in the universe, the man for Vincent, her dream lover, her husband-to-be. She intends, by all the powers at her disposal, to conjure him up in the circle of light thrown by the magic candle in her bedroom on Chestnut Street.

The first séance occurs on April 3, 1911. The title of her diary entry is "Consecration."

> To you who, tho yet but a shadow, are more real than reality to me: I consecrate myself.
> Confident that you are seeking for me even as I am waiting for you, I will fill the time until you come with preparation for you.
> I will make myself what you wish me to be. I will kill out of myself the little selfish vices that are trying to spoil me, and I will plant pleasing things in their places.
>
> You are strong, clean and kind. I know that I am weak. But I will grow strong thinking of you, never forgetting that I am not mine but yours, and trying to care for myself as you would wish me cared for, until you come.
> I will keep myself clean. Even the smallest of my favors I will keep for you.

Like a vestal virgin or a novice bride of Christ she means to cultivate, for *him*, purity, industry, and humility. Her yearning for him did not begin on the date she wrote the "Consecration." On the same date she wrote: "I have felt sometimes that you must come to me at once, I needed you so; times when my heart would cry out at the wrong I was doing you, because I had grown tired of waiting." She confesses that her own strength is not enough, "and with my whole soul I have called to you to come, to help me, to command me ... I have grown sick of having the whole responsibility of myself. I need your strength." It is notable that, having grown up without a male role model, Millay would invest her dream lover with the power to solve all her problems, and look to him for the signal to abandon her own will.

As she continues, page after page, to pour out her heart to this absent lover, she shows that he represents for her not only the promise of sexual fulfillment. She also seeks happiness, a feeling of peace that transcends erotic satisfaction. "For years I have not been happy, because I have been filled with an ache of longing for you. I have been glad; I have been joyful; I have been ecstatic; but I have not been happy."

This last phrase—"I have been ecstatic; but I have not been happy"—is a key to the personality and genius of Millay. She has an ecstatic nature. A

flower, a Bach prelude, a sunset, or her mother's gray eyes can send her into
an emotional transport, an out-of-body experience in which she feels double
or triple the thrill that the rest of us might draw from the same stimulus.
But the thrill has little to do with happiness, which consists not so much in
distinct delights or sensations as it does in deep and more sustained feelings
of wholeness and serenity. As much as Millay admired Wordsworth, she was
not the sort of poet whose verses were the fruit of what he called "emotion
recollected in tranquillity." She stands more prominently in the visionary
tradition of Blake, Shelley, and Coleridge, of Nerval, Baudelaire, and Rim-
baud, for whom poetry is an ecstatic response to experience, often induced
by violent or painful disorientation of the senses.

Her desire for this dream lover never leaves her: "It is the accompani-
ment to every song I sing. While I am at work the thought of you never
leaves me. All day long and all night long. . . . It is the undercurrent to my
life." If he does not come, then she will "never be free from the feeling
of something lacking, nothing quite perfect—quite full. Oh, I want to be
happy!" She would choose to have an hour with him now even if she should
die tomorrow: "That hour would be my life and my life would be full and
perfect."

The idea that there can be no true happiness apart from a perfect human
love will remain at the core of Millay's philosophy, even years after she has
given up hope for it. That she addresses the lover-to-be, the love of her
dreams, in so much the manner of a novice praying to Christ is peculiar and
highly significant. But she is more poet than saint, and her journal is destined
to evolve into a love poem, as evidenced by this entry, on June 3, 1911:
"When I have found a way to express the inexpressible, then will I tell you
how I love you."

❧

In her little room on Chestnut Street overlooking the commonplace world
of Camden harbor—the chandlery, the anchor forge and foundry buildings,
the coal warehouses—she arranges on the third of every month, the com-
memoration of what she calls a "consecration" in an effort to woo her love
o' dreams, to bring him to her from wherever he may be. "I will make believe you are in some distant country for a time and are surely coming to me
soon. And I will make myself so sweet that you will surely love me when
you come."

She waits until everyone else is asleep and the house is still. She gets into
her finest white nightgown, brushes her long copper-red hair until it shines,

slides the secret journal from under her mattress, and sits down at the writing table. She puts on the tin ring that came to her in the fortune cake, and then she lights the candle. Oh the candle, for which girls of all times and places have found so many comforting rituals and prophetic uses! She lights the candle to summon his spirit, and then she begins to pour out her soul to him—her sorrows, yearnings, and wishes.

During the first months she entertains him only on the third of the month. Later she makes him "welcome at all hours," privacy permitting, as any day of his coming "will make that day sacred too." So the secret journal begins to cover more and more of the calendar.

She writes and she whispers, and when her passions grow too large for the written page she lays down her pen and rises to act out the scene that has begun to fill up her room.

"Beloved—I have been true to you in thought and deed. I have been saving up for you my month's allowance of Heart's Adoration. . . . It grows most abundantly of all the flowers in my Heart-Garden . . . more beautiful even than Heart's delight or Heart's Lavendar or Bleeding Heart or even Heart's ease."

Her need to adore and be adored by the dream lover grew in direct proportion to the difficulty of living from day to day, particularly when her mother was gone and money was scarce. The summer of 1911 proved to be the most demanding of Vincent's life. The Maine summers usually came as a relief from the oppression of winter—the snow and ice, the bitter wind, the struggle to keep warm in drafty houses without central heat, without indoor "flush-closets." By July Vincent would be luxuriating in the flowers and soft breezes of the seaport, sailing and swimming daily in the bay, climbing Mount Battie, picnicking at Sherman's Point, and canoeing on Lake Megunticook. But this summer her mother was gone most of the time, working in Boston, Rockport, and other towns. Vincent was left with the management of the household and the care of her sisters, now seventeen and fourteen, neither of whom ever developed the self-reliance or domestic industry that Vincent had assumed, perforce, at age ten. Why she was cast in this Cinderella role, when Norma was only a year younger, and Kathleen was older than Vincent had been when she had taken on the role of surrogate parent, is hard to say. These family dynamics, once established, become rigid; and it seems that for a while Vincent (like mother, like daughter) took some masochistic comfort in the martyr's role.

In the same long letters to Cora wherein she describes what a wonderful time the three girls are having—on motorboat parties on the Bay, on evening picnics on Sherman's Point, in learning to swim—she apologizes for the shameful inadequacies of her domestic efforts:

> I am so sorry and ashamed about things. I started with the idea that I was an invalid and unable to do a thing. I really did feel pretty bum, but I might have kept things going. I am feeling fine now and I have been doing well at home lately. (July 7, 1911)

She has been ill again, but has sufficiently recovered to resume baking bread, beans, pies, cakes, and doughnuts, "and we are living almost wholly from home cooking." She describes her marketing, her wrangling with the grocer over the bill.

As published, Millay's letters to Cora do not reveal the onerous pressure under which the girl labored that summer, or the toll it took on her. She takes pains to conceal this from her mother, while emphasizing the robust pleasures she and her sisters are taking out of doors. But Cora's letters to Vincent, and Vincent's journals, tell a more dramatic story.

On August 3, Cora writes from Rockland where she is nursing three sisters who are dying. She has just received her week's pay, which she is sending in money orders immediately to Vincent to cover overdue bills. The Millays are deeply in debt, Cora is desperate over it, and she blames Vincent for mismanaging their money. Of the grocer, she writes, "Pascal's bill came yesterday and it made me sick on top of all my hard work here. I couldn't get to sleep last night even though I had a chance. It is $38.60 and I paid $15.00 [to him] while at Dr. Wargall's. I cannot stand it and it must be different. I thought earning what I am now I might get caught up a little." Then she gives Vincent elaborate instructions for going over possible mistakes in the bills, budgeting for meals, and cooking more cheaply. Then she adds, "Where are your fall outfits coming from? And for the Music Festival?" (In other words, have you begun sewing yet on yard goods we can't afford?) "I am just about discouraged and this is a very hard case and one little girl we have just pulled out of death if we can hold her there. See that Pascal and Mrs. Sherman get these [money orders] *at once*. And send me that bill *at once*. Write me how you are getting along. Have a good time, but talk it over a bit and plan for Mama's interest, which is nothing but your own interest as all I get is what I eat."

Talk about your Jewish mothers laying on the guilt—Cora Millay raised the pain quotient. "Have a good time," writes nurse Cora, while I am struggling here to save the lives of three dying sisters, and you frivolous girls with your picnics and motorboat rides are taking the food out of my mouth and sucking the very blood out of my poor veins. "Oh, we're having a good time," Vincent replies, brightly, her cheerfulness masking her illness, exhaustion, anxiety, and guilt. All the while she just wants her mother to come home and take care of *her*. Not the least of Cinderella's emotional stew was a load of unconscious, displaced fury at her mother, whom she adored.

"It is hard work being brave when you're lonesome," Vincent confides to her dream lover on August 3. "I've tried to be brave and I've done pretty well, but I've had to cry just a little tonight. It's no fun being in love with a shadow. . . . You must be somewhere in this world. God would not have made a heart like mine and not have made its mate. It would be too cruel. O, I know you are not very far away."

She is practicing, studying to be brave, and in the end her bravery will become her most admirable virtue, outlasting her charm and beauty, her wit and perseverance. In this soul-searching journal entry we can see how Millay's courage grew from a frail seed to a sturdy evergreen:

> Beloved, I need your strength tonight. Keep me with you and away from myself. Don't let me be a bundle of nerves and emotions, now up and upright at the top of the world, and now lying face-down at the bottom of everything. (July 27, 1911)

She has recognized in herself, at age nineteen, the manic-depressive dynamic that has destroyed so many artists.

> Oh, I am sick of myself! If I might have another self—more governable, more temperate. . . . Oh, I need your strength. I need calmness and restraint, I need a balance wheel.

> I depend more on you. . . . It's a dreadful feeling, you know, dear, to lean on something which isn't there. It makes you think for a minute that the bottom has dropped out of the world. But there has never been a bottom of the world for me, nor anything but a seeking and a breathlessness.

> I am all feelings. My emotions are wearing my body thin.

Manual labor is also wearing her body thin. On October 9 she writes that she is going to bed early because she has worked "from seven to seven, with just time out to eat. I've been washing—Oh such a washing! My poor hands are blistered in a dozen places." Now she must start on the ironing, which "will blister my hands in a dozen places and by that time the outside blisters will be all healed and I shall be ready for more." This becomes a recurrent complaint. The fair-skinned Vincent's hands are often so chafed she cannot play the piano or hold a pencil.

"I hope I will rest at the rate of an ache a minute tonight so that I won't feel tired in the morning. I am so anxious to get the work all caught up. You are my reward, you know, and I'm trying to earn you. Oh dear, I would so like to be rocked to sleep tonight!"

On one page she prays to her lover to make her a more perfect servant, sister, and daughter, stronger and more patient. The next evening she cries out for him to come and rescue her. "I am so tired . . . it isn't right . . ." And in a long and eloquent existential tirade she protests the futility and sadness of human toil. She grieves over the tedious labor that she, and all of human-kind, must do and do over again, like Sisyphus rolling his rock up the hill; and more deeply she mourns for the beauty that goes unseen, unappreciated, while she is scrubbing a floor.

She looks out the window and sees Mount Megunticook in its mantle of autumn leaves. "The color—Oh—there is never anything like their color in the fall! I want to climb Megunticook before the leaves are all gone. But I can't. I've got to work—work all the time. And for what?"

Once more she looks out her window, down toward the men at work in the coal yard. A man rides by on a bicycle, his hat paint-spattered. A boy walks up the road carrying a window frame. A whistle blows, the smoke pours from the chimneys. She hears the sounds of hammers, shovels, digging and dredging, sees trams going past filled with barrels and window frames. "Tired men and tired horses, everybody tired, and no one with a minute to call his own. No time to lift your eyes to the hills. Go in and get to work. Get into the house and scrub the dirty clothes till you rub the skin off your fingers. Sweep the floor and sweep it again tomorrow and the day after that . . . every day of your life—if not that floor, why then—some other floor."

Because of the mindless, ceaseless toil, she has no time "to practice my beautiful sonatas. I might sometime have a beautiful sonata all my own. . . . What good would that do? I couldn't take my hands out of the wash-tub long enough to play it over. . . . What's the good of books and poems? I don't get any time to read."

And not the least of the dreamer's worries is that she is getting "old and ugly. My hands are stiff and rough and stained and blistered. I can feel my face dragging down. I can feel the lines coming underneath my skin. . . . I love beauty more than anything else in the world and I can't take time to be pretty. . . . Crawl into bed at night too tired to brush my hair—my beautiful hair—all autumn-colored like Megunticook."

She fears that by the time her lover finds his way to her door, if he ever does, she will be so haggard and homely he'll take one look at her and beat a hasty retreat.

The secret diary of 1911 records such mood swings that any attempt to synopsize its hundred dense pages is likely to leave a false impression. Her sense of humor never completely deserts her. The diary, with its dream lover, was her "balance wheel"; alternating with pages of gloom and despair are passages of joy, hope, and exhilaration. "The weariness and the restlessness have left my heart—for a time at least—and in their stead is a wonderful feeling of calmness, confidence, and constancy, all in one." On such nights her love is different. On nights such as October 6, 1911, she has so much strength of her own that she does not need a man's company at all:

> You are my boy tonight—my own, dear boy, whom I do utterly love and adore. The mother heart in my breast beats steadily, and sends healthy blood through all my quiet body. The mother-heart: there is no strength like it.
> You are my boy tonight. I do not want to be comforted, but to comfort—to hold your head on my lap, and love you, and fuss with your hair, and cry over you, not stormily, not hysterically, but tenderly, and quietly, lest you see and be grieved.

The dynamic of these needs—to give comfort and to be comforted—will continue throughout Millay's life, influencing her many love affairs. It is noteworthy that she is in anguish while seeking the strength of the absent male and at peace when she has internalized the warm presence of her mother.

❧

The incantations at 40 Chestnut Street that began in spring of 1911 and continued into 1912 were a weird kind of courtship. "I will send out my love over the whole earth tonight—there is enough, Oh, love! there is enough—and wherever you are it will reach you."

She was casting a cosmic, psychic net. With words and candles, a "spirit ring," and a set of private rituals and fairy minions, the little sorceress was weaving a spell. "I am sitting now in the light of that candle which tonight [November 3] I have lighted for the seventh time. I shall light it five times more, and on the fifth night I shall let it burn out. Then, if you have not come by that time, I shall get another, and begin again."

We may well wonder, those of us who think we are above superstition, just how much power was generated by this demonic girl and her lares and penates, her chants and candles, what sort of immeasurable vibrations she was creating in the bowl of Camden Harbor, in the lee of Mount Battie. Her will, grimly affirmed in her incantations, is superhuman, terrifying: "I swear to you by our love, than which no oath can be more sacred, that I shall not fail. . . . The depth of my purpose has underscored these words more heavily than anyone else could possibly understand."

The months pass, the autumn leaves fall, the snow covers the streets and countryside, and the cold always makes her feel lonelier. Still, he does not come. On January 6, 1912, she writes:

> Although I loathe the position I am in, although my need of you is terrible and my desire for you almost annihilating, yet must I exert every atom of my will and lift myself body and soul—above my situation and my surroundings. I must. It has to be. . . . And if there is so much as an atom in all this universe that understands and desires to help me, let that atom come forth and stand by me now in this my last, desperate war against futility.

The atoms that will come forth to save Vincent are the words of poems. She is above all else a poet. There is much unintentional, informal poetry in her diaries and journals, and the ideas and emotions so lyrically described in her prose will soon find a more potent expression in her verses. In fact, the gaps in her diary correspond with dates that found Vincent absorbed in writing poems. For instance, her first substantial long poem, "Interim," a mysterious elegy of more than two hundred lines, was written in late September of 1911, in the same notebook that contains an extraordinary "Essay on Faith." This thousand-word essay is a precise philosophical statement of Millay's belief system, as it has emerged out of her recent crisis of faith.

> Things are real only as we believe them. Just as surely as each is the center of his universe, just so surely is his universe bounded by the circumference of his life. His believings are the radii he sends out to the edge of things and on the edge of things does each find its corresponding belief. [*The world stands out on either side / No wider than the heart is wide* . . . —"Renascence"]

> My soul is as deathless as God's soul, for there is no degree in eternity.

Faith is all that keeps the world alive. If faith were all at once to be taken away, the tide which is now high would forget how to fall, birds flying fearless across the sky would drop in terror to the earth, fishes would drown in the sea; the veins of the universe would fall tangled from the nerveless hands of God, and the worlds would gallop headlong to destruction.

Better die firm in the faith of immortality than live dreading an ultimate death.

A man's future is his own and he is its creator. Would you be a king? Only believe and your future is your kingdom.

This unpublished "Essay on Faith" serves as the philosophical groundwork not only for the elegiac monologue "Interim," but also for the sublime "Renascence," which the poet began a few months later. "Interim" is a curious and enigmatic poem, an elegy for a departed girl. When Millay submitted the piece to a writing class at Vassar in 1914, it so stymied the professor that he suggested she add the Browningesque stage direction "A Man Speaks." She graciously agreed, to please him, but later she deleted the stage direction when the poem was published in her first book:

> The room is full of you! As I came in
> And closed the door behind me, all at once
> A something in the air, intangible,
> Yet stiff with meaning, struck my senses sick!

Like "Lycidas," "Adonais," and other classic elegies Millay admired, "Interim" mingles memories of the lost beloved with meditations upon death, mortality, and the dynamics of faith.

> There is your book, just as you laid it down,
> Face to the table,—I cannot believe
> That you are gone!
>
> And here are the last words your fingers wrote,
> Scrawled in broad characters across a page
> In this brown book I gave you.

We know the book, the table, and the room very well. This is a picture of Vincent's own bedroom and secret diary, an 8½-by-6½-inch, brown bound notebook, and the description of writer and handwriting ("You were so small, and wrote so brave a hand!") and other details indicate that the subject of "Interim" is the poet herself. Written only two months after her "Journal of a Little Girl Grown Up," the poem is Vincent's formal farewell to and expression of grief for the girl (herself) left in the doorway of Auntie Bine's farmhouse. The speaker's sadness opens the door to painful religious questions: "Would to God / I too might feel that frenzied faith whose touch / Makes temporal the most enduring grief . . ." Although the long poem never wholly resolves the speaker's own doubts, it forcefully argues the urgent *necessity* of faith for survival in language echoing the "Essay on Faith."

> Not Truth, but Faith, it is
> That keeps the world alive. If all at once
> Faith were to slacken,—that unconscious faith
> Which must, I know, yet be the corner-stone
> Of all believing,—birds now flying fearless
> Across would drop in terror to the earth;
> Fishes would drown; and the all-governing reins
> Would tangle in the frantic hands of God
> And the worlds gallop headlong to destruction!

Aptly named, "Interim" captures the feelings and ideas during the season between Edna St. Vincent Millay's crisis of faith and identity in 1911 and the triumph of 1912, when she completed "Renascence."

The state of mind, the circumstances, and the sentiments of the young Vincent who wrote the masterpiece "Renascence" have long been subjects of keen interest and intense speculation. The poem is a cry of the heart, *de profundis*; but it is far less spontaneous and less naïve—more premeditated, more the product of a highly evolved intellect, engaging religious and moral problems of considerable weight—than has hitherto been recognized. The notebooks, diaries, and letters that anticipated the verses of "Renascence" were kept under lock and key for nearly a hundred years, like the secret devices of a stage magician. The poem has always seemed an American miracle of precocity; it may seem no less a miracle today, but somewhat less mysterious, once the scaffolding that supported it stands revealed.

In the "interim," things will get far worse for Vincent before they get better.

RENASCENCE

❧

*I*n September of 1911 she had written, "There is no time, no distance in my love. It is the supreme element. But it is too great to bear alone and the weight of it is crushing me. . . . I need your hand to cling to. . . . Oh, Sweetheart! How long will you leave me alone?"

By January 1912, in the icy grip of winter, she was terrified: "I am frightened. I do not know of what I am afraid. The thought of the universe makes me sick. It is dread that I feel, an intangible, fatalistic feeling. There is so little left of my winnowing on which to build a faith. . . . I love you. At least I think it's love. But it seems to me I'm drowning." If she had been reading Kierkegaard, which of course she had not, she could not have composed a passage more sympathetic to the angst of the Danish existentialist, whose influence would not be felt in America for another thirty years.

On February 3, her "anniversary" night, she entered in her journal only three sentences: "I have a lot of things to say but this is another death—this night. I've lighted my candle and I'm going to wear my ring all night. Perhaps I will tell you the things tomorrow."

But she will not tell him anything that day, or the next, because she has been busy writing verses.

> All I could see from where I stood
> Was three long mountains and a wood;
> I turned and looked the other way,
> And saw three islands in a bay.
> So with my eyes I traced the line
> Of the horizon, thin and fine,
> Straight around till I was come
> Back to where I started from . . .
>   (from "Renascence")

It might have been the view from the crest of Mount Battie, or it might have been the panorama from the waterfront anywhere along the western side of the harbor just down the hill from Vincent's room and across Bay View

Street. Anywhere south of the mast- and spar-makers you could see mountains in one direction and islands in the other.

> These were the things that bounded me.
> And I could touch them with my hand,
> Almost, I thought, from where I stand!
> And all at once things seemed so small
> My breath came short, and scarce at all.

The vision that follows takes up themes that haunted Edgar Allan Poe and Emily Dickinson, fearful feelings of claustrophobia and thoughts of premature burial. Sure that the sky is big enough for her to rest comfortably under it, she lies down to look at the heavens until she has got her fill of them; but soon she grows suspicious that "the sky . . . must somewhere stop."

> And reaching up my hand to try,
> I screamed to feel it touch the sky.
>
> I screamed, and—lo!—Infinity
> Came down and settled over me;
> Forced back my scream into my chest;
> Bent back my arm upon my breast . . .

Through the lens of infinity she is granted a unique and privileged revelation:

> I saw and heard and knew at last
> The How and Why of all things, past,
> And present, and forevermore.

The price she must pay for such knowledge is dear.

> For my omniscience paid I a toll
> In infinite remorse of soul.
> All sin was of my sinning, all
> Atoning mine, and mine the gall
> Of all regret.

For months she had been recording in her diary her sufferings of guilt, existential terror, and angst. On February 11 she wrote, "I do not think there is a woman in whom the roots of passion shoot deeper than in me. . . . It seems to me that I am, incarnate, rapture and melancholy. . . . I feel intensely every little thing. . . . Sometimes I think that I have experienced . . . every emotion, that is, the emotions I have not physically felt I have imagined so vividly as to make them real to me. And what life I have lived I have lived doubly, actually and symbolically." For example, waking in the morning so tired she dreads to get up, she envisions a world of workers filled with the same dread.

There can be no more precise account of the psychic burden of the poet, the *moral* poet, or the anointed saint. "Renascence" is perhaps the most striking expression of this burden in American literature, at least before the later poems of T. S. Eliot and some of the meditations of Thomas Merton. The poet and critic John Crowe Ransom, who was restrained but unequivocal in his praise of what he did not hesitate to call Millay's "genius," said "*Renascence* is genuine, in the sense that it is the right kind of religious poem for an actual young girl of New England." She resumes:

> I saw at sea a great fog bank
> Between two ships that struck and sank.
> A thousand screams the heavens smote;
> And every scream tore through my throat.
>
> . . . .
>
> All suffering mine, and mine its rod;
> Mine, pity like the pity of God.
>
> Ah, awful weight! Infinity
> Pressed down upon the finite Me!

Under this terrible burden she longs for death. And quietly the earth gives way beneath her until she is "full six feet under ground." There the onerous weight cannot follow, and she rests peacefully, "gladly dead," listening to the rain fall.

> For rain it hath a friendly sound
> To one who's six feet under ground;
> And scarce the friendly voice or face,
> A grave is such a quiet place.

Here, at line 116 of the poem that would someday be nearly twice that length, the poet looked up from her paper and desk, out the window overlooking Camden harbor. She did not know what would come next, but tried out certain lines aloud: "Long lay I listening to the rain / Conscious of blessed ease from pain . . ." And she imagined peace personified as a kind of domestic goddess "whose sandals fall / Softly along from hall to hall / Where Pain has held his wild carouse, / While patiently she rights the house. . . ." These lines played through her mind, and she tried them out with the pencil on the page.

The last lines were somehow wrong. Either the poem was finished before, or she was stuck. She left the work, returning days later to scribble disjointed notes: "I know not how such came to be!—I breathed my soul back into me." And then, "Bounding to my feet came I / And hailed the earth with such a cry / As is not heard save from a man / Who dies and comes to life again." These and a few other fragments she scrawled on the same unlined pages with the 116 finished verses. But the rest of the poem, if there was indeed more to come, would have to wait for a while.

❧

Writing the first half of "Renascence" greatly lifted the poet's spirits, as only working at the top of one's form can do. The diary entry on her twentieth birthday (February 22, 1912) is quite cheerful. "Good morning! I am just twenty years old this minute—half past nine—and you are the first person I've spoken to. Just think! Not in my teens anymore and never again. It seems so funny. I usually make resolutions on my birthday, and I usually keep them pretty well . . . but I think I'll not make any today, or perhaps just one . . . suppose that during the next year I try to be fairly decent. . . . Now I am going out and be fairly decent to somebody. Good-bye!"

The chance to do a good deed came a week later, and Vincent jumped at it. On Thursday, February 29, a long-distance call came from Kingman, Maine, where her father lived. Cora was working on a case in Rockland, so Vincent answered the phone.

"Your father is very ill, and may not recover."

Vincent was speechless, but eventually stuttered out the words that she would soon be sending a telegram. Then she rang her mother long distance. They decided that Vincent ought to go at once to Bangor and see how she might help Henry Tolman Millay.

Few references to Henry Millay appear in the family letters and diaries before this year. Vincent sometimes mentions that she has written to her father, but there are no letters from him before 1912 or mention of visits to him or from him. Though he seems to have sent the girls money irregularly, whenever he was able, there is no evidence that they depended upon it or that Cora received alimony.

From photographs and Vincent's letters we know that he was handsome: square-jawed, fair-haired, and blue-eyed, with a luxurious handlebar mustache. He was fond of jokes, laughter, and singing, and a devil with the cards. During long nights at the whist or poker table he was not averse to steadying his nerves with rye whiskey. It has always been believed that Cora (whose mother divorced *her* father) divorced Henry more or less amicably because he spilled their hard-earned dollars onto the card table and lost more than he won. Divorce was rare in those days. Detailed letters from Cora to her sister Sue speak of a pattern of abuse. The only witness at her divorce trial was Henry's brother Bert, who testified that Henry "had abused her bitterly." Another brother, Fred, said he did not know how she "had stood it so long." It is difficult to imagine the feisty, tough Cora allowing anyone to strike her, with words or fists, but we do not know how she became the "hard-bitten" woman who raised three girls by herself, or what she was like as a young bride. There is little room for doubt that Henry did treat his wife cruelly, that the girls witnessed this, and that Cora was bitter about it forever afterward.

Nevertheless, Cora seems to have encouraged her daughters to maintain contact with their father, in deference to the Fifth Commandment, not to mention the man's potential as a source of income. Henry evidently was dying up there in Kingman, and if he had a dollar left to his name after his compulsive gambling (he was still a notorious cardsharp), the money belonged to his daughters.

So Vincent threw some clothes and poems together into her Aunt Rose's borrowed suitcase, and the next day boarded the noon boat for Bucksport, where she caught a train to Bangor. She spent the night there with family friends, the Duntons, whose granddaughter Gladys Niles, a law student, read Vincent's new poem, as yet untitled. Vincent casually called it "the down underground poem." Gladys liked the verses and the Camden girl, and before Vincent boarded the train for Kingman the next morning they had vowed to keep in touch.

Ella Somerville, the daughter of Henry Millay's doctor, met Vincent at the train station. Arrangements had been made for her to stay at Dr. Somerville's home. According to Vincent's diary, after a cup of coffee there, the doctor and Ella took Vincent to the place where her father was boarding, a pale blue house owned by Mr. and Mrs. Yannis Boyd. As Vincent walked through the doorway she heard the sound of a man coughing upstairs. Only at that moment did she realize how long it had been since she had seen her father—eleven years.

An Irish nurse announced that Mr. Millay was expecting his daughter. Then it seemed to Vincent that all of them—the doctor and nurse, the Boyds and their sons, and Ella—were watching her carefully, piteously, advising her to brace up and keep calm, "which was really funny," she recalled, "as I was not the least bit nervous and everybody else seemed very much upset. Isn't that always the way? Perhaps I wasn't so calm though, as I was numb." She stood outside of herself, "hearing myself say things and watching myself do things," as if she were "an altogether different being, not in the least concerned."

Dr. Somerville led her upstairs and left her alone with the dying man.

"It didn't seem to me that the man on the bed was my father." She stood beside him and said, "Hello Papa, dear," just as she had planned, but her voice came out higher pitched than usual.

He opened his eyes, the bluest she had ever seen, and cried out, "Vincent, my little girl," struggling to sit up in the bed, as he held out his arms to her. She put her arms around him and made him lie back against the pillows, then sat on the side of the bed and talked to him.

"Oh, I wish my eyes were blue like yours so they might match my hat."

Now he could only whisper. "You can't very well change your eyes, Vincent, but you might have got a green hat."

She laughed then, and he smiled faintly, with his eyes closed. He had difficulty opening them, which made her all the more certain that he was going to die, a suspicion that the doctor confirmed later that afternoon, saying the man had only a few days to live.

That evening she wrote a card to her mother and sisters, telling them that she had "found Papa very low." That little postcard was, to their dismay, the last they heard from their emissary for three weeks. Whether or not the presence of his beloved daughter revived Henry Tolman Millay, the man did begin to improve, slowly. She visited him daily and read to him from the works of Kipling, his favorite, and the humorous story "Pigs Is Pigs," no more than an hour or two a day. And when she wasn't attending her father, the twenty-year-old girl, free at last from the dreary routine of housekeeping in Camden, was having the time of her life.

"He didn't die after all. In spite of everything he got well, and my sojourn in Kingman turned out to be a visit to Ella Somerville whom I grew to like very much."

Ella was twenty-four, a talented painter and pianist who had attended a good finishing school. Witty and funny, Ella delighted in poetry and dancing and certain boys. But she never loved anything on this earth as much as the red-haired fairy poet from Camden. She fell madly in love with Vincent Millay, in ways that Vincent found altogether welcome. According to her diary, the first night she spent at the Somervilles' home Ella asked Vincent if she would prefer staying with her in her room, or if Ella should just come and sleep with Vincent in her bed. Vincent said she would much rather Ella would come to her.

"After that we slept together every night—at least we spent the nights together." They talked, laughed, and giggled until the bed shook. They read poetry aloud, including Vincent's new poem. Ella particularly enjoyed hearing Vincent read Robert Burns, because she rolled her tongue so easily and joyously around the words. She loved Vincent's tongue and her little fingers, and it is not until the end of the month when Vincent has gone home and Ella, bereaved, starts writing her candid love letters, that we realize just how Ella loved Vincent Millay.

March 30, 1912

Dearie,
Did you think that Lovey had forgotten her own precious poppy laden canoe? Not so! She has only been so overcome by her loss that she has been incapable of transmitting even one rational sentence on paper. . . . She was so overwhelmed with anguish that she became temporarily deranged.

This is not playful sarcasm. After Vincent's departure Ella went into seclusion for two days. When she emerged she visited Henry Millay "thinking I might extract a grain of comfort by talking of my beloved." She stammered, "What a dreadful thing it is to be in love," a comment which Vincent's father took in with a kind glance of understanding but then dismissed "with an unseemly levity."

Of course, Henry had no idea what Ella was really trying to tell him, and modesty prevented her from being more explicit. But Ella's letters are graphic. "Say, it's awfully lonesome. No one to play with me, no one to call me 'grapefruit,' no one to roll on at night. . . . One thing is certain, old girl; when you make a place for yourself in someone's heart, no one else can fill it. . . ." This was the prototype of a thousand love letters, mostly from men, that Millay will receive during a lifetime abounding in love affairs. The specific carnal details of the girls' play, the flames of pretty tongues, "each little tongue will do a cunning dance . . . the *serpentine* dance, the *butterfly* dance," should not be construed as indicating the two girls were practicing to be lesbians primarily. They were both obsessed with men; most of their correspondence concerns their shared crush on a vaudeville fiddler, and Ella was lustily navigating a sea of romantic suitors on the way to marriage. But men were too dangerous to serve the physical needs of these hot-blooded Edwardian ladies, so they were relieved—delighted even—to turn to each other for warmth in the long winter nights, to touch each other in just the way they wanted to be touched. Praising Vincent's genitalia in the most liberated manner, Ella concludes: "It will afford much greater opportunity to give vent to the domestic side of your nature."

Their days together were as fun filled as their nights. They went to town meetings (where Henry Millay had always been "moderator") and attended dances almost every night. The Kingman fellows were renowned for dancing, not the old-fashioned contra dances, but waltzes and polkas and schottisches, and Vincent was a sensational dancer.

During the entire second week of March, the Kickapoo-Laguna Vaudeville Medicine Show played Kingman, and the girls went to it every day except for Tuesday, when they attended a lecture by the Dean of Education of the University of Maine. The medicine show's chief attraction was the Violin Man, described by Vincent "from our near front-end seats . . . was a good-looking man of thirty or almost, tall, rather, and slim, rather, with peripatetic eyes, three gold teeth, black hair, and the handsomest feet and ankles I ever saw. We could not keep our eyes away from—his violin."

She made eyes at him; he noticed her and returned the favor. "And he played to us and at us and through us, beautifully, just beautifully." The next night came the lecture, which the girls attended under duress "because all the nice people went . . . and Ella and I were nice people still, for we had not yet fallen in love with the violin man. We were just teetering round on the bias edge of it." But "our hearts were in the show-barn there with the fiddle."

So the next night they were back in the show-barn, sitting in the same seats, and this time they noticed that the Violin Man was looking at *them*. "When he had finished the overture, Ella said 'I wish he would play the Intermezzo from Cavaliera Rusticana.'" Ella had been playing the "Ave Maria" air from that Intermezzo to accompany Vincent's singing of it, which the duo planned to perform in the town's Methodist church. Imagine their surprise when, minutes later, the Violin Man played the piece they had longed for as his only solo of the evening!

"We began to think we had him hypnotized."

Indeed the flirtation between Vincent and the Violin Man became more and more flagrant as the week went by. She and Ella persuaded the Methodist minister to invite the Violin Man to play the Intermezzo as an obligato to Vincent's solo in the church on Sunday. And while the Violin Man was flattered beyond words, his schedule would not permit it, as he had to move on to the next town before the Sabbath. "The violinist was almost heart-broken, it seemed."

But eventually Vincent would get her man, in the only way that mattered to her. The medicine show nightly debauched into a dance party, for which the fiddler provided the music. Vincent was far and away the best dancer in the barn, and he could not keep his eyes off her as she spun and glided in the arms of the handsomest men in Kingman. "He didn't know it, but I was dancing for a prize, which was the Violin Man's admiration."

The fifteen-page letter that she wrote at last to her sisters on St. Patrick's Day "has more stuff to tell you than would fill a novel of Dickens." She can only begin to tell them what has happened to her, in the humorous and enthusiastic prose of a young woman who has discovered a new source of joy and vitality.

At the center of the Kingman experience is her father. "Papa sat up yesterday in a chair, partly dressed. I pop in and out all the time and we just love each other." The pale blue house where he was convalescing stood across the yard from the Methodist Church. Before she and Ella went into the sanctuary to rehearse Vincent's solo, she opened up Papa's window wide, despite the cold, and then they opened the church window so that he could hear his daughter singing a few lines of "Ave Maria."

"Papa thinks I have a voice with a future, said he thought it was [Madame Ernestine] Schumann-Heink a-bellering next door, had no idea I could sing like that. . . . Lord! How I do fool 'em all!" Her father who adores her, her pianist who is head over heels in love with her, the Violin Man who doesn't know what to do with her, the bedazzled swains of Kingman: it is a heady taste of power, far from home, where she can be free.

The letters from Camden came fast and furious before Vincent took time to write her long epistle of March 17. Her mother and sisters were frantic without her, could not understand why on earth they had heard nothing from her. On March 20 Cora wrote, "I have been so anxious about you that tonight I tried to telephone Dr. Somerville and the line was out of order. . . . We have watched the mails and I have come down from my case every night to hear from you. I have been afraid you were sick." On the contrary, Vincent never felt better. "It is time for you to come home. We need you. The girls are not having a fair chance for the last term. . . . I want you to be sure to be here to look out for things next week for them. . . . If I do not hear at once I shall telegraph." She enclosed a pathetic letter from Norma begging her sister to come back to her at once.

But Cinderella was taking her own sweet time. Ella was begging her to stay forever; at last Vincent decided that the two of them would go to Bangor together the following week, their date depending upon the theater schedule, as they wanted to take in a play before Ella put Vincent on the train to Bucksport.

In desperation, seeing the entreaties to Vincent's family loyalty were falling on deaf ears, Cora appealed to her daughter's literary ambitions: "I am going to try to catch you now with something that may interest and encourage you." Cora had seen an ad in a magazine announcing a "contest for writers of verse is being held by Mitchell Kennerley the publisher. . . . *One thousand dollars* [Cora's italics] has been set aside to be distributed in *three prizes* to authors of the best three poems submitted before June 1, 1912. . . . *Nov 1st of this year* Mr. Kennerley will put out the volume under the title 'The Lyric Year.'" It would contain the winning poems as well as others. "This seems to be a great chance for you. . . . Come home and make a good try so you can have chances to run up to school and use the typewriter."

This letter did not catch up with Vincent until March 28, when she was staying at her friends the Duntons for two days in Bangor, on her way back to Camden.

She arrived home on March 31, completely rejuvenated and ready to resume work on her long poem.

❧

The Kingman adventure is essential biography of the young woman who wrote "Renascence." The rejuvenation of spirits that had begun with the cathartic composition of 116 anguished lines in the winter of 1911–1912 was thoroughly accomplished and secured in March of 1912. Poetry had revived her, and love had restored her—paternal love, as well as a strong dose of erotic love, which she had found as strange and exhilarating as poetry. For the next several years, a critical transition in Vincent's life, the letters to and from her Papa are frequent and affectionate. As for the letters from Ella, though the correspondence will be short-lived it is intense. In her teens Vincent had felt the promptings of erotic love for nameless and insignificant boys. But never before had she known the erotic power of being *adored*, which Ella so finely expressed in her letters. Now that Vincent had experienced this passion, she would never be able to do without it.

Her crisis was over. Never again in her diaries or letters will she seem so frightened, tormented, so full of existential angst. She had found two sources of strength that would sustain her for years to come: poetry and erotic love. She returned to all of her work, domestic and literary, with a new outlook, joy, humor, and an irrepressible appetite for adventure. She came home to the exciting news that they were moving, from the dark tenement on the ground floor of 40 Chestnut, where she had suffered so deeply for more than a year, to a bright, two-story freestanding house with an upstairs bathroom and a coal furnace at 82 Washington Street. "A dear place," she called it at first sight, only a few blocks on the town side of the house in the field where she had spent her childhood.

April would always be a starred month on Millay's calendar. It was in mid-April of 1912, in a little room with a slanted ceiling under the eaves, at a table at the northeast window overlooking Washington Street, that the poet returned to her unfinished poem. There is a snapshot of her leaning out of this window, her long hair flowing like Rapunzel's. In reciting the visionary narrative to her friends Gladys Niles and Ella Somerville she had been calling it "the down underground poem." The first part she had written under the weight of two family dwellings above her on Chestnut Street. Now she sat in the light-filled aerie at the top of her house. And even when it rained there the drops on the tin roof made a happy sound. She wrote:

> The rain, I said, is kind to come
> And speak to me in my new home.
> I would I were alive again
> To kiss the fingers of the rain . . .

And she *was* alive again, joyously alive after a winter whose gloom had buried her so deeply she feared she might never arise from it.

> O God, I cried, give me new birth,
> And put me back upon the earth!
> Upset each cloud's gigantic gourd
> And let the heavy rain, down-poured
> In one big torrent, set me free,
> Washing my grave away from me!

In order to finish the poem she had started that winter she needed a poetic vision of regeneration to redeem the horrific nightmare of premature burial that had inspired her first hundred lines—and April and May would bring it. The rain in a black wave falls from the sky and strikes her grave.

> And as I looked a quickening gust
> Of wind blew up to me and thrust
> Into my face a miracle
> Of orchard-breath, and with the smell,—
> I know not how such things can be!—
> I breathed my soul back into me.

The last thirty-four verses of "Renascence" are an ode to joy whose exuberance and philosophical import know few parallels in American literature. Many of the lines are familiar even to those who have never read the poem in its entirety.

> Ah! Up then from the ground sprang I
> And hailed the earth with such a cry
> As is not heard save from a man
> Who has been dead, and lives again.
> About the trees my arms I wound;
> Like one gone mad I hugged the ground;
> I raised my quivering arms on high;
> I laughed and laughed into the sky;
> . . . .
> God, I can push the grass apart
> And lay my finger on Thy heart!

The twelve lines that end the poem, the "moral" or metaphysical coda, are drawn from her "Essay on Faith," a geometry of belief reminiscent of Pascal: "The world stands out on either side / No wider than the heart is wide; / Above the world is stretched the sky,—/ No higher than the soul is high." The elaboration of this Donne-like metaphysical simile leads her to a cautionary conclusion, which has been praised for nearly a century for its profundity cast in the cracker-barrel tone of the "Down East" porch philosopher: "And he whose soul is flat—the sky / Will cave in on him by and by."

From the kitchen door, their new house looked out on the mansard roof, high-arched windows, and the slender-columned portico of the Camden High School on Knowlton Street. Vincent had arranged to use the typewriter in the school office. Back and forth to the school, under the balcony of the Victorian portico, Vincent passed with her manuscript. At the end of May she was satisfied with her new poem, which she now titled "Renaissance." (The Americanized spelling was her editor's idea.) And on Monday, May 27, she sent the poem, along with her other long poem "Interim," and a stamped, self-addressed envelope to Mitchell Kennerley on East Twenty-eighth Street in New York City. Her greatest hope was for a generous portion of the one thousand dollars in prize money that judges Edward J. Wheeler and William Stanley Braithwaite would be awarding for the three best poems. She did not dream that the poem "Renaissance" was about to shoot lightning through the literary world. Even less did she think that the prayers she had offered up to her dream lover in the little chamber on Chestnut Street were soon to be answered. The poem she had written would bring the longed-for lover to her, in a myriad of forms, as befitted the nature of her longing:

> My love for you is something more than just thought, it is the love of Everywoman for Everyman. It is all primitive female life desiring its mate, it is all hunger crying for food, all weariness sighing for rest, it is the instinctive reaching out of the universal soul.

That June Vincent was joyfully preparing for Norma's graduation—sewing, baking, and rehearsing some duets they would perform at the commencement in the Opera House. Several of her friends, including Ethel Knight, were getting married, and there were wedding showers and weddings to attend, and gifts to be made for brides.

On July 19, 1912, she received a letter from an editor of *The Lyric Year*, saying that her poem "Renaissance" was accepted. He liked it "tremendously," and was requesting biographical information.

What happened to Edna St. Vincent Millay that summer and autumn has been told often and well by a hundred biographers, journalists, and literary historians. It has become a legend central to our literary heritage, like the death of Poe, Whitman's reviewing of *Leaves of Grass* under pseudonymns, Pound's editing of *The Waste Land*, or the vanishing of Ambrose Bierce. In Millay's case the events were so public, controversial, and widely discussed that the documentary accounts have given a false impression. It was generally believed that the apotheosis of St. Vincent Millay that year and the next was a thing that happened *to* the girl from Camden, a series of peculiar coincidences of which she was less an active participant than a passive spectator. This is far from true. From the day she received her first letter from *The Lyric Year*, the ambitious poet worked the situation for all it was worth, and it turned out to be worth a fortune.

To start with, thinking that the editor who had written to her was none other than Mitchell Kennerley himself (and that perhaps "her editor" was the dream lover she had been conjuring for nearly a year and a half), she set her cap to seduce him in a series of letters that range from coquettish to downright salacious. The editor, assuming Vincent was a man, addressed her as "esquire." At first the judge/editor wished to conceal his identity, and withheld his name, knowing it unethical to be corresponding personally with a contestant in such a competition. So during the months of July and August the two performed an epistolary striptease, as she, shedding a veil at a time, suggested to him she was a young, lovely, and passionate girl from Camden, and he divulged that he was one Ferdinand Earle, a thirty-four-year-old poet from England with a wife and baby daughter. He confided that the contest at Kennerley's *Lyric Year* was his very own brainchild "to reach just such budding geniuses as yourself." And in his second letter he addressed her as "Dear and true Poetess! You have indeed astonished me through and through—a *lassie* o'twenty—is it possible? I am not alone in thinking that your poem is very fine, original, strong, impressive." In short, "sometimes" he thinks it's the best in the book—that "sometimes" serving as the shade that keeps the concupiscent judge from completely giving the game away. Vincent sent him her photo and a four-leaf clover; he called her his "most captivating young authoress," and sent her a picture of himself on snow skis. By that time Vincent was ready to order a bumper of champagne and a new autumn wardrobe with her prize money, which was as good as in the bank.

Before he told her his real name she wrote to him, "It doesn't matter in the least who you are, for, whoever you are, you are perfectly charming and I am crazy about you. There! Such a relief to be able at last to confess it . . ."—as if this had been a page of her secret diary instead of a mash letter to a married English poet with an infant daughter. By October they were planning to meet in New York, he was teasing her to "write something decidedly immoral," and she was all but assured that the five hundred dollars in first-prize money was hers if he could only lay eyes on her.

In an exuberant letter to Gladys Niles she notes, "Isn't it wonderful, the way it has happened? I little thought when I sent my manuscript away last spring that today I should be on such intimate terms with the editor. . . . Isn't it lovely to make new friends? I've made so many this year: you and your grandmother and Sophie, and Ella Somerville and her people." And all of them are in love with her. This is the year, 1912, that she has discovered the rare power she has to make people fall in love with her, and the incomparable thrill of it.

She appeared at first to have no knowledge of the risks and dangers of the game she was playing with Earle, until, in a letter of October 19, he responded to one of her love letters with wise caution. "Dear impulsive child: What am I to say or think. . . . I should grieve to hurt you . . . and you could easily hurt me." Her love letters were so full of wit, badinage, and sexual wordplay that he did not know exactly how to take them ("Lay aside, very gently, the roguish mask behind which you write," he pleaded), but it is obvious she was driving him mad with desire and uncertainty. "I beg of you to write me immediately . . . a frank, serious intelligible letter. . . . Remember in spite of all you may suspect, I am just a baby boy in the woods. You must take me by the hand and lead me to the light. There is something bewitching about you. . . . You see, I need a letter, crystal clear!" This is an ultimatum. He is calling her bluff in this letter that is breathless with schemes about his sneaking into Camden or her coming to New York, this letter in which he coyly and parenthetically remarks "think of it, while I am writing to you I know the decision of one of the two other judges!!!!!!!"

Whether or not Earle was the dream lover Millay had been summoning with her candles and incantations, she implies in the letters that she was prepared to go to bed with him if it might give her a jump on winning the five hundred dollars. For top prize, the imaginative girl might convince herself he was the man she hoped he was.

Not all of the correspondence has been preserved, but it is clear from subsequent events, and from a letter written by Millay on October 28, that this is what happened: She wrote him the crystal-clear love letter that he demanded. It scared the daylights out of him. He left the billets-doux from the shameless Camden girl poet lying somewhere where his wife could find them, and she read him the riot act. Then during the last week in October he wrote a craven note in which he apologized for any part that *he* might have played in encouraging her amorous, wanton schemes. By then he certainly knew that Vincent's poem "Renascence" had finished the poetry tournament out of the money. She would not know this for another two weeks, nor would she learn until thirty years later that her correspondence with Ferdinand Earle had been the beginning of the end of his marriage.

In her letter of October 28, 1912, furious, she lambastes him as "the Patch-Work Letter Man," asking him to return her last love letter, of which she was proudest, granting him permission to read the others aloud to his wife, and offering to send all of his letters back to him (she didn't). She had wanted a flesh-and-blood lover, not a nervous moralist. "Let me congratulate you," she hisses, "on your convincing impersonation of a genuine man. . . . How can I be expected to understand a person who got his education in France, his business-methods in Siberia, his behaviour in vaudeville, and his brains in a raffle?"

So the search for her true love was only beginning.

That summer Norma Millay had a job waiting tables at the new Whitehall Inn on High Street, located on the slope of Megunticook overlooking the bay. The white-columned inn with its wide picture windows and broad porches with Shaker rocking chairs was a new guest house, which looked old because it had once been the Victorian manse of a sea captain. At the end of the summer season it was the custom for the inn's employees to put on a show for the guests, after which everyone would mingle at a masquerade ball. Vincent had written several songs, and Norma thought it would be fun if her sister would come along and sing some of them.

So on August 29 Vincent showed up at the inn dressed adorably as the pantomime character Pierrette, wearing a ruffled tunic. She sat at the piano and belted out her songs "The Circus Rag," "Sun's Comin' Out," and "Humoresque," which pretty Norma had sung recently at her graduation. Then someone asked for a poem. Vincent told the audience of forty charmed listeners about "Renascence" and its impending publication, and they begged to hear it.

At the piano bench she turned her profile toward them and delivered, by heart, the whole 214-line poem, intoning it through the archway of the music room to a spellbound audience lounging in wing chairs and on davenports, a group that included a Miss Caroline B. Dow from New York City. After long and enthusiastic applause, Miss Dow and others insisted that this otherworldly creature return from whatever planet she had descended from, and repeat the entire performance. Agreeably, Edna St. Vincent Millay returned and performed the next night; and on Tuesday, September 3, she went up the hill to the inn once more, having been invited to a tea. On that occasion Miss Dow asked Vincent's permission to call upon her and her mother the next day at their home.

Now the writer whose fame was growing so rapidly was almost twenty-one, and frankly confessed to anyone who asked her that she was a self-educated poet who had taught herself Latin and read the classics on her own, time permitting, having had no occasion to go to college. She did not have to tell anyone that she was poor—that tidbit would slip out between and around the lines of her conversation.

Miss Caroline Dow, a woman of means, was the dean of the YWCA Training School in New York City. Stolid, earnest, she resembled the actress Margaret Dumont, Groucho Marx's straight lady. In the parlor of the Millay residence on Washington Street, with its little bay window, Miss Dow explained to the poet and her mother that it was inappropriate, not to say an injustice, for the author of "Renascence" not to attend college. So she suggested a plan to send Vincent to Vassar, naming several wealthy friends who would be willing to put the plan into action.

This was not a novel idea. Abbie Evans, the preacher's daughter, had gone to Radcliffe by grace of wealthy patrons. By October Dow found herself in competition with Mrs. Julius Esselbourne, who had also caught Vincent's act at Whitehall, and was pulling strings to get Vincent a scholarship to Smith College. (In December Vincent would receive a letter from President Burton of Smith, offering to pay full freight if the poet would sign with Smith.)

Summing up the whole chain of events in her diary, Vincent wrote, "It was the most wonderful thing that ever happened to anybody, I think." At twenty she looked like a changeling princess in a fairy tale, and recently her life had begun to take on a fairy-tale unreality. But what she had seen so far was paltry compared to the wonders that were soon to come, some of them longed for, schemed for, others beyond imagining.

First she had to win that prize, and the fame and glory and five hundred dollars that came with it. She may even have feared that her college prospects hinged upon her success in the contest. "*The Lyric Year* is to come out in a week, and I'm almost dead with impatience and nervousness and wariness and anxiety." Just how much that money meant to Vincent, her mother, and her sisters—and how much "her editor" had led her to count on it—is painfully obvious in a drafted letter to Earle of November 5, 1912, upon learning of her defeat. The draft, unfinished and without heading or signature, probably was never posted:

> This, then, is what I have been waiting for, from day to day, from mail to mail, in such an agony as I had not known I could experience. This is the answer, this is the end. I wonder why I am not crying. My mother is crying. Did you ever hear your mother cry as if her heart would break? It is a strange and terrible sound. I think I shall never forget it.

After months of teasing the poetess with comments like "Were I a sport, I should wager odds on 'Renascence' for first honors," and "You will, I think, be quite pleased with the results of the competition," Earle had feebly written, "Would you be satisfied with a very honorable mention?"

No, she would not. And "the difference between first prize and no prize . . . is, in fact, the difference between the distressing poverty of my family and a comparative ease—a release from the heart-breaking, soul-sickening desperation of old debt. [It began with a loan Cora had taken out when they moved to Camden.] I have lived with this debt ever since I can remember. I have talked it, tasted it, breathed it. . . . And at last I had sighted help, I was made so hopeful I began to plan just what I could do with it." Cora's annual income in 1912 was probably between eight hundred and one thousand dollars. Five hundred dollars from the contest would have put them solidly in the black.

Vincent herself is numb, she says. She pities her mother and sisters, whom she has convinced the prize money was a sure thing; and she pities, disdainfully, the double-talking editor. "I would not be in your place, with my own capability for remorse, for anything on earth or heaven. . . ." What little she feels for herself is anger that she, like Earle, led others to believe in a chimera. "Perhaps this will be good for me in the end. It will make me so careful what I say to people."

It would be good for her in many other ways. Strange, is it not, the way certain themes in a life recur? Three years earlier the Camden boys had conspired to deprive the poetess of her rightful laurels; now the high judges Earle, Wheeler, and Braithwaite had denied her every last one of the cash awards for "Renascence," which she now had reason to believe was the finest poem in *The Lyric Year*.

The prizes went to Messrs. Orrick Johns, Thomas Daly, and George Sterling. History has had her little joke on them by leaving them out of all conversation except biographies of Millay. We will never know exactly what transpired among the judges in Mitchell Kennerley's office on East Twenty-eighth Street. But it is my guess that the discovery of Vincent Millay's sex, her dalliance by mail with a judge, and his wife's tantrum over it did nothing to help Millay's cause.

But Vincent's honorable mention in *The Lyric Year*, a handsomely bound red-cloth-covered book with a golden lyre stamped on its cover, turned out to be the consolation prize of the century. Most well-established American poets—Richard LeGallienne, Sara Teasdale, Edwin Markham, Louis Untermeyer, William Rose Benét, Joyce Kilmer, John Hall Wheelock, Witter Bynner, Arthur Ficke, and fifty others—contributed to the book that showcased "Renascence." They all read the poem, and it was universally acknowledged that the judges had made a colossal and outrageous error. To his credit, Earle singled out "Renascence" for special praise in his "Note by the Editor," implying that not he but the other judges had allowed the miscarriage of justice, the aesthetic blunder. Letters poured in from all over the literary world (this is not hyperbole: the bundle of mail is preserved in the Library of Congress collection) protesting the imbecilic decision and praising

Edna St. Vincent Millay. The winner himself, Orrick Johns, embarrassed, wrote, "I realized it was an unmerited award. The outstanding poem in that book was 'Renascence' by Edna St. Vincent Millay, immediately acknowledged by every authoritative critic as such." He excused himself from the awards banquet. Legend has it that one of the prize winners offered to give Millay his share of the money, and the proud girl refused. This seems incredible: not that he would have offered, but that she would have turned it down. The influential poet and critic Louis Untermeyer wrote to praise her poem in the *Chicago Post*, as did many others around the country (the *New York Times Book Review*, December 1, 1912; *St. Louis Mirror*, November 28, 1912) who reviewed the anthology. The secretary of the Poetry Society of America, Jesse Rittenhouse, wrote to Millay that " 'Renascence' is the best thing in the book," and invited her to give a poetry reading for the society.

An oft-repeated (though unattributed) comment came from one critic who called her "the young girl from Camden, Maine, who became famous through *not* receiving the prize." In the year when John Butler Yeats (W. B. Yeats's father) noted "The fiddles are tuning all over America," and such poets as Robert Frost, Ezra Pound, Amy Lowell, and Robinson Jeffers burst upon the scene, the same year Harriet Monroe founded the showcase of modern verse, *Poetry: A Magazine of Verse*—in that age of poetic renaissance, 1912, Edna St. Vincent Millay's poem struck the keynote.

❧

In her hillside bedroom overlooking Camden harbor the young woman had prayed to a mysterious spirit, a dream lover, to come and rescue her from loneliness and a bitter life of futile toil. In that same room where she made love ritually to a ghost, she also summoned Erato, the muse of love poetry. She had cast a spell over her room, her notebooks, pencil and paper, the air around her, and the streets of her hometown. Now through her poetry she was casting a spell over the whole world.

On January 10, 1913, in the dark early hours of the morning, Vincent gazed at her guttering candle. She braided her long red hair into one pigtail. She pulled the tarnished ring from her finger, placed it in a little white box, and holding the candle at an angle spilled a drop of molten wax into the box with the ring. Then she took up a sewing needle. "I did it. And I pricked my ring-finger and dropped in a drop of red, red blood. (I shall always have to do things like that. It is my *self* that does it)." So she whispered, then wrote in her book as she sealed the box: "We will have no more vigils."

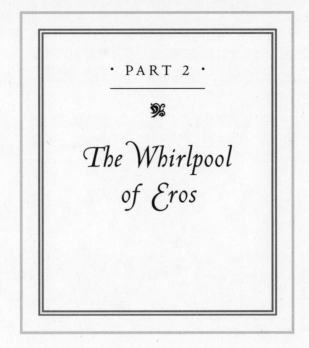

· PART 2 ·

The Whirlpool
of Eros

THE WHIRLPOOL OF EROS

❦

A poem breathing the spirit of love had changed her life. "Renascence" had translated her name far beyond the close society of Camden, and now the poem and Vincent's many new friends were going to lift the young poet up, with her suitcase packed with homemade clothing, and transport her to New York City in a Pullman car.

Vassar wanted Vincent, but she was not quite ready for Vassar; she needed some remedial work in mathematics and languages before she could pass the rigorous entrance examinations. So Miss Dow (Vincent had begun to call her Auntie Cahline, with a southern accent) arranged for her protégée to stay at the YWCA Training School during the spring semester while she attended classes at Barnard.

She arrived in New York on February 5, 1913. "I got on the sleeper Wednesday morning (my first sleeper!) after having tipped two porters, and I have been so very good that I haven't yet been sent home." She registered at Barnard the same day and the next evening attended a philharmonic concert at Carnegie Hall. Her diary entries for the first week are breathless with joy and excitement. February 10: "O today has been wonderful! I had my first experience alone on the subway—from 42nd Street to 116th Street, all around the college buildings, lunch at Milbank Hall, interview with Dr. Williams then home again. Tonight Mr. Downer [Ferdinand Earle's assistant, a professor at Columbia] came to see me right after dinner. I had only a few moments talk with him before it was time to get to the theatre with Miss Dow and Mr. Talcott Williams: Annie Russell in *She Stoops to Conquer*—and afterwards we went behind the scenes and met her, Her, Her! And also him, Him, Him, for he's a dear, just as dear as she is,—Oswald York. I'd like awfully much to know him. Still, as I'm half in love with him already, it may be just as well. Yet I don't know; I *have* to be in love, and it might just as well be a nice person as a horrid person—(The thought has just occurred to me that it might be a great deal better.) I *must* go to bed,—but oh, it was wonderful, wonderful!"

Millay arrived in New York City as a celebrity ingenue, a V.I.P. whose fame preceded her most places she went. The fan mail that had jammed the post office in Camden followed her to New York, where it increased exponentially. Doors opened magically; everyone made a fuss over the author of "Renascence" before they saw her. And then when they beheld the exquisite red-haired girl with the intense green eyes no one could get quite enough of her.

She was immediately taken up by literary "high society." On February 8, she received notes from Mr. and Mrs. Louis Untermeyer, and Sara Teasdale, inviting her to their homes. On the afternoon of the fifteenth she had tea with Sara Teasdale at the Martha Washington Hotel and stayed to dinner. This was the beginning of a lifelong friendship. She made the most of every social situation. If the excitement proved to be too much, or too little, for her delicate nerves, she had been known to faint dead away in a crowded room, drawing all hearts to her, as she did at the Macdowell Club on the evening of February 11.

Miss Dow had brought her there to meet Edward J. Wheeler, the editor of *Current Opinion*, and the president of the poetry society; Arthur Maurice, editor of *The Bookman*; the writer Parker Fillmore, and others. She was worn out from shopping on Fifth Avenue. In the middle of a lecture by the legendary publisher S. S. McClure, Edna St. Vincent Millay fainted, fell out of her chair, and had to be assisted out of the room. This caused quite a stir as gentlemen vied for the privilege of lending their arms and shoulders to rescue her. "All the lovely men were so sorry!" she wrote, and a number of them helped make her comfortable outside. She added, "I had a lovely time later out in the other room," where she did not have to compete with the droning editor of *McClure's* magazine for the party's attention.

On February 22, her birthday, among her many letters was one from her pastor, L. D. Evans, Abbie's father, a touching reminder of where she had come from: "The chance of your life has come to you, as it came to Abbie. Few girls, crippled by circumstances, like you and Abbie, get such unlooked-for helps to make good what is in them. I love to think that such good fortunes come from God . . ." He did not doubt she would make the most of her poetic gifts. But he urged her to make it "your supreme aim to be the finest *woman* in your power, so that the lustre of your trained gifts in future years may be intensified by the lustre of a superb womanhood." Then the dear naïve man went on to argue that the immortal poets were men and women of sterling moral character and Christian piety. "The men were greater than their works. Let this too be said of you," he prayed, "when genius brings you fame." (He apparently did not know the lives of Shelley, Byron, Villon, Baudelaire, or Catullus.) "Be true to your highest self, dear Vincent, and you shall never be false to God's gifts to you." This touching letter parallels those of Caroline Dow, Vincent's patron, who would apply pressures on her ward other than sentiment to get her to comport herself like a Christian lady.

The day after her first birthday away from home, she wrote: "Wore my hair down in a curl into the dining room tonight. I *won't* be grown up even if I am twenty-one." She was five feet one and weighed a hundred pounds. Even with her new wardrobe and her hair pulled up with side combs and back combs she still looked like she was sixteen. "I *love* my little black satin slippers with the rhinestone buckles. Wonder if Witter Bynner will be at the Poetry Society meeting Tuesday night? I hope so, but I don't believe so."

The young poet Witter ("Hal") Bynner (1881–1968) would indeed be present at the meeting on March 4; he would also attend the poetry society's Sunday soiree, given in Vincent's honor, on March 9. Bynner, one of the most gifted poets of his generation, was only slightly less susceptible to Millay's charms than his fellow poet and former Harvard classmate Arthur Davison Ficke (1883–1945.) The two friends had been so stunned by Millay's poem in *The Lyric Year*, where they also had poems appearing, Ficke wrote immediately to Ferdinand Earle: "Witter Bynner, who is visiting me, and I read through most of the book . . . suddenly we stumbled on this one, which really lights up the whole book. It seems to us a real vision, such as Coleridge might have seen. Are you at liberty to name the author?" They were convinced that Millay's sex was a hoax, that "no sweet young thing of twenty ever ended a poem precisely where this one ends: it takes a brawny male of forty-five to do that."

Earle gave them Millay's address, while writing to her humorously about Ficke's suspicions. On Thanksgiving they wrote her a simple letter. "This is Thanksgiving Day. We thank you. If we had a thousand dollars, we would send it to you. You should unquestionably have had the prize. All three prizes! Very Truly Yours, Witter Bynner / Arthur Davison Ficke." And Ficke's wife insisted that her "Me too!" be added in a postscript.

On December 5 Vincent wrote to thank them, a long humorous letter protesting, "I simply will not be a 'brawny male,' " and enclosing a copy of the photo she had been sending to every male writer or editor who expressed any interest in her. A rich and flirtatious correspondence ensued between the married poet-lawyer, Arthur Ficke of Davenport, Iowa, and the sweet young thing of twenty in Camden, Maine—an exchange of letters far more eloquent, intelligent, and rewarding than what she had ventured with the blundering Ferdinand Earle. This came closer to the romantic intimacy she had hoped for. Handsome, brilliant, Arthur Ficke really did have what it took to be Vincent's dream lover, including the manners of a gentleman. Not yet thirty, he called himself her "spiritual advisor," for a while confining his letters to affectionate, avuncular literary advice and criticism of her poems. He sent her his books of verse; he mailed her a volume of Blake, whom she had never read. Only after months of the girl's seductive teasing did the lawyer begin to drop his defenses, indicating with gallant subtlety (and sometimes by literally clipping out "improper" passages of his letters!) that his interest in her had overstepped the boundaries suitable to a married man.

By March of 1913, the epistolary seduction of Arthur Ficke was in full swing, with both parties apologizing for their too frequent "indiscretions." But in fishing for love, Vincent was not content to have only one line in the water—she had been trying to get Witter Bynner's attention, with less success. Before meeting him she even mentioned in her diary that she suspected "he's too mean," meaning that after four months of assailing him through the post she had not been able to get the rise out of him she had come to expect from men. What she did not know, and seemed not to understand or accept even after Witter Bynner had been a close friend for a decade, was that the handsome poet preferred men to women when it came to lovemaking. Perhaps he hoped to take some advantage of her confusion over this.

The day after she attended her first opera, *Die Walküre*, at the Met, she cut classes at Barnard so she could attend the luncheon at the Poetry Society of America where she met Witter Bynner and other well-known poets, such as Alfred Noyes and Edwin Markham. She must have been intrigued by young Bynner, his high, intelligent forehead, his heavy-lidded eyes, and his sensitive good looks. But it wasn't until the society's party in her honor at secretary Jesse Rittenhouse's, on Sunday the ninth, that Witter Bynner engaged her in conversation.

"Do you mind if I smoke?" he asked.

"Not in the least," she replied.

He offered her a cigarette from his silver case, and she declined. He raised his eyebrows.

"Oh, don't you smoke?"

"Not here, certainly," she said.

"Then you have no prejudice against it?"

"None whatever."

"I'm glad of that." Bynner had a way of making a sentence mean several things at once, with undertones and overtones, that she found thrilling. They talked for a long time. Soon they would enjoy many cigarettes together, bottles of wine, and books of poetry. He honored her by asking her permission to recite her verses and she was thrilled. That evening he read aloud, in his musical voice, the whole of "Renascence" to a rapt audience that included Mr. and Mrs. Markham, Sara Teasdale, Mr. and Mrs. Louis Ledoux, Anna Branch, and other poets of note.

On March 14, Miss Rittenhouse mysteriously confided to Vincent, and she recorded that, "Witter Bynner said some very nice things about me. I didn't ask what they were, but I'm dying to know."

Despite a social calendar listing concerts, plays, baseball games (she had a mad crush on the baseball pitcher Christy Mathewson), art exhibitions, and Poetry Society functions—a schedule that kept her out most nights— Vincent was working diligently at Barnard to pass the courses that would allow her to enter Vassar. She was also writing poetry, between classes, in the Barnard library. She wrote two poems in the afternoon of March 10: the famous "I'll keep a little tavern / Below the high hill's crest / Wherein all gray-eyed people / May set them down and rest," and "If we should die tomorrow." As in Camden, so in New York, she wrote, and studied, and socialized to the point of exhaustion. Then she would crash, take to her bed, and give herself up to the other girls' instincts to nurse her and wait upon her in the dormitory until she had recovered her manic energies.

After two months in the city, she was still a curious blend of sophistication and vulnerability. The night of April 4, the ink of her diary runs with teardrops. "While I was studying my Horace like a good girl, it got later and later and I don't have any clock, and the bell didn't ring and nobody called me and so I didn't get any dinner. You can talk all you want to about virtue being its own reward, but it's darn unsatisfying when you're hungry. And I think my tooth is ulcerating. . . . I want my *mother*."

A few days later she was ecstatic to receive a twenty-five-dollar check from Mitchell Kennerley for two poems, "God's World" ("O, world, I cannot hold thee close enough") and "Journey," to be published in his magazine, *The Forum*. After she'd crowed over the check for a while, she endorsed and sent it to her mother, to buy "shoes, dear,—or have your glasses fixed if they're not just right." And then she begged mother and sisters each to buy some little thing that she could always keep. Her desire to be mothered and her desire to care for her mother were indivisible.

A nine-page letter to Cora on April 22 shows how deeply Vincent con-fided in her mother, about everything, even the particulars of her love life. Mother had disapproved of her daughter's relation to Ferdinand Earle. Now Vincent proudly reported that despite being in the same city with him she had kept him at arm's length, meeting Earle only once at a Poetry Soci-ety function. She never gave him her New York address, even though she had, after his abject apologies, pardoned him for his false-hearted behavior during the contest.

"I am really getting a great deal more sense than I ever had before. A year ago I would have called him up in some desperately lonely fit while Miss Dow was away and had him come down. Which wouldn't have been so very dreadful, but which isn't the way I'm running things now. Mama, *pat* me!"

Hard as it is to imagine this popular girl in some "desperately lonely fit," she was eager to be in love, to take a lover. On April 14 she wrote, "Have fallen in love again,—thank goodness! I won't feel so lost-like now—with the red-haired boy who sat next to me at dinner." He's a recent Yale grad, and "a *darned sweet kid*" with "a *real* sense of humor, and he loves music." Then she hopes she'll never see him again "because I'd be awfully likely to spoil him. I wish I were a really *nice* girl!" In other words, Vincent wishes her sex drive were more in line with the Victorian standard for respectable women. Vincent Millay had a megawatt libido, and it would not be subli-mated much longer.

The nameless red-haired Yalie disappears from her diaries without a trace, but Vincent will have her lover soon, in a month. And that curious, consum-ing affair will become the emotional center of several less important rela-tionships that will orbit around it. On May 9, 1913, she realized a lifelong dream when she saw her idol Sarah Bernhardt in *Camille*. Bernhardt, as woman and as artist, was an essential role model to Millay; and like the beautiful courtesan Camille, young Vincent was eager to find some man worth dying for.

❧

The love of her life from 1913 until she graduated from Vassar in 1917 was yet another editor, another Englishman, another Arthur—this one named Arthur Hooley. Now, you will not find Arthur Hooley's name in previous books about Edna St. Vincent Millay. It is a surprise to find him in the biographical dictionary of 1916, because he was a Man of Mystery. He lived under assumed names and in disguises at shifting residences. He demanded of his acquaintances the utmost discretion. This suited young Vincent's romantic tastes, the mystery of her lover always hanging just out of reach, while it met her own need for liberty and secrecy in a love life that was soon to become a complex web. Millay was so discreet she never mentions Hooley in her diary, though she *does* mention him in letters to Cora. Even Edna's sister Norma, who knew nearly everything there was to be known about the poet's private affairs, having inherited her diaries and letters, could never figure out the fat folder of love letters addressed to and from Charles Vale. His were signed "Arthur" within; and in her hand, under the pseudonymous envelopes, Millay called him her beloved Arthur. Norma figured it was a ruse to protect the married Arthur Ficke. It was not. It was more important than that.

She addressed Hooley under the name Charles Vale because that was his pseudonym as a novelist and editor. (It is my opinion that Hooley had something to hide, but I can educe no evidence to prove this—it's only a biographer's hunch.) Born in Newcastle-under-Lyme, England, on December 29, 1874, Hooley attended Newcastle High School and the University of London before beginning his career as a freelance writer and editor. He came to America in 1908, and his cousin Mitchell Kennerley hired him as editor of *The Forum* in July of 1910. Kennerley also published Vale's only novel, *John Ward, M.D.*, in 1913. The first time Millay ever saw the name Charles Vale was on January 6, 1913, when Kennerley sent her a copy of the recent *Forum*. In this magazine was Vale's review of *The Lyric Year*. With trembling hands she "hunted up the page, and happened to strike the end of the article first so that I caught a fleeting glimpse of a whole page of my poem." Vale had quoted most of "Renascence," raving about it.

We would not be astonished to learn that she wrote to the reviewer, enclosing her enticing photo. In any case they were destined to meet soon, as both belonged to that society of avant-garde artists and writers centered around Mr. and Mrs. Kennerley's mansion in Mamaroneck, New York. Kennerley is a story in himself. He was one of the bold publishers—along with Alfred Knopf, Horace Liveright, and B. W. Huebsch—who were balancing lists of great French and Russian authors in translation and homegrown radical talents like Theodore Dreiser and Walter Lippmann with moneymakers like romantic novelists and writers on spiritualism. Kennerley was the chief rogue among these booksellers, a fast-talking hustler who liked to traffic in high-brow fiction, poetry, and sex; in Edna St. Vincent Millay he had the hunter's instinct that he had found all three rolled into one. It was Kennerley who brought D. H. Lawrence's scandalous *Sons and Lovers* to this country in 1913, and Kennerley who went toe to toe with Anthony Comstock's Society for the Suspension of Vice over a tawdry novel about a fallen woman, *Hagar Revelly*. Kennerley won the first major decision against censorship laws not long after he met Millay, who was to become one of his principal moneymakers.

Mitchell Kennerley wanted to publish a book of Millay's from the moment he laid eyes on her, in his office on April 18, 1913. In her diary she described the encounter as "very pleasant. He has invited me out some Sunday to see him and her and the kiddies! They are in the *country*!—I can eat grass! He wants to bring out a little volume of my stuff, but I don't think it feasible."

There were a couple of reasons why she might not think it feasible. First, she did not have enough poetry that came up anywhere near the standard of "Renascence." She may or may not have realized this. Second, Miss Dow and other ladies did not approve of Mitchell Kennerley's house as a proper imprimatur for their young protégée. The handsome, blue-eyed foreigner seemed a bit shady; he trafficked in books of questionable morals; if he had not yet been jailed for his imprudence he soon would be (in the summer of 1913). He parted his slick hair neatly in the middle. Swinging his silver-headed cane as he strolled from midtown Manhattan to the underworld downtown, he moved in a milieu of writers, publicists, loan sharks, and readers that were too relaxed in their attitudes toward drinking, smoking, politics, and sex. Aunt Caroline Dow would prefer to see her darling Vincent under the imprint of Harper's or Houghton Mifflin.

But Mitchell Kennerley would not take no for an answer. And while Vincent would not satisfy him by saying "yes," Mitchell and his wife Helen wooed the poetess by inviting her to weekend parties at their mansion in Mamaroneck where she could meet and commune with other artists, poets, and intellectuals, more and less famous than herself.

The first of these visits was on Sunday, May 18. She and Witter Bynner rode out on the train together to Mamaroneck, for a "poet's evening." In her diary that day and the next she refers portentously to a man she will not name but who has made her *anxious*. She returned to the Kennerleys' the next weekend to attend a country club dance, and at one in the morning after it she wrote: "I have not yet begun to regret this day and night, but I shall be sick about it in the morning. I have been intemperate in three ways, I have failed to keep, or rather to fulfill an obligation, and I have deliberately broken my word of honor. The cocks are crowing. It's later than I thought. I must get to sleep before I get to thinking."

And on Monday, back in the city, packing to leave school for home, she wrote: "It must be I am getting terribly calloused in soul. I don't seem to be regretting very much." Against her better judgment she went back to Mamaroneck, at Helen Kennerley's insistence, to a liaison that lady must have encouraged, but which had already scandalized Miss Dow, who somehow had gotten wind of it.

"Miss Dow called up. She's heard some new cussedness about me and is about heart-broken. Damn-em, I wish they'd keep their mouths shut."

And on the next day, Monday, June 2: "Didn't get much rest last night. Came down to breakfast looking like a ghost. Felt like dying and couldn't do anything. He came over this afternoon. He felt like dying and couldn't do anything. So we went off into the woods together."

Only from letters between the lovers years later, recalling the flowering trees of Mamaroneck in the spring, the dogwood blossoms, and their first meetings there, can we ascertain that the man who so troubled Miss Dow and her ward was the forty-year-old Englishman Arthur Hooley, who worked as an editor and writer for Mitchell Kennerley.

Arthur Hooley had a large aquiline nose, a long pointed chin, sunken cheeks and sunken eyes, heavily browed, and marvelous big pitcher-handle ears that almost lent humor to his otherwise gloomy countenance. In a tweed jacket, high collar, and thin tie, Hooley looked like an undertaker on holiday, his coarse straight hair falling to his eyebrows before he would rake it back with his fingers in a gesture at once languid and hopeless. The face was cadaverous, sepulchral. The word that comes to mind as we review the long, curious exchange of letters between the dour critic and the vulnerable poetess is: *doom-driven*. Arthur Hooley had not only the romantic's melancholy sense of destiny—the man was doom-driven, bearing in his grave carriage and wracked poet's soul the sorrow and pain of the ages.

Dark, mysterious, intuitively perceptive, the older man struck a romantic chord in Vincent that no man ever had, and no one would until she met and fell in love with Arthur Ficke in February of 1918. An unmarried man who would never marry, Arthur Hooley was on the one hand dangerously available, and on the other hand maddeningly remote. If she had been searching for someone whose remoteness might resemble her father's, she could not have done better. He appears to have begun by resisting the advances of the pretty "child," as he called her. Then, after surrendering a few times, to his distress and shame as an English gentleman he spent the next three years feeding the flames of her imagination while continually denying her the pleasure of his company in the flesh. Because he is the *only* one of a hundred certified lovers of our heroine ever to behave this way, his resistance to the irresistible girl, his overall status as an enigma, and certain remarks about homosexuality in his letters make me wonder if Hooley, like Bynner, preferred sex with men. In any case, Hooley had an enormous influence upon Millay's polymorphous lovelife during her Vassar years.

She passed her courses at Barnard and was duly admitted to the Vassar class of 1917. The summer of 1913 found her back home in Camden with her mother and sisters. Norma's graduation from high school and her income as a telephone operator, Vincent's patrons, and Henry Millay's increased financial support had somewhat eased the family's financial strain. Vincent spent her summer studying and resting, swimming, sailing on the bay, and canoeing on Lake Megunticook. She frequently mentions a local boy named Fritz with whom she passed the time; she and Fritz went on double dates with Norma and her longtime beau Kenneth. Fritz was in love with Vincent, and she was always holding him at arm's length, exasperating the poor fellow. One night she entertained him in her bedroom, wearing the red kimono he was so wild about. And three days later she "told Fritz he can't come up any more. He's dreadfully cut up about it. I wonder if I've done anything terrible. I think it would kill me to know I had hurt anyone like that." No, it really wouldn't kill her. Her comment is either disingenuous or naïve. This may be one of the last shreds of her innocence, but it sounds more like sublimated anger. In a few months the alluring ingenue would find herself in a web of erotic entanglements where hurting others was frequently, if not usually, the point of the game, a main pleasure. She was learning quickly that love, if it is a game, is one where power rests with the person whose passion remains a few degrees cooler—where one lover must perforce hurt the other if she is not to be wounded herself.

This was the lesson she learned from her older paramour Arthur Hooley, the strategy for lovemaking she packed up, with her dresses and combs and petticoats, to take with her to college in Poughkeepsie.

Vincent's college career is mostly a matter of public record, a scandalous legend at Vassar, and a story that many writers have told very well. These include Millay herself (rather guardedly) in her published letters, half a dozen biographers, and no less a personage than the president of Vassar, the late Henry Noble MacCracken, in his memoir *The Hickory Limb*. This is a subject ripe for comedy from the outset. A brilliant, beautiful, and celebrated poet goes to college—to a *very* proper, *very* staid, and rigorous girl's college where men are not allowed on the premises and the girls are not allowed off campus without official leave. She is four years older than the other freshmen. Almost impossible to imagine this today: but think of Bob Dylan, or better yet a twenty-one-year-old Ani DiFranco, revolutionary rock-poet hell-raiser, agreeing to matriculate at Vassar back when there were still parietals and a core curriculum. It was a recipe for disaster—a great credit to Millay's seriousness and to the institution's tolerance that she did (albeit under a pall) graduate from Vassar College on schedule in 1917.

She smoked cigarettes in the cemetery, she drank spirits, she cut classes when she pleased, she played hooky from compulsory chapel, she led classmates in insurrections, she was late for classes, and went absent without leave again and again. She broke every rule in the manual, and then turned in papers and exams that were so brilliant that her teachers, furious, had no choice but to give her good grades. She was the star of every play on campus (author of two original dramas there), and she wrote the class songs, valedictory poems, and anthems. She was the adored queen of the student body. In and out of young Henry MacCracken's office (he was only thirty-five) every other week for some infraction, she would storm and cry as he calmly reasoned with her, explaining why this or that college rule was necessary. But the bottom line was clear to both of them from the day she arrived: She wanted an education, and would work hard to make her academic performance beyond reproach. She was more famous than MacCracken and the whole faculty put together. Edna St. Vincent Millay would put Vassar on the map. Insofar as he had the power, the president would never expel her for her conduct.

"I know all about poets at college," he said bravely, handing her his handkerchief to stem the tide of tears. "And I don't want a banished Shelley on my doorstep!" They thought of Shelley at the same time.

That was good enough for Vincent. "On those terms," she sniffed, "I think I can continue to live in this hellhole."

In 1917, a Vassar education was well worth the effort to achieve. You didn't graduate from there in those days without a thorough grounding in the classics—Latin particularly—advanced mathematics, laboratory sciences, ancient and modern history, and fluency in one or two modern foreign languages. The kind of poet Vincent wished to be, and was swiftly becoming, was a lyric poet in the intellectual tradition of Percy Shelley. Critics from John Crowe Ransom to John Ciardi who have charged Millay with a lack of intellectual interest have done her a grave injustice, mistaking clarity and unity for triviality. She wrote:

Euclid alone has looked on Beauty bare.
Let all who prate of Beauty hold their peace,
And lay them prone upon the earth and cease
To ponder on themselves, the while they stare
At nothing, intricately drawn nowhere
In shapes of shifting lineage . . .

Vincent's bound notebook from her course in Euclidean geometry has been preserved, so neatly transcribed, drawn, and lovingly annotated that the volume might itself serve as a textbook to the Greek *Elements* if that sacred work were to be lost forever. It attests to a deep passion for the pure intellectual light of Greek thought, refined by burning the midnight oil at Vassar when she was not otherwise engaged—writing poetry, reading Virgil, Horace, William James, Mackail's *Latin Literature*, acting in one of her own stage plays, or hopping from one of her classmates' beds to another.

She had two nagging problems in college. The first she predicted in her diary at Barnard on April 27. She was supposed to be making up a list of studies, "then got mixed up in a poem and couldn't do anything. What shall I do with four years of college if this one semester is turning out like this? Here register I my first doubt." And two days later: "Worked on a poem. I am going crazy with the poems that I simply can't get time to write. It isn't a joke. I can't study now; I'm too old; I ought to be through college at my age, and I know it, and I have other things to think about, and *I can't study*." She would work it out. In spite of everything the poems made room for themselves, so that most of the contents of her first book, *Renascence and Other Poems* (December 1917), she composed before graduating from Vassar in June of that year.

The other problem was more complex. At twenty-one, after a winter of heady independence in New York City, Vincent, within the stone walls and adamant rules of Vassar, was like a caged tigress. She wrote to Arthur Ficke:

> I hate this pink-and-gray college. If there had been a college in *Alice in Wonderland* it would be this college. . . . They treat us like an orphan asylum.
>
> They trust us with everything but men. . . . We can go into the candy-kitchen and take what we like and pay or not, and nobody is there to know. But a man is forbidden as if he were an apple.

It is a very funny letter. "Mr. Ficke, are you fond of truncated prisms?—If you are I will send you a box. This is where they grow. I don't wonder Miss Blunt [Ficke's wife] went to the University of Chicago. I am thinking seriously of going to the University of Moscow, and taking a course in Polite Anarchy & Murder as a Fine Art."

She will have her revenge on the sexual restrictions and "impositions" of the pink-and-gray college, as only a true and instinctive sexual revolutionary could do. With Arthur Hooley occasionally available for heterosexual trysts in New York City and Mamaroneck, and a harem of sex-starved Vassar girls eager for same-sex experiments right there on campus, Millay found herself at the center of a four-year bacchanal, an early-twentieth-century clinic in the art of love.

❧

Vincent sat on the bed with her friend Katharine Tilt one idle evening in Katharine's dorm room in North Hall. As they chatted, Vincent leafed through a magazine. All at once she read aloud from a passage under the illustration of a young woman.

"She was a small, dark creature with lips that required no rouge. . . ."

"That's you," said Katharine.

"Me? What do you mean? Am I a dark creature?"

"No, but the other part certainly fits you. *Lips that required no rouge*," said Katharine admiringly.

That was the first time she realized that the color of her mouth was different from other girls'. "When their mouths are pale and chapped," she confided in a letter to her sister, "mine is like a poppy."

A few nights later Katharine, gazing fondly at her friend in a moment of silence after Vincent had stopped speaking, said, "Honestly, Vincent, you have a *gorgeous* red mouth." Twice in the past week another girl, Grace Roper from Washington, D.C., who meant to introduce her to President Woodrow Wilson, had asked her "What makes your lips so red all the time?"

Her coloring, the contrast between her white skin and the red integuments, lips, tongue, and more secret circles and folds her lovers would cherish, had become spectacular after the girl turned twenty.

> She is neither pink nor pale,
> And she never will be all mine;
> She learned her hands in a fairy-tale
> And her mouth on a valentine.
> (from "The Witch-Wife")

And then there was the crimson flame of her hair—not carrot-colored, let no one call it that—indoors the hair was deep red, and in the sunshine a dazzling strawberry blond. (Owing to her mother's profession as a hair-weaver, there is a beautiful switch of the poet's hair still kept in her bureau drawer in tissue, eerily as fresh and vivid as the day it was harvested. I have seen this relic in the half-light of the bedroom at her estate Steepletop, and in the direct morning light as it poured through a window. I have heard that a man before me fainted at the sight of it.)

Her looks and her sister Norma's and the need for women to be beautiful are the themes of a long letter she wrote days later to her sister, a few weeks before Christmas that first year at Vassar. It is a hard-boiled letter of advice to the lovelorn Norma, whose perennial boyfriend Kenneth had been worrying her to death. The letter is very much the kind but condescending lecture of an older, sadder-but-wiser woman to her kid sister, giving us a complete picture of Vincent's philosophy of love at age twenty-one, and just how she figured a young woman in 1913 ought to play the game.

She sat in her room, 603 North Hall, on her Indian-blanket-covered bed, dressed in bloomers, middy-blouse, hair braided in a pigtail, cross-legged, wearing ballet slippers. Her table was covered with books and papers and her mother's chafing dish (always known as "James") with the tea things, and jelly and bread Cora had mailed from Camden, and a knife she had snitched from Katharine Tilt's place setting at dinner ("won't she be mad though!"). On her bureau was a mess of standing framed photos of her mother and sisters, some combs and brushes, and a bottle of emulsion Dr. Baldwin had given her because she believed Vincent was "somewhat anemic. Fancy! That means run-down, bloodless, etc. (Don't tell mother . . .)" The costly new high boots she adored lay side by side on the floor next to the bed.

According to several accounts of the time, she looked not a day over seventeen, as she sat on the bed in the dorm where her advanced years had already earned her the job as "proctor." She sipped her tea, nibbled bread, and settled down to write a long letter to Norma, who was only nineteen. "I must just talk to you about your love affairs, child," she begins.

> Dear, Kenneth isn't worth it. Not for a minute. You can't help it, I know that, you are so used to him, but there are a great many men— not in Camden; but you won't always be in Maine, you know. Anyone who hurts you all the time as he does isn't worth while. . . .

Warming to her subject, she turns up the volume: "Let Kenneth go to the devil! You've given him his chance and he didn't have sense enough to know it." The problem, as she sees it, is that Kenneth is too restless ever to settle down long with one girl, and that "he is too old, and he knows too darned much."

You want a boy that can start about where you do—in most everything—getting drunk, and getting disgusted, and everything else. You're
too *good* for Kenneth. And besides you don't want to dust shoe-boxes
all your life, you know. You're too good-looking. Just remember that.

And while we're on the subject of good looks, writes Miss Lonelyhearts, "I'm
pretty! People use that word!" She drops in an anecdote or two about this
fellow or that who has raved about her, and how she's gotten wind of it.

For one thing, loved, I have something that I never had before—don't
die, please—a beautiful mouth! I don't know whether a sweetening of
my disposition has done it, or whether the fact that for some unknown
reason it never gets chapped anymore and is just the size it was intended
to be, but anyway it is now one of my first attractions.

Is it possible that no one had explained to her the ancient doctrine that
a young woman's mouth grows beautiful by doing what it is meant to do at
twenty-one: kissing, making love? Or at least thinking about it? Had she not
figured this out for herself? Kisses are more colorful and lasting than lipstick
and rouge.

"What a fool I am!" she exclaimed, suddenly embarrassed by her vanity.
"I wouldn't tell another soul but you." Then she excused herself to dress for
dinner.

The next morning she resumed her theme, congratulating Norma for taking up with handsome Billy Hanley in spite of Kenneth, assuring her that
she will not always miss Kenneth so awfully as she does now, and that other
men will have "his charms combined with virtues he never heard of." The
point she drives home, again and again, is that Norma must be sensible and
stay *in control* of her affairs—she must never let her heart and emotions run
away with her.

He's not good for you. He keeps you stirred up all the time, and you
must just be sensible about it. You are in love with him, of course you
are, but that doesn't mean anything. You'll be in love with a dozen
more, and one will be the kind you want to marry. I am in love with
three right this minute, and may see one at least in about two weeks,
but I'm not getting gray about it.

And she does not waste tears anymore for those she once loved. No, "it's
too disfiguring. You have to be sensible about these little things, and deny

yourself certain little luxuries of the sort. So don't get *nervous* about Kenneth. Repose is a beautiful and attractive thing. You need both. A girl *has* to be good-looking."

She closes with the exhortation to practice control of mind over heart: no matter how long Norma has "belonged" to Kenneth, she can, if she chooses, "withdraw from him *utterly*, and *refuse to remember one thing* that can possibly hurt you." She strikes the Olympian pose: "Be bigger than the situation, always. You don't have to hate Kenneth to stop loving him,—that is horrid. But just don't let him bother you any more." And all of this wisdom goes in service of the quest to find the perfect man "who will always be good to you."

It will be amusing to see how Millay follows, and violates, her own rules of courtship during the next decade as she finds that "the heart is slow to learn / What the swift mind beholds at every turn" (from the sonnet "Pity me not because the light of day"). The mind and will are no match for passions in circumstances that can swiftly spin out of control in the whirlpool of eros.

But there is ample evidence that from now until her marriage in 1923, Millay will adhere to a policy of "divide and conquer" in her love life, enjoying several partners concurrently with careful, clever discretion, compartmentalizing, plotting with the precision of a French farceur the entrances and exits of her lovers so that they might not collide, coming and going. She was notoriously promiscuous and notably discreet. A skilled actress, she could cast a spell on any suitor, making one believe for the moment that he or she was the center of Vincent's universe. The evidence of this is abundant in more than a thousand love letters that she kept—pathetic, many of them. The subjects caught in her web became, unwittingly, slaves, prepared to give up anything for her, marriages, friendships, fortunes, reputations, careers. Meanwhile she maintained a lofty emotional liberty; she was, before the present lover knew it, on to the next erotic adventure. Not the least of her magic consisted in her graceful skill in ending an affair—her lovers as often as not became devoted friends.

We cannot know for certain who the "three" were she was in love with when she wrote to her sister that autumn. One was surely the spectral Arthur Hooley. One was probably her adoring pen pal Arthur Ficke, the lawyer poet who was angling vaguely and guiltily for a tryst with her in New York City. He traveled there from Iowa, periodically, on business. The wonderful missives between Millay and Ficke, many of them in print, are passionate love letters coated with a thin veneer of humor and arch propriety. The third lover may have been any one of several "boys" such as Harrison

Dowd, with whom she played, as she had advised her sister to do, because a boy is so much more pliable than a man. (It was not the Nicaraguan poet Salomón de la Selva who, in all previous books about Millay, is incorrectly identified as her companion in New York in 1913. They did not meet until 1915.)

Arthur Hooley was the most intriguing and dangerous. Her secret affair with him, and the letters that document it, are the Rosetta stone to Millay's formative romantic and psychic life during her early twenties. All of the love poems in Millay's first volume, *Renascence*, and several from later volumes, are best understood as emanations from that curious arrangement with the English editor who lived on Lexington Avenue in New York, and on weekends had the use of a charming cottage in Mamaroneck.

The correspondence is particularly rich because we have both sides of it. (At some point he returned to her some of her letters after 1914.) But there are problems. The letters before 1914 are lost so we must reconstruct the affair by the lovers' romantic recollections of events a year and more past.

She arranged to spend a day or two again with Hooley at the cottage in Mamaroneck after Christmas 1913. She would always go to him under the cover of a weekend visit to the Kennerleys, who countenanced the affair. It may indeed have given Mitchell a bargaining edge in purchasing the poet's first book.

Arthur made a crackling fire in the hearth. He admired her long green dress and made a fuss over her "princess slippers." He was sad, always sad. The Englishman longed for his native land, and spoke nostalgically of the hills and heaths and castles, quoting for her the new verses of Rupert Brooke: "If I should die, think only this of me: / That there's some corner of a foreign field / That is forever England."

She believed they were soul mates, and that Arthur understood her in a way no one ever had before. He was so sensitive it seemed he could read her thoughts. She told him how much she adored him.

"Oh child, child," he scolded her, but at last he allowed her to kiss him, and do other things. But in the dark, only in the pitch dark. "If I were a fairy," she whispered, "I would take you back to England, to the Derby races." This made him laugh, dryly, and he said that she did look so much like a fairy with green eyes and red hair and her little body, less like a boy or woman than a fairy, really. When she begged him to stop calling her a child and regard her as the woman that she was, he confessed he preferred her as a child, and asked her please, never to grow up.

"In you there are so many beautiful possibilities—I would be loathe to leave you with any memory that you might ever wish to obliterate," he said in his doleful, lisping voice.

The first night she visited the brown-shingled cottage with the big fireplace, she took a seat across from the glowing hearth and he said to her: "Don't sit there Edna—I might want you there always." He recited some verses of his own, and then she read aloud to him Swinburne's "Triumph of Time."

> We had stood as the sure stars stand, and moved
> As the moon moves, loving the world; and seen
> Grief collapse as a thing disproved,
> Death consume as a thing unclean,
> Twain halves of a perfect heart, made fast,
> Soul to soul while the years fell past;
> Had you loved me once, as you have not loved;
> Had the chance been with us that has not been.

She recalled one night in the lamplit library of her publisher's mansion, when Arthur drew her aside and bid her smell his linen handkerchief, "*saturated*, it must have been, with eau de cologne." And he wickedly told her, who was giddy with love for him: "One can get on without women, if he has perfumes . . . and vermouth," a remark that she fondly recalled as unpleasant but characteristic, thrillingly decadent.

Yet another evening as they dined at the Kennerleys' and she wore a dress so near the color of the wine he praised it, she recited in his ear her new poem called "Sorrow."

> Sorrow like a ceaseless rain
>   Beats upon my heart.
> People twist and scream in pain,—
> Dawn will find them still again;
> This has neither wax nor wane,
>   Neither stop nor start.
>
> People dress and go to town;
>   I sit in my chair.
> All my thoughts are slow and brown;
> Standing up or sitting down
> Little matters, or what gown
>   Or what shoes I wear.

When she was done reciting, she kissed his hand where it rested on the arm of his chair.

He scolded her for this, and for childishly surprising him at work at his desk, and for the way sometimes she would cross her fingers about her knees, pulling one knee toward her. "Don't do that, Edna, it makes your hands look ugly." She would look at them guiltily, and quickly hide the hands behind her back. She loved his hands, loved nothing more than sitting at his feet, next to the fire, holding his warm palm to her cheek.

Most of all he scolded his "child" for loving him, even as he drew her to him. He was ill, he was getting old, he was dying of some mysterious illness neither he nor any physician could understand and that neither drug nor time nor love could cure. She must leave him, she must not telephone or write; they must be content with a love spiritual, above the flesh, eternal and divine. But then he sent her love poems, and after months of tormented correspondence on both sides he would wearily consent at last to another tryst, at his apartment on Lexington Avenue in New York. There in the darkness he would let her have her way with him, and he might use her in the way he would use a wicked little schoolboy who would not do as he had been told.

※

On September 8, 1914, Vassar sophomore Edna St. Vincent Millay sat down to breakfast in the dining room of the new Plaza Hotel on Fifth Avenue with her friend the dapper publisher. Mitchell Kennerley had grown up in England and she admired his accent. When they finished their cantaloupe and sweet rolls, their toast and marmalade, they sipped coffee and Mr. Kennerley offered the poet a cigarette from a silver case. She declined, concerned there might be someone in the room "who knows I do not smoke." But as soon as they returned to the publisher's office downtown she gratefully accepted her first cigarette of what had already been a long day.

She had arrived in New York from Camden on her way back to school at Vassar, and went directly to call on her patroness "Auntie Cahline" at her apartment. Miss Dow was hurrying out of town on another train so they spent only a few moments together. In the midmorning Vincent showed up at Kennerley's, and he dropped everything to take her to breakfast. Then back at his office he made such a fuss over her she had to laugh: he found a jar of Page & Shaw orange candies and stuck it in her bag. He pulled a big novel off the shelf he wanted her to read, along with a box of imported chocolates; and as the gifts piled up he rang for his stenographer to ship all of them to Vassar. Then he wanted to know what else he could do for her.

Kennerley picked up the telephone and rang up Arnold Genthe, the most eminent portrait photographer in New York. Vincent was already a name, which intrigued the photographer of celebrities. Herr Genthe could make her even more famous by taking her picture, which would profit Kennerley's *Forum*, where so many of her new poems were appearing. Her lovely face in magazines and on gallery walls would fan flames of interest in the book of poems, which the aggressive publisher knew she must consent to, sooner or later. It was just a matter of time. Arnold Genthe said he would be delighted to see the illustrious poet right away.

Herr Genthe's studio on Fifth Avenue and Forty-sixth Street was "everything a studio ought to be," Vincent recalled in a letter home, "all sorts of tapestries and wonderful colored draperies and cabinets of curious things, and photographs, photographs everywhere of beautiful women and famous people." There was Paderewski, the Polish pianist-statesman, and producer David Belasco; and there was actress Billie Burke, and the photo of Martha Hedman that had just lit up the cover of *Theatre Magazine*. And "a real yellow cat that lies and sleeps or walks around the room."

"To think," she wrote, "that he wanted to take *me*!" The irony will soon be apparent.

But first they had lunch in a Sixth Avenue restaurant, where he apologized to her because he had several appointments before he could give her his full attention. This worked out well, as she had hoped for a few bittersweet hours with her lover Arthur Hooley, whose apartment was near Kennerly's office, where she had left her bags. She wanted to take a bath and change her shirtwaist, and she knew that Arthur would not deny her his hospitality in such an emergency.

After a sad parting from Arthur (she always felt she would never see him again) she followed the black janitor out of the building. He carried her luggage down to the street and hailed the cab that took her back to the studio "to be immortalized."

Genthe's attentions inspired a delightful "self-portrait" in Vincent's letter to her family: "Let me tell you something you didn't know. Besides having beautiful hair, an extraordinarily good forehead in spite of the freckles, an impudent, aggressive, and critical nose, and a mysterious mouth, I have, artistically, and even technically, an unusually beautiful throat." Something of a poet himself, the German photographer was justifiably obsessed with the long throat and red mouth, the instrument that had formed the verses of "Renascence." He wrapped her in a rich light-blue cloak that set off her golden-red hair, sat her "side-to" in front of a pale gray plush curtain, and made her lean forward while lifting back her head. Then he disappeared under the hood of his tripod camera, and proceeded to photograph her throat a dozen times.

"Imagine to yourself that blue thing about me, and my hair, which is very red in the light, knotted loosely at the back of my neck, and that gray thing behind me, and *pray* that the pictures are good."

The pictures are lost. But Herr Genthe followed his muse out to Mamaroneck in the spring, where he captured her in an arch of magnolia blossoms, her classic profile, the delicate hands fingering the branches, dressed in a chaste A-line linen dress with square buttons of abalone. It is his most famous, enduring image, and now hangs in the Museum of Modern Art.

THE SAPPHO OF NORTH HALL

She had written in her diary three years earlier, "What life I have lived I have lived doubly, actually and symbolically," and her life in the autumn of 1914 lends that rich reflection a fresh nuance. She was living two lives—one in Manhattan and another in Poughkeepsie—and at times it must have been hard for her to know which was more actual, and which was the more symbolic.

Arthur Hooley belonged to her grown-up life in New York, her powerhouse career as a celebrity courted by publishers, patrons, editors, and portrait artists. But she had to return to her role as a student. Vassar meant long hours of study, play rehearsals and performances (she was in seven plays from 1915 to 1917), and writing poems and plays as the spirit moved her. Then there was her sex life on campus, which she pursued with gusto, with ingenuity, with a vengeance.

As an older student at Vassar, a woman with versatile experience in lovemaking, Vincent lost no time in taking advantage of the undirected lusts of the girls she found attracted to her. She was devilishly attractive, and her charm in these years, under the influence of her decadent Englishman, was decidedly androgynous. Amusing photos of Vincent from her Vassar days show her onstage playing the role of Marchbanks, the boy poet in Shaw's *Candida* who is in love with the heroine. Vincent looks convincing in her black suit, her black tie in an artist's bow, her hair bobbed. She relished the role, and wrote to her family: "I felt *perfectly* at home in the clothes. People told me I reminded them of their brothers the way I walked around and slung my legs over the arms of chairs, etc. . . . Somebody thought I really was a boy. Somebody thought it was wonderful the way I used my trousers and walked and stuck my hands in my pockets and crossed my legs—*as if I myself didn't notice I was doing it—*"

She probably knew exactly what she was doing. She wrote to Arthur that she was true to him "in her fashion"; and then presently, with stunning candor, explained that the main relief for her sexual urges came in the arms of her Vassar classmates. In days when birth control was difficult and sensitive women and men (with few exceptions) linked heterosexual intercourse with romantic love, sex between women who had a taste for it was safe fun and comparatively unburdened. It is impressive how blithely and openly Millay wrote to her family at large about her same-sex adventures, and how they welcomed her female lovers home for the holidays.

The element of androgyny in Edna St. Vincent Millay's childhood and youth has been much discussed and little understood. Journalists and biographers, pointing to her middle name, have guessed that Cora wanted a boy firstborn, which seems highly unlikely. Others mention the fatherless, husbandless family of four women, Vincent's role as head of the household in her parents' absence, and her using the name "Vincent" instead of the homely "Edna." Certainly these conditions led her to challenge gender conventions. The truth is that, like her mother, Vincent seemed to be aware early in life that virtues like courage, wisdom, and leadership are neither male nor female. She admired these qualities in herself even if the whole world preferred to consider them as masculine and the woman who vaunts them as something less than a proper woman. She was way ahead of her time.

Where Millay's androgyny becomes a powerful force is not so much in her life (though her homosexual adventures lend it a beguiling piquancy) as in her art. We see from first to last of the poet's oeuvre—as in the poetry and plays of Shakespeare—the cultivation of a multitude of rich voices from a profound and androgynous emotional center. If the male in her was not so firmly in touch with the female, she could never have written so insightfully of men and women in love.

She was aware of the peculiar nature of her sexuality by 1911 when she wrote "Renascence." It is her first great poem, and the first to speak out in a voice that is neither male nor female in its timbre (although men were eager to claim it as "male") but simply and magnificently human. The Millay "voice," the persona that is the basis of her early work, inhabits a meta-morphic creature, intermediate not only between the sexes but between the mortal and the divine, between the human and animal, and between the nun and the harlot. Remember her early verses, "Give her to me who was created mine! / Just as she is, half pixie, half divine!" One of the most stunning documents among her unpublished papers is a ragged draft of a letter to Ferdinand Earle, from the summer of 1912. In it she describes the agony of her "psychic hermaphrodism":

> If anyone but God had put a soul into a pixie, I should say it was done *just to see what would happen,*—out of the same curiosity that makes some children pull flies wings off. . . . I had no choice, I was an exper-iment. And I think it must have begun so long ago that the heart-breaking and grotesque antics brought about by this psychic hermaphrodism have long since ceased to be amusing. . . .

The gods that made her this way seem to have abandoned her "to zig-zag on alone. Rather shabby of 'em, seems to me," she adds. She supposes there must be others like her in the world somewhere, "gypsy souls following false paths in search of camping grounds that cannot be on earth, thirsting after poisoned springs, singers of forbidden songs, insatiable. . . ."

In this same astonishing letter, the young woman shows her enthusiasm for Ibsen (she had devoured all the plays) in comparing herself to Anitra of *Peer Gynt.* Peer has fallen in love with Anitra the dancing slave girl, and promises to make her "a Houri in Paradise!" if she will marry him. She says, "Impossible, Master! I've no soul!" When he assures her that he can get her a soul through education, she stubbornly refuses, saying she doesn't care so much about having a soul, but she sure would like to have that opal in Gynt's turban.

"Anitra was wise in her choice of the opal," wrote Vincent. "I would have done the same in her place; for I'm sure 'twould be far much pleasanter to dance a dozen years than to [go to] school for a million. But I had no choice." College had not been an option for her, though it soon would be. A life of Art (to "dance" a dozen years) seemed to be her fate, one she would gracefully accept as long as the jewels arrived on schedule.

What makes Millay's identification with the dancing girl even more sig-nificant is that the dancer is a conventional symbol of ecstasy. Like many poets and holy prophets, Edna St. Vincent Millay had an ecstatic nature given to transports of delight, terror, and melancholy, driven by the music in her to make poetry in the throes of those passions.

O world, I cannot hold thee close enough!

. . . .

Lord, I do fear
Thou'st made the world too beautiful this year;
My soul is all but out of me,—let fall
No burning leaf; prithee, let no bird call.
(from "God's World," circa 1915)

She would never be content with the quieter, subtler consolations of philosophy and spiritual love, the stoical disciplines that guide less restless souls toward peace. The poet craved ecstasy and could not live long without it.

❧

Her dance among the nymphs and houris of Vassar College caused lively commotion during her career there, furnishing gossip and tall tales for decades to come. Many readers believed that Lakey, the lesbian ringleader of Mary McCarthy's novel *The Group*, was based upon Millay's legend at Vassar, although McCarthy herself denied it. Years after the poet graduated from the pink-and-gray college, upon hearing that some distraught student had leapt from a high window there, Millay was heard to remark tartly: "Well, at least they can't blame that one on me." Vincent took no credit for any suicides during her college career, though she wrote a poem there called "The Suicide," of which Miss Dow did not approve.

Curse thee, Life, I will live with thee no more!
Thou hast mocked me, starved me, beat my body sore!
And all for a pledge that was not pledged by me. . . .

No one died there for love of Vincent, but letters from her admirers during those years prove that the Sappho of North Hall broke many a girl's heart.

"People, my friends and hers, are very much interested in a seemingly new friendship which has sprung up between Catherine Filene and me," she wrote in her diary on December 5, 1913. "Handsome great big child! Kim and Margaret made candy, and Catherine and I came in together. People are very much disturbed." They were disturbed because a sort of informal monogamy prevailed in the sexual subculture of Vassar in 1913, and girls tended to pair off with their "best friends"; by the end of that year Vincent was known to be Katharine Tilt's sidekick (the Katharine who so admired Vincent's lips), so the poet's appearing on the arm of Catherine Filene caused tongues to wag.

Social life on campus at Vassar in 1913 was a round of teas, formal lunch-eons, and fudge-making parties that were the fabrications of a long Victorian tradition of manners and social intercourse. Many of the events were posted, and the young ladies were expected to attend, correctly attired, and to observe at all times the etiquette appropriate to their class. This was meant to help them assume their proper roles in society as wives and mothers.

Vincent, of course, did not come from a "good" family—not by a long shot. She was not alone at Vassar in needing desperately to stake out her own turf in this rich, tradition-bound social milieu by parodying the quaint traditions and behaving in ways that would shock the more conservative of her teachers and classmates. This was the beginning of a pattern of rebellion that would carry her into middle age.

The customary teas in dormitory rooms—who hosted them and who attended—were often a public announcement of an alliance. The first week in December was Vincent and Katharine Tilt's turn to give a tea, and the couple was having a spat. Katharine mentioned in passing that she had found some other girl engaging, whereupon Vincent, on a stroll downtown to pur-chase the tea cakes, "told her about Catherine Filene purposely to make her jealous. . . . It worked beautifully."

The Sunday tea Vincent hosted with Katharine on December 7 was full of tension, after which Vincent recalled, "I just came home and howled over a little thing Katharine did. However, Catherine Filene came in and consoled me beautifully." The next morning she wrote, "Katharine feels nervous about what she did last night. She will feel nervouser before it's over. And it will be good for her." She means to teach her girlfriend a lesson in jealousy, practicing what she had preached to her sister Norma, always to stay in control of a romantic situation.

On Friday night they attended a "reunion dance." Vincent wore a thin, low-cut satin dress with a train and nothing on underneath it, "and felt just like dancing. Danced with Catherine Filene most of the time. Katharine Tilt came upstairs with me and asked to unhook me. I let her. It's all working wonder-fully. Did ten theorums in my mathbook," she wrote in her diary. Six years later mathematics and sex would add up to one of the finest sonnets in the lan-guage, Millay's "Euclid alone has looked on beauty bare." By then more than a handful of people knew that the poem was more about sex than math.

The next night she "was invited to and attended a very exclusive dance in Catherine Filene's room. . . . Love to dance. And Catherine makes a won-derful man. She was swell-looking and swell *feeling* last night!"

This was soon before Christmas vacation. On the way home to Camden

Vincent stopped for a night at the home of her mother's brother Bert Buzzell, who had been begging for a long time to see her. A brief diary entry on December 23 is poignant and haunting, considering the drama of her emotional life:

"I wonder why people love me so."

Was there ever a woman, with beauty and intelligence, who plotted so tirelessly and obsessively to get everyone to love her? Yet there it stands in her diary, that sentence, stark naked, surrounded by white space. *I wonder why people love me so*, as if the riddle of love still eluded her, the mystery of her own carefully wrought charisma. One day she was telling her sisters how beautiful she was, how fine an actress, how gifted a poet. And the next day, en route home from college, she was haunted by self-doubt, challenging the people who love her, including her family, demanding: *Why? What has made me worthy?*

She meant to keep working at it until so many people loved her so much the answer would become self-evident to her, and she would never feel unloved again.

Back at school on January 19, 1914, she wrote, "Tonight Katharine and I came together with a crash that smashed us all up, and when we picked up the pieces we put them together as they should be and now everything is quite wonderful. God, if you are looking, bless her, please." The benediction is formulaic, fascinating—each time she consummates a sexual relationship, she bestows the blessing. There ends the lively diary of 1913.

Vincent would not keep a strict diary again for many years, only intermittent journals. But her general correspondence continues to provide a full picture of her love life. Millay's constellation of friends and admirers at Vassar, which soon assumed the range and intensity of a cult, included her Latin teacher, Elizabeth Hazelton Haight, a history teacher, Mildred Thompson, her senior-year roommate Charlotte Noyes Babcock (they called each other "sister"), classmates Frances Stout, Anne Gardner, and the attractive singer Dorothy Coleman, whom Vincent immortalized in the sequence of poems "Memorial to D.C." after Dorothy died of the flu in 1918. Most of these women have been suspected of carrying on "affairs" with the androgynous poet. All that we know for sure about this is that several, including Elizabeth Haight and Charlotte Babcock, became Vincent's lifelong friends, and that Dorothy Coleman's mother, upon her daughter's death, discovered diaries that revealed a secret and tumultuous passion of the young singer for her older classmate.

These are the suspects that pop up when most biographers examine Millay's lesbian reputation at Vassar. But Vincent had the self-possession and good manners to keep her real lovers secret from the public and, wherever possible, from each other. The letters and diaries reveal unequivocally that she was engaged in both serial and simultaneous sexual relationships with Katharine Tilt, Catherine Filene, Isobel Simpson, and Elaine Ralli. There may have been others who left no paper trail, but certainly those four would have sufficed to keep Vincent entertained when she was not hard at work.

It is hardly an exaggeration to describe Vincent as the queen of a cult of personality at Vassar. There are romantic photographs in the college archives of her sophomore-year triumph in *The Pageant of Athena*. She stands with a golden crown and necklace, her dress designed after one of Maxfield Parrish's faerie queens, with a long, coarse white cotton skirt gathered into an elaborate girdle belted low on her hips. Two starry-eyed handmaidens in dark tunics and tights hold the corners of her ten-foot-long train. The pageant came as near to a literal coronation of their idol as the sophomore class could devise.

Written by Hazel MacKaye, *The Pageant of Athena* featured Vincent as Marie de France, the French medieval poetess and half sister to Henry II of England, famous for her Breton verse romances. In full regalia, she wound her way to the green grass of the athletic circle followed by fifty college girls, some carrying cushions, others rugs. One shouldered a parasol, another wielded a fan so neither sun nor wind should visit Vincent too roughly. The bleachers had been transformed with crepe and felt into a throne for the regal poetess to take her ease while they entertained her in anticipation of her longed-for poems.

"I recline there while they have their song-practice. They ask permission to do everything,—what to sing, who is to lead, and I stop them every once in a while to say that the sun is in my eyes and things like that," she wrote to her sisters. She sends someone off to the Lost and Found office after a ring she's mislaid, another to the bookstore to fetch her a theme pad, another to gather her mail. This is all in fun, of course, all part of the mock pageant that will culminate in Vincent–Marie de France, in her glory, reciting the sublime Breton *lais*.

The thing is, this playacting is not far from the truth. When Vincent fell ill and took to her bed, as she did every few weeks, a whole dormitory of girls fell over one another to wait upon her until she recovered her strength. For years after the *Pageant of Athena*, the students and faculty, with more awe than irony, addressed this undergraduate as if she were royalty: "Everywhere on campus now I meet people who say, 'Hello, Princess!' And yesterday, actually, in the laboratory, with many girls experimenting all around us, Professor Sanders came up to me and said, 'How is your Royal Highness this afternoon?' and then he said, 'I want to thank you for what you did for us Saturday. It was very lovely.' The committee thanked me when it was all over, and one of them said, 'There isn't another soul that could have done it.'" What had she done? She had brought the romantic spirit of poetry and beauty to life, in the flesh, on the Vassar campus for a few hours, and the school would never forget it.

"And I have more dinner dates than I can handle."

Her room often looked like a florist's shop. During the play, Elaine Ralli, a junior, sent her an armful of large tan-pink roses mixed with pussy willows, in a heavy dark-green Egyptian amphora. "Harry" (Harriet Wiefenbach, her freshman roommate) sent her a woven basket full of growing daffodils. Anne Gardner gave her a box of chocolates, and Isobel Simpson a filigree brooch. Anne Gardner also had delivered a corsage of roses and freesia, and Agnes Rogers a little rustic basket of purple crocuses and tiny lilies. When Elaine's roses had faded and her affection had not, she sent her favorite a corsage of pansies to wear and a great bunch of daffodils and pussy willows for her room. "I have had tulips and yellow daisies too,—my room seems to be always full of flowers. On the table behind me now are seventeen purple crocuses, some white lilies growing in a basket, and eight yellow jonquils in a green vase. On the tea table is my little straight old-fashioned glass vase mother gave me with some freak daffodils. . . ." And on the table with her Royal Doulton dishes another pitcher flared with jonquils and pussy willows.

"How'd you like to be an actress?" she wrote to her family after this flower show. The theater fosters the cult of personality. So does the mystery of sex. The right ingredients had combined to make the twenty-two-year-old diva an object of devotion.

Someday the complete letters of Edna St. Vincent Millay will be published, unexpurgated. There could be few more entertaining and revealing letters from any American woman of the twentieth century, and the correspondence will give us a view of adolescence and young womanhood as colorful as the diary of Anne Frank, yet broader and more various. In one of the funniest letters home from Vassar to her sisters, in October 1914, she writes in the role of "Bad Vincent." Good Vincent is considerate, well mannered, and diligent. "Bad Vincent doesn't like her family, she's having a glad time at college,—oh simply *marv*! And she really has forgotten all *about* her family. Last night,—which was Wednesday night at *this* college—Bad Vincent cleaned up his house and sat down and stood up and sat down and looked at his little bracelet clock and said, 'It's dinner time, why don't you come, you Belated Guest?' And Belated Guest said devil a word. He was so very Belated. So Bad Vincent ate his evening meal and ushered hisself to chapel."

A bit of explanation: "Bad Vincent" is Vincent as a bad boy, and Belated Guest and the other characters she is about to mention in the male gender are all women. (If Vassar won't let them have their men, then to hell with it, they'll be their *own* men.) Her letter tells us how the Belated Guest appeared at chapel and, "under the leadership of the gods came up to Bad Vincent and said without shame or guilt in his beautiful black eye, 'may I sit with you?' . . . Bad Vincent moved his gracious self aside and while Belated Guest prayed his prayers with his curly black head on the back of the next pew Bad Vincent said with glee and malice, 'Did you know you cut a dinner engagement with me tonight?'—Belated Guest went stiff all over."

After a long, stunned silence the girl said, "O, Vincent, I'm so mortified!" And she looked as if she would cry. "So Bad Vincent was pleased, and he showed pleasure. And Belated Guest said 'O *can't* I come again? *When* can I come again?' And Bad Vincent said, 'No, don't want you now. All out of the notion.' And Belated Guest died."

But during the prayers the poor recreant cried, and pleaded, and drew pictures of herself "all melted into weep" until at last the goddess relented a little, asking if she was really so sorry as that. "So Bad Vincent thought for a long hour and sometimes yea and sometimes no he thought . . . and at last he proclaimed, 'Tomorrow night, then, Base but Beautiful!'"

Then she describes the Belated Guest as a hockey hero, roommate of Katharine Tilt. "Bad Vincent loves him and makes Elaine jealous. Elaine is jealous when Bad Vincent loves anybody but hisself. He is almost even jealous when Bad Vincent loves him, because that is his nature. . . ."

As I have mentioned, Vincent confided to her mother and sisters her same-sex flirtations with extraordinary ease. She wrote to Norma on November 4, 1914, that Elaine Ralli was a junior, "another hockey hero, cheerleader, rides horseback a lot, very boyish, not tall, but *all* muscle. She's just naturally *taken* me, for better or worse." Vincent would be standing in a crowd of people conversing, and if Elaine "wants me for anything, first thing I know she has come and got me, just plain lugged me off. . . . Everybody recognizes the situation, and accepts it unquestioningly, and there's no fuss about it. . . ." In a joyful photograph of Millay and Elaine Ralli arm-in-arm, the handsome, dark-haired Italian-American girl, with her broad nose, wide-set eyes, and thick neck, looks as if she is about to whirl the delicate poet away in a dance.

Elaine had more of an interest in science than the arts, but was eager to learn from Vincent. The two girls spent happy weekends at an inn owned by Elaine's parents in Bellport, Long Island. And that summer Elaine was a welcome guest at Vincent's home in Camden, where they enjoyed sailing and swimming and hiking. Apparently their friendship caused no discomfort or embarrassment to either of the families. Vincent also spent enjoyable weekends at the Rallis' apartment in New York City. Once she wrote to her lover Arthur Hooley, on Ralli stationery, that if he would like to send her a letter the week before September 17, 1915, he should address her there, and "I am perfectly happy and can live without you. With much love nevertheless—Edna."

Letters from Millay to Ralli (except for one thirty years later when Ralli had become a physician and helped Vincent in an emergency) have not survived. But Ralli's letters to Millay prove that their intimacy was more than a platonic friendship with a sexual edge—this was an intense and carnal affair. And for Ralli (as for Dorothy Coleman) the falling out was devastating.

> How I want to come back to you—yes I know I have just left—but the longing in me never leaves and this is a night that seems made for you and me. Do not worry—we are friends but I am still in love. . . . If I am not careful I will be covering this paper with words that make a poor endeavor to tell you I love you. . . . I can find nothing to express the hunger, the yearning, and oh! the love for you—and you are so small!
> Have you heard the rain? It is cold tonight and I'm too restless for rain—only for the touch of you—will I ever not want that?

A long, undated letter from Elaine Ralli to Vincent at 603 North Hall tells of the lover's happiness that turned to ashes and gall in 1917 when Elaine graduated and Vincent broke off with her, probably to spend more nights with Dorothy Coleman:

> I'm sorry we had to disagree so decidedly and that out of all we had been we didn't have enough left to build up a friendship of some kind.—But I guess that's the usual thing—the more people are to one another the more decided is the break. . . . I grant you that I made a fool of myself but I learned an awful lot.

This painful letter is interlaced with verses that refer to their parting: "Too late I stayed—forgive the crime—Unheeded flew the hours," Elaine writes apologetically. Elaine had worn out her welcome in Vincent's crowded love life, and the lesson the poet was trying to teach her no longer desirable mistress is that it is best to quit an affair while there is yet life in it. As candid as Elaine's letters are, she takes pains to assure Vincent that she has written "a restrained letter" with every "attempt to be careful," and that her beloved is "perfectly safe" in her confidence.

After Elaine Ralli's melancholy letters, Vincent must have taken pure delight in the frolicsome company of Isobel Simpson, a Greek major with a lively sense of humor. Unlike the athletic Ralli, Simpson shared Millay's passion for books. The letters abound in allusions to Kipling's *Jungle Books* in particular, as they addressed one another as "Best Beloved." She called Isobel the "Little Sphinx" when she did not call the younger girl her "child" or her "daughter." Isobel in turn called her sexual mentor her "Little Mother," and more often "Dearest Little Slimey Serpent," reminiscent of the letters of Vincent's inamorata Ella Somerville. Simpson's letters are affectionate, funny, and lascivious.

> Now, when the roads are full of mud and the air is full of spring, I begin to think of you more particularly than at any other time of the year. Puddles, for instance, always remind me of you, because you always insisted that I should walk 'round them rather than thro' them as any right-minded person would naturally do. Then, I'm sure I saw a *tiny* bit of green on the ends of some pine boughs, and that made me think *very* hard about you.

Away working as a camp counselor one summer, she wrote Vincent letters about how much she wanted her. "I think of you when I brush my teeth because I use the same kind of toothpaste that you do—I think of you when I bathe—for obvious reasons. . . . I think of you from force of habit. . . . Best Beloved I want a picture of you, too. Where is that undressed, fairy one you promised me?"

> Please ma'am, will you send me a tiny little person, with inexcusably red hair, green eyes, and the saddest mouth in the world? I'd like to have her in a brown slip-over sweater, and a corduroy skirt with a peacock feather stuck in her belt, and in one hand she must have a cup of chicken broth—in the other a fruit salad. Oh—and she must wear brown stockings with little green things climbing around them.

The intimacy between Simpson and Millay, leavened by humor, continued intermittently until 1920, and then ripened into lifelong friendship, due partly to their shared interest in the Greek and Latin poets. Simpson became

a distinguished teacher of classics at the Brearley School. Under her guidance
Millay translated Sappho:

> Relaxing me from head to feet
> Love masters me, the bitter sweet
>   O'er thy limbs breathing;
> Yea, Eros now, the god born blind
> Sweeps my soul like the mountain wind
>   Through the oaks seething.

Millay the poet, Millay the scholar, and Millay the lover, working together,
had joined two famous fragments the poet of Lesbos had dedicated to Atthis,
making one lovely stanza.

❦

Having passed her midyear examinations in January of 1916, she was "tired
to death," she wrote to Arthur Hooley. She still had to complete her physical
education requirement, "which means that last fall I did not climb the
required number of ropes or leap the required number of bars . . . so that
now if I wish to play the part of Deirdre in Synge's *Deirdre of the Sorrows*
I have to spend all my time in the gym. . . ." The exertion reduced her weight
to an incredible ninety-six pounds, which suited her mood and her sense of
pathos—haunted, hollow-eyed as she was by her unrequited love for Arthur.

She tried to make him jealous, describing her upcoming junior prom in
sartorial detail that only her fastidious Englishman might appreciate, "an
affair of surpassing magnificence" she will attend with a very nice man that
Arthur would not like at all. And she will wear a dress of pale yellow chiffon
with butterflies on the shoulders and fur around the bottom, and gold slippers—"pure gold, *truly* Arthur, I think they must be, they *shine* so." A year
before, after a shopping trip on Fifth Avenue, she had written in her diary:
"I am *cursed*, and I know it, with a love for beautiful things. I can't *bear*
anything that looks cheap or feels cheap or is over-trimmed or coarse. I hate
myself all the time because I'm all the time wearing things I don't like. It's
wicked and it's ungrateful but I can't help it. I wish I had *one graceful dress*."
(Like Lord Byron, the mature Millay would dress so magnificently that her
unique clothing, eerily preserved, hangs in museums here and abroad. The
Paris-made dresses, encrusted heavily with pearls and semiprecious stones
and with their long trains, are like the regalia of a Renaissance princess. It
is difficult to lift one of these dresses with one hand.)

She told her insouciant Englishman that she would have a delightful evening at the prom with her young man, and she would be "*ravishing* to behold—or else I shall not go a step. And I shall appear to be only about seventeen,—who am actually—but there!—We will not discuss it! And I shall be tireless, and vivacious,—and no one will ever guess that I have a secret, eating sorrow, by which I mean to say *yourself*, my dear."

But her English lover's stone heart was unmoved. By the end of the month she had chosen another tack, challenging *his* sexuality, his notion of her as a woman, and his idea of himself as a man. He had suggested to his "child" that only if she were a man could she understand his sadness, his ennui, and his torment.

She answered him with a cry of the heart that would evolve into a romantic principle governing her life. "It really isn't necessary that I should be a man, Arthur, in order to know what the word *girl* sometimes means to you. What do you suppose the word *man* sometimes means to me? In a place like this?" She is scribbling on pale blue Vassar College stationery, a few doors away from the broad-shouldered Elaine Ralli. She has had four years to figure things out. "It is silly to say that men and women can't understand each other. They can understand each other quite as well as they can understand themselves."

> This is a strange place. I had known, but I had not realized, until I came here, how greatly one girl's beauty or presence can disturb another's peace of mind,—more still, sometimes, her beauty and absence. There are Anactorias here for any Sappho.

She goes on at length to defend the license of Greek philosophers and English poets from Plato to Oscar Wilde, and all those lovers the narrow-minded world has condemned for their homosexual acts and affections. And she rings changes on St. John's "He that is without sin among you, let him cast the first stone," by saying, "Let him among you who has sinned *all* sins, cast the first stone," concluding that a poet needs only to sin in her heart to know that "it is no question of stone-throwing at all. And it often happens that I am very, very sorry for everybody."

She was in rehearsals for her greatest performance at Vassar, the starring role in John Millington Synge's *Deirdre of the Sorrows*. The heroine from Irish legend was born, according to a prophecy, the most beautiful woman of Ireland, and destined to provoke strife and mayhem. Like Oedipus she was given to surrogate parents, by an old king who hoped to trick fate by raising her in seclusion then marrying her when she came of age. But Deirdre, hearing tales of the handsome young Noisi, persuades her nurse to bring him to her, then falls in love with the youth. The angry king hunts Noisi to his death, whereupon Deirdre kills herself at her lover's grave. This was a prophetic role for this Irish-American poet-actress, who dreamed of dying for love at the same time she was studying to become a world-renowned femme fatale. Someday she will know the danger of eros from all sides, as well as any poet who has ever written, and will write:

> Sweet love, sweet thorn, when lightly to my heart
> I took your thrust, whereby I since am slain,
> And lie disheveled in the grass apart,
> A sodden thing bedrenched by tears and rain,
> While misty night to cloudy morning clears,
> And clouds disperse across the gathering light,
> And birds grow noisy, and the sun appears—
> Had I bethought me then, sweet love, sweet thorn,
> How sharp an anguish even at the best—
> When all's requited and the future sworn—
> The happy hour can leave within the breast,
> I had not so come running at the call
> Of one who loves me little, if at all.
>   (from *Fatal Interview*)

Reporters got wind that something special was on the boards in Poughkeepsie the night of March 13, 1916—this girl wonder who wrote "Renascence" and those other poems that had been appearing in *The Forum* was chewing up the scenery as Deirdre in Synge's tragedy. They showed up in force, not only the daily critics from the nearby *Eagle* and the *Enterprise*, but also the drama reviewer from the *New York Tribune*. What they got was more than they hoped for, a virtuoso performance of profound emotion and exquisite subtlety. Until now, no one has ever known exactly why. It seemed a mystery as dark, perhaps, as the uncanny composition of "Renascence."

> Deirdre, small and bewitching . . . lovely in her little Irish costume, clinched the attention of the audience and the whole play with the increasing intensity of her acting, building to a successful crisis.
>   (*The Eagle*, March 12, 1916)

The "successful crisis" in the last act comes after the man Deirdre loves has been killed in battle. She stands beside the hero's grave and, unable to endure a moment more of life without him, takes the knife from his hand and plunges it into her own heart. The audience, at first terrified, dissolved in tears.

"It was very real to me, as always," she wrote to Arthur Hooley, "and when they picked me up from the floor after the fall of the curtain, I found that I had actually driven the knife right through my little leather jacket." It was Arthur she mourned. Her desperate love for him drove the stage knife through the leather jacket and pricked the skin over her heart.

She needed him, and the exact nature of her need is expressed in many of the letters. She wanted him to look at her, to listen and speak to her as an equal, as no one else could. "Nobody speaks to me. People fall in love with me, and annoy me and distress me and flatter me and excite me and— and all that sort of thing. But no one speaks to me. I sometimes think that no one can. Can you?" She had created such a dense and mobile mask, layer by layer, that almost no one could penetrate it. But now she had told him everything. She was quick to add that it was not a confession but an obser- vation, not at all irrelevant but in no way shameful. "For up here, while some of us are thinking of the rest of us, the rest of us are thinking of you, or men like you—I mean to say, unlike you."

Arthur responded quickly and kindly, eager, it would appear, to play the role of her sexual confessor in a matter he thoroughly understood. "Edna, Edna, even if you *had* cared for a girl, and even if you had given yourself (so far as you could) I do not think I should care, greatly. No. I should not." From his lofty eminence next to Ganymede on Olympus, Arthur Hooley grandly pours down the sunlight of his blessings: "Everything would have been beautiful, to you. As to Sappho. And so, to me. [signed] Arthur." And there he stands, her tragic Englishman, free at last of the girl child who wanted him as a father figure, as a husband perhaps, as a woman wants a man; at long last he is relieved of the pressure of her relentless heterosexuality.

In July she wrote to him that she thought of him less often because "my time and my thoughts and nearly all my love have been given to a boy my own age, the sweetest boy in the world. He is so sweet I cannot think what to do with him, and he is adorably stupid. We never converse. Of course I shall not marry him—I am too tragically wise."

Yet her letters to Arthur continued faithfully, though with fading hope, until the end of that year. She begged him for one last audience, in Mamar- oneck, in Manhattan, *anywhere*; and Arthur kept refusing, saying he was sick, dying, returning to England.

> And what are you that, missing you,
>   I should be kept awake
> As many nights as there are days
>   With weeping for your sake?

. . . .

> I know a man that's a braver man
>   And twenty men as kind,
> And what are you, that you should be
>   The one man on my mind?
>   (from "The Philosopher")

There is no evidence she ever saw him again. After a brief exchange of notes about the publication of her book in the autumn of 1917, Arthur Hooley disappeared from Millay's life without a trace. Coincidentally, her lesbian adventures faded away with the ghost of Arthur Hooley.

☙

The elusive Englishman, with all his sighs, dirges, and crotchets, had been pivotal in her coming of age as a lover and a poet.

What is left of this unique drama—in addition to a heap of unpublished love letters—is a dozen love poems scattered through Millay's first three books, *Renascence, A Few Figs from Thistles*, and *Second April*. Beginning with the "Three Songs of Shattering" in *Renascence,* with their references to the plum tree and the dogwood blossoms, the love lyrics in that book clearly recall the idyllic springtime in Mamaroneck and the yearning she felt for Arthur, the anguish for the passion and the sweet season that will come no more. Here are lines from the third of the "Three Songs."

> All the dog-wood blossoms are underneath the tree!
>   Ere spring was going—ah, spring is gone!
> And there comes no summer to the like of you and me,—
>   Blossom time is early, but no fruit sets on.

From the languid, morbid Englishman the young poetess absorbed the mood, the "dying fall" of the fin de siècle, the sweet misery of love doomed.

> Love, if I weep it will not matter,
>   And if you laugh I shall not care;
> Foolish am I to think about it,
>   But it is good to feel you there.
>   (from "The Dream")

A similar tone may be heard in early W. B. Yeats, in Swinburne, and some of the more romantic members of the Irish Rhymers' Club.

I lay,—for Love was laggard, O, he came not until dawn,—
I lay and listened for his step and could not get to sleep;
And he found me at my window with my big cloak on,
All sorry with the tears some folks might weep!

                                    (from "Indifference")

As graceful as these poems are, there is a false note about them. She is
trying on a costume and a mask that does not quite suit her. No, she has
too much humor to mourn long for that lost April. She also has a rich fund
of anger she has been storing up since long before Arthur Hooley chained
her to that futile obsession. The humor and anger will soon erupt in the wit
of half a dozen sonnets that will shake the landscape of twentieth-century
love poetry. Taking her cue from Shakespeare, she begins with the octet:

Thou art not lovelier than lilacs,—no,
    Nor honeysuckle; thou art not more fair
    Than small white single poppies,—I can bear
Thy beauty; though I bend before thee, though
From left to right, not knowing where to go,
    I turn my troubled eyes, nor here nor there
    Find my refuge from thee, yet I swear
So has it been with mist,—with moonlight so.

Millay's first sonnet (not really her first, just the first she prints in her first
book) is prophetic, as so much great poetry is, in anticipating the writer's
fate. Her reading of Plutarch had led her to the story of Mithridates, King
of Pontus (120–63 B.C.), who dosed himself with a concoction of toxins,
drop by drop, as an antidote so that his enemies could not poison him. (The
downside to the tactic was that when Mithridates wanted to poison himself,
he couldn't.) The sestet takes the classical turn:

Like him who day by day unto his draught
    Of delicate poison adds him one drop more
Till he may drink unharmed the death of ten,
Even so inured to beauty, who have quaffed
    Each hour more deeply than the hour before,
I drink—and live—what has destroyed some men.

Already the theme of beauty's danger was familiar to Millay ("Lord, I do
fear / Thou'st made the world too beautiful this year. . . .") Now she consid-

ers her lover's beauty as a kind of venom that she, "inured to beauty, who have quaffed / Each hour more deeply than the hour before," is supernaturally equipped to consume.

We need look no further than this first sonnet to locate a perfect expression of the poet's character and her approach to life and love. The virtue one must admire in Millay above all others is her courage, her absolute fearlessness. If beauty is dangerous, if it is a poison, then she will sip at it drop by drop until she can enjoy more of beauty than any man alive. If sex is dangerous, she will study and practice it until she has mastered all of its holds, feints, and attacks, and until she has learned to escape from sex without injury. If men say alcohol is deleterious she will drink with such gusto and diligence, her tolerance for beer, wine, and gin will render her free from every effect but the liquor's pleasure. And when alcohol has been tamed, there will always be hashish and morphine. It is quite wonderful that in her early twenties the young voluptuary identified herself with the King of Pontus, in a love sonnet meant to even the score with Arthur Hooley.

The suite of six sonnets in the last pages of *Renascence* is a farewell to the "dyspeptic Englishman" (as she calls him in her letter of March 10, 1916). They range from the tenderly affectionate: "Mindful of you the sodden earth in spring / And all the flowers that in the springtime grow . . . / But you were something more than young and sweet / And fair,—and the long year remembers you" (Sonnet III), to the bitterly ironic:

> If I should learn, in some quite casual way,
> That you were gone, not to return again—
> Read from the back-page of a paper, say,
> Held by a neighbor in a subway train,
> How at the corner of this avenue
> And such a street (so are the papers filled)
> A hurrying man—who happened to be you—
> At noon today had happened to be killed,
> I should not cry aloud . . .

Hardly. In this ultramodern, anti-romantic poem the woman of Vassar, soon to be a prophet of love in Greenwich Village, would instead

> watch the station lights rush by
> With a more careful interest on my face,
> Or raise my eyes and read with greater care
> Where to store furs and how to treat the hair.

This is a new Millay, tough as sailcloth despite her reputation for vulnerability, delicacy, and giving all for love. Because she has suffered so from her passion, she knows how to defend herself, to shut the book on an affair when it no longer brings her pleasure.

Also, she has learned by example to shut the door of her innermost being, the core of herself, against anyone who threatens to violate it.

> Yet this alone out of my life I kept
> Unto myself, lest any know me quite;
> And you did so profane me when you crept
> Unto the threshold of this room tonight
> That I must never more behold your face.
> This now is yours. I seek another place.

This is the sestet of the last poem in the book, "Bluebeard," perhaps the most important of these early sonnets, and surely the most famous (the only one she honored with a title). The date of composition, early 1916, disproves the long-held assumption (by Jean Gould and others) that "Bluebeard" was a response to her lover Floyd Dell's incessant prying into her private life. She did not meet playwright Floyd Dell until a year after the poem was published in the May issue of *The Forum*.

The ancient folktale on which the poem is based so fascinated Millay that she reworked the story over and over in her journals. Bluebeard, the pirate (or wicked king, depending on the version), marries three sisters, one after another. Each time he gives his new bride the keys to his castle and the freedom to unlock any room but one—then he rides off. She disobeys him and enters the forbidden chamber where she finds the grisly remains of Bluebeard's ex-wives. When he comes home and finds out she has betrayed his trust, he adds the live wife to his collection of stuffed ones. This goes on until the youngest and cleverest girl tricks Bluebeard into believing she never entered the room; then she magically revives and rescues her sisters. Years after Millay published the poem "Bluebeard," she published the story in straightforward prose in *Ainslee's* magazine.

The folktale features the taboo motif—the forbidden chamber, the locked door—and the fatal danger of breaking a taboo. Millay's use of the story is ingenious, extraordinarily subtle. The androgynous poet has cast herself in the role of Bluebeard, but this is a Bluebeard the likes of which the world has never known, a detached, nonviolent, swordless pirate. His strongest sentiment is his desire for privacy, and next to that is his lofty contempt for the traitor who has invaded it.

This sublime parable about privacy comes from the grafting of a woman's voice upon a man's, Edna St. Vincent Millay's voice upon Arthur Hooley's. By the end of the poem, as by the end of 1916, the poetic voice and space had become entirely hers, and so had her heart.

She and Arthur had worked out a curious arrangement. She might love him, and he might return her love; but under no circumstances was she ever to disturb his privacy, invade his space. One night she and a girlfriend sneaked into his apartment building on Lexington Avenue, and she climbed the stairs to his door, desperate to see him. She stood there in silence, her heart pounding, hardly able to breathe. But she was unable to summon the courage to knock on the door.

"Arthur, you should be glad that I love you so sweetly, without troubling you at all," she wrote him on November 2. "You did not tell me if you read or liked my poem 'Bluebeard' in the May *Forum*. I thought that you would like that." The poem begins:

> This door you might not open, and you did;
> So enter now, and see for what slight thing
> You are betrayed . . . Here is no treasure hid,
> No cauldron, no clear crystal mirroring
> The sought-for truth, no heads of women slain
> For greed like yours, no writhings of distress,
> But only what you see . . . Look yet again—
> An empty room, cobwebbed and comfortless.

There will be no more Arthur Hooleys in Millay's love life. From him she learned a crucial lesson. From now on *she* will remain in control of her love affairs; never again will she be in the painful position of loving someone more than they love her—with one earthshaking exception a dozen years later, a liaison that will inspire the poignant sonnets of her book *Fatal Interview*.

THE GODDESS

꙳

*H*ow "Bad Vincent" challenged the authorities of Vassar College, breaking rule after rule to the wonder and delight of her classmates, the exasperation of her teachers, and the mortification of her friend the president; how during her final semester Bad Vincent went AWOL so many times, galavanting on trains and in motorcars all over New York State, she was first "campused" and then "rusticated" (thrown off campus); how at last the faculty voted a week before commencement to cashier and suspend her, denying her the right to graduate with her class (though she had written their baccalaureate hymn, the "Tree Ceremonies," and the marching song); how the students got up a petition and sent it to the beleaguered president demanding their heroine's reinstatement; how the whole college was in an uproar; how at the eleventh hour President MacCracken sent the faculty a request that Miss Millay's suspension be ended the eve of commencement so she might go across the stage with her classmates to receive her sheepskin—these stories and many others continue to regale the alumni and undergraduates of the "pink and gray" college. Percy Shelley was her idol: she did a perfect female impersonation of the rebel poet Shelley in all things but her failure to get drummed out of Vassar as Shelley had been expelled from Oxford a century earlier. She really tried her best. Cora Millay kept a letter from Ella Caleb, the dean, dated June 13, 1917. It is a long and thoughtful letter to Cora about the pandemonium Vincent had created at Vassar that week, and I will quote only a few telling passages.

> All the way through college Vincent has found it extremely difficult to live according to college regulations, and she had been forgiven possibly too often. I kept hoping she would grow into a sense of responsibility for daily engagements, and into a more cordial support of college laws, and possibly we were too easy with her. . . . When the Warden's department placed her under penalties for calmly staying in New York to go to the Opera instead of returning at the appointed time at the end of the spring recess, she ought to have known that it was a serious matter, but when the impulse came to go off on a lark, she yielded as any little child might have done, hoping that she would not be found out.

Dean Caleb goes on to explain that it was no single infraction but a "culmination of disregard for college rights that broke the long enduring patience that has been accorded her in this place."

> Vincent has undoubted genius and ability but she is absurdly childish
> for a young woman of her years and experience in her attitude toward
> law. Let us hope that this experience, which has been bitter and trying
> for her friends as well as herself, may be a crisis that will be of per-
> manent value in her life.

It was not. She remained indignant and petulant, and she seems to have taken away from her Vassar experience only the confirmed belief that the rules and laws that apply to ordinary students, citizens, and mortals do not apply to the immortal gods, muses, goddesses, and poets.

She had been traveling in some noble company, breathing rarefied air. No account of Millay's love life during the Vassar years (and after) would be complete without mention of the Nicaraguan poet Salomón de la Selva. It was he who took her to hear Caruso sing *Aida* at the Met, the day after her spring vacation was done and she was supposed to be in class back at Vassar. This incensed the wardens; this was the incident Dean Caleb mentioned in her letter.

Born in León in 1893, the boy poet came to the United States to study English in 1906 at the age of thirteen, with the ambition of adopting our language as his literary medium. When Millay arrived at Barnard in 1913, the twenty-year-old Nicaraguan was teaching classes at Columbia, but there is no evidence that Vincent attended any of these, or that the two ever met before the autumn of 1915. She first mentioned "the Spanish boy who wrote 'Fall from Fairieland' in the July *Forum*" in a September 6, 1915, letter to Hooley. She reported that Salomón had written to her, and asked her lover if he knew the young poet: "Is he as good-looking as he ought to be?" The bid to make Hooley jealous, as always, fell upon deaf ears. Had Hooley the temperament for it, and read the letters Salomón was writing to his "child," he would have been plenty jealous.

Salomón de la Selva, the hot-blooded Latin American poet, had fallen in love with the author of a few lyrics he had read in *The Forum*: "Kin to Sorrow," "The Witch-Wife," and "Afternoon on a Hill." His rhapsodic let-ters to this girl he had never seen were the substantial beginning of the mystical process by which Edna Millay turned into a goddess. The adoring correspondence that Salomón began in September of 1915 became the cen-tral current of a river of love letters from half a hundred men that swelled to a raging torrent before 1923, when the poet's marriage at last stemmed the tide. How her pen kept pace with it we will never know. But certainly her love poems are an emanation of that ardent and laborious body of correspondence. The writers would soon include Edmund Wilson, John Peale Bishop, Floyd Dell, Llewelyn Powys, Arthur Davison Ficke, and others less celebrated but equally fanatical in their devotion.

No one wrote letters to Millay so passionate and beautiful as the Nicaraguan poet's. These rival the greatest love letters of all time, and it is a pity they have been hidden, unedited and unpublished for so many years. These are a literary treasure that rightly belongs to the people of Nicaragua, whom Salomón served as ambassador to France before his death in 1959.

As she had done with Ferdinand Earle and Arthur Ficke, Millay drove him to write letters. Her side of the correspondence has not survived (to my knowledge) but Salomón's letters show the earmarks of a fit response to a shameless flirtation. One day after writing to her, he was visiting his friend the poet Mr. Joyce Kilmer. "I was so full of you, I spoke of you," Salomón confessed. "He has never seen you; has had a little correspondence with you . . . but he told me that you are very beautiful." Now what could be lovelier to a poet than a beautiful woman he has never seen?

> You must be beautiful, he says—like a willful princess loved of many, loving some—with a little dagger in her hand, red with the blood of slaves. That is why, when you are tired, you send your visitants away. They return. I would not. But when you are tired, wouldn't you let me caress you—very gently—and lull you?
>
> I love you, ugly or beautiful. But if you are beautiful you will always be a thing apart from me, somehow, like a lovely music. But if you are ugly, I will take your face in my hands and kiss you very deeply, until your face pales and glows like a star and I feel how nothing that God made is ugly, and then you shall be beautiful with the beauty of a dream that I bear in my heart.

She has asked him to describe himself, is he fat or lean, dark or fair, as if she were about to buy him in a slave market. "No," he reports, "I am not fat. I hate fat poets. . . . Neither am I as lanky as Rose Benét. And my nose is not like Louis Untermeyer's. I am a little poet, not a bit tall, and thin, and sometimes—when night after night crawls over the world and I haven't slept—I am very pale." He assures her he does not look like a dark South American. Of mingled Spanish, Indian, and English blood, de la Selva's hair is fair, his eyes hazel. But his nose, cheekbones, and set of his eyes are Indian.

"All in all, I am far from being handsome. I would never do for an Arrow-collar advertisement. . . ." (Most of Millay's lovers, after Arthur Hooley, would do very well as fashion models.)

But this does not put her off, especially not while the pale poet is praising her verses and her beauty to the skies. "*Witch-Wife* is a precious wine . . . *Afternoon on a Hill* is the sort of song dear dead Emily Dickinson would have made had she been a singer as well as a 'poet of ideas.' " Millay has told him she is of a sunny disposition. He protests: "You do not tell me the truth. You say you are gay. You are not. You are sad. Your heart is pregnant with sadness, and day by day sadness grows in you, as the moon grows in the heavens." There is a grain of truth in this, which becomes a theme not only in Salomón's love letters but the general run of billets-doux, by many hands, that she will receive during the decade to come. Most of her lovers apprehend a sadness in her beyond anything she will admit to. Evidently she projected a tragic sense in her lovemaking, which I believe was compounded by her own deep conviction that love, so precious, cannot last, and her lovers' contrary desire to capture the woman and keep her forever. Edna appeared sad to Salomón, as she would to dozens of other men, because she made *him* sad—she was a promise of paradise too good to be true, the consummate femme fatale.

> Love, why do you build such dreams for my unmaking? Why do you say that I must teach you Spanish? [He will.] Why do you draw me to you and bind me so? I stretch my arms to you in the dark, and my lips seek yours in the dark. . . . I hear you, and you always call me, and I go on, and on, seeking, seeking, O Love! . . .

Salomón had not yet met Millay, but already he had identified her with a romantic abstraction, linked the flesh-and-blood woman with the Ideal of Love. This is how men make goddesses; this is how proud men become suppliants. "Why, Love, I'm human. It is you who are 'not made for any man,' " writes Salomón, quoting from "Witch-Wife." At the end of this long letter, he quotes Ruskin, who once said to Robert Browning, "No man could have the power that is yours and not know it."

Salomón de la Selva is an important character in Millay's story because he was a brilliant, eloquent, and otherwise sensible gentleman who became— between September of 1915 and his enlisting in the British army during World War I—an absolute, often abject slave to Edna St. Vincent Millay. He worked tirelessly to advance her career, lobbying for her poems to be published in Spanish and arranging a special dinner in her honor at the Pan

American Association at the Felix Portland Hotel in New York. He showed her Manhattan, took her to plays, to concerts, and for rides on the Staten Island Ferry.

In 1916, when Salomón left New York to take a teaching job at Williams College, he continued his suit from there, bombarding her with letters, pleading with her to come and visit him before Christmas. She finally relented, traveling to Williamstown the first weekend in December. The poets went to concerts, and they took long walks in the Berkshires, where one day she would make her home. But by that time Salomón had settled for a relationship that was only tangentially, potentially sexual. They had slept together once in New York, and he mournfully admitted that he had failed her. "I wish once and for all to dispell whatever fear you may have of my making love to you. I made love to you once, and you did not care for it. I will not make love to you again. I wish only that between us there may grow a wholesome friendship. I shall try not to be selfish. I shall try to give you the very best that is in me."

Salomón faithfully gave her his best, and would have given her anything she asked of him. He showered her with gifts, some of them extravagant. "I have received, from England, a little flask of Attar of Roses. Over a year ago I had written to England to have it sent to me for you. The price of it had so increased during the war that the friend whom I commissioned to get it for me, thought it wise to wait hoping the prices would lower." This perfume, then the most costly in the world, was the Christmas present with which he hoped to lure her to Williamstown. Not that she was indifferent to his company and his fascinating conversation. But physically he was not her type, so between them there arose the uncomfortable pressure of his sublimated desire.

In 1917 Salomón told his friend, Walter Adolphe Roberts, the editor of *Ainslee's*, that Millay was the best young poet in America. The editor dropped her a note asking her to please come by his office and bring some poems. He was dazzled by her—she put him in mind of a tiger lily, as he later wrote in his memoir *Tiger Lily*. He took her to Mouquin's restaurant on Sixth Avenue. That evening began a relationship (an affair, according to him) between the writer and editor that resulted in Roberts publishing dozens of Millay's poems and stories in *Ainslee's*, including the first of many prose pieces under her pen name, "Nancy Boyd." Her work for *Ainslee's* became her chief source of income until 1921 when *Vanity Fair* stole her away. Roberts was in love with her from the first, and though there is no evidence that she was in love with him, she never allowed the editor to lose hope that she might have a change of heart and choose him over the other men in her life.

We have no correspondence from Roberts. But from Salomón came such love letters as perhaps no woman has ever received before, worshipful letters meant to convince her she was a goddess. If only Arthur Hooley had written such letters! The English poet Alice Meynell once asked Salomón to describe Millay, and he relayed the answer to his beloved:

> One might take her somehow for a seagull's feather, ruffled, cast off on an Autumn meadow,—a thing for dream and pity, magic withal, for it has the sea to give you, in memory, and the wind, in remembrance. She has been in strange nests and known sweet warmths. Oh, God is a bird of the sea, and Edna his wings!

He recalled a day he met her at the station, when the snow was falling as her train pulled in. "I was thinking how terrible it would be for me when you had gone, how terrible if you should never come; how terrible, when the war is ended, for those whose loves would not return. I think my heart and the world's heart was one, just then." He wept over these letters to her, and then apologized for his lack of manly restraint. "*Linda!* [my dear!] Now I want to cry but I won't." Playing the fool for her, he signs some of his letters "Pierrot" with a serpentine flourish: "My letters must pester you in the eyes and ears like flies on a hot day. Please forgive me. I am selfish to demand of you even that you read these mad things I write. Bear with me: soon enough I will be sane and perhaps you will miss me."

She loved his letters, even if she did not love Salomón. They are a cornucopia of adoration, praise, and engaging commentary on world literature and art. Salomón was fluent in Spanish, English, French, and Italian, and an authority on the art of the Italian Renaissance. From Salomón, Millay was getting a first-rate correspondence course that not only covered the classics of the romance languages but also included insightful line edits of her new poems, as quickly as she wrote them. Most important, she was growing to fit Salomón's conception of her, the poet's ideal. He worshipped her, and she meant to be worthy of adoration. The voice of her poems to come, particularly the love poems, arose from her vision of herself as both human and divine.

%

In discussing Millay's love life and how the poetry arose from it, we must never lose sight of the other important component of the poet's emotional life: her affection for Cora, Norma, and Kathleen. There is another whole book to be written about this loyalty and the family dynamic. That story will be told most effectively when the family's voluminous general correspondence is published, which, it is hoped, it will be someday soon. Insofar as the young adventuress could take her mother and sisters along with her—to New York, to Vassar, to Europe and beyond—she would always strive to manage it, even if she had to borrow money. The bulk of her correspondence that has survived is to her family; they are quick to scold her when her letters come too slowly, and as quickly she is abashed. While letters to and from friends and lovers sometimes picture a languishing lily, mired in ennui or romantic melancholy, we may always look to her letters home for the tough practicality and humor that anchor her character. She is herself when writing to her mother and sisters; writing to a lover she often seems to be playing to an audience.

Her success was to be their success. The Millays had all been poor together and now it was Vincent's fervent wish that they should be rich together, or at least comfortable—one for all and all for one. She lobbied successfully to get Kathleen a scholarship to Vassar (amazing, considering her rebellion against the institution that had adopted her, that the college would take on *another* Millay). By the summer of 1917, after her melodramatic graduation from college, she was plotting and planning to get the whole family fixed up and on a cash basis. She writes to Cora:

> I have a scheme whereby in the fall *you* are to go to Bridgeport to live with Uncle Charlie and Aunt Jennie—they have a flat now—and do hair-work; Kathleen is to be in Vassar, not far away; and Norma and I are to be seeking our fortunes in some hall bedroom way down town in New York—Norma trying to get a millinery job . . . and I a theatrical engagement or work on a magazine (We are to store the furniture for future reference)—More darned fun! Love, Vincent.

Actually her plans included bringing Cora to New York to live with them as well. "Don't you suppose mother could get a job editing some dumb page in some newspaper?" she wrote to Norma. Cora would do much better than that.

But in the meantime, while considering a host of invitations and prospects for the coming year, Vincent went home to Camden after graduating, to write, rest, and to get her wardrobe in order. She records an ongoing concern about couture and footwear and millinery that will make her presentable for her assault on the theater managers and magazine editors of Broadway. In addition to Caroline Dow, the young poet-actress had found new patrons in the theatrical family of the actor-playwright Charles Rann Kennedy (1881–1950), author of the international hit *The Servant of the House* (1908), and his wife, the popular actress Edith Wynne Mattison. Millay's fame as an actress had spread far beyond the halls of Vassar. Her performance as Vigdis in the premiere of John Masefield's *The Locked Chest* (December 9, 1916) brought praise from the laureate himself, who wrote from England to tell Miss Millay that his theater friends in New York had informed him she had been superb in his play. And he wanted to see her poetry. Kennedy and Mattison (a renowned acting coach) first saw Millay star in one of the plays she wrote at Vassar, *The Princess Marries the Page* (May 12, 1917), and were so swept away they went backstage after the performance to meet the playwright-actress, aglow in her princess costume. Edith Mattison embraced and kissed the proud girl, and prophesied for her a brilliant career on the stage. She offered to do anything in her power—as teacher, as sponsor, as patron—to get Vincent started on the road to fame in the theater world. Soon after her graduation, the Kennedys began calling upon powerful friends, theater managers in New York and in regional theaters, to audition the budding actress as soon as possible.

Vincent went to stay with the Kennedys late that summer, most of July and August, at their home in Hartford, Connecticut. There she worked on new poems and prepared the manuscript of *Renascence* for Mitchell Kennerley. At last he had gotten his favorite poet under contract. (He promised her $500 and never paid it.) And she studied acting technique with Edith. The generous Shakespearean actress had a significant influence on Millay's diction, both onstage and in her theatrical-style poetry readings. One night she read the title poem in her revamped diction to a crowd at the Kennedys' that included the celebrated actress Laura Hope Crews. Crews was so impressed she invited the ingenue to call on her at home; subsequently she gave her letters of introduction to the Selwyns and other theater managers that the Kennedys had overlooked.

By now the poet had every reason to believe a glamorous career on the stage was hers for the asking. It was just a matter of time. Meanwhile, her book would be coming out, and friends of the Kennedys, and Caroline Dow, and Elizabeth Haight and her wealthy friend Blanche Hooker, were booking poetry readings for Vincent in private homes and schools and theaters for as much as fifty dollars per appearance.

A charming story she tells, in a letter of September 22, is how she was to give a poetry reading at Mrs. Hooker's in Greenwich Village on Monday night the seventeenth, and her trunk failed to arrive. "So she [Mrs. Hooker] dressed me up in something of hers, a gown with a train and hanging about six inches on the floor all around, made out of three rainbow colored scarfs. And, family, I discover that I have nothing to give readings in, I *must* have long dresses, trailing ones. The short ones won't do. If Norma hasn't yet done anything to the greenish chiffon and rose scarf then *that* dress ought to be made up very long and drapy—more like a negligee than a dress, really—very graceful and floaty." And that is how she would dress for her poetry readings for the rest of her life, as a Pre-Raphaelite vision who seemed to hover between heaven and earth in auditoriums and theaters, at public readings more electrifying than any that were ever heard before Dylan Thomas took to the hustings in the 1940s. The "graceful and floaty" negligees with their long trains were her charmed mantles, just as her theatrical stage-English was the melodeon of her magic on the platform. The Pulitzer Prize–winning poet Richard Eberhart heard her read in a red dress at Dartmouth in 1924. He was so captivated he "followed her back to the Inn, lagging a hundred feet behind her. . . . I was not only enraptured but afraid of the greatness of poetry. I worshipped Millay as a possessor of immortality. She was too beautiful to live among mortals. She symbolized Platonic beauty."

One could quote a hundred other witnesses echoing Eberhart, poetry lovers under the spell of a sorceress whose gift was as much the genius of poetry as it was the studied technique of a stage actress. For this, she owed a debt of gratitude to Edith Wynne Mattison's coaching, and to thirteen years of her own serious dedication to the art of drama.

Since the day she had published "Renascence" she never lacked fans and patrons. Now, upon graduating from Vassar, she had so many of them they began to break down into jealous factions, vying for affection and influence. Between the Mattison Kennedys and senior benefactress Caroline Dow, a battle for Vincent's allegiance raged in 1917. Was she to be a poet or a showgirl? The second week of September the Kennedys packed Vincent off to New York where she was to audition for Winthrop Ames, George Tyler of the New Amsterdam Theatre, and several other prominent managers. Customarily she would have stayed with Miss Dow. But Aunt Caroline was dead set against her protégée getting mixed up in that Broadway crowd, so Vincent secretly stayed at the Kennedys' pied-à-terre on West Eighty-sixth Street, where Arthur Hooley wrote his last letters to her.

Theater roles did not come easily or quickly even for a talented actress with the best connections. And Vincent's luminous presence in New York City could not be kept a secret from Miss Dow for very long. Aunt Caroline took advantage of one of Vincent's inevitable bouts of exhaustion and illness ("I flopped in a faint on the sidewalk at the corner of Fifth Avenue and 50th Street") to argue her case that the mad, catch-penny theater world was no place for a serious lyric poet to waste her time. She convinced her ward to take advantage of an offer that she could hardly refuse: a Mrs. Thompson, one of the syndicate of wealthy patrons who had paid for Vincent's Vassar education, wanted the poet to act as her "social secretary." This was to be a sinecure with minimal responsibilities and luxurious benefits including a salary, her own bedroom suite at Sparkhill, the Thompson estate, her own maid, excellent meals, and plenty of time to write poetry. She was to come and go to the city as she pleased. Mrs. Thompson just wanted the poet in residence, creating her immortal works on the grounds of Sparkhill. Vincent arrived in late October.

But she chafed against the role of the society woman's conversation piece. The Kennedys were still pulling her toward the theater, arranging for her plays to be produced at the Bennet School in Milbrook, where she was paid handsomely (fifty dollars) to direct them. One of these performances caused unexpected excitement as the head of the Bennet School sent her limousine to Vassar to collect President MacCracken and his wife, Kathleen Millay, Elizabeth Haight, and as many more of Vincent's former teachers as could squeeze into the car so they could attend. Vincent wrote to her mother, "I wish I could take the time to tell you how beautifully they were done and how everybody loved them." When it was over President MacCracken told her, "Oh, you're a wonder!" She recalled that he "is quite convinced I can do whatever I like with the world."

She would have her poetry and her theater too, but not in the gilded cage of Sparkhill where Miss Thompson and Miss Dow as duennas watched vigilantly over her personal life. By late November of 1917, Vincent and Norma had taken a walk-up apartment in Greenwich Village, at 30 West Ninth Street.

THE VILLAGE

✣

The fruit-carts and clam-carts were ribald as a fair
    (Pink nets and wet shells trodden under heel)
She had haggled from the fruit-man of his rotting ware
    (I shall never get to sleep, the way I feel!)
                    —from "Macdougal Street"

*V*incent and Norma Millay arrived in Greenwich Village during the spring-tide of bohemia, a time and place that is the subject of so many good novels, histories, scholarly studies, and legends that its major characters and political themes are now familiar to even the most casual readers of twentieth-century history.

Once a fashionable residential district, in the second half of the nineteenth-century the Village began a steady decline, as Manhattan developed skyward and northward toward Central Park. By the time Millay arrived in the old downtown neighborhood it had become a picturesque slum where only the redbrick mansions to the north of Washington Square maintained their former dignity. Buses, cabs, and victorias encountered a bottleneck along Greenwich Avenue, on the other side of which the maze of narrow, crooked streets led to nowhere; before the West Side subway and Seventh Avenue cut into the Village, it was too isolated for wealthy people of business and fashion. So rents there were cheap. It proved a perfect haven for poets, painters, musicians, and anarchists—not far from the Jewish Lower East Side, which had its own bohemian energies. In the Village for thirty dollars a month you could rent the entire floor of an old house, with two high-ceilinged rooms, fireplaces, tall embrasured windows, a "hall" bedroom, a kitchen, and a bathroom.

At Chumley's bar, between Bedford and Barrow streets, you could get a good meal for a dollar. During Prohibition the bar naturally became a speakeasy, where the Millay sisters joined other writers, actors, and artists to drink beer and bootleg liquor, argue about art, sex, and politics, and play chess. The Liberal Club on Macdougal Street, just south of Washington Square and a few doors down from the Provincetown Playhouse, served as the community center of downtown's artistic and political life. In the basement of this club was a restaurant run by Polly Holliday, who, as Floyd Dell put it, "presided with benignant serenity over the wild and noisy horde of young people, seeing to it those truants and orphans were properly fed." Holliday's cook and waiter was Czech anarchist Hippolyte Havel, whose favorite insult to those who disagreed with him was "Bourgeois pigs!"

Dell's *Homecoming* (1933) is a classic book about those days, as is Max Eastman's *Enjoyment of Living* (1948) and Allen Churchill's *The Improper Bohemians* (1959). Later years produced Casey Blake's *Beloved Community* (1990), a study of the cultural criticism of Randolphe Bourne, Van Wyck Brooks, Waldo Frank, and Lewis Mumford, as well as Christine Stansell's lively history, *American Moderns: Bohemian New York and the Creation of a New Century* (2000). The mere titles of these books tell the story in a nutshell: Between the turn of the century and 1920 the Village became a mecca for creative writers, artists, and leftist intellectuals who meant to do away with their parents' middle-class manners, sexual mores, and politics. The bohemians planned to replace those timeworn hand-me-downs with more versatile and attractive equipment. The major players were the writers profiled in *Beloved Community*, playwrights Floyd Dell and Eugene O'Neill, writers Max Eastman, Theodore Dreiser, Edmund Wilson, John Reed, Malcolm Cowley, and Kenneth Burke, free-love advocates Mabel Dodge, Hutchins Hapgood, and Neith Boyce, and artists John Sloan, George Bellows, and Stuart Davis. In a loft on lower Fifth Avenue, Isadora Duncan was putting her dancers through their paces.

The hub of bohemian intellectual life (until 1918) was the sparkling left-wing magazine *The Masses*, where Millay's friend Louis Untermeyer served as literary editor. Socialist Max Eastman quit his job as professor of philosophy at Columbia to take over the magazine's editor's desk in 1913, guiding it boldly until the war with Germany approached. The magazine's shrill criticism of America's involvement in World War I resulted in Dell and others being indicted for violation of the Sedition Act, and in August of 1917 the U.S. Post Office barred the magazine from the mail. Its editors quickly launched *The Liberator* to replace *The Masses* in March of 1918.

In the 1920s Edna St. Vincent Millay became a figurehead of the bohemian life of Greenwich Village, an image she has maintained in the popular imagination. But there is little evidence that at the time she harbored more than a passing interest in any political movement apart from the right of women to have sex with whom they chose, when and where they chose, in or out of wedlock. Economically she was a proto-conservative, a natural capitalist.

She did not ever "cross the line" to attend an Emma Goldman speech, and she did not run to comfort the patron saint of birth control Margaret Sanger outside the Brooklyn courthouse in 1917. Millay was frantically busy day and night composing poetry, writing and acting in plays, writing love letters, and plotting trysts with lovers from Hartford to New York to Washington, D.C.—so many concurrent liaisons with so many lovers that it makes a biographer cross-eyed to look at her calendar. (How she avoided venereal disease and pregnancy is a question for medical historians. Likely she practiced reliable techniques for satisfying lovers besides coitus, minimizing the risk to herself. She was known to be pregnant only once.) Millay wrote her most famous love poems during her three-year residence in the Village, a time when the number and the intensity of her love affairs seems incredible, considering the volume of work she was producing, onstage and in books and magazines.

❧

In his 1933 book about his years in the Village, Floyd Dell wrote that "a serious love affair is a matter of so much importance in anyone's life that a wholly true account of such a life would present the story in detail." For many reasons he avoids detailing most of his love affairs in that memoir. But for Vincent Millay, who "flashed into my life like a meteor," the writer makes an exception. A notorious professor of "free love," Dell was to learn its high price from a girl he presumed to take on as a pupil.

Upon an intellectual like himself, Dell declared, a love affair has certain effects. The stark reality of it would shatter most "theories with which it had been approached, and reveal in blinding glimpses something truer about love, and perhaps more terrible in its splendor, than was set forth in any philosophy of freedom." There is nothing like pain, he recalled, to teach us the nature of life; and some hearts, such as his, must be broken "before they are much good for the simple purposes of life and love." Edna Millay broke Floyd Dell's heart, and he was forever grateful to her for it.

With his handsome, boyish Irish face, high prominent brow, strong chin, and humorous, mobile mouth, Dell was dynamic and charming. His reputation as a wit and rebel had preceded him from Chicago when he came to New York in 1914 to become associate editor of *The Masses*. Arthur Ficke's friend, Dell had collaborated with the lawyer-poet on a play that was staged at the Liberal Club. Dell's theater ambitions led him to join his buddy

George ("Jig") Cook and Cook's wife, the playwright Susan Glaspell, in turning a stable on Macdougal Street into the Provincetown Playhouse in 1916. The hundred-seat theater was about fifteen feet wide and forty-five feet long. Dell's play *King Arthur's Socks* was on the first bill—Dell was the self-styled "Village satirist."

Days after arriving in the Village in late November 1917, Millay sought work onstage, answering a call to audition for the ingenue's role in Dell's one-act *The Angel Intrudes* at the Provincetown Playhouse. "A slender little girl with red-gold hair came to the greenroom over the theatre, and read 'Annabelle's' lines. She looked her frivolous part to perfection, and read the lines so winningly that she was at once engaged—at a salary of nothing at all, that being our artistic custom." Somebody asked her if she was English—no, she retorted, she was Irish (like half the Provincetown company). Then they laughed and said admiringly *that* accounts for it! She filled out the form with her name and address, dropped it on the table, and disappeared into the traffic on Macdougal Street, leaving Dell and Cook and the others staring after her and scratching their heads, wondering if that really could be the author of the poem "Renascence."

Floyd Dell was thirty-one, recently divorced, and a man of considerable sexual experience in the freewheeling bohemian neighborhood. He had just gotten out of jail after being held briefly for publishing seditious articles in *The Masses*, making him something of a political-artistic hero. She was twenty-five and eager for adventure, with at present only one vaguely romantic interest (within reach), the devoted Salomón de la Selva, who was not really her type. Dell moved in on Millay quickly, with wit and savoir faire, not to mention that elixir to which the woman was never indifferent—the power to advance her career.

He took her to the theater and to dinner at the Brevoort on November 29, and she took him to bed with her in her cold room on Ninth Street. On the afternoon of December 1, he escorted his new leading lady to tea at the Liberal Club. In his 1933 autobiography he recalls her impact on him: "I fell in love with her voice at once; and with her spirit, when I came to know it, so full of indomitable courage. But there was in her something of which one stood in awe—she seemed, as a poet, no mere mortal, but a goddess; and though one could not but love her, one loved her hopelessly, as a goddess must be loved." This seasoned writer nearly ran out of adjectives trying to capture "the lonely, unreachable, tragically beautiful, inhuman, remote and divine quality" in Vincent that so disturbed his days and nights. At one moment she seemed "a scared little girl from Maine," and the next "an austere immortal." Dell, of all people, ought to have understood the common denominator that held these

personalities together: Millay was a consummate actress onstage *and* in the privacy of the bedroom. She was "unreachable" and "remote" to him when it
pleased her. When she really decided to give herself to a lover, which she
would do only two or three times in her life, that man would tell a very different story from Dell's, Salomón de la Selva's, or Edmund Wilson's.

She was pleased to go to bed with him, and whisper all sorts of endearments in response to his during nights of lovemaking that left them both
exhausted by dawn. They had much to discuss. Three days after she'd won
the role in *The Angel Intrudes*, he begged her to play the lead in his next
piece at the Provincetown, *Sweet and Twenty*, in late January. She seemed
altogether comfortable for a few weeks to let him think he was speaking for
both of them when he rhapsodized over their unique and exquisite love. He
was a great talker, with the Irish gift of gab: "Always the teacher whenever
I had the slightest excuse, I earnestly discoursed upon Pacifism, Revolution,
Soviet Russia and Psychoanalysis to her. She was very much a revolutionary
in all her sympathies, and a whole-hearted Feminist."

He saw what he wanted to see. And then he saw some things he really
preferred not to see. According to an "unpublished interview" Dell granted
to Norman Britten, later quoted by Anne Cheney in her biography *Millay in
Greenwich Village*, Dell was uncomfortable with Millay's "preoccupation
with lesbianism." When he asked her to address the "problem" through
psychoanalysis, she refused, saying she disliked Freud.

A good deal of nonsense has been written about this relationship (perhaps
too much being made of it altogether), because it meant so much to Dell,
so little to Millay, because she spurned him, and now only his side of the
story exists. He wrote about her proudly and at length, but often without
much understanding. There is a list of standard excuses a man cites when a
woman spurns him—one of them is that she prefers women. We know all
about Millay's "lesbian tendencies," far more than Dell ever knew, and by
1918 this part of her love life had dwindled to an occasional romp with her
dear little "Sphinx" Isobel Simpson, for old time's sake. Otherwise she was
absorbed in sex with men, feverishly, as if to make up for lost time.

Yet Dell had some perceptive things to say about Millay's same-sex sentiments, and he published them in *Homecoming*, where she and everybody else
could read them: "She was also to give dignity to those passionate friendships
between girls in adolescence, where they stand terrified at the bogeys which
haunt the realm of grown-up man-and-woman love. . . ." A mature, sensitive
man who was adept in the art of love, Dell must have realized that at age
twenty-five his ingenue had developed techniques of giving and receiving pleasure in bed that were better suited to girls in adolescence than grown-up men

and women. Like any devoted lover he wanted to please his partner: he would take his pleasure and give as he could in return. But there were problems having to do with the young woman's inexperience with his gender. And Dell, as much as he wished to be, was not the man to transform Vincent Millay into a man's ideal mistress. It would take more than one man to bring that about.

It is almost certain that her short poem "Daphne," first published in November of 1918, was addressed to Dell.

> Why do you follow me?—
>   Any moment I can be
> Nothing but a laurel tree.
>
> Any moment of the chase
> I can leave you in my place
> A pink bough for your embrace.
>
> Yet if over hill and hollow
> . Still it is your will to follow,
> I am off;—to heel, Apollo!

She was determined, from the first to the last of this relationship, to keep the upper hand, and *not* to abandon herself to Dell as she had to Arthur Hooley. Dell was strong, bright, and arrogant, a know-it-all, so she might deal with him more high-handedly than with the tenderhearted Salomón. Millay kept a sad letter from Dell, undated but certainly arriving toward the end of their affair. He had been waiting for her, somewhere—at her apartment or the theater (men were always waiting for her, or lying in wait for her)—and at last he decided to write her this valedictory:

> The pain . . . which prompted me to wait for you tonight leaves me no alternative but this note. It seems I have made certain vain boasts. The pretentions I have made to being equal to being in love with you are . . . a bit beyond my strength. I cannot endure a change in status which implicitly denies and discards some moments of our mutual dreaming, a change which leaves me remembering certain things which you have forgotten.

He had asked her to marry him. At some point, according to Dell's remarks half a century later, the lady said she would. Now the only decent thing to do, since he could not ask her to remember, was for her to ask him to forget.

> I am asking you to end a one-sided love relationship because it seems to be one-sided. . . . If this is true, then—I really think we can be the

best of friends, and I hope you will want to, as I do. If this were a conversation, I should somewhere in the course of it, I know, ask you again to marry me. Will you . . . let the happiness which is possible between us come to be?

He closes his letter with assurances he will graciously accept her decision, whatever it may be.

Little more is known about this love affair. According to Dell it was on again and off again until the summer of 1918. When the second trial of *The Masses* for sedition began in October of that year, Millay faithfully accompanied Dell, along with Max Eastman, John Reed, and others, to the courthouse. But Millay and Dell were most intimate during the winter months of 1917 to 1918 when the actress and the playwright were collaborating at the Provincetown Playhouse, where Dell's *Sweet and Twenty* premiered on January 25, 1918. By February she was head over heels in love with another man, with a passion she never felt for Dell. But her sexual affair with Dell soon evolved into a friendship that lasted most of Millay's life.

"We always quarrel so delightfully," Dell wrote to her. He was her perfect straw man. The four bitter sonnets at the end of *A Few Figs from Thistles* (1920), addressed to Dell in 1918, are her declaration of erotic independence, her revenge upon Hooley, and they should serve as fair warning to any future suitors. In the first, "Love though for this you riddle me with darts," she dares the god himself (in terror only the faithful can know) to subdue her, "who still am free, unto no querulous care a fool." The second sonnet, "I think I should have loved you presently, / And given in earnest words I flung in jest," is a cruel rejoinder to Dell's plaintive letter about their "mutual dreaming," a poem in which she states her preference to "walk your memory's halls, austere, supreme / A ghost in marble of a girl you knew / Who would have loved you in a day or two."

Even more cruel is the last sonnet, "I shall forget you presently, my dear / So make the most of this, your little day," in which the modern woman demolishes the romantic edifice of courtship and courtly love in a few tart epigrams.

> If you entreat me with your loveliest lie
> I will protest you with my favorite vow.
> I would indeed that love were longer-lived,
> And vows were not so brittle as they are,
> But so it is, and nature has contrived
> To struggle on without a break thus far,—
> Whether or not we find what we are seeking
> Is idle, biologically speaking.

Down with Sir Walter Raleigh, to hell with Robert Herrick, Richard Love-
lace, and the whole sweet-talking army of two-faced cavaliers! Long live Dar-
win and Herbert Spencer! For anyone to write and publish this sonnet, with its
Byronic flavor, before 1920 would have been a surprise. For a woman, not yet
thirty, to compose and market such a poem, along with the others, and lines
like "I am most faithless when I most am true," and "After all's said after all's
done, / What should I be but a harlot and a nun," was a scandal, an alarm, and
a red flag to the censors, who were not about to tangle with publisher Mitchell
Kennerley, a bulldog defender of the First Amendment, over a thirty-nine-
page book of verses. The slender book with its famous epigram

> My candle burns at both ends;
>   It will not last the night;
> But ah my foes, and oh, my friends—
>   It gives a lovely light!

became a cause célèbre, quickly selling out edition after edition, as fast as
Kennerley could print them. The *Figs* book established Millay's reputation
as the sex goddess of Greenwich Village.

※

But let us return to the winter of 1917–1918, a cold winter made more bitter
by the war, fuel rationing, and a coal strike. High up in a brick building on
West Ninth Street, Vincent and Norma had a little coal stove in their room,
but the bathroom was two floors below, and they nearly froze going up and
down stairs at night in their dressing gowns. Any excuse to go and sleep in
someone else's apartment or hotel was welcome. On December 5 Vincent's
book *Renascence and Other Poems* was finally published, a volume bound in
black ribbed cloth with the title in gold capitals on the cover, hand-set type
on Glaslan watermarked paper, and the edges uncut. Though he didn't pay
her a dime for it (dodging more dangerous creditors, he wouldn't even
answer her phone calls), at least Kennerley had made her a handsome book.

The girls were exhilarated. They were living in New York on poetry and
dreams, running on adrenaline, fearless as only the young can be. They were
dining out in restaurants on the strength of their charm and good looks,
eating bar food in Chumley's and the Hell Hole, and acting in plays for
nothing or a tiny percentage of the gate. Norma worked as a seamstress.
Vincent earned a few dollars from selling poems and stories to magazines; it
would be a while before she got a paycheck from an acting job.

Meanwhile Cora had given up nursing. She was up in Bridgeport weaving hairpieces for a dollar and a half per switch, as Vincent had told her to do, and sending money to her daughters. She was not hearing nearly enough from her wayward girls—and what she was hearing she did not like one bit, not the cold stairways, nor the lack of warm clothing, nor the scarcity of gainful employment. It was the latter, perhaps, as much as the cold, that got to her the most. She had not reared her daughters to be courtesans. Bohemians, yes. But showgirls who displayed their charms for little more than applause in drafty theaters and free meals in the Hell Hole, no. This was not adding up to a picture that looked good to Mother Cora up in Bridgeport.

On January 8, 1918, she wrote a long letter to Vincent and Norma that is a blend of maternal solicitude, wisdom, hysteria, humor, and common sense. Here are some excerpts:

> My dear, dear girls,
>   There is no way in which to commence a letter to you, for I am all at sea, and so far away from any knowledge of how you are faring . . . or what you are going to do, as if I were on some other planet. I haven't been much good for a few days . . . my head is bad, "confused," I guess.
>   What a terrible time you poor babies have had out there (freeze up of even gas) alone and penniless in the biggest city in the world, in the hardest year in history. And you are just the same as friendless. I realize that now, and I guess that is where I feel lame. My last prop has been kicked out from under me.

Kathleen had telephoned from Vassar, worried about her sisters' temperature, then a letter from Aunt Jennie told Cora that Vincent and Norma had run out of coal in a building where there was no gas heat, either. Cora was worried. And she was hopping mad.

> And I thought you had some real friends out there upon whom you could call in a matter of life and death. Even without car-fare, you could have telephoned on credit, or reversing the charges to Mrs. Simpson or Kennerley. I would have thought, rather than to starve or freeze, when such dangers were not peculiar to you but general enough for a call for help to be a thing to be expected.

Then she gets down to business. She trusts neither of the girls to be able to earn a living. "If you cannot, either of you get the kind of work you want, you must get something at once. . . . Now it is very probable that neither of you could now pass a Civil Service Exam," she writes, and you can hear her teeth grinding, as she urges them to go for it, to take what the government has to offer. After a few more sarcastic remarks about Vincent's "influential friends out there," Cora Millay opens fire on her daughters with both barrels.

> And if you are the only two girls who are not smart enough to get work out there, you'd be better go back to Camden and go into the Plaster or Shirt factory. This is a year for practicalities. Arts and amusements, and even ordinary schooling may have to give way for a time to the needs of the masses and armies for fuel and supplies.
>
> So you must be sensible, and find somewhere under the surface of temperament, the sub-strata of good common-sense I always credited you with but which is getting rather shaky just now. A live poet is worth a half a dozen frozen ones or starved ones, even in Greenwich Village, and things that make good stories may be too costly experiences. Don't carry things so far again. Get out somewhere and yell for help.

A live poet is worth a half a dozen frozen ones or starved ones, even in Greenwich Village. Cora's epigram deserves to be cross-stitched on samplers to hang on the walls of middle-class families who glorify the "creative arts," and then wonder why their children quit law school to join dance companies.

"I've stood about enough," she wrote. "If I had done this, how would *you* feel?" She encloses $2.50, money that just walked in the door for a hairpiece she had stitched.

The main subtext of this marvelous letter is that fifty-three-year-old Cora Millay is bored to death and lonely in Bridgeport, Connecticut, while her daughters are in glorious Gotham having all the excitement and adventures, with no better sense than to freeze their toes off in a flat with no heat and the water taps jammed with ice. "For the first time in our history I feel myself pushed entirely out of things," she confesses.

The upshot of this was that on June 3, 1918, Cora Millay arrived at Grand Central Station with her suitcase, a pound of tobacco and cigarette papers, and a quart of gin for her girls. Vincent met her at the station. They went to a nearby tavern where John Masefield once tended bar, and drank a beer together. Then they took a cab to the girls' new apartment at 25 Charlton Street, where they had moved recently from 139 Waverly Place (they had lived there since January) in order to make room for Mother. Cora hauled her suitcase up the stairs at 25 Charlton. She peered through her wire-rimmed spectacles at Norma's bobbed hair, sighed deeply over the loss of the precious blond tresses, called for scissors, and bobbed her own. She became as bohemian as the rest of them—writing poetry and stories for the Village magazines, singing and acting in the Provincetown Playhouse, sewing costumes—while serving as den mother to these rowdy children and their parade of suitors.

It was soon after this that Edmund Wilson met Cora Millay. He called her "the most extraordinary" of all of them, "a little old woman with spectacles who, although she had evidently been through a good deal, had managed to remain very brisk and bright. She sat up straight and smoked cigarettes and quizzically followed the conversation. She looked not unlike a New England schoolteacher, yet there was something almost raffish about her." He believed she was the first bohemian in the family. He recalled that her remarks were often startling, coming from the lips of a woman her age, and that "even more than with Edna," he felt that Cora "had passed beyond good and evil, beyond the power of hardship to worry her, and that she had attained there a certain gaiety." Wilson knew and loved Edna, and he wrote the most perceptive memoir in the vast literature on the poet's life; but no comment of his is more piercing than this one, which takes in the symbiotic characters of mother and daughter in a single sentence. They had passed beyond good and evil, and it was hardship that had led them to that mysterious state of gaiety.

%

Cora Millay's scattershot diary of the years she lived in Greenwich Village, 1918–1920, provides a wealth of precise information about her daughter's social and professional life. Vincent was too busy to keep a diary (or balance a checkbook—after they got evicted from Charlton Street for nonpayment, Mother handled the money). Cora's unpublished memoir gives a rough accounting of Vincent's income, which was *very* impressive for a poet. Norma called her sister "the little red mill," and the sheer mass of her creative output during these years—the poetry, drama, and short fiction—is simply staggering. How she managed to write many of her greatest works in that roar and tumult from Charlton Street to Macdougal, from theater rehearsals to all-night "bull sessions," how and where she slept or found sufficient quiet for reflection, remains a mystery.

The summer of 1918 Floyd Dell was in the apartment a lot of the time, and so was a keenly jealous Salomón de la Selva. He wept and made scenes; sometimes Salomón refused to go someplace if Dell was invited too. Gallantly, Dell would withdraw, confident that the Nicaraguan poet was no real threat to his bond with Vincent. Her sonnet "We talk of taxes, and I call you friend," which she started at Waverly Place and finished at Charlton Street, is addressed to Dell and portends the end of their affair. But evidently he had not gotten the message and did not realize that Vincent was using Salomón as a wedge between them. She had also begun seeing Scudder Middleton, "a poet with the romantic profile of a matinee idol," on July 23. That evening Middleton took her to the Lafayette for dinner, and then "for a ride." To S. M. she dedicated her poem "If He Should Lie A-Dying."

> I am not willing you should go
>   Into the earth, where Helen went;
> She is awake by now, I know.
> Where Cleopatra's anklets rust
> You will not lie with my consent . . .

The love poem ends with the complaint, "You leave me much against my will." Inasmuch as this is a rarity in the poet's experience, and Middleton has left no more footprints in Millay's biography or in history, it seems likely he left on a troop ship, as did de la Selva and Arthur Ficke, to join the Allies in Europe.

Ficke was the man who really should have shaken Dell's confidence. Dell's old friend showed up in New York on February 16, 1918, in the uniform of a major in the army, "Sam Browne belt," and puttees. En route to France with dispatches from Washington to General Pershing, Major Ficke used his three-day layover in New York before boarding a troop ship in Hoboken as the perfect chance to meet Edna St. Vincent Millay, with whom he had been corresponding since the debacle over her poem "Renascence." His friend Floyd would arrange it.

So on Saturday night Dell led Ficke to the Millays' apartment. The sisters had just hung pale blue curtains on the two windows that looked out on the street. The head of their bed narrowly fit between the tall windows. They had rolled the pillows up like a long bolster, covering them and the bed with cloth patterned with orange moons and green trees Kathleen had sent them, then tossed on a couple of golden throw pillows. Vincent's trunk, under the window where the radiator wasn't, also covered with the same cloth as the curtains, made a cozy window seat. Then there was space for a bureau and writing table, and not room for much else but the sisters and a few guests and the mice, which they had named "Wee-Sleekit" and "Mousushka Ratovitch."

Floyd and Arthur found the Millay sisters and Norma's future husband, the actor-painter Charles Ellis, preparing for dinner. The five of them enjoyed a picnic of delicatessen sandwiches, pickles, and beer on the rug. They sat on the bed and on the floor, and talked and laughed and improvised silly verses about the food. Ficke lifted a pickle and declaimed: "This pickle is a little loving-cup. / I raise it to my lips, and where you kissed / There lurks a certain sting that I have missed / In nectars more laboriously put up." One cannot imagine what was going on in Dell's mind (he thought she would *marry* him!) as he watched the handsome Ficke make eye contact for the first time with his longtime epistolary dream girl. If you have ever seen a man and a woman fall in love at first sight, you know it is an awe-inspiring, disturbing spectacle. The event often clears the room of everybody but the stricken couple, leaving them standing alone in terrified silence or stammering some nonsense that only they think they can understand.

That is what happened to Arthur and Vincent: love at first sight. This is clear from their later correspondence (much of which has been published, at least her side of it) and the dozens of sonnets that the two lovers wrote to each other in the years thereafter. Many of these are among Millay's best, including "Into the golden vessel of great song," "And you as well must die, beloved dust," and "Oh my beloved, have you thought of this." There has been considerable speculation about their intense encounter that February weekend in 1918. It piques curiosity because so many poems and letters came of it, and because afterward the couple spent no time alone together (as can be best determined) before Arthur's second marriage, to Gladys Brown. The Fickes became Millay's closest friends after her marriage in 1923.

Millay's letters to Ficke during the war have been lost, but here is what she wrote to Kathleen on the Tuesday after she had met him.

> No less a person has been here than Arthur Davison Ficke,—you know we used to correspond at one time very feverishly and fast and, well, he was in New York for three days last week and played around with us all the time . . . and he's exceedingly handsome, tall and curly-headed and with a lovely voice and—oh my God, *everything*! He's gone to France!—I am crazy about him, and he's gone, he's gone . . .

The day he left on the troop ship she fell ill, and took to her bed to grieve, unable to face the daylight without him, dragging herself downstairs after dark to her favorite tavern. "There's no comfort left me on earth except one beer on top of another all night long at the Hell Hole." A hundred pounds of Irish gamine, at twenty-six she could drink with a stevedore twice her weight, matching him beer for beer, until her bitter speech thickened and her eyes grew narrow and cold, and one friend or another would see to it she got back to the door of her apartment building safely.

On the Atlantic, on his troop ship, Arthur sat in the blue light of the officers' smoking room where so many men were writing letters to their loved ones. On February 19 he wrote to her how sorry he was that "the vulgarity of the war should have broken so rudely across the subtlety of our inter-course." And three days later, "Wasn't it a scream that we should have met at last after so long an acquaintance—and didn't fate stage the event with a sure and restrained touch? Can't you come to Paris? I'll come to see you every three months. . . ." And he sent her sonnet after sonnet. "This was the perfect discord of good-bye—/ This was the jangled, long-to-echo note—/ As inexpressive as your sleepy throat—And yet it seals us indissolubly" (from his poem "Vale.") And "Wakeful, I pace the deck and watch the stars / That also have no kinship unto rest: / I who am wounded by those greater wars / That storm across the spaces of the breast./ . . . Thou hast dazed me with a loveliness. . . ."

They had made the most of the few hours together they had been able to steal from the Argus-eyed Floyd Dell and from Vincent's busy rehearsal schedule. (According to Dell, he and Ficke were Vincent's shipmates on the Staten Island Ferry crossing that inspired the famous "Recuerdo.") That weekend she skipped her afternoon rehearsals, and in the winter light from the tall windows on either side of the bed in Vincent's apartment they made love for the first and perhaps the last time. He wanted never to leave her. But Floyd and other friends had arranged a round of farewell parties in Arthur's honor he could not disregard. At 4:00 A.M. the day his ship was due to shove off, Arthur wrote her a letter. He had just returned from a party. He would not wake the Millay household but he could not go to sleep without telling her how much he loved her. He had always known it, and she had known it too. "But this new way of loving you,—it has left me dizzy and bewildered.

> I did not know that I should love your body so much. I had tried for so long to forget that you had a body. And now—well, I see nothing but pictures of you. I did not know that anyone was so beautiful as that.

Put aside, for a moment, Ficke's infatuation. The man was not only a poet and an admirer of women, he was a notable art critic who became curator of prints and drawings at Harvard. He was not just *any* man claiming the woman he loves is ideal because he loves her. His impressions in this brief letter ought to be considered in the light of Millay's general impact on her lovers.

You have cut me with a sword, Vincent dear. I cannot forget. . . . Oh
you were so right to give me that unforgettable beauty. It is burned
into my brain now: You can't take it back even if you wanted to. Mine
for ever!

Of course, she did not want to take it back, her beauty was an infallible lock
upon a man's imagination, as was her poetry. *He* would be more likely to
wish someday he could be rid of it.

If she had looked like Edith Sitwell, Edith Wharton, or any other Edith;
if she had resembled Amy Lowell or Emily Dickinson; if she had not had
the effect on men that she had, and therefore the intimacy, she would not
have written the sonnets that are now under discussion. Her impact on men
(and some women) was a rare and curious phenomenon, a force usually
associated with movie stars like Marilyn Monroe or Ava Gardner.

There are hundreds of photographs of Millay. The most widely known
and reprinted are the most misleading: the famous publicity photos—from
Arnold Genthe's 1915 virginal Quaker-lady portrait of the poet among the
magnolias, to the severe Mishkin portraits of the twenties where Vincent in
pageboy, gentleman's coat, and necktie looks like Rupert Brooke needing a
haircut; to the *most* awful and enshrined of all, the last Berenice Abbott
portrait of Vincent. She was then in her thirties, enthroned just before a
poetry reading at Vassar, smiling faintly and primly, trying her best to look
like the severe Elinor Wylie or Elizabeth the Queen Consort. This is not,
nor was it ever, Edna St. Vincent Millay. It is obvious and completely under-
standable that Millay, acutely conscious of her public image, was taking no
risks with her publicity pictures. In some circles she may have been known
as a libertine, the sex goddess of Greenwich Village, but she wanted no hint
of this in the book jacket portraits or the newspaper photos. In these she
always looked like a nun, a librarian, or a lady lawyer. She meant to be taken
seriously, and she meant it grimly.

But many other photographs of Millay display her humor, intensely seductive glances, her raw and forward sexuality, and her unique physical grace.
One night she sat with two friends, Edmund Wilson and John Peale Bishop,
and the three writers decided to write comic self-portraits. A few verses of
Vincent's self-portrait will serve as a perfect opening to the main topic.

> A large mouth,
> Lascivious,
> Asceticized by blasphemies . . .

A small body
Unexclamatory,
But which,
Were it the fashion to wear no clothes,
Would be as well-dressed
As any.

We have heard Vincent and her friends at Vassar go on at length about the "lascivious" mouth. Now we have Vincent's word, and Arthur Ficke's, about her body, and these words are simply the truth. She was not keeping any secrets from Wilson and Bishop, who had both slept with her. Millay's impact had to do with the "small body, unexclamatory." The stylishly dressed poet had the look of an attractive, petite woman with a secret. This secret she might just share at the right time and place, but only with a very special man, the man who had the eye and the heart to appreciate it.

Vincent, standing five feet, one inch, had measurements of 34-22-34. Her breasts were surprisingly large and perfectly formed, and the rest of her, from fingers to toes, would have served the purposes of any sculptor of the neoclassic mode who cultivated an ideal of human form. We have already remarked upon her vivid coloring, the red hair, green eyes, and red mouth against the milk-white skin, features that strangers could admire. But clothing, in the teens and much of the twenties, was modest: above the waist, particularly, it concealed more than it showed. So when this small, mysterious child-woman took her clothes off, and stood naked before a man for the first time, the light of her beauty was blinding. There were many men who were never able to get over it.

She was not at all camera shy, so quite a few magnificent photographs of Millay in the nude have survived, most of them in the possession of the Library of Congress. The pictures are under an embargo until the year 2010, so it will be the advantage of some future biographer to publish them. The photos confirm the words of Arthur Ficke: "I did not know that anyone was as beautiful as that." This wonder that the man recalled was a pang that would be echoed in letter after letter, as one lover after another learned Millay's dangerous secret.

❧

Arthur Ficke was married, he was off to the war, and she would not see him again for several years. Longing is a powerful catalyst for the romantic poet. Ficke's inaccessibility, in addition to his personal and poetic virtues, made him infinitely desirable to Millay. Her love letters to Ficke are the most lyrical and intense in her published correspondence. On October 29, 1920, she wrote to him:

> I love you, too, my dear, and shall always, just as I did the first moment I saw you. You are a part of Loveliness to me.—Sometimes at night, when you were in France, I would read over the sonnets you had sent me—just as you have been doing now with mine—& long for you in an anguish of sweet memory, & send all my spirit out to you in passion. . . . It doesn't matter at all that we never see each other, & that we write so seldom. We shall never escape from each other.

The date is important—at the time she was sexually involved with a half-dozen men. The words above are like those she had written to the other Arthur, Hooley, four years earlier. But Ficke, a worthier subject, inspired Millay to greater heights of eloquence: "It is very dear to me to know that you love me Arthur,—just as I love you, quietly, quietly, yet with all your strength, & with a strength greater than your own that drives you toward me like the wind. It is a thing that exists simply, like a sapphire, like anything roundly beautiful; there is nothing to be done about it. . . ."

There was one thing she could do about it: write poetry. Ficke inspired the greatest sonnets of her book *Second April*.

> Into the golden vessel of great song
> Let us pour all our passion; breast to breast
> Let other lovers lie, in love and rest;
> Not we . . .

His sonnets to her, inferior but authentic, prompted more and more from Vincent, perhaps none more moving and memorable than this:

> And you as well must die, beloved dust
> And all your beauty stand you in no stead;
> This flawless, vital hand, this perfect head,
> This body of flame and steel, before the gust
> Of Death . . .
> . . . .
> In spite of all my love, you will arise
> Upon that day and wander down the air
> Obscurely as the unattended flower,
> It mattering not how beautiful you were,
> Or how beloved above all else that dies.

These poems, she eventually confessed to Arthur, were meant for him. Others, too, belong to him, such as the tenth sonnet in that book, "Oh my beloved, have you thought of this," which takes up the theme of their age difference (he was almost a decade older), and how "Time, more cruel than Death, will tear you from my kiss, / And make you old, and leave me in my prime?" are obviously for Ficke. In the latter she recalls "that on the day you came / I was a child, and you a hero grown."

The armistice was signed on November 11, 1918, and Arthur Ficke returned, as a colonel, to his wife in Iowa. He saw action at the front, "the whole show from Rheims to St. Mihiel:—shells screaming over my head, machine guns popping away through the woods, German planes overhead that chased my car down the roads trying to bomb me." Through it all her love poems and his memory of her were talismans. From France, and then from Iowa, he wrote to her of his undying affection, promising to visit soon. But for some reason, for many reasons, he never did, though she longed to see him, and told him so.

The year 1919 would be Millay's annus mirabilis, the time of her greatest artistic productivity in literature and drama. But it got off to a rocky start. Just before Christmas 1918 her landlord at 25 Charlton, fed up with her delays in paying the rent, sent Vincent an eviction notice. She had to vacate by February 1 and was obligated to find someone to take over the lease and pay the back rent. Her savior turned out to be Rollo Peters, an actor at the Provincetown who was also director of the Theatre Guild. When the Millays moved their furniture and books to 449 West Nineteenth Street near the Hudson River wharves, Peters took over their old flat.

In a letter of January 15, Peters proposed marriage to Millay, a gesture by now so familiar to her that she had learned to take her time responding, knowing there was little to be lost in an affectionate delay. She and Peters had a good deal to do with each other that winter, as she acted with him in *The String of the Samisen* at the Provincetown, which opened on January 17. Then he offered Millay her first high-paying stage role at the Theatre Guild—Columbine in *Bonds of Interest* at fifty dollars per week.

The whole Millay family was so absorbed in theater activity that winter and spring that it is hard to see how they found time to do much else. While Vincent was playing the lead in *The String of the Samisen*, Cora acted in Otto K. Liveright's *Portland to Dover*, and Norma took a lead role in *5050* by Robert Allerton Parker. Unfortunately, none of this produced any income.

The eviction from Charlton Street had been a humiliation and a wake-up call to Vincent. In January she began seeing more of Walt Roberts, the editor of *Ainslee's* magazine. He took her to the Lafayette bistro on University Place, where they had a good long talk over a bottle of wine. He escorted her to the famous Kit Kat Ball, which was hosted by various Village artists and illustrators. Roberts persuaded Vincent to write fiction and essays for him under the pen name Nancy Boyd. She could stay in his apartment if she liked, and work there if there was too much noise and distraction at home; they did not scruple to call this business arrangement "potboiling." Millay's pot had gone too long without meat in it, and she had decided to be poor no more.

According to Cora's diary, "Vincent sent story 'Young Love' to *Ainslee's*, and they took it. $75.00." (Remember, rent on a grand apartment in the Village cost thirty dollars per month.) That was toward the end of January. On January 31, Vincent paid twenty-one dollars in rent on their new flat and ten dollars to the New Amsterdam Gas Company. During the next few months she wrote "The Poor," "The Dark Horse," "Innocents at Large," and "The White Flamingo," earning seventy-five dollars for each. Then she recast her play *Wall of Dominoes* in story form and got paid for that, too. Roberts wanted a novella. So in June—right after she finished playing Columbine for the Theatre Guild—she began working on *The Seventh Stair*, night and day, according to Cora. "I got Vincent a dinner at three o'clock in the morning just the same as if it were noon." She completed the novella in a week, then collapsed from exhaustion. *Ainslee's* paid her four hundred dollars. She had grossed more than one thousand dollars in the five months since their eviction.

Only then did she turn her hand to poetry, and what a river of poetry poured from her pen! According to Cora, Vincent wrote verses, sonnets mostly, around the clock throughout the summer and well into the autumn. These included "What lips my lips have kissed," "Cherish you the hope I shall forget," "Ode to Silence," and (almost certainly) the great "Euclid alone has looked on beauty bare," although the last may have been written during the winter of 1919–1920. She was not deeply in love with anyone (excepting the distant Arthur Ficke) at the time. The sonnets she wrote, then, are addressed to lovers and love in general. The justly renowned sonnet "What lips my lips have kissed" is a summing up of her love life to date, and an occasion to invoke the classic themes of elegy, the *tempus fugit* and the *ubi sunt*: Where has the time gone, my life, my lovers?

> I cannot say what loves have come and gone,
> I only know that summer sang in me
> A little while, that in me sings no more.

Millay wrote the dates on very few of her manuscripts. Handwriting, paper, biographical context, and dates of first publication must all be considered in determining when she composed individual poems. We know that "Wild Swans" was finished in October 1919 ("Tiresome heart, forever living and dying, / House without air, I leave you and lock your door") and that "Pity me not because the light of day," one of her most adored sonnets, was written on July 26, 1920. From the summer of 1919 to the summer of 1920 Millay created most of the poetry that appeared in *Second April* (1921), as well as half of *The Harp-Weaver and Other Poems*, which did not appear until 1923. There is a sadness about these poems and a disillusionment that arose directly out of painful experiences.

But meanwhile, somehow, in the midst of writing some of her greatest poetry, acting in plays uptown and downtown, and dodging suitors such as Rollo Peters, Walter Roberts, and William Harris, Jr., the manager of the Hudson Theatre—letters from him confirm an affair with her in the summer and autumn—Millay finished writing her greatest play, *Aria da Capo*, in early November. "You know the one," she wrote to her mother, away in Newburyport, "Pierrot & Columbine & the shepherds & the spirit of Tragedy. . . . Well, it's a peach—one of the best things I've ever done."

The harlequins are caricatures of Village bohemians—he's an artist, she's a "flapper." Their farcical banter is interrupted by the "stage manager" Cothurnus (spirit of tragedy), who gives them the hook so that two rustics—Thyrsis and Corydon—can play a pastoral tragedy. These shepherds devise a game of building a wall across the stage so "that over there belongs to me / And over here to you." The game that starts in fun with making a wall of colored crepe ribbons soon turns serious. All the water is on Thyrsis's side, and Corydon's sheep are thirsty; and then Corydon finds jewels on his land, making Thyrsis jealous. Their conflict and bargaining becomes an allegory about private property, nationalism, and greed. This ends with the shepherds murdering each other, whereupon Cothurnus, spirit of tragedy, slams the prompt-book shut. The harlequins return and comment ironically on the corpses. Hiding the bodies under a tablecloth, they resume the banter they began at the start of the play, giving the audience a shudder of déjà vu, "Aria da Capo" (Italian, meaning: "Sing it again, from the top").

The little play has an immediate and timeless appeal. At once the Provincetown company voted to put it on the next bill, with Vincent as director. *Aria da Capo* opened on December 5, 1919, with Norma Millay as Columbine, Vincent's old friend the composer Harrison Dowd as Pierrot, artist Hugh Ferris as Cothurnus, and Charles Ellis and James Light as the shepherds. Norma's lover Charles Ellis also designed the colorful set.

Vincent had told Kathleen on November 20, "If the thing gets over big, dear, as I think it must do, it will be a sensation." The words were prophetic. Alexander Woollcott, the redoubtable drama critic for the *New York Times*, urged his audience to hurry downtown to see *Aria da Capo*, "the most beautiful and interesting play in the English language now to be seen in New York." Many more people wanted to see it than could fit into the tiny playhouse on Macdougal; soon *Aria da Capo* would be thrilling audiences all over America and the world, so there was scarcely a weekend it was not running somewhere. Figures available for the decade 1950–1960, thirty years after its premiere, indicate that there were 471 licensed *productions*—not performances—during that time.

⁂

While *Aria da Capo* was making headlines and breaking box office records on Macdougal Street, in the process transforming Edna St. Vincent Millay from a bohemian cult figure to a household name, she was also the central figure in another drama unfolding in secret—in hotel rooms in New York and Washington, D.C.

Vincent was in love again. His name was Jim Lawyer, and he was a construction engineer working under contract to the Red Cross in Washington, D.C. Later he owned his own company with headquarters in Washington and a branch office in Albany. He had been a war hero, an army captain much decorated for his bravery under fire in France. He was married, one of Millay's many lovers whose conjugal loyalty served her as a firewall. The married man was predictably "safer," unlikely to make awkward claims upon her emotions or free time, and more likely to enjoy a dalliance for the sheer excitement it provided in stolen moments. It is not known how they met or when, but several affectionate references to Millay's family in his letters suggest that he may have been a friend from their days in Maine.

The first letter we have from Lawyer comes upon his return from New York on November 20, 1919. From Washington he writes to "Edna My Darling" that it seems he has had a wonderful dream. "It is hard to realize that you love me." The letter indicates that the affair, which began in the fall, had recently taken a more serious turn. We do not have her letters to him (he burned them at her request), but his many letters to Edna from November 1919 until February 1920 make plain in their responses that her letters matched his in their frequency and intensity.

His prose is nervous, ungraceful, and often pathetic. His letter is meant to assure her "that everything is all right. . . . Everything worked out perfectly." In other words, he had gotten back from his New York tryst without his wife, Louise, finding out he was with Edna. He says this over and over, as if to convince not her but himself that everything was all right.

> God knows, Edna, that I adore you. My love for you has certainly been tested very thoroughly. I feel so sorry for my poor wife and I really love her you know. . . . She just suspects something, she doesn't even know herself what, and she tries to be particularly attractive and nice to me. . . . I do hope that you have rested a little. You were so very tired. I felt that I might have been more careful of you. There is nothing I wouldn't do for you, My Darling.

Judging from Lawyer's prose style, he was not a man Millay pursued for his intellectual and spiritual strengths, as she did Arthur Ficke. Yet she did pursue the engineer, from hotel room to hotel room in Manhattan, whenever he could steal away from his wife. Jim Lawyer had something she sorely needed, something she could not get from Floyd Dell, Salomón de la Selva, Rollo Peters, Walter Roberts, William Harris, et al., because she did spend a remarkable amount of time in bed with him, clearing the decks whenever he hit town, during a winter when she needed all the sleep she could get. She was so crazy about Lawyer that she briefly considered marrying him if he would divorce his wife. The poet could not conceal the affair from her mother. Cora was horrified, but she neither interfered with Vincent nor judged her.

"Please try to love me a lot for I do need your love to help me over the rough places. It is easier for you," he observes—because she is not married. The "rough places" he mentions in mid-November are the trenches and barbed wire he must pass through on his way to divorce and freedom to join Edna in bliss eternal. Things moved along with wonderful alacrity. By January Jim's wife knew about the affair and was treating it "as a joke most of the time, and she doesn't seem to mind telling people about us. She laughs about it and teases me about you when other people are around." But when they were alone, Louise was sullen, troubled. Dreaming one night, he touched Louise's hair, and called her Edna. The next morning she "mentioned casually that if I wanted a divorce I could have it." But he was not sure that she really meant it.

Edna, as she promised, would love him as much as she could, and her many letters were meant to help him over the rough places. "Through all of the trial and worry," he writes, "I can see your Dear Face and that is the only thing that keeps me going now. I want you all of the time and especially at night. . . . The world seems to go along just the same but I am all upside-down somehow." He was working feverishly to make enough money to change women, but it was an uphill battle, and his divided attention had caused his work at the Red Cross to suffer.

She wrote him a letter in response to his of January 6 that was "gushing" (so he quotes her), begging him to love her at least as much as she loves him—he joyfully paraphrases it in his answer of January 9. Without her letters, it is impossible to know if she was urging Lawyer to leave his wife, but it is clear from his words that she was nurturing his belief that she was meant for him. He was counting the days until he would see her again, six days until he would be in New York. He advised her not to work too hard, and to take care of herself. "Just relax once in a while like you told me to do and think of the wonderful things that are coming to us. I am so very badly off financially at this moment that I can hardly make it seem possible that soon we won't have to worry about those things." The train fare to New York, the bills at the Hotel Judson on Washington Square, the midnight snacks, the whiskey and wine . . .

"Edna, don't ever doubt that I adore you. It is so silly to think that I don't. I worship you, actually, my Own." That is what she wanted to hear.

With his next letter he enclosed a memo from his boss, the general manager of the Red Cross. Jim had been applying for jobs in New York listing F. C. Monroe as a character reference. In a memo of January 10, Monroe says he can testify favorably as to Jim's ability as an engineer. However, "I have felt constrained to explain to a personal friend who wrote concerning you, the exact status existing between you and your wife, for which, after careful investigation, I find you are entirely to blame." And Monroe asks that he refrain from giving his name as a reference in the future.

Obviously Jim sent this to his beloved Edna as further proof of his devotion. She kept the trophy. We have no record of the beloved's response.

At last the long-awaited weekend arrived, the fifteenth of January, and the rendezvous was as wonderful as ever, until the telephone rang late at night at the Hotel Judson and kept ringing no matter how he tried to ignore it. The doctors in Washington explained to Mr. Lawyer that his wife had poisoned herself by drinking a quart or more of bootleg rotgut, and now she was completely blind and might or might not ever regain her vision, if she lived.

Edna St. Vincent Millay arose from the bed, put on her clothing, and sadly but graciously bid her lover return to his stricken wife on the first train leaving New York for Washington.

He went home and nursed his wife back to health, reading to her aloud (sometimes Millay's poetry) until the bandages were removed from her eyes. Weeks later, when he felt confident "she would not do anything so foolish again," he returned to the Hotel Judson to take up where he had left off with his darling Edna. But something was lacking—the thrill was not quite the same—and they had a hard night of it. When he woke up the next morning Edna was gone, and he wrote her a letter that though he loved her more than ever, he had to go back to his wife. "I knew as we have both known for some time that it was the only thing to do." He wrote to her instead of telephoning because he was afraid that if he heard her voice on the line he might weaken.

"I am telling everyone that you sent me back to my wife, which is true. Please tell them the same."

The affair had lasted about three months. When the poet was done with Captain James P. Lawyer, she sent him back to his wife, Louise—what was left of the poor woman. Millay was certain that Lawyer's professional and personal life was utterly ruined. In one of his last letters to her, February 10, he tells her he has destroyed her letters, and his wife has destroyed her photograph, adding "but the memory of you no one can ever destroy." Millay had borrowed from him a Corona typewriter, which he asked her to return to the Red Cross in New York where it belonged. She kept it. The poet wrote her great love sonnets of the next several years on the purloined Corona, and then took it with her all over the world.

This episode, which transpired during one of the busiest and most triumphant periods of Millay's life, defies understanding while it sheds light on events in the following years.

It is inconceivable that Millay could ever have seriously considered a long-term relationship, let alone a marriage, with Jim Lawyer. His letters show him to be weak, foolish, self-pitying, and rather humorless. There was no poetry in him. He had none of the virtues she wanted in a man except the one we can only deduce was his because he had no others. We have only a passing reference to him in one of her letters to Norma, in which she refers to him as "that poor fish." That Millay used him so cruelly, so mercilessly, while he forever believed that his beloved was a blameless paragon, suggests a cynicism, callousness, and anger that seem unfathomable in a lyric poet who, eight years earlier (in her letter to Ferdinand Earle), had called attention to her "own capability for remorse." Such are the paradoxes of personality. Perhaps she meant to punish the man for being imperfect. And surely there was a purple streak of sadism in the author of "This beast that rends me in the sight of all, / This love, this longing, this oblivious thing, / That has me under as the last leaves fall, / Will glut, will sicken, will be gone by spring" (from *Fatal Interview*).

In all fairness, she was not entirely without remorse. But she meant to drink deeply from the spring of Eros, as any man might, as men had been doing since the beginning of recorded time. It was a game that could not be played without someone getting hurt now and then, and the excitement did keep her pen moving.

MÉNAGE À TROIS

The sadness resounding in the sonnets written in 1919–1920 is the sadness of her lovers. The disillusionment is in them and in herself—but the cynicism is all her own. "Pity me not," she wrote, in one of her most famous poems. And knowing what we now know about her affairs we are only too happy to oblige her.

> Love is no more
> Than the wide blossom which the wind assails,
> Than the great tide that treads the shifting shore,
> Strewing fresh wreckage gathered in the gales . . .

Jim Lawyer seems to have whetted Millay's appetite for "fresh wreckage," and that year, 1920, the twenty-eight-year-old woman became a sort of avenging angel of Eros, engaging lover after lover and dashing their hopes in a pattern it is fair to say is pathological. The "poor fish" went back to his wife on February 10. Beginning on February 7, someone named Harkness Smith began writing Millay love letters from the Biltmore Hotel in Midtown—in answer to her own—that testify to a sexual affair that began in mid-February and continued until the summer when his heart was broken. His prosaic, passionate letters tell us almost nothing about him except that he was married, he worshipped the poet, and he felt sure that he could not live long without her. After a night together in New York, February 19, 1920, he wrote begging for her to arrange a tryst with him in Buffalo. Millay was in Covington, Kentucky, en route to a poetry reading in Cincinnati.

Her career as an actress was winding down at the point when she began to make good money as a writer and receive more and more invitations to read her poems publicly for handsome fees. She wrote to her family from Cincinnati, "I have never made such a thorough success of anything as I made of my lecture here." The letter shows a zest in the public performance that would vanish after 1926 when the poetry readings became big business, the zest to be superseded by ennui and a sense of professional duty. In the same letter she mentions that Max Seeger, a young writer friend, "is going to motor me up to Springfield for Fran Bauer's wedding." Here was an opportunity not be wasted. That motor trip inspired a half-pound of billets-doux from Max, who raves about what a wonder Millay is in bed, and how grateful he is—and when can he see her again? She would be too busy with work, and making love with other men, ever to see him again.

From February 1920 through February of the following year, more than fifty of her poems and three short stories appeared in periodicals. Millay composed most of these poems between the summer of 1919 and the autumn of 1920, a prodigious outpouring of poetry of the highest intensity, poetry that many readers consider her finest. In late October 1920 she wrote to Witter Bynner, "I am becoming very famous. The current *Vanity Fair* has a whole page of my poems [including "Pity me not because the light of day," "What lips my lips have kissed," and "Singing Woman from the Wood's Edge"] and a photograph of me . . . and there have been three reviews of something I wrote, in New York newspapers, in the last week alone." *Aria da Capo* had made her name familiar to newspaper readers in December 1919; her "Twenty Sonnets," published in *Reedy's Mirror* in May 1920, had proved to general readers her mastery of that classic form. So now she was "cocktail party famous," a phrase that was later used to refer to Leonard Bernstein, who was invited to every party, and whose name was as likely to come up in conversation if he were absent as when he was present.

By the late autumn of that year she would be so exhausted by work and the weight of her lovers that she could think only of escaping from all of them, and she began planning to leave New York for Europe.

❦

Edmund Wilson and John Bishop met her at the zenith of her bohemian celebrity, at a cocktail party in Greenwich Village during the last week of April 1920. A Princeton graduate and a war veteran, Wilson was working at *Vanity Fair* with his friend Bishop, a poet. A Princeton classmate of Bishop's named Hardwicke Nevin had invited a crowd of writers and artists to his apartment. Millay swept in the door, having just come from the Provincetown Playhouse where she was starring in a "review bill," a revival of Floyd Dell's *Sweet and Twenty* on the same program with her own *Aria da Capo*. Wilson had seen the performances only a few days earlier. Impressed by the actress, Wilson was also "thrilled and troubled by [her] little play; it was the first time I had felt Edna's peculiar power." (After 1919 most of her friends called her Edna.)

Wilson, born in Red Bank, New Jersey, in 1895, was two weeks shy of being twenty-five. According to biographer Jeffrey Meyers, when the writer met Millay "he was still a sexually inexperienced and innocent young man who had not yet succumbed to the awful daring of a moment's surrender." The fair-skinned, sandy-haired Wilson was short (five-foot-six) and had not yet put on the jowls and extra flesh that soon would make his contemporaries describe him as "plump" and "soft-bodied." He had a classic profile: perfect nose, strong chin, a sensuous mouth, and wide-set, fawn-colored eyes. But it was his piercing intelligence that many women found irresistible.

He seems to have been infatuated with the poet before he met her, having first read her work in a magazine in 1916. He reviewed her poems "Interim" and "The Suicide" for the *New York Evening Sun* later that year, commenting that "the contemporary verse sounds a new note of frankness, intensity and dramatic feeling." In March 1920 he saw her sonnet "To Love Impuissant" ("Love, though for this you riddle me with darts") and got it "by heart and found myself declaiming it in the shower . . . How I hoped I might someday meet her!" His wish was granted when the poet showed up at Hardwicke Nevin's party a month later, fatigued from her performance at the theater. Wilson recalled:

> She was dressed in some bright batik, and her face lit up with a flush
> that seemed to burn also in the bronze reflections of her not yet bobbed
> reddish hair. She was one of those women whose features are not per-
> fect . . . but who, excited by the blood or the spirit, become almost
> supernaturally beautiful.

Though tired, she gave in to the company's requests that she recite some of her poems. Wilson recalled "her power of imposing herself on others through a medium that unburdened the emotions of solitude. The company hushed and listened as people do to music—her authority was always complete; but her voice, though dramatic, was lonely." Wilson was uncannily perceptive.

Edmund "Bunny" Wilson was to become a linchpin of American letters—as a writer of fiction, editor of F. Scott Fitzgerald, a master scholar (fluent in Russian and Hebrew as well as the Romance languages), a literary historian, polemicist, and memoirist, and by acclamation the most important American literary critic of his generation. (T. S. Eliot, for the sake of argument, was British.) I have already remarked that no one has ever written so eloquently and perceptively about Millay as Wilson did in his reviews and personal essays. His fifty-page memoir "Epilogue, 1952," closing his literary chronicle *The Shores of Light*, written not long after Millay's death, is considered by Meyers and other scholars to be one of the finest personal essays Wilson ever published. The book remains in print, and the essay is essential reading for anyone interested in Millay and her work. I will not reduce to a cold synopsis the moving story Wilson tells of their love affair that ended much too soon for him, or the friendship that continued until her death in 1950, only a year after he last saw her and her husband at home in the Berkshires. But certain features of their romance, and several questions that Wilson raises concerning the poet's character, directly bear on the discussion of Millay's poetry in relation to her love life.

John Bishop and Edmund Wilson fell in love with Millay simultaneously that spring. Bishop, twenty-eight, was slender, stoop-shouldered, with eyes of pale blue in a narrow but handsome face. He was an aesthete, self-conscious, and, in his youth, self-centered. Bishop had published an excellent book of poetry, *Green Fruit*, in 1917, and now he was the managing editor of *Vanity Fair*, where he hired his friend Wilson to read copy and write reviews. Wilson recalled: "The more we saw of her poetry, the more our admiration grew, and we both, before very long, had fallen irretrievably in love with her. This latter was so common an experience, so almost inevitable a consequence of knowing her in those days. . . . One cannot really write about Edna Millay without bringing into the foreground of the picture her intoxicating effect on people, *because this so much created the atmosphere in which she lived and composed*." (The italics are mine.)

Wilson goes on to write, "There was something of awful drama about everything one did with Edna, and yet something that steadied one, too." The "something" that steadied Wilson was her genius, and what he called her "magnanimity," her indifference to personality in men (so he believed) that allowed him to be her friend when he could no longer be her lover. John Bishop, on the other hand, taking himself so seriously, could not regard Millay that way. While Wilson courted the woman with passion leavened by humor, his fellow editor was consumed and nearly destroyed by her.

Falling in love with the two friends simultaneously appealed to Millay's sense of fun. She encouraged them impartially. What began as an innocent friendship in April, with the three of them dining out in restaurants and going to parties and concerts together, ended farcically as a ménage à trois

in early winter on the daybed in Edna's apartment. That drunken evening
the three wound up in the bed together. Edna apportioned her body from
the waist up to John Bishop, while leaving everything from the waist down
to Edmund Wilson—"With a polite exchange of pleasantries about which
had the better share," as Wilson recalled. *A Few Figs from Thistles* had just
been published, and the sensational quatrain "My candle burns at both ends"
was on the lips of poetry readers all over Greenwich Village, while the author
was demonstrating the source of the poem in her bed on West Twelfth
Street.

She called them "the choir boys of hell," and Wilson heard (and recorded
in his diary) that she complained that their being in love with the same
woman had not broken up the men's friendship—a comment that, if not
spoken in irony, suggests a curious perversion of vanity, maybe even outright
malice. But in his affectionate memoir of 1952, he insisted upon her "invin-
cible magnanimity, and the effects of her transitory feminine malice would
be cancelled by an impartiality that was amiably humorous or sympathetic."
As a gentleman he understated the pain Millay caused him and his friend:
"Between John Bishop and me relations were, nevertheless, by this time,
becoming a little strained."

She was the woman who relieved the twenty-five-year-old Wilson of his
virginity. He was younger than she, and more vulnerable, and she took him
on as an apprentice in the art of love as she had other "boys," knowing she
could depend upon them to be docile.

"Edna ignited for me both my intellectual passion and my unsatisfied
desire, which went up together in a blaze of ecstasy that remains for me one
of the high points in my life," he wrote toward the end of his own, with
more than thirty years of perspective. "I do not believe that such experiences
can be common, for such women are not common." Wilson—who loved and
married several brilliant and beautiful women—never loved anyone as much
as he did Edna Millay.

In June 1920 the Millay family rented a small summer house in Truro
near the tip of Cape Cod. Edna invited Edmund there for a weekend in
August, having evenhandedly summoned John Bishop there on a different
weekend. And it was there one hot night, on the porch, as they sat side by
side on the swing, the mosquitoes buzzing around them, that Wilson formally
asked her to marry him. Wilson, like Salomón de la Selva years earlier, felt
for a moment like one of the insects. "She did not reject my proposal but
said that she would think about it." He never recorded her answer. But it
became clear presently that she would never accept his proposal. On August

3, 1920, she wrote to him from Truro: "I don't know what to write to you, either,—what you would like me to write, or what you would hate me for writing—I feel that you rather hate me, as it is. . . . I have thought of you often, Bunny, and wondered if you think of me with bitterness."

He had the common sense to see that he was not fit to be this woman's husband: "My subsequent chagrin and perplexity, when I discovered that, due to her extreme promiscuity, this could not be expected to continue, were rather amazingly soothed by an equanimity on her part." Surely it was Wilson's own rare equanimity that soothed both of them.

What this ménage à trois illustrates is that the woman became a mirror in which her suitors could see little that was not already in themselves. Wilson saw her genius, her equanimity, her magnanimity, her "disarming impartiality," and "this power of enhancing and ennobling life," which he observed was felt by everyone who knew her. He recognized these virtues not only because they were there (except for the "disarming impartiality") but because he possessed them to some degree. Her affection for him as revealed in her published letters is unusually tender, suggesting that for her love was only possible between equals.

But John Peale Bishop, as he reveals in dozens of tormented letters, saw an entirely different woman: thoughtless, or intentionally—deviously—cruel. The philosophical Wilson appears to have gotten out of Millay's way for the most part by the autumn of 1920, cutting his losses. Bishop kept pursuing her, desperately, obsessively, after she had made herself as hard for him to grasp as a wisp of smoke. On June 5 he writes to her from the Princeton Club on Forty-fourth Street to her summer retreat at Truro, apologizing for not writing "because I am trying to shake you a little from my mind—without great success. I am still restless with desire to feel your cool white hand against my temples. O Edna, why do you have power to torture me so?" He bemoans the distance she has put between them. "I wonder sometimes if you do not hurt for the sheer pleasure in hurting." He also wonders, accusingly, if she is disposed to "*épater*," a revealing word choice. The French word means "to flatten" or to "stun," and by the 1920s it was common parlance among intellectuals for bohemian behavior calculated to shock people, to overturn conventions for the sake of effect. Everybody in bohemia knew that Millay was playing Wilson off against Bishop. It quickly became a Village sideshow as Frank Crowninshield, the editor-in-chief of *Vanity Fair*, struggled to keep peace in the office between the rivals for Edna's attention. She was, after all, one of Crowninshield's prize contributors.

She had "flattened" Bishop in a month's time, hurting him badly by playing him false with other men. "And yet I think, wise one," he writes, "you tried not so much to hurt as to save me from later and more desperate pain. Edna, I love you because you are passionate and wise. And if your passion had been less than your wisdom I should not have felt you so cruelly."

What had hurt him was this: On Monday, May 31, Edna came to John's apartment to make love with him. They quickly got down to business. But either just before or after the act she casually mentioned that she had just been in the arms of another man, which is why she had been a bit late. And then before leaving him she announced she must not tarry because she had an appointment to make love with a different man altogether. (This is what used to be called during the Swinging Sixties a triple-header.) She had meant for her candor with Bishop to be a tonic, morally bracing. She was frank with him about "unsatisfied desire left after the ever so shattering ecstasy." He didn't really expect to detain her then or ever, or for his goddess to be any different than she was. Yet he was stunned: "I think really that your desire works strangely like a man's. And that desire has few secrets from me."

He was thinking in exactly the right direction. Her desire was indeed working like a man's, if in fact there is any natural distinction between male and female desire. If not, then Millay may have been one of the first modern women to indulge her nature as men had been doing for centuries, without apologizing.

Bishop's letter of June 5 also contains the first historical reference to the famous sonnet "What lips my lips have kissed"; he asked her to send it to him, what he termed her "last sonnet." As she was in the habit of reciting her new poems to friends shortly after finishing them, here is strong evidence that that particular melancholy summary of her love life was written in May 1920, when the ménage à trois with Wilson and Bishop was in full swing.

If she had meant by her candor to save him "from later and more desperate pain," her consideration was completely lost on Bishop. He continued to enjoy her favors now and then, wholly on her terms, until November, when she began to cut him loose. Then his letters grew desperate, pleading. From November 24: "I hope you haven't forgotten your promise to see me this week. . . . I do love you, Edna, more than I have ever loved anyone, more than I shall ever love anyone again. It seems such a cruel jest that you should be so fond of me—I believe you are—and yet love me so little."

Hers is the iron fist in the velvet glove. She caresses him with one hand and then cuffs him with the other. She did forget her promise, instead deciding that the wise thing was for them never to see each other again, which sent Bishop completely off his hinges: "For God's sake, Edna, don't forbid my coming to see you this week—I can't stand it. . . . I love you till no vein in my body is quiet without you. I am ill, really, with the thought of losing you."

This is strong stuff, and seems to have gotten the attention of the Great Queen (as Bishop had begun calling her in Wilson's presence). So she promised the poor fellow Monday, December 13. But their tryst that day only served to rub salt in his wounds. She had tenderly explained to him that her love for the new man in her life was but a sensual thing, and that was not something he wanted to hear. As he wrote to her on December 18: "The remembrance of your hair was a bitter thing, and the thought of your flesh a desperate thing. . . . Pondering on your beauty I am struck through with a new helpless longing that can only end in desperation. . . ." (The new man in her life was probably Luigi Laurenti, the Metropolitan opera tenor, who taught Millay Italian and other things, if it was not Llewelyn Powys, the English essayist.)

It began to dawn on John Bishop that he might not be the man for Edna Millay, who needed a brigade. This sadomasochistic pair seem to have escaped from each other only when Edna left for France on the *Rochambeau* after New Year's Day, 1921. Extraordinary letters from Bishop, just before his marriage years later, confess that he cannot give himself wholly to his fiancée, despite how much he loves her, because of the searing memory he has of Edna's flesh.

Bishop apparently had no inkling of Millay's difficulties that autumn and winter. For his part, Wilson knew she was ill, and from his apartment on West Thirteenth Street he did what he could for her in her cold flat on West Twelfth. He brought her an electric heater. He typed for her when she could not get out of bed. Where Wilson adapted himself to become a permanent friend, Bishop was unable to accept a similar role.

On December 20 she wrote to her mother, after a long silence, saying that she had been ill with bronchitis "& another small nervous breakdown after that. I didn't want you to know." The previous breakdown occurred in early April, fallout from the disastrous affair with the construction engineer, Jim Lawyer. The ecstasies of her love life sometimes came at a high cost.

Edmund Wilson and John Bishop, still friends on the date Millay sailed for France, decided not to see her off. "We were both afraid of the possible unknown others we might have to confront on the pier," Wilson wrote, with admirable humor. He gave her a beautifully bound edition of Verlaine to read on the voyage. She wrote to thank him on January 20, a week after arriving in Paris: "Such a lovely book . . . Poor Bunny—it will never be right between us, will it, my dear?—I have wronged you greatly. I know that.

Whatever my motives may have been, as far as you are concerned it is all a great wrong.—However, I shall try to do better in the future. . . ." She would become his loyal friend and an important critic of his fiction.

She wrote a poem called "Portrait," about an evening in January 1924 that they spent together, Wilson reading aloud to her the Latin elegiacs of Housman, and some new poetry of Yeats. "Portrait," which appeared in 1928, contrasts her joy in that occasion with Wilson's bitterness and regret: She had married another man, and Wilson would never possess her. She recalls his "reading aloud to me immortal page after page conceived in a mortal mind."

> I could not ever nor can I to this day
> Acquaint you with the triumph and sweet rest
> These hours have brought to me and always bring,—
> Rapture, coloured like the wild bird's neck and wing,
> Comfort, softer than the feathers of its breast.
> Always, and even now, when I rise to go,
> Your eyes blaze out from a face gone wickedly pale . . .

She wanted him to understand and share that peace she felt in intellectual fellowship. But in the poem she repines, "you cry me down, you scourge me with a salty flail; / You will not have it so."

"Portrait" is an incisive naturalistic poem about the conflict between a man's desire for erotic satisfaction and a woman's desire for the serenity of friendship. Edna was not sentimental about her "Bunny," but she definitely loved him and felt an abiding sympathy, as one might feel for an opponent one had wounded accidentally in a game, a regret that she had hurt him. As for the more egoistic John Bishop, he soon dropped out of her life altogether. Wilson was wrong about her "magnanimity," as he was wrong when he claimed that she was indifferent to personality in her suitors. Millay was cruel to men she perceived as weak in character. Those whom she admired, like Wilson, Ficke, and Dell, she rewarded with continuing affection and ultimately the prize of enduring friendship. She learned to be an exemplary friend. She collected male friends, as she once collected badges, valentines, and play programs, and one day would collect rare seashells.

※

In discussing how Millay "rewarded" her lovers with affection, bestowing on the worthiest of them her loyal friendship, the name of Llewelyn Powys must not be passed over. The younger brother of the English novelist John Cowper

Powys, Llewelyn, born in 1884, was an essayist, novelist, and memoirist of
notable skill and distinction. Traveling in America in the autumn and winter
of 1920–1921, the thirty-six-year-old writer visited Greenwich Village in
December. He met Millay early that month. She called him "Lulu," as did
many of his friends. Incredible as it seems—given her illness and her affairs
with Bishop and others—she managed to squeeze Lulu into her bedroom
and take him into her arms enough times, before January, to inspire an
obsession and a stack of love letters that rival Salomón de la Selva's in their
beauty. He wrote:

> Do, I pray you, let me see you again. I am simply tormented by you—I
> can't get you out of my mind day or night. . . . I can't tell what has
> happened to me since I saw you: I feel like some wretched child under
> a spell.

Bear in mind, if possible, that Powys was a gentleman, a genuinely admirable
man and not a crank.

There is a mystical streak in the whole Powys family (there was a third
brother, P. F. Powys, also a writer of fiction), and Millay seems to have
sparked Llewelyn's belief in an extraterrestrial, angelic being:

> There is nobody I have ever seen who can approach you. . . . I can hardly
> believe you are really alive. It is as if I had seen in a street, in a chamber,
> on the stairs, some being from outside the visible world, a being of moon-
> light, of imagination, intangible. . . . As long as I am alive I shall be
> haunted by your beauty—I can't tell you how deeply it is lodged in my
> brain—the look you had as you lay on that sofa, as illuminating and
> thrilling to me as anything I have ever seen in art or nature, like the
> very embodiment of all that is most tragic and imaginative and won-
> derful in life—the very essence of the mystery we all follow, seen now
> for the first time in my life, by me.

He begs her to let him visit, or just see her for a moment, for lunch, or for
a quick drink in a speakeasy. She replies that she is too busy, she is ill. But
then she relents. They spend an hour together, then he is even more miserable than before, writing to her: "When I am with you I can bear you—
almost—but when you are not there—then it is I enter hell and am
tormented." He can't get her out of his mind for a single moment. Obsessed,
he can hear over and over in his head every word she has ever spoken to
him, "even half finished sentences" that he dares not interpret as he would

like to. He and a friend walk into a church where he hopes to find sanctuary. But what does he see on the steps leading to the high altar? "The name of all names to madden me. What were the priests about to write your name on the high altar stairs? VINCENTI DABO MANNA ABSCONDITIUM." (Powys slightly misquoted the Latin passage from the revelation of John 2:17, meaning: "To the victor I will feed the hidden manna.") He humorously remarks that he knew this already, having just spent the night with Vincent. With his classical and High Church education he no doubt knew the context of the quote, a tirade against Jezebel "who calleth herself a prophetess, to teach and seduce my servants to commit fornication. . . ." The joke was probably lost on Edna, who was not a devoted reader of the Bible.

Her letters to him from this period are not available, but his letters suggest that she never "led him on." She advised Powys to cultivate in himself the same sort of cynicism about love that she had adopted. In that attitude, needless to say, he found himself way out of his depth: "If I live to be eighty I shall say I have seen beauty only once and it was your beauty."

Powys would not live to be eighty. He would die of tuberculosis in 1939, but not before he had seen the best side of Millay's friendship. Gracefully she managed to transform this idolator into a devoted friend, and to make friends with his wife, too. They spent a great deal of time together in England and America. Lulu became not only an object of affection and admiration (she encouraged his writing), but when he was poor and ailing and she was well-to-do, Powys was the beneficiary of Millay's extraordinary, and characteristic, munificence.

EUROPE

By the end of 1920, Edna St. Vincent Millay's power to drive men mad, whether or not it arose from a pathology, had become a compulsion. However much that potency had nourished her sonnets it had spoiled her, and now was beginning to undo her. It was not her work or a frail constitution that was occasioning these illnesses and nervous breakdowns, but rather a centrifugal dissolution, the emotional entropy caused by all of her affairs. No person with a shred of genuine feeling could have endured it for much longer.

Edna's sister Kathleen had fallen in love and married the playwright Howard Young in December 1920. Edna, still fundamentally lonely, may well have envied the stability of marriage that seemed so far out of her reach.

She had woven a constricting web. The only way out that she could imagine was to flee—get out of Greenwich Village, out of New York, get away from all these madmen in America and go to Europe where she might find lovers with a better sense of humor. For some time Frank Crowninshield had been asking her to go to Europe, partly at his expense, to become a correspondent for his magazine *Vanity Fair* under her pen name Nancy Boyd. (He had offered to pay her double to sign her real name to the prose pieces, but for years she refused to put that name on anything but her poetry.)

Arthur Ficke had gone abroad with Witter Bynner in the autumn, and she entertained a fantasy that she and Ficke would be reunited in Europe, never again to part. Passionate letters between Millay and Ficke, many of them already quoted, attesting to their sublime and enduring love, had continued since the day he left on the troop ship early in 1918. These only serve to underscore the curious nature of their connection—the ultra-romanticism, the nympholepsy, the pair's unconscious avoidance of meeting. On December 26, 1920, he wrote to her from Hong Kong: "Yes, my dear, we love each other and to know it is for me a consolation like that of a deeply felt religion. . . . The thought of you, and the love of your spirit which you give me is a happiness to me always: it is one of the handful of secret weapons which, when I cannot sleep at night, I use to fight spectres with."

Be that as it may, Ficke seems to have loved her absence more than her presence, traveling all over the world making jokes about how they were always "just missing" each other. His letter from Hong Kong did not arrive until weeks after she sailed for Le Havre on the *Rochambeau* on January 4, hoping to join Ficke in Europe. She wrote to him from Paris on January 25, "God knows where you are, but here's where I am—so near to 20 Rue Jacob that it makes my mind sick to think of it, and my heart so lonesome for you I could cry. I went over there the other night and walked way down to the end of the dark court-yard, & stared at all the windows. . . . Oh, if only you were there now, just around the corner from me!" Not three weeks later, on Valentine's Day, he wrote to her in Paris, from Iowa:

This does seem an unnecessary touch of ironical perversity on the part of life! Yesterday on the train coming home, I said to myself—"Well,

in March I must go to New York and see if Vincent is a real person"—
and now I find that you have not only gone, but gone to the identical
quarter-mile of the earth's surface that I love best.

He could not have received her last letter, because he begged her just once
to go to Rue Jacob and look at his windows: "Such lovely rooms. The garden
and the chimney pots are absolutely magic country when you look out on
them at evening from those windows."

She had closed her letter to Ficke with the plaintive question, "Shall I
ever see you again, my dear?"

※

Millay's adventures in Europe, except for her sexual escapades, are beautifully detailed in her published letters from Paris, Rome, Vienna, Budapest,
Albania, and Dorset, England. Many more unpublished letters are just as
good. What is most impressive about this chapter of her life is her fearlessness, notably the ease with which she took on the languages and customs of
unfamiliar countries, particularly France. An excerpt from a letter she wrote
aboard the *Rochambeau* on January 11, 1921, symbolizes her pluck and daring. A few days out to sea the going got rough, and the ship's doctor was
handing out anti-seasick pills all around.

> I stood in my cabin and looked at the damned things and couldn't make
> up my mind to do it. I wanted to dam well find out, & no fooling with
> pills and powders, whether E.St.V.M, who writes all those heart-interest
> poems about the bounding main, would or would not be a sea-sick
> ocean voyageur. And I ain't.
> For two or three days I didn't feel exactly secure, the boat kept
> dropping out from under me and doing the darndest things, but I simply
> made no resistance against it at all, just relaxed to the motion.

She went with the flow. She settled into her steam-heated room in the
Hotel des Saints-Pères at 65 rue des Saints-Pères near St.-Germain-des-Prés.
On January 18 she wrote to her mother that she'd already started working
(on prose, not poetry). She had agreed to write two pieces per month for
Vanity Fair. That commitment, plus work on a novel and her play *The Lamp
and the Bell*, left her no time for poetry. She had been to the theater and to
two parties, where she found the French people extremely amusing. "I have
walked and driven in a taxi about Paris quite a bit. Taxis cost almost nothing
here at the present rate of exchange." The dollar was strong in Europe after
the war, one of the chief reasons Hemingway, Pound, Fitzgerald, and other
writers settled there in the 1920s.

She loved the French theater, where "they say terrible naughty bad words right out loud on the stage, and between the acts you go to an adorable little café right in the theatre . . . and have liqueurs and cigarettes, and nobody arrests you!" The French considered Prohibition a unique American barbarism. So did Millay.

A natural Francophile, Millay became fluent in French in a matter of weeks. She enjoyed her wine and liqueurs at the Café de la Rotonde on Boulevard Montparnasse, and the Café des Deux Magots on Boulevard St. Germain. She relished the conversation there with other visiting Americans: poet Edgar Lee Masters, composer Deems Taylor, the brother poets Stephen Vincent Benét and William Rose Benét, and writer Djuna Barnes accompanied by her lover, the artist Thelma Wood. Thelma liked to dance with Edna, and this made Djuna Barnes jealous.

The only things Vincent disliked about France were the coffee and the milk products. In letter after letter she complained about constipation, blaming it on the coffee and cream. She could not live without laxatives in Europe, and would become so ill from an intestinal fistula the next year that radical surgery would be required in order to save her life. While in Paris in 1922 she received a five hundred dollars advance from publisher Horace Liveright to write a novel; the hero of the satirical novel was to be named "Hardigut," in honor of the intestinal fortitude the writer suffered so for lacking.

As for her love life, soon after arriving in Paris Millay rapidly and perfectly reproduced the sort of web she had escaped in New York: the turmoil of multiple lovers and its consequences, including illness and depression. It points up Emerson's belief that your giant always goes with you. While the passionate correspondence with Ficke continued, her other American lovers also pursued her by mail—and sometimes in person—all over Europe. They found her preoccupied. In June of 1921 Edmund Wilson quit his job at *Vanity Fair* to court Millay in Paris. He wrote this dispatch to John Bishop on July 3:

> I found her in a very first-rate hotel on the Left Bank and better dressed,
> I suppose, than she has ever been before in her life. You were right in
> guessing that she was well cared for as she had never been before.

It was not *Vanity Fair*'s largesse that was maintaining the poet in such high style. She had discovered the nexus between men's wallets and their affections. Wilson thought Millay looked more mature and seemed more serious and sincere about herself. He writes to Bishop, "[She] told me she wanted to settle down to a new life: she was tired of breaking hearts and spreading havoc." She was happy with her current lover, "a big red-haired British journalist named Slocum [*sic*], the Paris correspondent of the London Herald (a Labor paper) who had spent three years in France and had two teeth knocked out in the war."

Slender George Slocombe, thirty-seven, with his mane of golden-red hair and beard, was as handsome as a Nordic god. He had a wife and three children in Saint-Cloud, and was dividing his time between that western suburb of Paris and the Latin Quarter where Millay was notoriously known as his mistress. She told Wilson she meant to marry Slocombe if he got a divorce, and expressed pain at having wrecked another home. This made Wilson laugh in spite of himself. Slocombe would never leave his wife, and he would not give up his mistress. She wrote:

> Mild we were for a summer month
>   As the wind from over the weirs,
> And blessed be death, that hushed with salt
>   The harsh and slovenly years!
>
> Who builds her house with love for timber
>   Builds her a house of foam.
> And I'd liefer be bride to a lad gone down
>   Than widow to one safe home.
>   (from "Keen")

These astringent verses published in 1923 were probably inspired by her affair with Slocombe. The cadences have a lilt similar to "The Ballad of the Harp-Weaver," also written in the summer of 1921, when Slocombe and Millay were sleeping together.

She enjoyed as much or as little of Slocombe's company that year as she liked. Meanwhile she maintained the leisure and privacy to entertain various other men, as she had done in New York—at least when she had the strength. She had inflammatory bowel disease. In an unpublished letter to Kathleen, September 9, 1921, written in Dieppe, France, she describes herself as "flat on my back with a physician in attendance." But she found plenty of time for the journalist Griffin Barry, who had introduced her to Slocombe while he was having an affair with the English poet Anna Wickham; then there was John Carter, who had been Stephen Benét's roommate at Yale, an aspiring poet who now was serving as an attaché at the American embassy in Rome. By the autumn of 1921 Millay's affair with Carter was providing her with a pleasurable and lucrative counterpoint to Slocombe, whose marital woes and remorse had begun to weary her. She traveled from Paris to Italy in the company of Griffin Barry—a false friend of Slocombe's, a merry prankster who was enjoying Edna's favors under the guise of chaperoning her in Vienna and elsewhere—in order to join Carter in Rome. Carter, like Slocombe, worshipped Millay, and would have done nearly anything for her. He even squired Millay to Albania—then, as now, an inhospitable place.

With the possible exception of "Keen," no poems arose from these liaisons. It was as if she realized she had begun to repeat herself in life, and was too good an artist to repeat herself in verse. Millay wrote little poetry at all in Europe, and no certifiable love poems. What she got out of the men that year was laughs, distraction, and money to keep moving. In the Old World her cynicism ripened to that point of sophistication where she did not shy from confiding to her lovers (including Ficke) just how much she needed money for clothing, for meals, for travel; and she was never too proud to take francs, lira, dollars, or bank checks when a friend offered them. John Carter gave and/or loaned Millay thousands of dollars during their intense affair in France, Italy, and Albania. Not until she had thrown him over did he try to collect it. (She repaid him after she met her fiancé in 1923. And Carter never spoke unkindly of her.)

On a stroll with Edmund Wilson in the Bois de Boulogne that summer of 1921, she told him she was broke, and raising her lovely eyes to his she asked him if he would take her to the South of France. But Bunny had grown sadder and wiser. "I knew that she was not to be relied on and would leave me for anyone who seemed more attractive," he wrote in his diary. Tough words from a man who loved Millay, a friend who appreciated her virtues better perhaps than anyone else in the world.

Norma married Charles Ellis in October. Edna, who had always imagined she would marry before the age of thirty, saw the clock running out. She wrote to Arthur Ficke from Albania: "It is wicked and useless,—all these months & months apart from you, all these years with only a glimpse of you in the face of everybody—I tell you I must see you again.—" But she was in *Albania*, for God's sake, the dark side of the moon. She sensed that Arthur was interested in another woman, and she was right.

In New York City, in January of 1922, he fell in love with a charming young painter named Gladys Brown, and he would confess it to Millay by the spring. Confused, desperate, and surely furious at Ficke (while protesting she would love him forever no matter what), in December she was angling for a marriage proposal from Ficke's best friend Witter ("Hal") Bynner, in letters bristling with phrases such as "It is true I love Arthur. But we have all known that for some time. . . . But why should that trouble you, Hal?

Don't you love him, too? Don't you love several people? . . . Surely one must be either undiscerning, or frightened, to love only one person, when the world is so full of gracious and noble spirits." The sexual rebel was making her first formal case for an open marriage. That winter a comic three-way exchange of letters (Millay's are in print) ensued among Millay, Bynner, and Ficke, with letters crisscrossing in the mail from Budapest to Iowa to New York in the most hilarious manner—letters lost and letters to Ficke misaddressed to Bynner. Bynner did propose, earnestly, not knowing how to say no to her, and she couldn't wait to tell Ficke: "We should make such a beautiful design, don't you see,—Hal and you and I. Three variable and incommensurate souls automatically resolved into two right angles, and no nonsense about it." Ever the geometer! She reminds Ficke she loves him as she will never love anyone, "But that's no reason why I couldn't marry Hal, and be happy with him. I love him, too. In a different way."

Was this her final, desperate attempt to get Ficke to marry her? If so, she got nowhere with it. Apparently, first Arthur, then Vincent, had realized after all these years they were not marriage material; with so much fire and romanticism on both sides, they would likely go up in flames. Rather, the droll engagement to the kind homosexual Bynner appeared as a plan to nullify marriage, *reductio ad absurdum*, leaving them all free to love one another pell-mell. She was hoping that Ficke might arrange something similar in his marriage.

For several months Ficke played along with this harlequinade, journeying to New York to discuss with Hal the pros and cons of the proposed alliance. Remember that these were the mischievous coauthors of one of the greatest literary hoaxes in American history, the "Spectra Hoax." In 1916 Ficke and Bynner had invented an entire school of crazy avant-garde poetry: false poets and tongue-in-cheek poems, and an anthology that was seriously reviewed everywhere. The two men shared a marvelous sense of humor. But they saw little in this situation with Edna. Ficke wrote a letter addressed jointly to Dear Vincent and Dear Hal, to wit:

> I have the idea that somehow you two have got yourselves snarled up over this marriage idea. . . . Now I, by virtue of the authority entrusted to me by my intuitions, *hereby call this marriage idea absolutely and utterly off.* You are, I order you, both of you to consider it a thing that has never been suggested. . . . I order you to laugh good and hard. . . . Now, children dear, I hate to be stern, but *what I say, goes.*

Ficke mailed a copy to each of them on August 2, 1922. And there was no more talk of marriage between Vincent and Hal after that.

❧

There is desperation and illogic—even hysteria—in Millay's letters that year, strongly suggesting that by the end of 1921 the poet was beginning to lose her bearings. While she continued to meet her deadlines for *Vanity Fair*, she managed to write only one significant poem, the moving tribute to her mother called "The Ballad of the Harp-Weaver," which she composed in Paris during the summer. The ballad transforms her childhood experience of poverty and her mother's heroism into a mythic parable: A mother and her son in a cold house are so poor she cannot afford the material to make him clothes to keep him warm.

> Men say the winter
>   Was bad that year;
> Fuel was scarce,
>   And food was dear.
>
> A wind with a wolf's head
>   Howled about our door,
> And we burned up the chairs
>   And sat upon the floor.

They own nothing but a harp (with a woman's head) that no one will buy. And one night before Christmas she magically weaves magnificent clothing out of the harp strings.

> She wove a child's jacket
>   And when it was done
> She laid it on the floor
>   And wove another one.

The miracle and the mother's inevitable martyrdom are a perfect allegory for the poet's life. Cora Millay, the hair-weaver, was the "harp with the woman's head" who had taught her daughter Shakespeare, how to play piano and sing, how to tell stories, and how to make clothing to show off her beauty. She taught Vincent how to transform her rage against poverty and injustice into work and art that would rescue her from despair. The daughter had played mightily upon that harp, weaving miracle after miracle upon it.

Vincent sent her mother the poem in midsummer. She was worried when she got no response from Cora before leaving for Italy on October 7; then she sent her mother fifty dollars and a promise to have Frank Crowninshield send one hundred dollars directly from New York. In that same letter she mentions that she has been quite ill with stomach trouble, but adds that a French doctor has put her on a special diet and "tonic" that seem to be helping.

She missed her mother terribly. After just six months away she had written to Cora: "A long time. Mother, do you know, almost all people love their mothers, but I have never met anybody in my life, I think, who loved his mother as much as I love you." This was around the time she wrote "The Ballad of the Harp-Weaver." She first conceived of bringing Cora to Europe that summer, and much of her time and effort during the winter of 1921–1922 was given over to earning, begging, and borrowing enough money to make this dream come true. The reason she did not hear from her mother for so many months is that Cora had taken ill after "The Ballad of the Harp-Weaver" was written. Norma finally informed Vincent of this. On March 1, 1922, Vincent wrote to Norma from Budapest: "Your letter put some things straight in my mind that had been a little cluttered before. Your telling me that mother had been sick, and all that,—*you* know—made me realize that nothing in the world is important beside getting mother over here with me. . . . A possible marriage, for instance, is not important beside it. Anybody can get married. It happens all the time. But not everybody, after the life we have had, can bring her mother to Europe."

Vincent Millay met her mother in Le Havre in April 1922, and the two spent an idyllic spring together in Paris, going to the Louvre, to many churches, and to organ recitals in St. Eustache. It turned out that Vincent needed nurse Cora far more than her mother needed her. Cora was in robust good health, a tireless tourist who "saw more of Paris in a month" than Vincent saw in a year, while the daughter was unraveling, both physically and emotionally. She kept writing to Horace Liveright and others that she was working on the novel *Hardigut*, that indeed it was nearly finished (his designers drafted the book jacket) when in fact she had only incoherent notes for the *Candide*-like satire. It was not Millay's habit to lie outright; she seems to have been in denial, not admitting to herself there was no novel.

In late summer they crossed the Channel to England and settled in Dorset, where they hoped the food and water would improve Vincent's chronic stomach problems. There they rented a thatched cottage in the village of Shillington. An American pianist Edna had befriended in Paris, Esther "Tess" Root, followed the Millays to Dorset, taking rooms nearby. And by a curious coincidence another of their neighbors was the painter Gladys Brown, the young woman Arthur Ficke had fallen in love with in America during the winter. Arthur had not told Millay that Gladys was going to England to show her paintings. Edna and Gladys struck up a friendship, went on long walks together along country lanes, and Gladys, an expert equestrian, coached her new friend in horseback riding.

Now and then Vincent would leave Cora to go to London on business (she was acquiring English publishers for her poetry) or for a quick trip to Paris where she was having a fling with a French musician. By September 1922 she was acutely ill, partly due to the chronic stomach ailment, and partly due to morning sickness. Norma Millay Ellis told her friend Elizabeth Barnett (now the executor of Millay's estate) that sister Edna had become pregnant that summer "by the French musician." Cora, a masterful herbalist, had induced an abortion with a brew concocted from the native flowers and herbs of Dorset.

Ficke was divorced on November 20, 1922, and in his letter to Millay on that date he rejoiced in the fact that he and his new love, Gladys Brown, were to be together at last. Though Vincent had seen it coming, this hurt her; she would never let him know how much it pained her, and would only congratulate him on his happiness.

Hoping to recover her health, Millay and her mother wintered in the South of France at Cassis-sur-Mer, Cannes, Nice, and Monte Carlo. On December 17 she wrote to Ficke that she was so ill "I can just drag about," and that she had come close to contracting peritonitis. Mother and daughter decided they had best go home early, and booked passage on a ship that sailed in late January. By the time they returned to America, a month before her thirty-first birthday, the poet was fairly certain she had left all of her lovers behind. And Edna St. Vincent Millay was a very sick woman.

· PART 3 ·

❦

Marriage

MARRIAGE

❧

The weary traveler arrived in New York from France in late January 1923, returning to her old neighborhood in the Village. Millay rented rooms on Waverly Place in the same building as her friend Tess Root, the pianist she had met in Paris who had accompanied her and Cora to England. Cora went back to Maine after a frustrating effort to arouse Vincent from her torpor and get her to seek the medical attention she so obviously needed. The poet had never felt so alone.

The Harp-Weaver and Other Poems, which Arthur Ficke helped Millay prepare for publication that year, includes three poems about marriage. Two of them are bitter: "Keen," probably based upon her affair with the married George Slocombe in the summer of 1921, and "The Betrothal." The latter poem reflects Millay's feelings after she proposed an open marriage among herself, Witter Bynner, and Ficke in January 1922. Addressed to Bynner, the stanzas evoke her longing for Ficke—referring to his dark hair—and Millay's strong message is that happiness for her is not to be found in matrimony. "Oh bring me gifts or beg me gifts, / And wed me if you will," sings the devil-may-care maiden.

> I might as well be easing you
> As lie alone in bed
> And waste the night in wanting
> A cruel dark head.
>
> You may as well be calling yours
> What never will be his,
> And one of us be happy.
> There's few enough as is.

How different this viewpoint and mood are from the joy expressed in "The Return from Town":

As I sat down by Saddle Stream
To bathe my dusty feet there,
A boy was standing on the bridge
Any girl would meet there.

As I went over Woody Knob
And dipped into the hollow
A youth was coming up the hill
Any maid would follow.

Then in I turned at my own gate—
And nothing to be sad for—
To such a man as any wife
Would pass a pretty lad for.

This poem, written at least a year before "Keen" and "The Betrothal" (she sent it to Bynner in August 1920), prophesies Millay's rare good luck in finding "such a man as any wife / Would pass a pretty lad for" after she returned from Europe in 1923, ailing and depressed.

The poet's life was full of surprises and stunning reversals of fortune, but perhaps none is so remarkable as her marrying, in this gloomy season of her life, the only man who might satisfy her strange, complex desires and needs.

❧

His name was Eugen Boissevain. He was born in Amsterdam on May 20, 1880, descended from French Huguenots who immigrated to Holland in the seventeenth century. The Boissevains made their fortune in banking, shipbuilding, and international trade. His grandfather started the first shipping lines between Holland and Java; Eugen's father, Charles, was the owner and editor of the *Algemeen Handelsblad*, the foremost liberal newspaper in the Netherlands. His mother's father served as provost of Trinity College, Dublin. Educated by tutors and in private school, early in life the bright, athletic boy showed a lust for travel and adventure. He first visited America in 1901; President Theodore Roosevelt received the Dutch publisher's son at the White House.

Although Eugen read widely in history and the classics, his interests were too diverse, his energies too explosive for him to settle into an academic life or a business career in his twenties. Instead he became a wanderer, a sportsman, and a seeker: He hunted big game in Africa, rowed in the Henley Regatta in England, and journeyed to Zurich to be analyzed by Carl Jung.

The young man became fluent in French, English, and German. At the age of thirty-two he went to work for Guglielmo Marconi, inventor of wireless telegraphy. His job with Marconi in 1912 brought him back to America, where he had always wanted to live.

Just under six feet tall, 160 pounds, Eugen had the physique and grace of a middleweight boxer. With his twinkling, close-set gray eyes, high forehead, strong chin, large straight nose, and long upper lip above a small mouth, the Dutchman was quick with smiles and booming laughter, ready with wit, his charming accent irresistible to women and men alike.

It was Boissevain's destiny to marry great women. On a ship bound for London in 1913 he met Inez Milholland, the woman suffrage leader. Like Eugen, she had a sprightly mind in a powerful body. Inez had been a star athlete, a sprinter, and a champion shot-putter at Vassar. A tall, striking woman with abundant dark hair, big blue eyes, and sensitive mouth, the brilliant, strong-willed lawyer won the heart of the thirty-three-year-old bachelor. The two were married secretly in London that July. The secret could not be kept for long, because Inez was the daughter of the *New York Tribune*'s editor. From the time she had been a student at Vassar, the press had charted Inez's radical political activities in England as well as in America. She was still a student at Vassar when she began organizing meetings to discuss prison reform and suffrage and the emancipation of women. She spent her summer holidays in England, raising her voice on behalf of women there, and had been arrested once in London for disturbing the peace, as she had been jailed in America twice for her role in a strike of shirtwaist makers.

On July 16, 1913, the marriage of the illustrious Inez Milholland and the obscure son a of a Dutch newspaper magnate made headlines on the front page of the *New York Times*, and Eugen Boissevain returned to America in the shadow of a living legend. They rented a house in Harmon-on-Hudson, New York, where Inez introduced her husband to Max Eastman and other leftist intellectuals connected with the magazine *The Masses*.

Boissevain was a gentleman of such hardy self-confidence and good humor, and so in love with his wife, that he was never uncomfortable when he saw his name, in parentheses, in news articles about the heroic suffragette that referred to him as "the devoted husband" who drove her car or brought her a glass of water on the podium. The man was so sure of his virility that no woman could threaten it, and he was a serious feminist who shared his wife's political vision. Eugen soon gave up his job with Marconi to accompany Inez on her lecture tours and campaigns.

In an unpublished letter from Vincent Millay to her sister Norma on

March 3, 1914, she writes from Vassar: "Inez Milholland (the great Suffragette of America) a Vassar grad, was back here and played a little skit for the college, a little play. She's wonderful."

Milholland was spellbinding on the platform. Her voice was a resilient trumpet, and her eyes blazed as she flung back her flame-lined cloak and challenged her audiences. She spoke without emotional reserve, as if to move heaven and earth, and as though each speech were her last and only chance to win the day. Sometimes she would hyperventilate and fall in a faint, mid-sentence, to the horror of the spectators. Eugen would fetch the smelling salts, set Inez back on her feet, and the fiery orator would continue.

In 1916 she engaged in an exhausting effort to commute the death sentence of a farmhand convicted of murder in New York. Despite her fatigue she felt bound to honor a prior commitment to tour the western states to gather support for the federal amendment for women's suffrage. She called on the enfranchised women of Wyoming, Idaho, Oregon, Washington, Montana, and other western states to use their power as voters to force the major parties to pass the bill. Eugen went with her, concerned that the length of the journey and her manic energy on the platform might consume her altogether. One evening he watched his wife address the crowd in a street of Carson City, Nevada. The setting sun made her fair cheeks glow with an otherworldly light, as the entire town of men, women, and children pressed toward her.

"We are bound to win," she cried. "There never was a fight yet where interest was pitted against principle that principle did not triumph."

By the time they reached California, Eugen was begging Inez to stop and rest, as she seemed to have no life in her at all except when she was addressing a crowd of people. On October 24, 1916, at a thronging mass meeting in Los Angeles, she reached a climax of her speech with the desperate plea "How long shall women wait for liberty?" then collapsed like a rag doll onstage, and could not stand up again.

Eugen lifted her up and took her to their hotel. Doctors discovered the twenty-eight-year-old firebrand had pernicious anemia and ordered blood transfusions. Suffragettes lined up in the hallway to give blood to their martyr, but to no avail. She died within hours, in her husband's arms. Later he told his best friend Max Eastman that in the panic and grief of that terrible hour he had asked his dying wife if she wanted him to go with her, and she whispered, "No, you go ahead and live another life."

So he had become known as the husband of the martyr—and then Milholland's widower. He chose to "live another life" surprisingly different from

the playboy existence of his twenties, and unlike the life of radical ideal-
ism he had enjoyed with Inez. As if in fulfillment of family destiny, Boissevain took up his grandfathers' vocation, launching an import business
with the Dutch East Indies, bringing coffee, sugar, and copra to America.
He and Eastman moved into a modest apartment on East Eighth Street in
the Village. And "Gene," as his friends now called him, threw himself into
this new venture in high-stakes capitalism to distract himself from thoughts
of his late wife and the grief that was slow to subside. He could not think
of marrying again.

Of course, as Eastman recalls in his memoir *The Enjoyment of Living*,
there were other diversions in Greenwich Village in 1917. Whenever Max
could drag his friend away from the obsessions of the office and the docks,
Eugen played the consummate bon vivant, a man with "the daring to enjoy
life." It was Boissevain whose gusto inspired the title of Eastman's book.
Max and Eugen shared the appreciation of good wine, tobacco, well-made
suits, the love of women, and a freewheeling attitude toward sex. The
Eastman-Boissevain ménage moved to a house on Washington Place, then
into a large apartment on St. Luke's Place. Their home became a popular
meeting place for artists and intellectuals, and the scene of much merrymak-
ing. Parties were presided over by the Dutchman, who possessed a rare gift
for cooking, entertaining, and running a household with servants. This was
all part of what Eastman called "a strain of something feminine that most
men except the creative geniuses lack."

Boissevain also loved literature and the arts, continuing throughout his
life to read widely and intensely. His own library from this period—books
underlined, annotated, and in many cases inscribed, attests to this eclectic
intellectual passion. Books by Theodore Dreiser, Walter Lippmann, John
Reed, Sinclair Lewis, Upton Sinclair, and the poets Alfred Kreymbourg and
Edna St. Vincent Millay lined his shelves. An affectionately inscribed copy
of Claude McKay's first book, *Harlem Shadows*, indicates that the importer
knew the great black poet. With Eastman as his guide, Boissevain kept up
with the latest trends in bohemia—literary, artistic, and political.

By 1920 Boissevain was managing a fleet of merchant ships steaming
across the Atlantic laden with coffee and sugar from Java, Sumatra, and the
Moluccas. He owned a twelve-story building downtown at 137 Front Street,
where his business was headquartered; in fact, his name was carved in granite
over its archway. Eastman swore that his friend never took moneymaking
seriously; rather, he thought of it as a harmless practical joke on his custom-
ers and competitors. Nonetheless, by the early 1920s Boissevain was seriously

rich. His versatility, resourcefulness, and indomitable high spirits put one in mind of the Homeric hero Odysseus.

A little more than six years after his wife's death, on an April evening in 1923, Eugen Boissevain would encounter Edna Millay at a house party in Croton-on-Hudson.

%

In her apartment on Waverly Place, Millay introduced Tess Root to her friend Franklin P. Adams (F.P.A.), the clever poet-columnist of the *New York Tribune*. Tess and Franklin fell in love, and would soon be married. F.P.A., who recalled Millay during that dark period in 1923, said that her appearance was disturbing, her "high bright gaiety" and nervous chatter typical of an effort to conceal intense pain. She spent much of her time that winter in seclusion in a final listless effort to write *Hardigut*, which she abandoned at last to prepare her new volume of poetry for the press.

Edmund Wilson, ever faithful, came to call upon—but not to court—his old flame. During the winter he managed to bring together his friends Edna Millay and Elinor Wylie, the sophisticated, aristocratic-looking poet whose marriages and divorces caused such scandal. She had been flattered and deeply grateful for Millay's enthusiastic review of her first book, *Nets to Catch the Wind*, in the *Literary Review* the previous November. Millay commented: "The book is an important one . . . important in itself as it contains some excellent and distinguished work and . . . because it is the first book of its author, and thus marks the opening of yet another door by which beauty may enter into the world." This judgment launched Wylie's career in the 1920s as a love poet second only to Millay herself, who proved memorably generous to spirits with whom she felt artistic kinship such as Wylie and, later, Louise Bogan. From the day Millay met Wylie, the two women were devoted to each other, corresponded, and visited each other's homes.

Millay's third book, *Second April*, published while she was abroad, enjoyed such good reviews and sales that she had no trouble attracting the best publishers. This was a good thing because Mitchell Kennerley, as might have been expected, was bankrupt and invisible. On December 29, 1922, Frank Shay, an independent bookseller on Christopher Street, had published a pretty edition of "The Ballad of the Harp-Weaver," twenty pages stapled together in an orange wrapper with a woodcut of a mother and child on the front. The poem had already caused a sensation when it was published in *Vanity Fair* in June. Despite its whisper of sentimentality, the ballad was the most widely admired of Millay's works since "Renascence." By early April 1923 the Pulitzer committee at Columbia had all but decided, on the basis of "Harp-Weaver," *A Few Figs from Thistles*, and eight sonnets that had appeared in the miscellany *American Poetry, 1922*, to award her the Pulitzer Prize.

This is a mysterious passage in Millay's history, one about which there is scant information, a period made more intriguing by that undated letter from Arthur Ficke quoted earlier, in connection with their brief New York encounter in February of 1918. "I did not know that I should love your body so much," reads the text. "I did not know that anyone was as beautiful as that," it continues, indicating they had gone to bed together. The letter was preserved in an unpostmarked envelope addressed to 156 Waverly Place, where Vincent was living in early 1923. If Ficke did write the letter then— while he and Gladys Brown were in New York and engaged to be married— the revised chronology gives a poignant twist to the melodramatic romance of the two poets. It seems incredible, but the data, in all its maddening ambiguity, must not be dismissed. If Millay and Ficke did at long last consummate their passion in 1923 instead of 1918, it may have been all the more saddening to them that he would marry Gladys anyway, despite the fact that Vincent "had cut him with the sword" of her beauty. And it might have prompted these star-crossed lovers to seek a "solution" vis-à-vis matrimony that would not rule out their having sex together when the spirit moved them. Events over the next decades do suggest that marriage did not interfere with Arthur and Edna's enjoyment of each other in any way.

❦

As the Village became more "touristy" in the 1920s, a colony of writers and artists, including John Reed, Floyd Dell, and Max Eastman, began to spring up along the Hudson. Eugen Boissevain and Eastman bought a small house on Mount Airy, near the Croton-on-Hudson residence of Dudley Malone and Doris Stevens, who gave wonderful parties. The convivial couple had met Tess Root and Edna Millay in Paris.

Tess had attended several of the Malones' parties already that winter, and she had been trying to persuade her sick friend to join her for one. Finally in mid-April the poet dragged herself out of her lair on Waverly Place, and with Tess boarded the train that would take them to Croton for the weekend.

Millay found the Malone-Stevens house full of old friends and lovers: Arthur Ficke and his fiancée Gladys Brown (who had become secretary to Mrs. Harry Payne Whitney), and Floyd Dell and his pretty blond-haired wife, the socialist B. Marie Gage. Dell had met and married Gage soon after his affair with Millay ended.

Boissevain went to the gathering alone. Although Edna had not seen him

in five years, she recognized him at once. In 1918, Dell had taken the Millay
sisters to a party at Gene and Max's house on Washington Place, and weeks
later, Gene dropped by the Millay apartment and met Cora. At that time,
so soon after his wife's death, the businessman seemed invulnerable to Edna's
charm. "It was impossible to guess," Dell recalled, "that Edna Millay and
Eugen Boissevain would one day be married to one another." In 1918, when
Dell had taken Millay to Boissevain's, "They were certainly not in the least
interested in one another." But years had passed, Millay was weary and ill,
and the company of these former lovers and their wives made her wistful.
She was struck by the Dutchman's strength, exuberance, and radiant good
health. His smiles and laughter illuminated the room, reviving even her low
spirits.

Someone suggested charades. Ficke had a clever idea that might make
better use of the dramatic talent in the room and bring poor Edna to life.
He decided they should improvise scenes from the timeless story of the
bumpkin who goes to the city and falls among thieves—but instead the
victims would be city folks lost in the country. Dell recalled:

> Eugen and Edna had the part of two lovers in a delicious farcical inven-
> tion, at once Rabelaisian and romantic. They acted their parts wonder-
> fully—so remarkably, indeed, that it was apparent to us all that it wasn't
> just acting. We were having the unusual privilege of seeing a man and
> a girl fall in love with each other violently and in public, and telling
> each other so, and doing it very beautifully.

Gene and Edna fell in love that day in April. He took her home with him
in his big Mercer motorcar, and there she stayed. Perhaps no one, even
Millay, realized how ill she had been until Eugen did. He was what is today
called a "take charge" sort of guy, and he took charge of his new girlfriend
and her illness at a time when she badly needed it. We are fortunate to have
Floyd Dell's account of their meeting, so there can be no doubt of the powerful chemistry between this couple from that day on. Otherwise the poet's
cynicism, her recent mercenary approach to her liaisons, as well as her immediate need, might lead one to believe that Millay wanted this man for his
money. Some people cried "gold digger" at the time, and even after many
years together, when her income far exceeded his, the question lingered. It
is untrue and unfair. To believe this is to misunderstand one of the most
meaningful events in her life, as well as important qualities of her fate and
character, not to mention Eugen's.

Who could marry such a woman? Whom would such a woman marry, after

Cora Millay.
Library of Congress.

Henry Tolman Millay. *Library of Congress.*

Edna St. Vincent Millay before Mount Battie, 1910. *Library of Congress.*

The Whitehall Inn. Camden, Maine.

Edna St. Vincent
Millay, Camden, 1912.
Library of Congress.

LEFT: Witter "Hal" Bynner. *Library of Congress*.
RIGHT: Edmund Wilson, circa 1920. *Author's collection*.

LEFT TO RIGHT: Charles Ellis, Jan Boissevain, Norma Millay Ellis, Arthur Ficke, Gladys Brown Ficke, Edna St. Vincent Millay, Eugen Boissevain, and justice of the peace. Croton-on-Hudson, July 18, 1923. *Library of Congress*.

Edna St. Vincent Millay and Eugen Boissevain after their wedding. *Library of Congress.*

Steepletop.
Courtesy of the Edna St. Vincent Millay Society.

Edna St. Vincent Millay, circa 1924. *Library of Congress.*

Arthur Ficke, Edna St. Vincent Millay, and Eugen Boissevain, circa 1926. *Library of Congress.*

Vincent, Norma, and Kathleen, circa 1930. *Library of Congress.*

George Dillon, 1930.
*Courtesy of the University
of Syracuse Library.*

Edna St. Vincent Millay, 1939. *Library of Congress.*

Edna St. Vincent Millay,
circa 1948.

all? The answer to these questions is the name of a unique man, Eugen Boissevain. He was, literally, the "dream lover" she had summoned with candles and incantations when she was nineteen back in Camden, Maine. He was about ten years too late (but then, who would have written those sad sonnets?), yet perhaps only now was Boissevain ready for her. If she did not know this immediately, instinctively, as astral lovers sometimes recognize their mates, she quickly figured it out. As for him, he had fallen under the same spell as had countless other men, although he was more practical, more firmly grounded in reality and a self-knowledge gained from those long sessions with C. G. Jung.

Edna's meeting Eugen at this moment of her history was providential. It is hardly an exaggeration to say that she was dying in 1923, and that he saved her life. When Edna returned from France, her sister Norma found her haggard and depressed, and recalled her intimating that life was mostly behind her. "What were once mountains will perhaps be only little hills," she whispered, alluding to her prophetic poem "Renascence." She was suffering from a poisonous blockage of the intestines—"adhesions," the surgeons called them then. Now the disease is called Crohn's. Little was passing in or out of her in the way of nutrients or waste. She was starving, hollow-eyed, and hollow-cheeked, as the few photos from this period show. As she herself insisted that she "lived doubly, actually and symbolically," it is suitable to consider her illness as metaphor for her artistic obstruction: too much had gone into her delicate body, and now it had shut down, sealed itself off. Nothing more could go in or out of it—not even poetry. Everywhere she looked she saw failure: the ruins of *Hardigut*, the collapse of her lyric inspiration, even the will to love. To Norma it seemed that Edna was not long for this world.

The poetry she had already written bid fair to make her immortal—she was the most famous poet in America, hands down. On April 30, 1923, Frank Fackenthal of Columbia University wrote to her that she had been awarded the 1922 Pulitzer Prize in poetry. On May 24, the committee sent her a check for one thousand dollars. *That* pleased her. She wrote to Cora it was money "I ain't going to bust for god or hero."

Meanwhile, Boissevain sought out the finest internists and surgeons in New York City, and during that spring, while he was taking care of her in Croton, he insisted she go to the doctors until they got to the root of her problem. She had been too listless to get help herself; now she was too weak to resist his. He drove her to and from New York in his Mercer, sometimes several times a week, waiting while the doctors questioned and poked and probed and X-rayed her insides. Also, after years of neglect and incompetent dentistry, she needed a lot of work on her teeth. Eugen paid for that, too. In May he gave her the Mercer.

That spring the poet who had been too drained by life and love to write love poems wrote a delicate one, "Hyacinth," to her new lover.

> I am in love with him to whom a hyacinth is dearer
> Than I shall ever be dear.
> On nights when the field-mice are abroad he cannot sleep:
> He hears their narrow teeth at the bulbs of his hyacinths.
> But the gnawing at my heart he does not hear.

She saved the first draft for him. She inscribed it "To Eugen with all my heart, this first draft of my first poem to him," and sealed it in a small envelope with a lock of her hair and a snapshot of herself.

On May 30, 1923, she wrote to her mother apologizing for not corresponding in ages or sending money, but pointed out that she had a very good excuse: Eugen Boissevain. "I love him very much, & am going to marry him. *There!!!* Will you forgive me?" (Her mother's ensuing remoteness suggests she *was* rather put out about this sudden turn of events.) "My mind has been pretty much taken up with all this, & I have neglected my mummie.— We shall be married sometime this summer." A week later she wrote to her mother that "I have six doctors at work on me for different things." Millay was allowed to work only one hour a day, and had to lie down for fifteen.

In early July she wrote that the doctors were still perplexed about "the condition of my insides" and had decided they better perform exploratory surgery before it was too late. Because of her Pulitzer Prize, reporters were following the poet's every move, phoning Boissevain and pestering the doctors. They informed the press the operation was to remove her appendix.

※

Her decision to marry Eugen on July 18, 1923, the very day she was to go under the knife at New York Hospital, is so loaded with dramatic symbolism the occasion cannot be mere coincidence. It cries out for interpretation more than most of her poems. The scenario seems almost like the work of a clever press agent, and the double event did reap a bonanza of publicity for the recent Pulitzer winner. There were front-page headlines with glamorous photographs in all the New York newspapers. (Newsmen reported that the wedding scheduled for Friday was moved up to Wednesday because doctors ordered an emergency appendectomy. But emergency appendectomies do not wait upon pastoral marriages and wedding breakfasts.)

Obviously the couple wanted to be married *before* the risky operation, but in view of Millay's letter to Cora of May 30, any day in June would have served them just as well. The dramatist, the poet, expert manipulator of symbols and situations had to underscore the connection between medical catharsis (purification) and the life-giving sacrament of marriage. She would be married on the same day she was healed. The only way a playwright might have improved upon the allegory would have been to have the surgery *first* and the nuptials just afterward.

So, with the operating room booked at New York Hospital on West Sixteenth Street, and with scalpels honed and surgeons scrubbed and ready, Eugen and Edna were married in a grove outside the house of the painter Boardman Robinson at Croton-on-Hudson. The groom wore a three-piece suit of brown English worsted and a dark necktie subtly striped; the bride wore a green silk dress with a boat neck, golden mandalas embossed at the waist, and golden fretting on the skirt. At the last minute her sister Norma gathered up some white mosquito netting from the side porch, and (as if in memory of the lovers who had swarmed around her) draped it around Edna's head and shoulders to make a long white veil fit for a bride. Her corsage was of roses and lilies of the valley. Jan Boissevain, Eugen's brother, served as best man, and Norma as maid of honor. The other guests were Arthur Ficke and Gladys Brown, Charles Ellis (Norma's husband), and Eugen's longtime black cook and housemaid, Hattie. When the bridegroom realized that he had misplaced the ring, Hattie lent her wedding band for the ceremony. In the heat of that bright July morning, under the trees, Edna and Eugen said their vows before the justice of the peace, who pronounced them man and wife.

After a quick brunch Eugen and Arthur drove Edna down to New York Hospital. Before entering the operating room she told Arthur, "Well, if I die now, I shall be immortal." According to the *Evening Telegram*, the doctors found her happy, "one of the most cheerful patients." At noon "she had been under the anaesthetic for more than one and a half hours, and the surgeons were still at their task." The doctors expected her to be out of the hospital in two weeks, barring complications.

The transverse incision ran parallel with her waistline, seven inches long, and to the right above her navel. Her appendix had been the least of the doctors' concerns. According to Millay's letter of August 8 to Kathleen, Edna's lower intestines were so "tied down by membranes, which could not be removed" that the surgeons had to virtually rebuild the tract by cutting holes in the intestines and sewing them "together in such a way as to make a new channel." She was pleased that the scar was healing well, and "will be very soon just a tiny hairline."

Back home in Mount Airy, Eugen nursed and cared for her like a mother, like a ministering angel, as if Providence had given him another chance to save his first wife from dying. Edna thrived under his care. In August she had strength enough to work with Ficke—in his capacity as friend and fellow poet—on the final manuscript of *The Harp-Weaver and Other Poems*. At the end of that month she produced the first sonnet she had written in nearly a year, the death-haunted "I see so clearly now my similar years / Repeat each other, shod in rusty black." According to Ficke's account, she composed the sonnet in her head, without pen or paper, and dictated it to him line by line as he listened in amazement to her inspired voice. This was not a poet who would ever rest on her laurels.

※

Millay's Pulitzer Prize had made her a celebrity. Now everything she said or did was of interest to her public, particularly this unlikely marriage to a Dutch importer.

"Edna Millay Goes Under Knife After Wedding Wealthy New York Importer," read a typical headline, in this case from the *Evening Telegram*. The press loved the story, and clever journalists such as Julia McCarthy of the *Evening Journal* made sport of the ironies, great and small, of the thirty-one-year-old poet's midsummer marriage to a rich man twelve years her senior. McCarthy's headline was "Famous Love Lyricist Belies Her Own Philosophy by Marrying," followed by "Perverse Attitude Toward Grand Passion and Mockery of It as Fleeting Affair Characterize Several of Miss Millay's Best-Known Verses." Millay happened to get married on a Wednesday. So the journalist quotes from *A Few Figs from Thistles*:

> And if I loved you Wednesday,
>   Well, what is that to you?
> I do not love you Thursday—
>   So much is true.
>
> And why you come complaining
>   Is more than I can see.
> I love you Wednesday,—yes—but what
>   Is that to me?

"Whether Mr. Boissevain retained on Thursday the love he won Wednesday we do not know," McCarthy quipped. Then she mentioned the rare attitude toward love revealed in Millay's lyrics: "teasing perversity, an extreme candor, and a willingness to take love as men are reputed to, to be fickle and to be off with the old love when the fervor is gone."

Edna and her husband were about to surprise the whole world, beginning with Millay's mother and sisters, who were reasonably skeptical. But Eugen turned out to be not only a doting husband but a most considerate son-in-law and brother-in-law. While Edna convalesced, first in Croton, then at the Holley Hotel on Washington Square in the autumn, Eugen took over her correspondence, personal as well as business. His writing for her, and with her, gives us a charming view of their intimacy, as they clearly took enormous pleasure in the hours they spent together writing letters. The joint correspondence began with her recuperation from surgery, but the practice continued throughout their long marriage, because Millay would have many bouts of illness, and she could always rely upon Eugen to be a faithful and clever amanuensis. He wrote to Norma in the late summer:

> Edna is so well now that she is positively uninteresting: therefore I do not phone you any more. She sleeps like a guinea pig, eats like a trooper. The doctor is tickled to death.

Cora's correspondence from this period is not available, but it seems that she felt estranged: She had not been invited to the wedding, and she had not gone to visit her daughter at the hospital or during her convalescence in Croton. Evidently, in all the rush and confusion, Vincent neglected to tell her mother that she was getting married. So Cora was communicating via Norma. Eugen acknowledges Cora's inquiries, then asks Norma if she will be kind enough to answer his mother-in-law's indirect questions:

> Say that I was very wealthy, but lost in a sugar speculation, but will be very wealthy again in a little while. That I'm a Hollander, Irish mother, French grandparents . . . am housebroken, and am unlikely to beat Edna unless she really deserves it.

Cora seemed concerned that in haste her sick child might have married the wrong man. (Eugen's mother in Holland was happily uninformed about Edna's backward domesticity: she wrote glowingly to her new daughter-in-law how happy she was that at last her boy would have a wife to take care of him!) But Cora really had nothing to worry about. Despite his comment about the failed sugar speculation, Eugen was very well-to-do, devoted, and unfailingly generous. When at last Edna dictated to Eugen a letter to Cora, it is affectionate and high-spirited, with jokes about her scar, which she says is healing so well that "I can still be an oriental tummy-dancer and get you and me a lot of sheckels in our respective old ages." Then she teases her scribe:

Eugen is having some trouble with the spelling, have you noticed?[He isn't.] That is what occurs when a plain business man marries a literary body of colorful vocabulary and insubordinate intestines. All well and good—oh, by the way, did you hear about my getting married? Well, I'm happily married to a kind and thoughtful man, a little bit slow in the head but all the steadier for that . . . (The hussy! Don't believe her. E. B.). Now that Eugen is beginning to call me names I will discreetly close. . . .

She at last signs her letter "Edna St. Vincent Millay Boissevain. P.S. This is the first time I have writ my name in the above screamingly funny manner. I do not intend to do it often, but it is fun."

The question of Boissevain's net worth and income is interesting, pertinent, and impossible to determine. He must have had a considerable legacy in order to spend his youth as he did, and there are hints that some stream of income from a family trust continued for most of his life. One does not start up an import business without capital. It is certain that his business had made a fortune by the early 1920s, though like any fortune his ebbed and flowed. He lived and entertained well, dressed in fine English suits, drove expensive automobiles. And from the day he met his future wife he believed that nothing was too good for her, showering her with costly—and very thoughtful—presents. He bought her a solid gold mechanical pencil and a diamond watch and a bracelet of the finest oriental pearls. He sent her to the most exclusive shops on Fifth Avenue to buy whatever shoes and dresses she liked (and she liked only the best) with orders never to look at the price tags. In an unpublished letter to him in January 1924 she refers to "my $42,000 emerald ring you bought me, my beautiful ring, so much too valuable for me to wear with any degree of safety." When she was not wearing the emerald ring (which perfectly complemented her green eyes and red hair) the gem resided in a safe deposit box, and sometimes in a showcase at Cartier's on Fifth Avenue. This is crucial data. Boissevain had tied up more than half-a-million dollars in today's currency in a single token of his affection.

Eugen helped Edna pay off her debts to Arthur Ficke, John Carter, and other lovers who had helped her in times of need. That autumn Edna wrote to her mother, ecstatic and proud that she had paid off her mother's outstanding debts in Camden. "I suppose it is a mean pride in me, but, oh, I wish I could have done this before I got married!—because of course everybody thinks it is my rich husband who has done it, when in fact it is really I myself, every cent of it, with money I made by writing—nearly a thousand dollars, in all, since you went to Camden."

She was deceiving herself. She had been living with Boissevain for nearly seven months, a man to whom her one thousand dollars Pulitzer Prize money was pocket change, and who, at this point in their marriage, would not let her pick up the tab for even so much as a cup of coffee.

On October 26, 1923, Eugen took Edna and her sisters on a luxurious trip to Montreal for a weekend at the Ritz-Carlton. As the Boissevains had not yet enjoyed a real honeymoon, Norma and Kathleen were greatly impressed with Eugen's breadth of spirit, not to mention the depth of his wallet, in sharing his bride with her two sisters.

Millay was well enough to travel alone to Washington, D.C., on November 18 to attend the unveiling of statues to Susan B. Anthony and other founders of the Women's Party. There she recited the sonnet "The Pioneer" ("Take up the song; forget the epitaph"), which later she dedicated to Inez Milholland. But she caught cold on the train. In a letter to her mother a month later she observed that "somehow, ever since my operation, I catch cold twice as easy, & the dentist hurts me twice as much, etc." This early mention of her pain threshold is significant. Her doctors would have given her opiates to recover from abdominal surgery in 1923, before they learned to administer them in safe moderation. Morphine, taken in excess, reduces pain tolerance even as it loses its own effectiveness in assuaging pain. As a result many patients suffered from the overadministration of morphine.

November 19, 1923, the day she returned from Washington, was also the date on which Harper & Brothers published *The Harp-Weaver and Other Poems* to resounding praise on both sides of the Atlantic. Poet and publisher had gained the unique advantage of having the Pulitzer announced long before the book's publication. The committee awarded the prize based on part of its contents, which had appeared in periodicals a year earlier. And after the blitz of publicity attendant upon Millay's illness and matrimony, this book of poems was poised for a spectacular success—equally popular with the public and the critics. The prominent English poet-critic Arthur Symons compared her to Keats and Poe. The *Times Literary Supplement* proclaimed, "Hers is 'the naked thinking heart' of a modern Donne. There is an ascetic hardness, an almost algebraic precision, about the form of her shorter lyrics which creates the illusion of moving in a world of pure idea. And yet she never chills us with casuistry because her heart is intent as well as her mind, and out of the clash of the two almost all of her best poetry is born." She cherished the comparison with Donne because it was apt and her poetry was becoming more complex, moving in a "metaphysical" direction;

later her detractors would conjure Donne as a standard by which they found her deficient.

※

Eugen had signed a lease in November to rent a house in the Village, 75½ Bedford Street, one year for $2,400. The main entrance opened within a courtyard and garden across from the Cherry Lane Theatre. The three-story, six-room brick row house with fireplaces in every room was only 9½ feet wide by 30 feet deep. They called it the "dollhouse," furnished it, and moved there in December, hosting their first formal dinner as a married couple, for family and friends, on Christmas Day.

"Any day I may have an hour of extraordinary beauty in my life," Boissevain informed the journalist Allan Macdougall, who interviewed the husband about his marriage. "It is so obvious to anyone that Vincent is more important than I am." He consecrated his life to his wife's freedom—a paradoxical marriage plan, because the institution opposes freedom. Yet the marriage flourished because of their mutual generosity and irrepressible humor. Boissevain's values were admirably clear-cut. "If she wrote *one* sonnet a year it seems to me important that she be free to write that sonnet," he told Macdougall. "Anyone can buy and sell coffee."

A letter from Boissevain's mother on the second day of the New Year mentions that he has recently had to liquidate his business. There were several reasons for this, but debt was not one of them. At forty-three years of age, after seven years as an importer, Eugen had made enough profit to live off his investments; he was tired of the East India trade. He wanted to devote his life to Edna St. Vincent Millay and her career, just as he had devoted himself to Inez Milholland and hers. He did not, in 1924, foresee that the stock market would melt down before the decade was done, any more than he could imagine that his wife, the lyric poet, would soon become the highest-paid poet-dramatist in American history. But between husband and wife there would never be a harsh word about who made, or who spent, the most money.

Their plan for the year was to take a trip around the world (to make up for the long-delayed honeymoon). Millay and her publishers had been scheduling a poetry reading tour to promote *The Harp-Weaver*. So while Boissevain attended to the liquidation of his company in Manhattan, she left for Washington, D.C., on January 15, alone, on the only lecture tour she would ever undertake without Eugen at her side. She did not see him again until late February when she returned to New York for two weeks. Then she and

Eugen headed for Cheyenne, Wyoming, where she had a poetry reading, en route to San Francisco where she had another. This reading tour, which included Charleston (West Virginia), Louisville, St. Louis, Pittsburgh, Columbus, Cleveland, Rochester, Chicago, Milwaukee, Minneapolis, Indianapolis, Omaha, and Cedar Rapids—more than thirty readings in twenty cities—was grueling but profitable. She netted more than two thousand dollars. Millay was delighted by the size of her audiences and their enthusiasm, amazed by how many people had read her books and how many readers knew her poems by heart.

From trains and hotel rooms, she wrote to Eugen almost daily. Her letters to him are love letters unlike any she had ever written, overflowing with affection, endearments, and expressions of how much she misses him—yet they are as finely detailed and humorous as her mail to Cora. When she returned to her suite at the Shoreham in D.C. late on the night of January 17, after her poetry reading, a bouquet of long-stemmed roses awaited her. She wrote to him: "Darling—The beautiful roses came. Thank you, my sweetheart. I am taking them with me to Louisville. How did you manage it so quickly, with your own writing on the card?"

Passing through West Virginia she wrote:

> This is a desolate place,—steep hills dotted with tiny shacks and rows
> of coke-ovens, rising straight from the wicked, wicked river, full of rap-
> ids here. Someone has built a little house directly in front of and at the
> foot of an enormous, isolated boulder, though the river below, cluttered
> and distraught with just such rocks as this, must tell him what is in the
> boulder's mind.

All night she had kept her husband's roses wrapped in wet paper and a towel. "My roses are dying now. I could put them in the water in the woman's dressing room . . . but I believe they would rather die privately here with me, than live in a public bowl where undistinguished people wash their hands. They mayn't live forever. I send a petal from one of them. I have kissed it."

The long reading tour was crucial in consolidating Millay's reputation as well as her self-concept as an important artist and celebrity whose destiny set her apart from others. After that arduous tour of 1924, Millay's thirst for public applause was permanently slaked. The reading tours she undertook in later years, under Eugen's supervision, were done strictly for the money and to deliver the poetry personally to her public. She did not relish the performances ("Oh, Jesus! If ever I felt like a prostitute it was last night"), and after 1939 no amount of cash could lure her back onto the sawdust trail of American poetry.

At times the poet's sense of her own uniqueness expresses itself in curious, meaningful ways, as in her personal hygiene:

> My hands are so dirty it's almost theatrical. Everybody who looks at me wonders why such a nice girl, with such a beautiful gold pencil, & such expensive cuff-links, & such a refined and elegant address-book, has such dirty hands.—I don't care. I'm tired of washing my hands. It's a great waste of time. Besides, in the winter it's dangerous. It is likely to roughen the skin.

This is the famous woman who had been the frail girl in a Camden tenement, scrubbing clothing and washing dishes until her hands cracked and bled—Cinderella, who had grown up and married a prince.

On February 15 a journalist reviewed her performance at Catherine Strong Hall at the University of Rochester, New York. He described her as slender, with bobbed hair, and noted that she more resembled a shy undergraduate than a successful poet and playwright. In a simple blue dress, with a brilliant yellow silk scarf wrapped around her shoulders, she was "wistful, appealing, and in every way lives up to the image of the poet-girl of fiction." She read selections from her earlier books—"When the Years Grow Old," "God's World," "Elaine," and "Travel"—before giving a spirited recital of "The Ballad of the Harp-Weaver" that brought tears to the eyes of many. Then for comic relief she recited her children's poems in her brightest little-girl voice:

> All the grown-up people say
> "What, those ugly thistles?
> Mustn't touch them! Keep away!
> Prickly! Full of bristles!"
>
> Yet they never make me bleed
> Half so much as roses!
> Must be purple is a weed,
> And pink and white is posies.

Many years as an actress and playwright had taught her how to script and pace a program, and how to work an audience. Playing all four characters in her new drama *Two Slatterns and a King*, she brought the comedy alive

by herself. Of course, the climax of her reading was the haunting "Renascence," which audiences always found spellbinding. After this she closed
with a few short poems, the "Figs" from her second book, and "Recuerdo":

> We were very tired, we were very merry—
> We had gone back and forth all night on the ferry.
> It was bare and bright, and smelled like a stable—
> But we looked into a fire, we leaned across a table,
> We lay on the hill-top underneath the moon;
> And the whistles kept blowing, and the dawn came soon.

The reporter noted, "At times the reading of her verses was as quiet
and simple as the blue dress, at times as flaming as the flame-colored scarf
that clung about her." Between poems she chatted with the audience in an
informal manner, but as soon as she began to recite (she held the book
before her but rarely glanced at it) "she withdrew herself entirely within
the poem." Most remarkable to the journalist was that with all the power
and enthusiasm of her expression he saw no trace of "artificial rhetoricism.
The fine lyric quality of her verses was allowed to stand forth unobscured
by posing and affectation." This is the art that conceals art: the actress had
learned to appear natural and spontaneous performing the same set pieces
night after night.

Millay granted this reporter a rare personal interview in a taxi on the way
from the train station to her hotel on the day of her reading. He met the
poet as she stepped off the train, a petite young woman dressed in a big fur
coat and a cloche hat of periwinkle blue, her auburn hair curling out from
under it. Millay sat scrunched in the corner of the taxi, "so frail and appealing and so very little that one hesitated to ask too many questions. She has
an unusually sensitive face, rather small features, and serious eyes with a
direct gaze which convey the impression that Miss Millay is giving you her
entire attention."

The reporter confined his questions to the subjects of love and marriage,
and the poet answered straightforwardly:

> Marriage, if not abused, is one of the most civilized institutions . . .
> but swimming is one of the most wonderful sports, and yet there are
> always some people who cannot swim who insist on going into the
> water and getting drowned. Many people spoil marriage in like man-
> ner. One should be sure she knows how to be married before rushing
> into it.

Asked if she were a "Lucy Stoner" (a follower of Lucy Stone, who advocated married women keeping their maiden names), she replied, "I am not a rabid Lucy Stoner and shouldn't feel at all insulted if I were called Mrs. Boisse-vain." She shyly conceded that she was terribly in love with her husband. And when challenged about maintaining her identity in marriage she replied: "Anyone who is a real person will never lose his or her identity. But as in any partnership, where one member has a stronger mentality and will he eventually tends to submerge the other. So it is in marriage. It isn't the fault of marriage. It is a matter of the human equation."

※

Eugen and Edna sailed on April 19 from San Francisco on a Japanese ship bound for Honolulu, Japan, China, Java, Singapore, India, and Marseilles. Despite bouts of illness in India, their journey was exciting, challenging, and memorable. Toward the end, in October, when Eugen was laid up with phlebitis at the Hotel Prince Albert in Paris, his left leg in a wire frame straight out in front of him, his wife nursed him and shaved him, applying the cotton wadding and rubber sheeting as the doctor ordered. When called upon she could—and would—step into nurse Cora's role. They spent months in Paris, where Eugen once saw Edna rush into a flower shop to water some forced apple blossoms she feared were dying of thirst. He loved to tell that story; he adored his wife the more time he spent with her.

Just after Thanksgiving they sailed for New York on the *Aquitania*, return-ing to their "dollhouse" on Bedford Street more in love than when they had left it. In that happy home Arthur Ficke married Gladys Brown on December 8, 1924. The newlywed Fickes moved into a studio apartment above the Cherry Lane Theatre. From their windows the Fickes could look out at the Boissevains' residence across the courtyard.

STEEPLETOP

❧

When she grew tired of the crowds and traffic noises of Manhattan and wanted silence and clear views of the horizon at sunset and the stars at night, he bought her a seven-hundred-acre berry farm in the Berkshires.

They found the property, a retreat nestled on a hillside ringed by wooded mountains, in March 1925, and settled on it quickly. Edna called it "Steepletop," after the steeplebush (hardhack) flowers that grew wild there. They took great delight in remodeling the house and landscaping the acreage to conform with their ideal of country living. An extensive and lucrative poetry reading tour that spring helped to pay for extensive renovations of the old farmhouse in the mountains, and the Boissevains moved to the country in June.

Two miles up a winding dirt road from the hamlet of Austerlitz, New York, stood the iron gate on fieldstone stanchions that guarded the circular driveway. The main entrance to the house, in the west elevation, faced the driveway. The doorway—with its sidelights and semicircular transom—was covered by an arched entrance porch with a gabled roof. The two-story clapboard house with its steep roof and central chimney was built just after the Civil War. Steepletop would be the poet's home for the rest of her life.

The main door led into a stair hall with a stone floor. Directly ahead was the dining room. To the right was the parlor, which extended the whole length of the house and took the southern light through the side door and windows. Here Millay kept her two pianos, with her bust of Sappho in a corner. She hung the windows with flowered linen curtains. She and Eugen enjoyed many intimate meals here before the hearth.

North of the entrance hall was the kitchen and a small pantry, and beyond the kitchen another small room with a wood-burning stove.

Just up the steep narrow staircase, which took a single turn at a landing near the base—where the poet liked to sit and chat as guests arrived and departed—was the poet's library. Covering all four walls of this long room across the front of the house ranged the poet's vast book collection: her reference books (dictionaries and grammars in many languages, law books, complete works of naturalists such as Fabre and Burroughs, twenty volumes of the American Stud Book, and other books on racing), as well as her personal library of poetry, fiction, history, and philosophy. She kept every book that she and her mother had ever owned, some heavily annotated. She also kept the books that Eugen and Inez had collected. There was scarce room for pictures: above the south window was an ancient portrait of the Pompeii lady holding her stylus; above the library table was an etching of Shelley; and in a nook of bookshelves hung a small photograph of Robinson Jeffers. The large room north of the library was Millay's study, with a doorway to the bedroom and another to the bath.

Through the short hallway at the stair landing was the main entrance to Edna's bedroom, located on the northeast corner of the second story. She often wrote in bed, when ill health or inclement weather discouraged her from walking through the pinewoods to her cabin studio. The mahogany headboard of the bed stood between the windows against the north wall; to its left was a tall mahogany chest of drawers. A few feet from the foot of the low-postered bed she could see a small semicircular fireplace with a brick mantel. At the southeast corner upstairs, off Edna's bedroom, was a long, bright, beautifully tiled bathroom with vanity table, shower, bidet, and a towering old-fashioned body scale with a big round dial. She weighed herself daily, and during the 1920s her weight varied from 97 pounds to 115, depending on her nerves.

On the other side of the stairway, to the north over the kitchen, they had built an addition to the old farmhouse—an ell with a gabled roof. Upstairs a booklined hallway led to another bathroom, a guest room, and the bedroom occupied by Eugen. (In the manner of European high society, husband and wife each kept a separate boudoir.)

The house faces a terrace that falls off sharply toward East Hill Road. They planted a fabulous rose garden leading down the driveway to a flat clearing where they installed a roofed wet bar and, in 1934, a large swimming pool. Below the swimming pool they landscaped a small park and amphitheater, with benches and a few small statues of nymphs and fauns. The many outbuildings included a two-story eighteenth-century guest house with gable roof and two brick chimneys across East Hill Road, and farther down the road an enormous barn with a curved roof.

On the top of the highest hill, ten minutes' walk from the house, they cleared an acre of land with a spectacular view of the surrounding hills and valleys (not another house or barn in sight). Up there they built a tennis court, where they played with their visitors and neighbors almost every day in good weather.

Between the house and the tennis court, about fifty yards' walk uphill through a pine grove, past an enormous rock of white flint, stood Millay's writing studio. The small cabin of unpainted boards with a gabled roof had sash windows in two side walls and a narrow door on the south side. It was furnished with a small desk and chair, a bureau, an armchair, a chaise longue, and a table stacked with books. An ornate iron "Sylvan Red Cross" wood-stove kept the space warm.

Millay's friend, the composer Deems Taylor, had been commissioned by the Metropolitan Opera to write an opera just before the Boissevains bought Steepletop, and he wanted Millay as his librettist. In this pine-shaded cabin during 1925–1926, Millay wrote the ingenious libretto for *The King's Hench-man*. And here in 1927–1928 she composed many of the poems included in the pastoral, pensive volume *The Buck in the Snow* (published September 27, 1928).

Meanwhile the resourceful, versatile Eugen became a gentleman farmer, cultivating the farmland and livestock for what profit it might yield. He pursued this agrarian enterprise with the same enthusiasm, common sense, and determination he had brought to Olympic rowing, the import business, psychoanalysis, and his wife's career, which henceforth he managed with a steady hand and shrewd eye on the bottom line. Some years the farm turned a profit; other years it was a tax write-off against his wife's bountiful royalties. But the farm was always a pleasure to him—perhaps even more than to his wife who was often too ill to enjoy it. Like Edna, Eugen was an amateur naturalist. He delighted in learning the names, colors, and habits of every bird and plant species to be found in Columbia County.

Master chef and connoisseur of wines (he published articles on cooking), sportsman, gardener, breeder of dogs and horses, Boissevain lived for plea-sure, and his wife's was his own. They always dressed for dinner: there are amusing photographs of the two of them, Eugen in tux, pouring the wine, Edna in furs, eating dinner with full service in front of their house on a terrace white with snow. He was bursting with energy. Snowbound in early winter, with a hip flask of brandy in his pocket and a cigarette dangling from his lips, Eugen, dressed in his red coat, would snowshoe the two miles down the mountain to the post office in Austerlitz, and return, rosy-cheeked, with Edna's heavy sack of fan mail. As long as there were plenty of cigarettes and a cellarful of wine and gin, nothing much ever disturbed the Dutchman's equanimity.

His mission at Steepletop was simply to make way for Millay's poetry. "She must not," he told reporter Macdougall, "have too many of those other mundane moments in a woman's life—moments when her world is filled with making lists, housekeeping matters. . . . She must not be dulled by routine acts; she must ever remain open to fresh contact with life's intensities." He found her restless and impulsive. By July of 1925 she was plagued by headaches. Eugen would say, "I must start something else—invite dangerous, stimulating people here; make things happen." He had observed that she did not keep regular hours for work, dining, or much else. "If I let her struggle with problems of order . . . she doesn't write." His solution was simple. "I look after everything."

The writer Joan Dash, in a perceptive 1975 monograph on the Boissevains' marriage, commented that Eugen assumed the role of a devoted parent. While Millay gratefully accepted it, that role, like the routine that inevitably goes with marriages, would eventually demystify their romance and take some of the shine off it. But this would not happen for several years. In the meantime Steepletop became the ideal dwelling place for the poet, a sanctuary where she concentrated fully on her poetry—a spacious, picturesque homestead where she could entertain family and friends from near and far. Witter Bynner came to visit, and Elinor Wylie arrived with her husband, Bill Benét. Max and Eliena Eastman spent time there, as did Floyd Dell and his wife. Cora loved it, joining them for their first Christmas holiday there in 1926. Arthur and Gladys Ficke spent many weeks at Steepletop before purchasing a small farm nearby in April 1927. They called theirs "Hardhack," another name for the steeplebush blossom. As Millay and Ficke had prophesied, nothing would ever come between them; now geography, which had frustrated them for so long, brought them together.

The Boissevains' easy-come, easy-go approach to financial planning is evident in a letter of September 16, 1926, from Edna at Steepletop to her sister Kathleen in New York. Eugen and Edna had lent Kathleen's husband (the playwright Howard Young) two hundred dollars. Now Edna wanted the money back because "in two weeks we leave for Santa Fe to visit Arthur and Gladys for a few weeks. No, we're not flush—we're broke! Arthur is sending us railroad fare and expenses." As they lived beyond their means, there was often a cash-flow problem. Edna explained to Kathleen that she and Eugen had just bought the farm across the road, paying cash. They were afraid someone else would buy the land and build something ugly there. So at the moment they hadn't a dollar to put gasoline in the Mercer.

Yet they boarded the train to Santa Fe; they went on living and spending as if money would never be more than a fleeting problem. Incredibly generous, by the 1930s they would be supporting half a dozen people, family and friends. The increasing sales of her books, the soon-to-be-published libretto of *The King's Henchman* (which was cleverly designed, produced, and marketed), and a new poetry collection promised to Harper's meant a ceaseless stream of royalties. And now she was so valuable to her publishers they could not deny her requests for whopping advances on those royalties. During the second half of 1928 her royalty income from Harper's would total fifteen thousand dollars (in today's currency, worth more than two hundred thousand dollars). This was modest compared with what was to come. So however Eugen's fortunes, dividends, and annuities ebbed and flowed, Edna's books, plays, and readings guaranteed the couple would never be broke for long.

That winter she wrote to her mother that from now on the three sisters would each send Cora thirty-five dollars at the beginning of every month. And she reminded her mother that she must come down from Newburyport to New York in February for the opening of *The King's Henchman*. "There will be at least four performances, the 17th, the 28th, and two later. But of course you'll want to be there for the premiere. And Harry Dowd's Mozart opera *La Finta* opens January 17 just a month before mine, and Norma is singing Serpetta. . . . Isn't that thrilling?" Cora could see both shows in the same week. "What a lovely life it is! Isn't it, darling?" After a few lines about practical matters, Vincent writes: "Golly, the snow's getting pink. I must go!" And an hour later she returns to her stationery. "I had to run and look at the color. It was marvelous tonight,—that deepest rose-pink that you get once in a while, you know, with bright blue shadows. It's so beautiful here. *You* know."

⁂

Dressed in a red velvet gown with a long train, Millay sat with her husband, in white tie, and the composer Deems Taylor and his wife Mary high in a theater box in the golden horseshoe of the Metropolitan Opera House. Nerves had whittled the poet down to her low weight of ninety-seven pounds. Cora watched the opera from the orchestra, where she sat with Norma and Kathleen and their husbands.

Millay had based the story on Aethelwold, the King's henchman. Sent forth to fetch a bride for the King, Aethelwold falls in love with the girl and marries her himself, a tragic mistake (shades of Synge's *Deirdre*). Tenor Edward Johnson sang the henchman's role, while a young baritone named Lawrence Tibbett brought down the house with his performance as the King. The premiere that Thursday night, February 17, 1927, was an important event in the history of opera: "It is almost incontestable that the lyric drama of Miss Millay and Mr. Taylor is the greatest American opera so far," decreed *The New Yorker*. And as far as the Millay family was concerned, this was the greatest public triumph yet of Vincent's career.

The first-night success commanded more performances, fabulous book sales, and eventually a thirty-city tour for *The King's Henchman*. On March 9, she wrote in her diary:

> Today on the front page of the *World* we came upon "$100 a day for Poet of King's Henchman" and an article about how my book has already sold 10,000 copies. . . . I was thrilled to death. That the amount of royalties I get for a book of poems should be of front page interest to the great New York public—well I just sat for ten minutes with my eyes sticking out, drinking it in—oh what a thrilling winter this has been! Ugin and I—what fun we've had!—how happy we are!

The next day the sun shone brightly, and she announced that this was the first day of spring. "All I wanted to do was sit in the sun. And Ugin [the familiar Dutch spelling of Eugen is Ugin] and the dog and the cat and the cows and the horses and the pigs all felt the same. We went to Austerlitz for the mail with Bonnie [the horse] and the red sled. The snow was so nearly gone on much of the road that I believe the next time will be on wheels."

But winter was not yet done with them. Not wanting to miss her curtain calls at the Met, Edna had Eugen take her to New York on Friday, March 11—first by horse and sleigh to State Line, then four hours by train to Manhattan to hear the opera. The next afternoon they took the 3:20 out of Grand Central for State Line. One of their field hands, named Baily, met them at the train with a wagon and drove them to a livery stable where he stayed while Eugen and Edna went on in the sleigh. The night was dark and overcast, and the lanterns on the sleigh shed only a ghost of light on the hills of snow. They had not driven far before Eugen, trying to avoid deep drifts, misjudged a gap in the hedge and turned off the road too early. The horses foundered in snow up to their flanks, then spooked, reared, and plunged whinnying into a thicket. A tree branch whipped Edna smartly across her open left eye. "Incredible pain, a million constellations, very sick for a few minutes," she later recalled in her diary. "But I said nothing, not considering it very serious, and went back to fetch Baily and Stanley while Eugen held the horses." It took the two men with axes to cut the team and sled out of the thicket. When the Boissevains finally arrived home her eye was "frightfully swollen, discolored and disfigured, and extremely painful."

STEEPLETOP · { 193 } ·

She had scratched her cornea. "The slightest increase of light, causing the pupil to contract, is like the stab of a sword. The sudden striking of a match in the room, untold agony. Cannot open my eyes at all—to open the right brings on loathsome scraping pain in the left as well."

She lay in the dark and Eugen fed her dinner with a spoon. The next day he took her to the oculist in Pittsfield, who pronounced the wound "terribly serious," and prescribed belladonna drops three times a day until it healed. Ophthalmologists now treat this with saline petroleum ointments to prevent the damaged cells from adhering to the eyelid. The painkiller belladonna would not help the wound to heal. She could not read or write for weeks. Abrasions of the cornea are notoriously painful and take six months to a year to heal, sometimes longer. The eye trouble made her headaches worse.

※

The great baritone Lawrence Tibbett gave his librettist a white leather-bound diary with gold-leaf edges as an opening-night gift on February 17. She wrote in it faithfully until November of that year, and the 1927 diary reveals a climacteric personality change. In the six months from the February premiere of *The King's Henchman*, through the pain of her accident in March, to the execution of the anarchists Sacco and Vanzetti on August 23, Millay steadily descended from the giddy pinnacle of ecstasy to the depths of depression. She suffered from a combination of physical, mental, and nervous ailments, all of them vague except for the scratched cornea. The treatments were sometimes more troubling than the complaints. She drank heavily. Psychiatrists, in casual conversation about Edna St. Vincent Millay, have glibly described her as "manic-depressive and death-obsessed," as if those few words might make short work of the poet and her personality. Give this patient lithium and her problems would vanish. But the poet's psyche defies simple analysis. If Millay chose to medicate herself with alcohol, it is impossible to determine which disease she was treating—eye pain, headaches, jittery nerves, or chronic depression.

April started with a delightful visit from Elinor Wylie and Bill Benét. "Elinor, Bill, Gene & I walked up to the top of the hill and looked at the Catskills & all the beautiful hills spread out" (April 3). They spent their evenings before the fire, reading poetry. They discussed "the relative weight of 'St. Agnes Eve' and 'Epipsychidion'—not as poems—but as love poems, Elinor holding that the last 20 lines or so [of "Epipsychidion"] are highly sensuous and impassioned, I insisting that, except for a phrase or two, they are so much rhetorical hot air. . . . Finally she read [Shelley's] the 'West Wind.' 'The best poem ever written!' she cried when she finished. I did not dispute her," although Millay suspected she liked Keats's "Grecian Urn" better. The next morning Elinor sat reading her own novel *Mortal Image*, "while I played first Chopin, then Bach, then Beethoven on the piano. I play so badly. But not too badly, I think, to be not allowed to play them. It was fun, Elinor there reading, & listening too" (April 5).

Her old friend, composer Harrison Dowd, visited in May, and Cora also came then to help plant the rose garden. Witter Bynner would visit that spring, and Max and Eliena Eastman, too. Friends and family brought diversion, and Edna's colorful diary records her joy in the flowers, birds, and other wildlife on the farm—from the first mayflowers to the "crow driving its hawk from its neighborhood, swooping at it & rising & swooping" to "the song of Sebastian, one of last year's song-sparrows." She joined Eugen in some of the gardening and housekeeping chores: "Ugin and I worked all day digging up & transplanting the snow-ball bushes . . . & raked and burned the driveway circle and other odd jobs" (April 9).

But she was not happy, and her sadness sometimes came in response to the natural landscape that she admired so romantically. On April 12 one of her Russian wolfhounds, Altair, "found a nest of baby moles. They must have just been born, three of them, all red & grey. . . . We remembered that they were moles, and that we are farmers, so we killed them. It made me really sick. And I cried. It is true that my tears come easily, at times." When she was younger she cried *only* when she was angry. "But life is cruel, & on a farm very cruel—there's no getting around that. It was thinking of their mother that made me cry. She had just that moment given birth to them, strange little blind creatures."

Two weeks later in her diary she described her encounter with the "Juggernaut":

> From the onrushing wheels of the tractor I saved, for the present, at least, my favorite patch of wild strawberries—covering an area not quite so big as my bathroom. But everybody was very much upset because I was interfering with the straight line from X to Y. And I knew that soon the day would come when all the wild strawberries, & all the daisies and hawkweed would be ploughed under to make a straight line for the tractor.—So I went down into the clearing below the blueberry pasture, & cried & cried & cried.—The most dreadful day, physically, that ever dawned, icy cold & the wind blowing a gale, deafening and confounding.

Her main outlet for her furies and frustrations was never, so far as one
can tell, her husband; it was, sadly and embarrassingly, the servants and the
farmhands. When Baily and Pinnie accidently cut down a bush she had
meant to transplant, because it stood in the way of a fence they were building, she wept bitterly and called them "great flat-footed, fat-headed gal-
umphing dumb-bells." Her feuds with housemaids and cooks were unending,
as she hired and fired one after another.

Eugen was continually going behind her, sweeping up emotional wreckage, consoling and rehiring fed-up servants. The vehemence with which she
curses them is Olympian and Rabelaisian. One cook is so fat her mistress
calls her The Three Graces; another she suspects of poisoning her. "She is
the foulest and most venomous slut I have yet had in the house, which is
going some." But beneath the humor her cruelty is profoundly disturbing.
At length she concludes, in October of that year, "The only people I really
hate are servants. They are not really human beings at all. They have no
conscience, no heart, no sense of responsibility, no memory of kind treatment
or past favors. Even their sins are not human sins, but the sins of spiders
and magpies, of monkeys, serpents and pigs."

Millay is not altogether leveling with us: She does hate other sorts of
people, and her diary will be more and more explicit about them in years to
come. But by the end of 1927 she seems to have internalized the cruelty in
nature she has witnessed on the farm and recorded in her diary on April 12.
And she has divided all of conscious life into two distinct species: those
worthy of her love and tenderness—including her family, her poet friends,
dogs, cats, birds—and everybody else, servants foremost among the hateful.

Something has gone wrong here. This is not the girl whose diary from
1909 overflows with all-embracing love and charity. Something is going hay-
wire. Remembering the vulnerability of her early years and her perfectionism,
perhaps the woman could not abide vulnerability or flaws in anyone around
her. Such psychology scarcely accounts for such vast rage.

Plenty of evidence this year and later indicates that the flaws and kinks
in the poet's psyche were aggravated by physical disease. The headaches date
back to 1925, after her complete recovery from abdominal surgery; these
were probably related to the heavy drinking that she chronicles in her diary,
with her consumption of liquor increasing in 1927. Nearly every writer drank
too much during Prohibition, and Millay was no exception. But she weighed
only a hundred pounds, and would match a grown man like Eugen drink
for drink from noon until midnight. Alcoholism is progressive, and one can
chart the inexorable advance of Millay's drinking in her diaries. The painful

scratched cornea colluded with her headaches. After her eye injury there are frequent "humorous" references to "getting tight." The pain made her irritable; alcohol relieved her for the evening, and a hangover made her short-tempered again.

On June 27, 1927, she had a D&C (dilation and curettage) at Mount Sinai Hospital in New York. She wrote in her diary, "They are lovely here and give me all the morphine I want—ply me with morphine." Doctors were less careful with opiates in the 1920s then they are today; they probably prescribed enough morphine to keep the poet free from all discomfort for weeks after her operation. But by August, her nerves were a wreck.

The Boissevains went to Boston on August 21, joining novelist John Dos Passos, poets Lola Ridge and Dorothy Parker, and other writers in a last-ditch effort to save the anarchists Sacco and Vanzetti from the electric chair. The cobbler and the fish peddler had been charged with murdering a paymaster and guard at a shoe factory in South Braintree, Massachusetts. In July of 1921 the men were found guilty of murder. But because the defendants had been draft dodgers and philosophical anarchists, many observers believed their radicalism had influenced the verdict. Judge Webster Thayer denied motions for a rehearing, and the Supreme Court of Massachusetts would not intervene. As the case dragged on for six years, it polarized the nation, liberal vs. conservative, poor vs. rich; intellectuals almost unanimously defended the condemned men. In early August, Millay wrote a bitter poem.

> The sun that warmed our stooping backs and withered the weed
>   uprooted—
> We shall not feel it again.
> We shall die in darkness, and be buried in the rain. . . .
>   . . . .
> Evil does overwhelm
> The larkspur and the corn . . .
>   (from "Justice Denied in Massachusetts")

Millay's campaign for the Italian anarchists was the most public political act of her life. While it is impertinent to question her motives, the action begs for perspective: She never did anything else like this. She was not Inez Milholland. Heartfelt, the demonstration was completely impulsive, yet on the basis of it—and on a tract she published called *Fear*, reflecting on what she termed the "Tragedy"—the public regarded the poet as a "parlor pink" until the 1940s, when she wrote so emotionally on behalf of the Allies during World War II.

Edna and Eugen stayed at the Copley-Plaza, where Millay arranged to give out her poem "Justice Denied in Massachusetts" to the press. In her diary she notes that "though all the New York papers used this, none of the Boston papers did." Her entry of August 22 is humorously self-conscious:

> Began this terrible day in an absurd fashion, shut in the hotel while a tailor across the road struggled with the only dress I had brought, and which I found, having recently put on at the doctor's orders 17 pounds, I could not nearly get into. Went down to the Joy Street Police Station and bailed out picketers up to about $800. Shocked to find how few people whose names I know were here in Boston to protest. Went with Dos Passos, Lola Ridge and about four others to picket the state house, carrying a placard saying 'Free Them and Save Massachusetts. American Honor dies with Sacco and Vanzetti.'

They marched up and down for ten minutes, while an enormous crowd watched them, and photographers popped away at the notables, before police arrested the literati and took them to that same Joy Street station house where Millay had just bailed out others.

She wrote in her diary, "Bailed out by Eugen, and Art Hays. Went to see Governor Fuller; talked to his secretary; finally admitted. Very courteous, but gave me no hope." Millay wrote to the governor pleading for a stay of execution, a letter that has been admired and reprinted for generations. ("I cry to you with a million voices.... Exert the clemency which your high office affords. There is need in Massachusetts of a great man tonight. It is not yet too late for you to be that man.") The Boissevains and the various writers sat up all night in lawyer Art Hays's hotel room keeping a death-watch. She wrote in her diary of August 23: "I knew that even at that moment Vanzetti was being strapped to the chair. Agony, agony in my heart to think how late I had come there ... there must be thousands here already and I would be just an intruder if noticed at all.... Barbarous, loathsome capital punishment ... the act of a frightened state against two radicals, who may or may not have committed a murder." She believed they were innocent. "But this was never the point, their innocence or guilt of anything save anarchy." Millay, Shelley's disciple, was appalled that anarchy might prove a hanging matter to the state.

She need not have worried about being noticed. When she made her entrance in court the next day with 150 others on a charge of "sauntering and loitering," Millay would be singled out, showcased, and made an example of by a Judge Sullivan. Interrupting Art Hays, the judge pointed to Millay and several others, saying, "Mr. Hays, I'm afraid this is just a waste of time. My mind is pretty well made up. I shall find these defendants guilty." In her diary she described him as "a very refined and clean little pig in his black robe, pulling his tiny grey beard and chuckling to himself."

The liberal press dubbed her an American Joan of Arc. Her trial was set for mid-November. On August 25, before returning to Steepletop, she visited a Dr. Myerson at the psychopathic hospital in Boston, "and had him examine me for a possible nervous disorder which might account for my head and eyes. No trouble at all, excepting that my reflex actions are much quicker than in the normal person. . . . He says I must try not to react so thoroughly to the least little thing about me—not to throw myself into things the way I do.—Well, I'll try—God help me." She was hypersensitive and lucky to have her husband as a buffer between her and the world. Eugen rarely left her side.

She returned to Boston on November 16, and wrote to her mother that her "trial is postponed again here. Heaven knows when it will come up now—I don't imagine anybody will go to jail—It would have been marvelous publicity (not for *me*—, I mean for the Sacco & Vanzetti defense people) if the trial had been today, as *The King's Henchman* is playing here all this week." Many in the packed opera house that night thought of Millay's trial when they heard her words sung: "I tell thee, a man that cometh to a crossroads / Must turn his back upon the one way / To follow the other." Her opera played to sold-out houses in twenty-seven cities in the United States and Canada between November 4 and January 4, and everywhere was talk of how the poet had fought for Sacco and Vanzetti.

She was acquitted in December. Although she failed to save the anarchists, who were executed on August 23, 1927, she had succeeded once more in making spectacular headlines. Millay would never do anything like this again—henceforth her not inconsiderable political contributions would be literary and monetary.

There is much to admire in the marriage of Eugen Boissevain and Edna St. Vincent Millay, and much to be learned from it. They were devoted to each other. They had no children and no intention of having any. They lived for their own pleasure, and for the glory of art. They were unfailingly generous with their friends and family. Eugen was committed not only to his wife's happiness, but also to her absolute freedom to create poetry. How he tried, and failed, to make his wife happy; how he succeeded, and fell short, in nurturing her poetry, is a complex story with more than one moral.

After a decade of marriage she proudly claimed that "We never quarrel." A man does not quarrel with a goddess. This does not mean they never disagreed, nor does it imply that Edna always had the last word. In practical matters the level-headed Dutchman often prevailed over the impulsive and messy bohemian. She cared little about most practical matters. What Millay deeply cared about was the welfare of her senses and moods, which sometimes entailed stimulants and often demanded anesthesia.

Millay was not inclined to suffer physical discomfort where gin or drugs or a climate change might alleviate it. And if and when she lusted for another man, she would have him, and that was that. Boissevain saw to it, as long as he lived, that Millay had whatever anodynes she wanted to keep her comfortable (sometimes at great cost), and when she wanted to be with another man, he discreetly got out of the way. This was not one-sided: What was good for the goose was good for the gander. We know from Max Eastman that Eugen had made a similar agreement with his first wife, "a vow of unpossessive love. Not a vow either, for it was the natural motion of love in the heart of each to wish thus to protect the freedom of the other." For Eugen and Inez it was just so much high-minded rhetoric. They were so young and in love for so short a time before she died that they remained faithful to the end.

But Eugen would be married to Edna for twenty-five years. Knowing her history as he did, he had to be prepared—for his part—for some restless nights, months, and perhaps even years, if their noble love was to weather the storms of lesser passions and intrigues. For the first five years of this union there is not a hint of an extramarital affair on either part. It is notable that in those years, during which she composed several poems included in *The Harp-Weaver*, as well as the entire contents of *The Buck in the Snow*, the illustrious poet, known the world over for her amorous verses, wrote almost no love poetry. She wrote instead:

Being Young and Green

Being young and green I said in love's despite
Never in the world will I to living wight
Give over, air my mind
To anyone,
Hang out its ancient secrets in the strong wind
To be shredded and faded. . . .

Oh, me, invaded
And sacked by the wind and the sun!

She had gone against that youthful vow in marrying Eugen. The paradox of marriage, and Steepletop, is that the perfect sanctuary left her no hiding place from her husband in which to practice that secret sorcery out of which she had brewed her love poems. She had been "invaded, sacked by the wind and sun," until every nook and cranny of her life was drenched with air and light—an enviable fate for most people. But not for Millay. Whatever else may be said about the blessings of matrimony, it does not often foster great love poetry. Marriage relieves the couple of the longing that brought them together, and it is this unsatisfied longing that has inspired lovers to sing since Sappho wooed Anaktoria. Most love poems are written in search of love—rarely by those who have found it. The exceptions: Donne's "Valediction Forbidding Mourning," Spenser's "Amoretti," Ransom's "The Equilibrists," and Levertov's "Marriage" are the more precious for their rarity; and all have a religious dimension that Millay's love sonnets and lyrics never broached. Hers is the poetry of savage desire, "this beast that rends me in the sight of all," a beautiful and ferocious god, a force of nature without grace or mercy. No doubt she felt other kinds of love for her husband, but these gentler affections did not often stir her to write verses.

"She must not be dulled by routine acts; she must ever remain open to fresh contact with life's intensities." These were Eugen's words to Allan Ross Macdougall when he was interviewed for a magazine article. And he stood by them: "To be in love is a terrific and continuous excitement. I want to keep that excitement, never be quite sure, never knowing, so that I can ask myself: Does she love me? And have the answer: I don't know."

The Buck in the Snow was published in September 1928 to tepid reviews on this side of the Atlantic, and wildly enthusiastic notices in England. Thomas Hardy went so far as to say that America's greatest contributions to the 1920s were its architecture and the poetry of Edna St. Vincent Millay. A. E. Housman thought her the greatest living American poet. But the famous woman had been silent for so long that expectations in her own country were impossibly high. She was a legend here, and critics had come to expect from her a certain kind of bold lyric, the quintessence of love poetry, the erotic sonnet. This new book was more meditative and abstract. If the American critics had made too much of her before, now they would compensate by damning her with faint praise. This had no measurable effect on the book's popularity—it would sell forty thousand copies in the first three months.

From October to December 17, she was on the road constantly, giving poetry readings to promote The Buck in the Snow. On All Souls' night, November 2, she gave a reading in the main auditorium at the University of Chicago. In the audience was a handsome young poet, a recent graduate of the university, twenty-one-year-old George Dillon. He had recently made a name for himself with the publication of Boy in the Wind, a book of poems he had written before he was twenty. At the university he had belonged to the famed Poetry Club, which included Glenway Westcott and Yvor Winters, and Dillon had launched a successful poetry magazine called The Forge; with the proceeds he started a reading series in the school's main auditorium. Dillon was tall and athletic with curly brown hair, blue eyes, sensual lips, and the long face of a rather austere cherub. The night he went to see Millay he was basking in the acclaim for Boy in the Wind. Critics hailed it as the decade's best "first book" of poetry, and the reviewer from the Chicago Daily News avowed that he had not felt "quite the thrill of discovery in poetry" to such a degree since he first read Keats. Like Millay, Dillon worked in traditional forms, and he had a gift for making enchanting word-music. Along with the rest of the audience that night, he was looking forward to hearing Millay's love sonnets in her own voice.

By this time Millay's aura was so potent that it had become a popular topic of newspaper columnists. "There is a story that the favored few strangers admitted to her presence are so awed that they approach her on tiptoes," noted one writer. Like others in the Chicago audience under the spell of the auburn-haired poet with the sibyl's voice, George Dillon could hardly believe what he was seeing and hearing.

Not with libations, but with shouts and laughter
We drenched the altars of Love's sacred grove,
Shaking to earth green fruits, impatient after
The launching of the colored moths of Love.
(Sonnet III from *Second April*)

Draped in long black satin, the poet seemed incredibly dainty—fragile, even—so that the voice coming from the frail form, organlike and laden with feeling, seemed for an instant almost like an act of ventriloquism. A reporter wrote: "Tenderly, wistfully, always with a hint of tears not far away, even in gladness, she brought the emotions of each verse unto her mobile, sensitive face."

"The sonnet form is very beautiful to me," she told the audience. "I think I would rather write sonnets than anything else."

The reporter observed that toward the end of the reading: "Already her voice was breaking, and one felt a collapse must not be far away. Tossed by the emotions of the genius, her body is not strong . . . as witness the pathetic gesture with which she sweeps back her hair, sips often from the glass of water at her side, and thumbs the slim gray volumes. . . ."

As a poet himself, Dillon was perhaps more deeply moved than others. At one point during the performance, he reached over and squeezed the wrist of a friend, as if to secure his hold on a world that was slipping away from him. Dillon was tall and strikingly attractive. Perhaps he made eye contact with Millay during the reading. After the applause, the young poet, drawn to her and privileged by his reputation as a writer as well as an associate editor of *Poetry*, made his way through the crowd of starstruck fans backstage to her dressing room. There he found her seated, sipping from a slender silver hip flask her husband had just produced from his pocket. She gazed at the youth, her eyelids lowering slightly, her nostrils flared. The look has been captured in photographs, and even there it is hypnotic. Someone introduced them, she took his hand, and the two poets—the thirty-six-year-old Millay and the twenty-one-year-old Dillon—began a fatal interview that continued later that evening at a small reception in the home of a mutual friend near Jackson Park. The moon was full. Had there been an astrologer in the house he could have read the future of the Scorpio Dillon and the Pisces Millay in a twinkling: even their sun signs show they were doomed to fall in love, deeply, desperately. Dillon recited some of his poems, and Eugen Boissevain made himself scarce, somewhat to the young man's surprise. But Boissevain thoroughly understood his wife, and had no doubt she was undergoing a seismic emotional disturbance.

> No lack of counsel from the shrewd and wise
> How love may be acquired and how conserved
> Warrants this laying bare before your eyes
> My needle to your north abruptly swerved . . .
> (Sonnet III from *Fatal Interview*)

Dillon was a southern gentleman with perfect manners. If he dared to think that the divine poet had fallen in love with him, he certainly did not suspect that he would soon be in the married woman's bed. The young man would have to be persuaded; he was in for a big surprise.

⁕

He was born on November 12, 1906, in Jacksonville, Florida, the only child of Adah Hill, a kind and beautiful woman from an old Kentucky family, and William Dillon, who was descended from a long line of Georgia preachers and physicians. The poet's father was a restless, if ambitious, businessman. In 1910 he moved the family to Henderson, Kentucky, where for two years he operated a bookstore. They moved often: to Covington, Louisville, Cincinnati, St. Louis, and to Webster Groves, Missouri, where George graduated from high school at sixteen. In 1923 the family finally settled in Chicago, where Dillon's father established a business as an electrical contractor, designing layouts for the stockyards. George worked for his father for a few months before enrolling at the university.

As an only child who never lived anywhere long enough to establish lasting friendships, George was a loner, a voracious reader who learned to live in the world of his imagination. He also loved magic; his doting parents bought him costumes and tricks and illusions so that he could put on magic shows for other children in the neighborhood, who regarded him as something of a wizard. At age six he memorized all of Longfellow's *Hiawatha*. When his teacher Nell Smith realized this, she led little George from room to room at the Center Street School to recite a few hundred lines here and there, much to the delight of the teachers and the dismay of the other children, who were supposed to profit from his example.

"Oddly enough, I wasn't stoned by the entire school," he told Francele Armstrong of the Henderson *Gleaner & Journal*. "An ironic fate decided that I should escape, and continue to indulge my bent for poetry,"

When he met Millay, Dillon was writing copy for an advertising agency, extolling the virtues of men's ready-to-wear, motor oil, and airplanes. In his spare time he wrote poetry, while living with his wealthy parents at 2000 Lincoln Park West in a magnificent apartment overlooking Lake Michigan. A powerful swimmer and long-distance runner, George also loved to take long walks on the shores of the lake, composing poems in his head as he walked. He would come home and proudly announce to his mother, "I have a poem," and then go to his room and write it down. Like young Millay, Dillon wrote poems for his mother:

> From summer and from the city I take what I need.
> You will sit here and read.
> You are happier than I shall be when I have done.
> I am afraid. I think how the wind will put us apart.
> I wonder, will I learn the quiet in your touch?
> Will I love someone so much?

One of the interesting questions in the unwritten biography of George Dillon is whether or not he ever loved anyone as much as he loved his mother. If so, it was probably Edna St. Vincent Millay, who was to forcibly remove him from his parents' home. All of his life he was a man of mystery who moved in shadows. This is because so much of his time was spent in secret with Eugen Boissevain's wife.

The "goddess" of American poetry and the handsome youth had a great deal in common, including a belief in magic, poetry, and the enduring power of myth. The harvest moon was not lost on either of them. It would be their fate to enact, in real life, the myth of Endymion, which they both knew well from Keats. A young shepherd of incomparable beauty, Endymion tended his flock on Mount Latmus in Caria. The moon goddess Selene (she of the cold heart) was so moved by the sight of him as he slept on the mountain that she slid down from the sky, kissed him, and lay by his side. He awoke to find her gone, but the memory of the sweet dreams she had given him was so vivid and intoxicating that he thought he would perish without them. He prayed to Zeus to make him immortal so that he might sleep forever on Mount Latmus and have such dreams. In many versions it is the goddess's kiss that casts the magic spell on Endymion, making him immortal and preserving his features forever in a Latmian cave where she can visit and kiss him whenever she likes.

Endymion's dreams have always been a symbol of the poet's vision, as Selene's kiss has been a symbol of the desire to possess the beloved for all time in the fullness of his beauty. Edna Millay would kiss George Dillon, and cast a spell upon him from which he would never waken, willing or not. And she was as bound by the spell as he was:

> Oh, sleep forever in the Latmian cave,
> Mortal Endymion, darling of the moon!
> Her silver garments by the senseless wave
> Shouldered and dropped and on the shingle strewn,
> Her fluttering hand against her forehead pressed,
> Her scattered looks that trouble all the sky,
> Her rapid footsteps running down the west—
> Of all her altered state, oblivious lie!
> Whom earthen you, by deathless lips adored,
> Wild-eyed and stammering to the grasses thrust,
> And deep into her crystal body poured
> The hot and sorrowful sweetness of the dust:
> Whereof she wanders mad, being all unfit
> For mortal love, that might not die of it.
>
> (*Fatal Interview*, Sonnet LII)

Here is such a poem as Boissevain had in mind when he said, "If she wrote *one* sonnet a year, it seems to me important that she be free to write that sonnet." He would set her free to write it, but the cost to him—to all of them—was beyond reckoning.

It is impossible to know exactly when Millay and Dillon first slept together. Knowing the heat of her desire once aroused and her low tolerance for frustration, it probably happened soon after they met. A great blow to Millay scholarship is the loss of most of Dillon's love letters to her. They were preserved in a trunk at Steepletop until the 1980s, when they were loaned to a biographer. After Norma Millay's death in 1986, neither the trunk nor the letters could be found. But in the Library of Congress, scattered among Millay's unprocessed papers I was able to identify half a dozen love letters from Dillon to Millay, all unsigned, but written in Dillon's distinctive hand. In 1999 the library acquired a cache of twenty-six love letters from Millay to Dillon—found wrapped in aluminum foil in his room after he died in 1968. With these sources at last the story can be told.

After her reading November 2 at the University of Chicago, Millay had no further bookings until November 9, when she addressed the Syracuse English Club. That left her and her new admirer a week in Chicago to continue their "fatal interview," and for Millay to pursue him. As a married woman, it would be up to her to take the initiative. Of the many sonnets that emanate from this long love affair, only Sonnet VIII may be construed as a poem of pursuit: "Yet in an hour to come, disdainful dust / You shall be bowed and brought to bed with me. . . . / If not today, then later; if not here / On the green grass, with sighing and delight, / Then under it, all in good time, my dear / We shall be laid together in the night." Her letters to Dillon indicate that while they stole a few moments to embrace during that week in Chicago, most of their time was spent *à trois* with Eugen. He was always the picture of conviviality and self-confidence, and was quite taken with the brilliant, soft-spoken lad with the Kentucky accent. Eugen allowed them time alone together, enough time for them to confess that they had fallen in love with each other and to seal the confession with kisses.

But under the circumstances she had a long way to go to persuade the innocent young man that her heart was in the right place. Trust, in an extra-marital affair, is hard won. While continuing her tour—Syracuse, Boston, New York, Bryn Mawr, Minneapolis, Nashville, and Indianapolis—she kept in touch with her new love via letters now lost, an exchange in which she presumably argued that her intentions were honorable. The first letter that has survived, from Edna in New York City on December 15, finds her in the middle of her rebuttal.

> My darling,
> You must never doubt me again. Truly, that is the one thing I could not bear. For indeed that is the only ugly thing that ever could be between us. I remember that just for an instant once I questioned some-thing you said; I said 'Is that really true' and you said in such a strange way, 'You don't believe me.' And your face was just as if somebody had blown out the candle there. You were right to feel like that. For we have two precious things that we share: that we love each other; and that we have told the truth about it.

Then she quotes John Donne's "I am two fools, I know, for loving and for saying so." Donne will be her guide on this journey—it is from his "Elegy 16" that she takes the name of her new sonnet sequence: "By our first strange and fatall interview, / By all desires which thereof did ensue." She tells Dillon how happy and proud she is "that I neither fought against this love when once I had caught a glimpse of its grave face, nor even for a moment thought to keep it from you."

Then she returns to her opening line, "You must never doubt . . . that I shall love you always, and that I shall never let you go out of my life" (as Selene who enchanted Endymion). She had already sent him Sonnet VIII, with its dragon image: "Life is no friend; her converts late and soon / Slide back to feed the dragon with the moon." She had begun wordplay upon his name: St. George, the dragon slayer, who saves the maiden from sacrifice and wins her hand. Dillon soon responds, to her delight, that he *will* play that role for her if she likes.

She writes: "What will come of all this none of us can tell, I think. The situation is a strange one truly: I am devoted to my husband, I love him more deeply than I could ever express, my feeling for him is in no way changed or diminished since I met you." Yet she thinks of Dillon all the time, and "an enchanted sickness comes over me as if I had drunk a witch's philtre." If she doesn't see him again she believes she will "dwindle in true fantastic style until I snapped in two." Although she tells him again she does not know what is to come, she is sure she will not give him up: "I have never once turned my back on the beautiful thing. And surely the goddess is not offended." These are crucial words, as close to a religious creed as she will ever utter.

On December 17 she received a letter from him that left her "dithering with relief & happiness," because he had assured her he would take her at her words. She replied:

> So you will kill the dragon for me, will you, my St. George?—Oh, I am
> sure you will!—For have you not this moment slain with that blade
> whose name is mightier—Than-the-Sword—this most noble & imposing
> monster, two-headed scaly DOUBT [the dragon], that has been steam-
> ing at me for so many hours now with his great breath?

The mock epic tone, the high rhetoric and diction are about to enter the sonnet sequence (for better and for worse), as Millay in life and art begins to see herself as a heroine in a classic romance—as Selene, Cressida, Isolt, and Helen all rolled into one lovesick American woman.

> Oh Lord, what fun it is to be happy again, & to be writing romantic
> ardent nonsense to the only infant dragon-killer since Hercules wore
> didies!

She says she is happy. In fact she was ecstatic, as she had not been in years, transported as only erotic love and the writing of poetry had ever been able to transport her. But she was in for a dreadful shock and a painful letdown. That very night, backstage at the Brooklyn Academy of Music, on December 17, just as she was preparing to give a poetry reading, someone casually mentioned to her that Elinor Wylie had died the day before.

Stunned, shaken, Millay made her way to the podium and, waving aside the fanfare and applause, began reciting Wylie's verses, poem after poem, from memory. Millay's next book would be dedicated to her late friend.

> *To Elinor Wylie*
> When I think of you,
> I die too.
> In my throat, bereft
> Like yours, of air,
> No sound is left,
> Nothing is there
> To make a word of grief.

Not only had Wylie been an exemplary poet, she also set an example for Millay in her personal life, following the promptings of her heart, risking scandal and the world's censure to be with the men she loved. Desolate, Millay wrote the next morning to Dillon: "I heard of the death of Elinor Wylie. I am so destroyed by it." Wylie's untimely death harshly reminded Vincent of her own mortality.

Edna and Eugen were planning to sail for Europe on January 19, 1929. On Christmas Eve she wrote to Dillon from Steepletop: "I do so long to see you. I know how you felt, that if you could just leap aboard a train & come to me, everything would be all right. It would, too, somehow, I think. . . . I feel that I must see you before I go. . . . I shall try. . . ." Her tone switches to outrage: "I will not have it, to go without looking at your face once more. . . ." And finally she confesses to a paradoxical ecstasy mingling triumph and surrender: "I am glad that I love you truly, glad that I am in for it, glad that I have no choice, glad that I am up to my mouth in love with you, and that the sand is dragging at my feet."

Dillon began to appear in Eugen's dreams, and Jung's former patient kindly shared these dreams with his wife—vaguely suggestive encounters among the three of them. On December 29 she wrote to Dillon, "You must come to Steepletop . . . as soon as possible, and stay as long as possible." She doesn't want him to risk losing his job or irritating his boss, *but*, "Tell him it is a matter of life or death." As she wrote this sentence Eugen handed her a note he had just penned:

> Vincent is writing you, asking you to come to Steepletop.—I, too, want you to come: I am going to make you love me and you must make me love you—So put on a gay tie, and pack your evening clothes and a

clean, clean shirt, and come and we'll drink wine together and laugh together.—And we'll take a walk and we'll go to the top of our mountain, High Hill.—

Affectionately, Ugin

What was the boy from Kentucky to make of all this? Perhaps it was all as innocent as *My wife loves you and I love my wife; ergo, we shall love one another* in the Euclidean, Platonic sense. *We shall all be gay, joyful friends up here on the mountain*—that sort of thing.

Edna hastened to clarify her intentions: "My lovely thing, my darling, darling—don't be apprehensive that I am trying in desperation to change your passionate beautiful love for me into something less—into simple friendship, I mean,—which is less." Maybe someday they will be mere friends, but she hopes that day is far off. "You do not understand all this perhaps. It may seem contradictory. Please don't try to understand then. Just come. Believe in me. Trust me, I beg of you. Do what I ask."

Reading over what she had written, she feared it was inadequate, confusing, chaotic: that she had failed to express just how much she loved him, and had left his greatest concerns unanswered. So she added "Let me swear to you, then, that through me nothing ugly, false or base shall ever touch your life."

What was he to think of such a vow? This heir of Georgia preachers, this poet, like most poets, knew the verses of Solomon: "Though the lips of an adulteress drip honey yet in the end she is more bitter than wormwood, and sharp as a two-edged sword. Her feet go downward on the path to death. . . ." And, "A prostitute can be had for the price of a loaf, but a married woman is out for bigger game." Solomon was a poet's poet and wrote those proverbs in his own blood, out of profound knowledge of erotic love. He bore its scars.

What was Dillon to think of Millay's vow, or the qualification that followed upon it: "But I refuse to shield you from life or death or sorrow—only from ugliness"? His mother had shielded Dillon from those things for most of his life.

"If you cannot come here, I will come to Chicago," Millay declared. "I must & I will see you before many days pass."

On January 4, 1929, a very bewildered young man boarded a train in Chicago to make his way to Steepletop.

"I want to sit on the edge of your bed while you have your breakfast—I want to laugh with you, dress up in curtains, be incredibly silly, be incredibly happy, be like children, and I want to kiss you more than anything in the world," she had written to him.

She would do all that she had dreamed of doing with George Dillon for several days in January, under the paternal, indulgent protection of her husband.

> Love in the open hand, no thing but that,
> Ungemmed, unhidden, wishing not to hurt,
> As one should bring you cowslips in a hat
> Swung from the hand, or apples in her skirt,
> I bring you, calling out as children do:
> "Look what I have! And these are all for you."
>   (*Fatal Interview*, Sonnet XI)

The three of them drank wine and took meals together and went on long walks over the snow-covered fields. And when Edna wanted to be alone with her boy, to show him her studio or go for a stroll or spend an hour or a night in her bedroom, Eugen graciously retired. He was no more threatened by this charming poet than he would have been by a puppy that his wife had gone mad about for a fortnight. Since his marriage to Inez Milholland, he had insisted that husbands and wives remain free to love, and now at the age of fifty he had acquired the equanimity to put the theory into practice. He had told Allan Macdougall that absolute conjugal fidelity was "like an ice-box with always some cold chicken in it." Soon the boy would be gone, Edna would be rejuvenated and writing, and Eugen would have her to himself again.

But it would not be so simple. The second sonnet in *Fatal Interview* records the impression Dillon made on her:

> Unscathed, however, from a claw so deep
> Though I should love again I should not go:
> Along my body, waking while I sleep,
> Sharp to the kiss, cold to the hand as snow,
> The scar of this encounter like a sword
> Will lie between me and my troubled lord.

The "lord" of Steepletop may have underestimated the impact of the beautiful youth or his wife's need for Dillon's peculiar strengths. They put

Dillon back on the train to Chicago on January 8, and Edna returned to Steepletop bereft, tormented—a soul torn from its body, in perfect ecstatic condition to write love sonnets of longing, despair, and grandiose aspirations.

> Nay, learned doctor, these fine leeches fresh
> From the pond's edge my cause cannot remove:
> Alas the sick disorder in my flesh
> Is deeper than your skill, is very love.
>
> (Sonnet IV)

No one can minister to her soul's or body's needs "but one mortal on the teeming globe." And he cannot come to her.

In another poem she imagines that love has imprisoned her, and while she shrieks for freedom till her dungeon shakes, "my chains throughout their iron length / Make such a golden clank upon my ear," she would not use her strength to break "out of here / Where thrusts my morsel daily through the bars / This tall, oblivious gaoler eyed with stars." Dillon is the tall jailer. Daily he feeds her the inspiration for poems.

> Shall I be prisoner till my pulses stop
> To hateful Love and drag his noisy chain . . .
> Perfidious Prince, that keep me here confined,
> Doubt not I know the letters of my doom . . .
>
> (Sonnet XVIII)

Her pain was so awful that by February her letters to Dillon became strained, cruel. In New York, preparing to leave for France, she apologized. "My darling, forget what I wrote about feeling further away from you. . . . It's not true any longer. Perhaps I wanted to hurt you—I don't know. Please forgive me. I love you terribly. . . . Sometimes I long so to see you that I want to hurt you, I think, just because you're not there." She had not been able to keep up her correspondence with him because in Manhattan she had been "going to theaters and parties & dancing & staying up all night & being ever so gay." She never went to bed before 4:00 A.M., and she never had a moment to herself. "I hated myself for not writing—and there was never a night when I didn't wish many times & oh so passionately, dancing with somebody else, that it were you.—Please don't be sad, sweetheart. Be sure that I love you always."

Bound for Europe on March 11, 1929, as she stepped aboard the S.S. *Rotterdam*, following Eugen and the baggage, she scribbled a brief note to

Dillon: "The pilot is just leaving, & I'm sending this ashore by him. Good-bye, goodbye, my darling." At that moment she may have wished for an end to the painful ordeal of this affair, but it had just begun. Notwithstanding the beauty of April in Paris and its social whirl, she missed Dillon. She wrote to him:

> Everybody wants to give a party, and I'm swept from Armenonville in the Bois to a terrifying little dive on the Left Bank called Oubliettes Rouge[s], full of subterranean torture chambers, and real skeletons, where one drinks crème de menthe, awful stuff, I hate it, through a straw, and listens to a girl who sings over and over a song about Les Temps Perdu[s]! And after that everybody goes some place to dance and we all drink quarts of champagne and presently I begin to sing aloud the words of all the songs the orchestra is playing even when I don't know them very well. . . .
>
> And all day long I shop and between shops I sit at a table on the boulevard with my head in my hands, while somebody feeds me brandy and soda and when the last shop is closed I stagger to a taxi and am whirled to my hotel just in time to hear the telephone ringing and explain why I am late to something or other. There! So will you please forgive me and love me still and not hate me at all?

One evening she was sitting in La Closerie des Lilas, and under the linden trees a boy passed by who looked like Dillon. She glimpsed his face as if George had been there—then he was gone. "And I was trembling terribly so that I didn't dare lift my glass, wave after wave of an indescribable passion rose and broke over my head for moments afterward, and I felt very strange and sick."

> Breathes but one mortal on the teeming globe
> Could minister to my soul or body's needs—
> Physician minus physic, minus robe;
> Confessor minus Latin, minus beads.
> Yet should you bid me name him I am numb;
> For though you summon him, he would not come.
>
> (Sonnet IV)

The lovers delighted, teased, and tormented each other with writing and not writing, with poems and silence. She was thoroughly inspired, ecstatic with desire as she had not been in many years.

That April, in a notebook in which she kept a photo of him, she worked on sonnet after sonnet to Dillon. As she finished poems, she mailed them to him a few at a time. They were not written in the order in which they appear in *Fatal Interview*. The last in the book, "Oh sleep forever in the Latmian cave," was one of the first composed. And, as she wrote Dillon in a letter in mid-1929, "Parts of these [sonnets] were done before"; that is, she had been building up an inventory of lines and sketches for sonnets since 1923. It was falling in love with Dillon that forced the fifty-two-poem sequence into flower, and the majority of the poems were brand-new.

She had started writing the poems in January 1929. Before the end of that year she sent him a batch of five along with a giddy letter: "These are samples. Enclosed is an order blank, etc. Indicate the type you prefer and the number of sonnets on that subject which you wish me to supply. At the rate at which I am working now, I shall easily be able to meet the most wholesale demand. Oh, God, did I say 'Easily'? I have never worked so hard." By May 15, 1930, Boissevain wrote to Eugene Saxton, Millay's editor, "Miss Millay wants me to say that she will have a group of sonnets ready for spring publication, i.e. about December. They are love sonnets, more or less a sequence, a loose sequence."

Fatal Interview hangs loosely upon a simple narrative frame: the story of a passionate love affair, from the first meeting and seduction through the drama of painful separations and joyful reunions to the final farewell. The woman who tells the tale is the wooer throughout, pursuing, like Sappho, like Shakespeare, an elusive, sometimes defiant beauty. In the end she must come to terms with her rejection and find peace within herself after bitter defeat. Millay's lifelong, career-long experimentation with role-playing (Deirdre, Marchbanks, Sappho, Melusina), including roles of the storied male lovers—Romeo to Don Juan—culminates in *Fatal Interview*, in which the voice, as in Shakespeare's sonnets, can easily assume an androgynous tone.

> Love is not all; it is not meat nor drink
> Nor slumber nor a roof against the rain,
> Nor yet a floating spar to men that sink
> And rise and sink and rise and sink again . . .
>   (Sonnet XXX)

But when she chooses to be "feminine"—as she remains throughout most of the story—then the poet works that other magic that distinguished her art from the first: the power to occupy an intermediate ground between the real and the mythic, between the mortal and the divine.

> I dreamed I moved among the Elysian fields,
> In converse with sweet women long since dead.

In this famous sonnet (XVI) she dreams of meeting the women of Greek myth—Danae, Europa, Leda—who had coupled with Zeus, thereby partaking of immortality.

> Freely I walked beside them and at ease,
> Addressing them, by them again addressed,
> And marvelled nothing, for remembering you,
> Wherefore I was among them well I knew.

Some readers, particularly women, considered this poem arrogant—the very idea that a woman would claim kinship with Zeus's mistresses! Likewise Sonnet XII, in which she claims that "the harm is done / Enraptured in his great embrace I lie; / Shake heaven with spears, but I shall bear a son / Branded with godhead, heel and brow and thigh." And, no less presumptuous, Sonnet XXVI, wherein the poet declares that while "women have loved before as I love now," it's been a few thousand years, more or less, since such a wonder has occurred. "Of all alive / I only in such utter, ancient way / Do suffer love; in me alone survive / The unregenerate passions of a day / When treacherous queens, with death upon the tread, / Heedless and wilful, took their knights to bed." There were women who heartily disagreed.

In fact *Fatal Interview* sharply divided Millay's audience. Edmund Wilson (who did not admire all of Millay's poetry) believed this was one of the finest sonnet sequences in the language, and certainly the greatest ever written by an American. Poet Robinson Jeffers agreed. John Crowe Ransom compared the sonnets to Donne's and found them wanting—imprecise, overwrought, and artificial. Many readers who had always appreciated the classical clarity of Millay's lines felt the same.

A poet of the people, as Millay was considered and as she regarded herself (compared to T. S. Eliot or Marianne Moore), took huge risks giving herself such airs—putting on the queen's crown, donning the dusty robes of ancient heroines, or assuming the mantle of a goddess (Selene). She might place herself too far above her readers, distancing her audience—the high diction and artificial rhetoric of much of the book already threatened to do that.

But this woman was never afraid to take risks in life or in art. She would end up with a book of fifty-two sonnets, a handful of which are sublime, fifteen more genuinely superb, and all of them interesting. Most poets would be satisfied with that.

In 1929, Edna St. Vincent Millay was beyond caring what anybody thought about these poems. She was in love, in ecstasy, and in the power of the muses. Poets have been arrogant from Homer to Omar Khayyam, from Whitman to Poe. Why should a woman be any different? Poetry is the art of transformation, the exercise of hyperbole. If Millay wanted to play the queen or the goddess in order to turn her passion into song, who could stop her? Her life for the past twenty years certainly had prepared her for these roles.

Not all of the sonnets were written to Dillon. In a letter she tells him, "Two were written to Eugen. They are the two beginning 'Believe, if ever the bridges of this town,' and 'If in the years to come you should recall.' " The first of these, Sonnet XXXVII, is an oblique poem sharply illumined by this new biographical data. The speaker instructs the listener (Millay to her husband) that if ever the structure of their city (marriage) "builded without fault or stain, / Be taken, and its battlements go down, / No mortal roof shall shelter me again . . ." She tells him to "take ship unto some happier shore / In such event, and have no thought for me." She will remain there in the ruins to cheer their dwindling army, to beg "from spectres by a broken arch." Millay thought twice before sending Dillon this poem—which rightly understood is testimony of loyalty to her husband—or the other one, Sonnet LI, which is movingly laudatory and tender: "of all men I honored you the most, / Holding you noblest among mortal-kind." True to her word, she loved Eugen as much as ever, although she pined for George day and night when they were apart. At last she had fulfilled the dream of her girlhood: to have an admirable man to shelter and worship her, and a boy to nurture and adore.

❦

Sometime that summer of 1929, after the Boissevains returned to Steepletop, Dillon visited them again—not for long, he never stayed more than a few days. But long enough for Millay to renew her love for him and fuel her desire for the boy after they parted. She wrote:

> I shall never kiss you goodbye again. There should never be hello kisses and goodbye kisses,—just kisses. Anyhow it is four weeks and a night and half a morning and a minute, since you went away from me. That's long enough, I think, indeed I think it's more than long enough. I want to see you. If I don't see you soon, I shall lie on the floor and kick and howl till something is done about it.

But the separation would be a long one, nearly a year. On January 14, 1930, she wrote to him referring to a recent phone conversation or lost letter:

"Yes, I really mean it.—What's the use? This seeing you for a day or two every year or two—it's no good—it makes me too unhappy." Well, one "use" of seeing Dillon infrequently is that he inspired her. By this time she was fairly desperate, and while it is never wholly safe to deduce biography from poetry, both her poetry and letters imply that it was Dillon's resistance that was keeping them apart. Sonnet XXXVI through Sonnet L tell the tale of a lover's quarrel and the end of an affair, although she composed the poems before autumn 1930, years before the affair ended.

The sonnets are prophetic, indicating that the seeds of discord were known, feared, and sown less than a year after the lovers first met. These are some of the most powerful and natural poems in the book, beginning with XXXVI, the celebrated "Matinicus" sonnet.

> Hearing your words, and not a word among them
> Tuned to my liking, on a salty day
> When inland woods were pushed by winds that flung them
> Hissing to leeward like a ton of spray,
> I thought of how off Matinicus the tide
> Came pounding in, came running through the Gut,
> While from the Rock the warning whistle cried,
> And children whimpered and the doors blew shut;
> There in the autumn when the men go forth,
> With slapping skirts the island women stand
> In gardens stripped and scattered, peering north,
> With dahlia tubers dripping from the hand:
> The wind of their endurance, driving south,
> Flattened your words against your speaking mouth.

Matinicus is an island off the coast of Maine. Its women were afraid their men would die in autumn storms; Millay is afraid love will die, but she has the endurance to make it prevail.

Among so much jewelry and scene-painting in the splendid *Fatal Interview* sequence—props that elevate the lovers to mythic stature—this searing poem stands out as vividly as a farm woman hoeing a potato patch. You can hear her speaking those words to Dillon off the top of her head, in plain American. She was terrified by what he was saying. "Most wicked words, forbear to speak them out. / Utter them not again. Blaspheme no more / Against our love with maxims learned from Doubt, / Lest Death should get his foot inside the door" (XXXIV). Death was as real to her as gray hair. She wanted him to assure her that their love would never die, that he would be her Endymion, ever beautiful, always available. But sometimes he just couldn't do it. He was twenty-three, the handsomest poet in Chicago, and about a year from winning his own Pulitzer Prize. She was thirty-eight, married, transparently neurotic, demanding, manipulative, and an alcoholic to boot. He certainly loved her, but he was not about to become Endymion, a shepherd boarding at Steepletop. He could not out-and-out lie to her and promise to satisfy her desire "to be with you day & night, and no questions asked, do things with you, see things with you, without compromise, without strain," as she begged of him in her letter of January 14, 1930. In Dillon's every show of resistance, the middle-aged woman could sense, with a sinking feeling, the loss of her famous magnetism. She was afraid to look in a mirror.

The week of July 21, Eugen and Edna hosted a four-day party to celebrate the completion of the Fickes' house at Hardhack. Among the fourteen houseguests who were expected at Steepletop were Mr. and Mrs. Deems Taylor, Floyd Dell and his wife, Max and Eliena Eastman, and George Dillon. Eugen invited Dillon on June 28, writing, "Our house will be full of pretty girls, but we have not enough beautiful men, so you'll have to come. . . . Come for a day, a week, a month, a year—love, Eugen."

After that summer Millay would not see Dillon for many months, during which she grew increasingly despondent and physically ill. By autumn she no longer had even the excitement of the sonnets to divert her. The book was finished. There are references in an unpublished note from Arthur Ficke dated October 28, 1930, that she was considering having surgery in New York in early November: "Vincent said yesterday that she would die on the operating table next week," Ficke wrote. "I don't believe it: it is improbable, ridiculous and immoral: furthermore, I shall not permit it." On the same date she wrote to Dillon: "Darling, for God's sake don't go to California. I shall die if you do.—It's been almost more than I could bear to have you as far away as Chicago. . . . —But California—oh please don't! I shall die if you do. I mean it. They'll call it something else, but it will be that."

Dillon had lost his job at the ad agency and was considering an offer from California. As there is no further reference to Millay's illness in November, it is certain that she did not have an operation, and probable that her illness was merely hysterical. "If I have to go to the hospital, & you haven't got a job by then, would you really come east to see me, before I go, if I asked you to?" He had not written her a love letter in a long time, and she archly commented: "I don't think I could just now stand the excitement . . . but it would be worth the risk. I wish awfully you'd conduct the experiment. . . ."

But something had gone awry in Chicago. Dillon had gotten into some kind of trouble that had been reported in a news column, and it would seem from Millay's letter to him of November 15 that the "trouble" linked a woman's name with Dillon's in a scandalous context. Or perhaps the trouble concerned his former employer. In any case, he told her they must not see each other for a while, and he declined to come to Steepletop.

If she had not been hysterical before, she certainly was when she heard that news. She wrote: "You should have known that anything you could have done, in the papers or out of the papers, would be without effect on me." Her letter is shrill, desperate, and imperious. She and Eugen were on their way to New York. She insisted that Dillon telephone her at the Vanderbilt Hotel and reverse the charges. "And I want you to be prepared to tell me whether or not you will come to Steepletop at once. If not, Ugin & I shall leave for Chicago at midnight Monday. . . . If you think I care at all what the whole world says about me, in comparison to being absent from you at this time, you have never really loved me or anybody else. Let them spy, let them follow, let them listen on the telephone, let every loose-tongued gossip in the country know that I love you & that I came to Chicago to see you."

In short, she concluded, "Either you come here & at once, or I come to Chicago. You have nearly killed me. I won't stand it any longer." The Boissevains waited forty-eight hours, then ordered the concierge to book passage to Chicago.

They were about to leave the hotel for the train station when Dillon telephoned. He calmed her down, promising to come to Steepletop soon. She wrote to him, abashed, remorseful: "Poor child, how I have harassed you. I will never do it again. I should not have done it now but that I was so sure you were in trouble & was very worried. But in any case, I'll never do it again—So breathe freely." She was granting him permission to breathe.

THE MOUNTAIN LAURELS

 ❧

$\mathcal{D}$uring the year that she was obsessed with George Dillon and the frenzied composition of the sonnets in *Fatal Interview*, Millay had neglected her mother. In mid-June 1929, Cora had visited Steepletop, where she came down with severe stomach trouble that was vaguely diagnosed as either ptomaine poisoning or food allergies. No letters passed between mother and daughter from then until late September when Vincent wrote a chatty letter to Cora about the farm and the servants; she wrote again after Thanksgiving, concerned about Cora's sparse correspondence and persistent head cold. Then she promised to visit her mother: "If I get anywhere near you this winter, I'll try to make it to Newburyport." She did not. But after the stock market crashed Eugen sent Cora one thousand dollars with the comment, "Things all around look dark and sad and what is worse it does not look as if times are going to be much better in the near future. We are hit along with the rest of the world." His letter maintains his usual confidence and good humor. He reassures his mother-in-law that there is "nothing to worry about," just try to "drag the old money out as long as you can," advising her against buying a Rolls-Royce on the installment plan.

Vincent did not hear much from her mother in 1930, and by July she was worried. In late August, the third anniversary of the Sacco and Vanzetti executions, Millay went to Cambridge to read her poems about the tragedy in the Old South Church. Afterward she and Eugen drove up to Newburyport to visit Cora, carrying four small mountain laurel bushes from Steepletop in the backseat of their Cadillac.

Cora was overjoyed to see her daughter after such a long time, and delighted with the bushes, which they planted in a row in front of her cottage. These reminded Cora of a happy day she had spent as a girl with her mother, a sunny spring day when they strolled among the blossoming mountain laurel. Cora was now sixty-six. She looked frail but she was in good spirits, and told them how hard she had been working on her poetry.

The rest of that year Millay was so preoccupied with keeping, or losing, George Dillon, and immortalizing their love in sonnets, that she did not think much about her mother until she received a letter from Cora on the evening of February 2, 1931, the day after Eugen's mother passed away. Death was foremost in their thoughts as she opened it. The letter was cheerful: "I am so happy I am at work again, doing I think as good work as I ever did." And she enclosed a poem. But the last stanza of the poem, "My Little Mountain-Laurel-Trees," made Vincent burst into tears—she could hardly bear it.

> My Little Mountain-Laurel-trees
> If you should ever grow
> Where I was very sound asleep,
> I think that I should know.
> Then I needn't dream of Cypresses
> Where cold their shadows fall
> But of the Mountain-Laurel-trees I loved
> When I was very small.

Eugen tried to comfort her, saying she mustn't interpret the references to the cypresses and sleep as meaning Cora had a premonition of death. Still, his wife could not keep from crying.

Two nights later as the Boissevains were having dinner, a taxi drove up the circular drive bearing the telegram: COME MOTHER VERY SICK ANSWER IMMEDIATELY TO ME signed UNCLE BERT. They answered that they were on their way.

The starter on the Cadillac was broken and the hand-throttle was stuck, so they had to drag the car out of the garage with horses. But finally they got it going at eleven, driving in fear of the engine stalling somewhere in the woods where no one could help them in the middle of the night. But Eugen swore to her he wouldn't stall the Cadillac, and he didn't. They drove for twelve hours straight, and as they motored up the Maine coast the day was dawning. Vincent felt a sudden chill and was sure her mother would never see the sun again.

Cora had moved back to Camden since their last visit. They entered town by the back road from Rockport, around the Lily Pond. Driving down Chestnut Street, Vincent began looking for the house. She had the address but was not quite sure which house her mother had purchased. "And then suddenly I saw the door, and there was crepe on it."

❧

Cora had died of the "stomach trouble" that had been plaguing her at least since 1929. For months Vincent kept telling herself and her sisters and everybody else that her mother "was not sick, she was quite well, then suddenly she felt sick, in her stomach," and before anybody knew it was anything other than a little indigestion, Cora fell asleep and never woke up again. But Millay had suspected her mother was not in good health since June 1929; and had they been paying attention, Vincent, Norma, or Kathleen might have gotten the sixty-seven-year-old woman the medical attention that Vincent herself had received in 1923 when she had nearly died of gastroenteritis.

The next night she wrote to Kathleen, sobbing, "Baby, my typewriter is smashed and I have to get back the one I lent to somebody before I can type the poem mother wrote about the mountain laurels." When Vincent passed through the door with the mauve bow on it, she went straight to her mother's desk, where she saw the draft of a new poem scrolling out of the typewriter carriage. She put the typewriter in its box with the sheet of paper just as she had found it, then set aside the machine for Kathleen, now a published poet of some note herself.

Norma and Charlie drove up from New York. And on Saturday night, "We thought we would have a wake for her, we thought she would like that. Norma and I wanted to watch up with her all night, but Charlie and Ugin wouldn't let us, we were so worn out." They had brought a bottle of champagne from Steepletop to celebrate Cora's getting well. Instead they poured out six glasses (one each for Kathleen and Howard who were absent) and drank to her anyway. "Every time we went to look at her—and it was hard to keep away, she looked so beautiful, so peaceful and asleep—we would look at her for you, too; and when we would stroke her lovely hair, we would do it for you, too, and say, 'This is for Kathleen.' "

They took Cora by auto-hearse to West Stockbridge through a snowstorm, then Eugen and the hired man John Pinnie drove the corpse to Steepletop in a sleigh. "Steaming black horses, a soft silent snowstorm, a swinging stable lantern on the side of the sleigh, over that beautiful road through the silent hills," Eugen wrote to Llewelyn Powys.

Edna stood at the door waiting to receive her mother's body. They put the coffin in the parlor, surrounded by flowers. Edna wanted to bury her in the mountain laurel patch on the east side of the hill, but the ground was frozen very deep, and they had to blast with dynamite for days to hollow a grave.

They buried her the night of February 12. Two farmhands with lanterns led the way, climbing the hill ahead of the sleigh with the coffin, followed by two pallbearers with lanterns, then Norma and Edna, Norma carrying a big basket of flowers, Edna with her rifle. Charlie and Eugen, swinging lanterns, brought up the rear. As the gravesite was about a mile from the house, for two days Eugen had had men digging a path through the snow.

After the farmhands lowered the casket into the ground, Eugen sent them away. Charlie and Eugen, Norma and Edna covered the coffin with flowers and pine boughs, and Eugen broke a bottle of good champagne (Lanson, '21) over the coffin, as if he were christening a ship. Then they took turns firing rounds over the grave into the woods with Edna's rifle. Eugen shot a few rounds toward the east for his mother, too.

"We went through a rough time," he wrote to Powys. "Poor little Vincent is broken-hearted." Guilt magnified her grief. Of the three daughters, she was always the one who assumed responsibility. She jotted lines she would never publish:

> At least, my dear
> You did not have to live to see me die.
>
> Considering now how many things I did that must have caused you pain,
> Sweating at certain memories, blushing dark blood, unable
> To gather home my scattered thoughts
> . . . .
> You kept no books against me! In my own hand
> Are written down the sum and the crude items of my inadequacy.
> The most I ever did for you was to outlive you.

(In 1954, Norma would revise the thirty-line fragment and publish it post-humously in such a form that it appears to be addressed to Edna's late husband. But it was written in 1931, for Cora.)

Even more revealing of Millay's state of mind is a pathetic elegy (unpublished) in which she apologizes to her mother for not visiting her grave, although "healing from this hill alone" can deliver her from torment. "Mother have you understood / Why you lie neglected here?" It is because Vincent is ashamed that the burial ground is so ugly.

> You shall have your pretty grave,
> Fine as any, all in time,
> Everything that others have,
> Rose and cypress, urn and rime
>
> Folded angels nothing missed,
> Iron fence, and wrought by hand—
> When I can unclench this fist
> At my throat, when I can stand

> Leaning on no other arm
> Than this knowledge: that you died,
> You, that never did me harm,
> Set this anguish in my side.
>
> . . . .
>
> Music, books, to talk, to think,
> All is torment that I do;
> Travel, dancing, love and drink,
> Nothing takes my mind from you.

The idea that her mother, whose love had so long sustained her, now in death holds so much power to torment her presents a macabre and nearly insoluble problem.

> You that were my torch and shield,
> Showed me honor, gave me life,
> Held within your hands concealed
> All that time, it seems, this knife . . .

It is a cruel thought, unrelieved by any spiritual grace, that the dearly beloved is in death no longer loving but vengeful. And the poet's answer to it, in her grief, is the mourner's cannibalism:

> In this mound, and what's beneath,
> Is my cure, if cure there be;
> I must starve, or eat your death
> Till it nourish me.

Edna St. Vincent Millay would never really recover from her mother's death, nor would her sister Kathleen. After a painful divorce in the late 1930s, Kathleen descended into clinical paranoia. A series of hospitalizations (paid for by the Boissevains) did little to help her. She would die of acute alcoholism in 1943. Vincent survived Kathleen by seven years, but from 1931 until 1950 she courted oblivion—in alcohol, in sex, in drugs, playing Russian roulette with death.

%

Eugen tried to make the acceptance of the harsh reality as painless for his wife as possible. He would deny Millay nothing. In late February he took her to the St. Regis, their favorite Manhattan hotel, where they stayed until early April, drowning their sorrows. She was grieving for both her mother and George Dillon, who had not written her a letter in weeks. When at last she received a note of condolence from him on March 29, she wrote him immediately from the hotel to tell him how happy she was to hear from him, how relieved.

> Probably you don't know that Ugin's mother died just a week before mine did. We're pretty sunk. . . . And we've been so dazed with liquor ever since that we didn't even notice until a few days ago that our letters weren't being forwarded. I'm not sober yet, and I don't intend to be.

Then she begs him to write to her.

> It was pretty hideous thinking I had lost you, just when I needed so seriously everything I had in my life that was beautiful, to remind me that life could be borne at all. Very likely I was right, and I *have* lost you, but don't let it go into effect just yet. Wait until I have become accustomed to this pain, which grows worse every day.

She tells him she is looking forward to returning to Steepletop, hoping it will ease her pain to work in the garden. "But it's funny. You can't tell. Sometimes things that shouldn't hurt at all, hurt most. And more than one flower that she was fond of has it in for me this summer, I expect." The idea of retribution was never far away.

Dillon wrote to her promptly, a letter that, according to her response of April 14, "healed so many wounds. Even though I'm still in the dark as to your strange repudiation game, I'm comforted. You say that you do still love me, that you did want to see me. I don't care about the rest. Except that I know you have been in torment." In the same post as her letter, she sent a copy of *Fatal Interview*. The book would be published the next day, April 15, 1931.

One revealing love letter from Dillon to Millay is undated, but it explains his "repudiation game," as he likely would have played it during 1930 and 1931. In this communication he refers to a previous "depressed, drunken letter I wrote you." That letter was so flatly a repudiation that she did not answer it. So he wrote:

> Forgive me for being crude and ungrateful. It's just that I have to pay for being with you by being plunged into a worse despair every time you go away. The rest of my life seems so useless, then, that I can't bear the thought of picking it up again. So I hide away a while, and drink and read, and take long walks, and sleep.

Just like Endymion: If he accepts her, he is only alive when she kisses him awake. The rest of the time he's a zombie, in a trance or sound asleep. He sent her these verses, a magnificent tribute to her flesh:

> Finding her body woven
> As if of flame and snow
> I thought, however often
> My pulses cease to go,
> Whipped by whatever pain
> Age or disease appoint,
> I shall not be again
> So jarred in every joint,
> So mute, amazed and taut,
> And winded of my breath—
> Beauty being at my throat
> More savagely than death.

The vampire imagery is not to be ignored. She was nearing forty, but Millay's physical beauty and charisma still had the power to drive a man out of his wits, and Dillon was smart enough even at twenty-four to know the danger of the succubus—if he was not careful she would consume him.

Fatal Interview was exactly what Vincent's audience had wanted (despite the controversy over her technique), what they had been waiting for since *The Harp-Weaver* was published nearly a decade earlier. The book's success owed much to the scent of scandal that clung to it, the controversy over the story: Fact or fiction? Did the married woman have an extramarital affair that inspired the sonnets, or was it all a fantasy? Under the circumstances Millay as well as Dillon had good reason to lay low, to keep away from each other. It seems that as of 1931 even the Boissevains' close friends were not aware of the liaison between Millay and the Chicago poet.

She and Eugen traveled widely in the United States that summer and autumn. They visited the poet Robinson Jeffers in California. He loved *Fatal Interview*, and called it her finest book, "flamelike and powerful and very sweet," with a charm that cannot be described but only felt, like a fragrance or a beautiful face. "It is yours," he wrote to her, "no one else has it."

They paid a surprise call on forty-four-year-old Georgia O'Keeffe, who was vacationing at Lake George. In an unpublished letter to Edna written after that visit, O'Keeffe said that Millay reminded her of a humming-bird that once flew into her studio and got trapped there. When she finally caught the creature, the painter could hardly believe the tiny thing had such intensity of life in it. She wanted to look at it, but as soon as she opened her hand the least bit, the hummingbird would escape and go fluttering against the windowpane. On the fourth try she finally caught the bird and got a glimpse of it before letting it fly out the door. She told Edna that she was like the hummingbird—and that if *she* did not understand what was meant by that, her husband Eugen certainly would.

This whole story was O'Keeffe's response to Edna's invitation that they get to know each other better—that they spend more time together. But the wise O'Keeffe was cautious, guarded. Millay appeared troubled. The beautiful painter, explaining that she was now so absorbed in her work she could not visit Steepletop, intimated that she and Millay knew the best part of each other *without* having to spend much time together. Edna wanted Georgia's attention, but Georgia was not ready. The painter says in her letter that when she *is* ready for such intimacy, she begs freedom to visit the poet, but makes Edna promise her that if *she* is not ready then, she will be frank and not allow herself to be disturbed. As one goddess to another, O'Keeffe will understand, and will always love her poet-sister.

Edna and Eugen traveled from coast to coast, but they avoided the city she most wanted to visit.

❧

Millay did not get to Chicago until the first week of December, and this time she traveled alone. After the first days of joy in being reunited with Dillon and fantasizing about their future, the prospect of living without him again— the anguish of parting—made her furious. It seemed more than she could bear. As she admitted in her letter to him afterward, she turned vicious in defense. She called their last night together, Saturday, December 7, the most horrible ever.

> My mind was in torment—it was the most hideous parting—I talking
> & forcing you to talk about other people & hateful things [i.e., husbands
> and lovers], when all the time I might have been in your arms & you
> kissing me. I was awake all night after that first drunken slumber, & I
> could not keep my mind from exploring every anguish or distraction
> possible to us—that I might never see you again—that you might stop
> loving me. . . .

But sometime that weekend, before this horrible night, they had made a plan "about Europe, being in Paris [together] or having a little chalet on the side of a mountain with a balcony right over the lake, & a waterfall," and the thought comforted her. Dillon had applied for a Guggenheim Fellowship he would likely win, and with the money he would go to France, where he and Edna might be free to live together. But there were so many "ifs," it made her angry. "Oh, darling, I wanted to say so many things to you, not at all the things I said. Why did I have to tease us at the last moment with such painful things, leaving us both with our minds full of cruel images—And I wonder seriously today if you have not at last succeeded in hating me."

Those cruel images were the same as spiteful lovers often use to torment each other, visions of other lovers, the phantoms of jealousy. Dillon started it by confessing that in his loneliness he had sought comfort with other women. Now she wished they had more time to talk it out, so they might really understand each other.

> For I too have had my periods of insane depression when only the wildest and most extravagant excesses seemed to have any value or even any beauty, such as last spring, for instance, when I had lost both my mother & you, & tried my best to drink myself right out of the picture, lapping up one speak-easy after another, & hardly knowing who was holding my hand.

She wrote this letter to him on Monday, December 8, while her train was standing in the station in Albany. At the time she was in the thick of an "insane depression," and her alcoholism had progressed to a point where she was having frequent and total blackouts that efficiently took her "right out of the picture." On Sunday she had been so drunk that Dillon had to carry her onto the train. She remembered that and little else. "I must have been good and drunk last night. I drew one blank after another—can't remember taking the train—can't remember being in the station."

> There is a word I dare not speak again,
> A face I never again must call to mind;
> I was not craven ever nor blenched at pain,
> But pain to such degree and of such kind
> As I must suffer if I think of you,
> Not in my senses will I undergo.
> (Sonnet XLIX)

When the conductor came for her ticket in the Pullman car he found her facedown on her berth completely clothed—even wearing her fur coat—

weeping. "The two of us had a great hunt for my ticket which seemed to be nowhere at all, or I was too drunk to be at all interested in the business. . . ." She passed out. When she woke up a few hours later she found her coat on one hanger and her suit neatly folded on another, and was fairly certain that she had not been conscious enough to undress herself. She thought the kind conductor must have tucked her in.

PARIS OR STEEPLETOP

*M*illay had dreamed of being in Paris with Dillon. And now she would not rest until she made that dream come true. He waited for the announcement of the Guggenheim Fellowship, hoping to see his name among the winners, so he could use the money for travel.

Edna and Eugen sailed for France on February 19, 1932. She telephoned Dillon just before the ship sailed that night, and from Chicago her lover wrote to her the next day: "It was thrilling to hear your voice on the telephone. You have the most beautiful voice in the world." After talking to her he felt so sad and lonely he couldn't sleep. "I try to think what a good time you're having. . . . I wonder why these things don't make me glad. They make me perfectly miserable. I'm in a nasty jealous mood today."

That night Dillon went to a party, but he was too melancholy to enjoy himself, so he went home early to write her a love letter.

> At times like this when I ought to forget you—when the sense of your absence is made intolerably keen by your going farther away—I can't think of anything else. Everything I do, everyone I see, seems an intrusion. I just want to be quiet and remember you. There is happiness in that, and that is why I am happy at the moment.
>
> I love you, my dear, more than anything. You know this—with some clairvoyance of yours . . . in spite of the neurotic moods that come between us—in spite of my bad manners and insane behavior. You have been sweet and patient always, and I am really grateful. *If I can amount*

to anything, it will be because you loved me, and continued to love me through these terrible years.

He was about to "amount to" a great deal, actually, within about two months' time. He had made up his mind to go to Paris in April with or without the Guggenheim money. In March, he won it. On May 3, Dillon was on a ship steaming across the Atlantic bound for France when his parents radio-wired him the news that he had won the Pulitzer Prize for his new book of poems, *The Flowering Stone.*

Stepping off the ship in Le Havre, on his way to be reunited with his true love, in Paris, the city of love, George Dillon must have been the happiest man alive.

No letters between Dillon and Millay have survived to tell if the young poet was aware of the thoughtful arrangements that Eugen and Edna had made for his arrival. While Dillon approached Paris, Eugen was westbound out of Paris for Le Havre—he literally saw George's train pass his, going the other way. Eugen was sailing to New York on May 10, on the M.S. *Lafayette,* leaving Edna behind at the Pont Royal Hotel to welcome Dillon.

The Boissevains' letters indicate that they were in accord. They still loved each other, but Edna was *in* love with Dillon; and at last Eugen—in a spirit of adventure—agreed to leave his wife alone with the boy. Not that Eugen had much choice. She had pretty much insisted upon the trial separation; Eugen would have preferred to stay in Paris and be a player in the game there. While her letters contain grace notes and innuendos of regret, Eugen's continually refer to his bravery in the experiment.

Eugen's courage, like his wife's, was such stuff as legends are built upon. The man had made international headlines just weeks earlier for an impulsive act of heroism that almost cost him his life.

On Friday, March 13, Eugen and Edna were to be the guests of honor at a formal dinner at the American embassy. As they dressed for the affair they drank cocktails out of crystal glasses, and lit cigarettes from his gold cigarette case. She had put on a white evening gown, low in front and back and very full in the skirts, and a red sash. Eugen wore a tuxedo dinner jacket and black butterfly tie, a new scarf of white silk, and a high silk top hat. They looked the picture of continental glamour—à la Fred Astaire and Ginger Rogers—as they got into a taxi and headed for the Right Bank.

As the cab approached the Pont Royal, Eugen noticed three men running across the bridge. On an impulse he rapped on the glass and ordered the taxi to stop. The driver pulled over to the curb.

"I want to see what's going on," Eugen said to his wife. "I'll be back in a minute."

He got out. Later, Edna told a reporter, "I am rather accustomed to Eugen's impulsive movements." And with a wink she added that she thought maybe he had had "too much to drink that day."

Eugen stepped to the parapet of the bridge and looked over the edge. Instantly, in the swift, swirling current of the Seine he saw the white face of a woman tossing past. She flung her hand up as if in appeal to him. And then she went under.

Behind the bridge, a footpath led down steps to the muddy water. Eugen started down the footpath, running. As he ran he tossed away his silk hat, then his overcoat. He unwound the scarf, and just before reaching the brink of the Seine, he shed his dinner jacket. He took off his shoes.

The crowd on the bridge and the bank was yelling, "It's no use! She's dead!"

Later he told a journalist: "I saw myself as in a picture, going back, after this heroic gesture in front of that gathering crowd—picking up, first my jacket, then my scarf . . . No, it was too ridiculous. I had to finish what I had started. So I jumped in."

The Seine is a treacherous, inhospitable river. Not a man in Paris but Boissevain jumped in it to rescue that woman.

"As I swam toward the woman—who might already be dead—I wished I were not there. I was afraid that if she were alive she might grab me and drown me. Something like that had almost happened to me once in Holland. I resented her. Why did she have to pick this time to jump into the river, just when I was passing by, on my way to a beautiful dinner?

"I did not feel at all heroic. I felt sorry for myself. At the same time I remembered her white face and her hand flung up in appeal to me." And he felt an affection, as if this were not a stranger, "but someone whom I had an absolute obligation to save."

Eugen began swimming downstream diagonally to the opposite shore, toward the Pont du Solferino, where he reached the woman and grabbed her cloak. But it came off in his hand, a ratty-looking fur piece. For some reason he could not let go of it, even as he lost her, and he kept holding on to the fur as he swam after her and finally caught her again. He managed to swim with the woman under his arm to the bank, where the crowd was cheering and shouting. But she and Eugen were too low in the tide for anyone to reach them. He yelled for the spectators to make a chain, which they did—a human chain of Frenchmen, one holding the ankles of the next, reaching down into the icy waters of the Seine to pull the girl and the hero up to the bank. He still held on to the fur piece.

Eugen, weeping, refused to give his name to the gendarmes. The girl, twenty-three-year-old Pauline Venys, in despair over the extreme poverty the Depression had caused her and her family, as well as over her husband having left her for another woman, had thrown herself from the Pont du Carousel just upstream from where Eugen first glimpsed her. The fur was her only piece of finery.

He was quite proud of himself, and Edna was proud of him, too. But Millay was cool, puffing cigarette after cigarette in the taxicab, the unflappable sophisticate of the 1930s. She knew exactly how to play a scene like this for the reporters—as if this were no more than a routine and rather annoying bit of grandstanding on the part of an American husband who had made her late for a party, where now he would show up looking like a *clochard,* a Left Bank bum.

In the reporter's presence, she scolded him: "You can't just come along and pull her out of the river and then leave her as she was. You've taken a serious responsibility on yourself. She must have been in a very desperate situation. If I were she I would resent your intrusion upon her private affairs. I'd say 'Either make life worth living for me, or else take me off to some secluded place where I can drown myself without being interfered with.' "

They visited Pauline Venys at the Hôpital de Charité, where she told Edna and Eugen her sad story of starvation and betrayal: "When I was a girl of seventeen, a fortune-teller told me I would come into great sorrow, but at the last moment God would step in and save me." She had prayed and prayed to God, and when praying to the Holy Virgin in Notre Dame brought no relief, she had thrown herself into the waters of the Seine. Only then did God save her.

Eugen gave the girl the money she needed to get back on her feet. And later Edna hired her as a cook and maid. Boissevain rescued Venys, as he had rescued Millay. This was the man she was sending back to America so she could be alone with George Dillon.

On May 10, Edna in her yellow dressing gown stood on a balcony of the Pont Royal Hotel and waved to Eugen as he stood in the rue du Bac. And he would never forget "that desperate, desolate feeling I had then, that it was goodbye, that it was the King is dead, long live the King, that the Queen-bee had left the hive with all the young bees and the old bees stayed back to die silently and without complaints."

※

There are 110 pages of unpublished correspondence—not including an equal number of cablegrams—between Eugen and his wife from May 10 through July 4, 1932. These provide a full picture of how they spent their two months' separation and the way they felt about it.

Eugen's letters are passionate, constant, and lyrical. His devotion to his "Freckles, Bibs, or Scaramoodles" (his pet names for Edna) is never in doubt. Her letters to "Skiddlepins" (as she called him), while richly detailed, are by turns wistful, elusive, mysterious, and passionate. He left her alone so she could figure out which man she loved more, and right up until the last minute she kept him guessing. It is difficult to ascertain if she was as perplexed as she led him to believe. And it is impossible to know which of the spouses was more miserable.

His first letter, written aboard the *Lafayette*, conveys the essence of his feelings as well as the nature of their discussions back at the hotel. "Rainbows on the starboard side all day long," he observed, "and I thought of all the rainbows we had seen together." In his opinion there was only one attractive woman on the ship, "a lovely smile and she is small and dainty and reminds me of you." He downed a glass of gin in the bar, thought of Edna, and sipped another.

> I love you more than even you can know. . . . Be happy and without a care. Button up your overcoat and be careful about booze and crossing streets. I made the rainbows I saw into rainbows for you. I kiss you on your soft sensitive lips. . . .
>
> Thank you for your wire. It made me happy. You must have sent it from Gare St. Lazare. Poor Bibs! Loving so much two galumps! And one is more than an ordinary girl can stand! Never you mind. You can manage it. And you'll have a life richer than any girl, but not rich enough to scare me.—Go to it, Scaramoodles, and no heartaches or feeling sorry for ANYBODY!

They saw themselves as pioneers, explorers on the frontier of free love and open marriage. There is constant reference—on both sides—to courage. "I'm fine," he reassured her, embellishing the margins with X's for kisses. "Goodbye my courageous lion. When I come back [which was his hope] you must be again the roaring lion." He signed this letter, and most of these letters, "Skiddlepins the Brave."

A few days after arriving home, in response to a wire from his wife, he sent her a prescription for painkillers: "Here is Dr. Lambert's prescription, in case you want to start taking it again." In the same letter he reassured her that he was "really *very happy*. I'm getting brown, I'm getting healthy (have not drunk today and only 3 cigarettes) am *very* busy. I didn't know I loved you as much as all this. It is fantastic, it is ridiculous, but it is a terrible lot of fun and I'm quite proud. Nobody ever loved anybody the way I love you . . . and nobody ever loved anybody the way you love me. So I'm very happy. But will be happier when I'm once more near you."

Eugen's life on the farm, his work in the fields and the garden, his pheasant hunting, cooking, and swimming, was an open book. Even his casual sexual escapades with girls in New York and at Steepletop he described to his wife—at her insistence. Part of the thrill of the trial separation was epistolary voyeurism / exhibitionism on both sides. (The more explicit erotic passages of the letters have been expurgated, probably by the Boissevains themselves, but perhaps by Norma, the literary executor. On June 14 he reassured his wife the letters were being handled with the utmost discretion, agreeing to burn any she wanted destroyed. The letters refer to pages that are missing.)

Nevertheless, Millay's weeks in Paris are carefully veiled and screened. It is easy to imagine her in the yellow dressing gown, wild with excitement as she greeted Dillon, with his fresh laurels on his brow, at the Pont Royal Hotel, and how they must have celebrated, making love all night and half the next day. George was a late riser. But as soon as she could get him up and out into the sunshine (her sleepy Endymion), they would walk and ride all over the city of Paris, in the Jardin du Luxembourg, up and down the Champs Elysées, and along the Seine in the shadow of Notre Dame. Her dream had come true.

While she sent many affectionate cables to Eugen, starting from the day he left, she wrote no letters to him until May 25, at breakfast. She did not avoid mentioning Dillon, but she was extremely discreet, at first, in referring to his presence. "George has found a charming apartment, very cheap, two rooms and a bath for 800 francs a month [about seventy-five dollars in today's currency]. It is on the Boulevard St. Germain, just opposite the lovely old church St.-Germain-des-Prés, by the Deux Magots." She wanted to find an apartment, too, because the hotel was too expensive. She would soon move to 5, rue Benjamin Godard, in the fashionable 16th arrondissement.

Millay was moving in the highest circles of transatlantic literary society, and apparently she did this while keeping her affair with Dillon under wraps.

This must have made him uneasy. Her first letter gives a full account of Elsa Maxwell's dazzling party at Les Ambassadeurs on May 24, dinner and dancing for a hundred guests. Maxwell, an American vaudevillian and prolific songwriter, was also a professional hostess who threw parties bankrolled by the Prince of Monaco. She knew exactly whom to invite.

The poet wore her new white dress and red jacket; she stepped in white slippers with sparkling buckles; she wore long white gloves, and carried a silver-sequinned handbag. Millay was seated at a round table with Edouard Bourdet, the playwright whose works explored homosexuality and lesbianism, three French counts and countesses, Noël Coward, a Russian prince, and Dicky Gordon, the lesbian lover of Elsa Maxwell. George Dillon was not present.

> Everybody was sweet to me, but I had the curse (of course I would have—came on just as I was dressing to go) & I felt blue & the music was awful for dancing, Hungarians playing jazz. . . . Anyway I was shockingly lonely, & I stayed on and on long after I wanted to go, because I hated to go alone.

This wistful tone must have been calculated to make Eugen ecstatic. After mentioning the company of Noël Coward and others she admitted, "I really enjoyed it a lot,—but you know, I had the curse, & I wanted my Skiddlepins." And she covered the page with X's.

There he has it, not two weeks since he sailed—she has her period and is not feeling well, and she wants her husband. It's their original domestic dynamic; and somewhere in his heart Eugen probably suspected, reading this on June 1, that all he needed in this game was patience.

But she did keep him wondering. On May 27, she sent him her social calendar for the week, including "George Dillon is coming here to have cocktails with me at 6:30 today, after which we are going out to dine and to the theatre." On June 1, she wrote: "Darling, this is your mother's birthday, & I just want to write you a line . . . —When you write tell me every different flower that's in blossom now at Steepletop. I'm having fun here, but I wish I could be at Steepletop at the same time. Love to Skiddlepins the Brave."

He was writing more letters than she was, and he began to interpret the imbalance as her effort to let him down gently. His long letter of June 2 submits apologies and resolutions: "I have been a fool, darling, a conceited, flat-footed fool. I am ashamed to have bombarded you with all my letters and cables." And now that he had had time to think about it, he made up his mind that he would not go back to her until she asked him, and not before he was certain she was not doing it out of some mistaken kindness for him.

> I am not going to be the black shadow between you and George and make you think that you must snatch your happiness whenever the ogre is away. Settle down quietly, Edna, take a place for a year or come back here with him, do what you like, but do not think of me as the plague of Egypt, or as a husband who with a cold hand any day can be expected to separate two young lovers. Please tell him and tell yourself, that you are going to be together for ever and ever, or as long as you wish to.

Was there ever such a letter, or such a husband? If Millay or Dillon were taking any pleasure in cuckolding this fellow, he meant to put a stop to it pronto. "I do not want you and George to think that you are snatching and stealing happy moments from a cruel world. *I am giving you eternity: all your life.*" How on earth could any woman answer such a statement? To her credit Millay, as clever as she was, did not even try.

This letter fatefully crossed his wife's of May 30, somewhere in the ship lanes of the Atlantic, a little note in which she inquired about her beloved dog, Ghost. The overleaf of her hotel stationery reads: "Wham, wham, Freckles could never, never love anybody so much as you, or ever, ever give you up for anybody." But he would not receive that pronunciamento until June 7, and in the meantime he was ready for anything. He wrote: "I will not do anything drastic and will live off your money for a year, unless we make some definite decision before that time. But in a year, all three of us ought to know what we want." After that she need never worry about him. He reminded her he had an income. "I made certain inquiries, and I know now that at any time I can go and live by myself and be economically independent."

Then he received the letter saying that "Freckles could never love anybody so much as you," and his landscape shifted. He replied: "I do believe your letter and I have not drunk one solitary drink today and I'm drunk with happiness. . . . And I curse myself for ever having left you for reasons too strong and beautiful"; that is, principles that are too lofty for any mortal such as himself ever to grasp. He would pronounce them with conviction one day; then the next day he would denounce them as inhuman. To celebrate the good news from Paris, the next night Eugen went to New York to make love with an old friend of his named Erica Willrich. She was overjoyed to see him again, and wrote a long and passionate love letter on June 9, assuring him of her undying devotion.

From June until July Eugen's letters have two themes: the exquisite beauty of Steepletop in the summer, and his desire to sail to France and be with his wife.

> The daisies and heliotropes are fighting for place. So far the heliotrope wins. . . . They are lovely and their fragrance is marvelous. What with them and the Jasmine bush under the maple where the white bench is, it is impossible for a man to work and not think of you. Oh, yes, my dear, listen: amongst the stones and under the white bench, in fact the whole throne under the maple, is full of pennyroyal.

He enclosed some fragrant pennyroyal in the envelope. He visited Cora's grave, and sent Edna some mountain laurel blossoms from the hillside. The garden was heavenly, and never had he loved any place as he loved Steepletop then. "Edna, darling, do you remember the moss-rose you planted near the garden house? It is the loveliest thing; like a little Irish peasant girl in a shawl. I am sending it to the flower show at Hillsdale. I am sending some columbines, too." He won top honors in the flower competitions.

He was breeding pheasants, and dogs, and going to the horse races at Belmont with his neighbor Bill Brann, then listening to the Sharkey-Schmelling fight on the radio with him. William L. Brann, an ex–advertising executive, was now part owner of a horse farm in Maryland; secretly he owed a great deal to the Boissevains' increasing interest in his thoroughbreds.

Eugen swam and sunbathed daily. He was the same, strong, fun-loving, high-spirited fellow, but down deep he was pining for his wife. "I lost 12 pounds and I am very strong, and Max [Eastman] told me I was very beautiful, and I would crush you in my arms and break all your little bones and eat you up."

By turns his letters to her were lyrical, poignant, and ribald—as when he wrote: "Couldn't you take a small handkerchief and put it in your Kitty before you take a bath, and mail it to me? I'm longing for your perfume."

When he grew serious—especially after reading some letters she had written while depressed—he argued forcefully that she must cable him at once and grant him permission to go to her. Eugen had agreed to stay out of her way until she was ready to see him again. Now he was sure she needed him, yet still she held him off. There was trouble in paradise: Dillon was jealous of Eugen, so many thousands of miles away, and dissatisfied with Edna's ambivalence.

On June 22, 1932, Millay wrote Eugen a thirteen-page letter, in which she admitted that on Sunday, June 19, she had told George that they better not see each other for a while. She insisted this was her idea and "very much against his will." She told Eugen it was one of the hardest things she had ever done.

> He said that he would give up anything for me, even his work, that just to be with me was more important than everything else & why didn't we forget everything else & just stay together & be happy & let every-thing go to smash. . . . To hear him talk like that made me realize how desperate he had become. And I couldn't stand it.

This is significant—that she "couldn't stand it." Millay never seemed to be satisfied until she had pushed an affair to that extreme. Dillon knew how much his mistress longed for her husband, and he wanted her to choose between them. It made the young man crazy with jealousy that Edna—if put to it—would not choose him. She never told him this outright, but he knew it in his heart.

"Finally I practically put him out of the apartment. . . . Probably if I hadn't been on the verge of getting the curse I shouldn't have had the nerve to do it." Millay almost never wrote to Eugen when she was not suffering from her period. She seemed to miss him most during those times—and she wanted him to know she was not pregnant. This worried him, that she might be pregnant with Dillon's child.

"I'm keen about his poetry, & I helped him get this Guggenheim thing, & I'm not going to be the one to bitch it all up for him now.—Oh, I know you think he's a mess, & has no stamina, & you're probably bored by all this. But you've been urging me to write you how things are. And this is how they are." It was only Wednesday, but to Edna "it has seemed like a long time because I realize we may never see each other any more. That's probably not the case, but it might turn out that way."

Millay's published letters (to Mary Kennedy, June 23, 1932) refer to a mishap on June 21, when Millay was drunk and disorderly at a Paris dinner party for Kennedy's friends. Her excuses were: "a pain amidships, and some-thing on my mind besides. But who cares who tripped a fallen woman." It was the breakup with Dillon that was on her mind.

This long letter to Eugen is flashing mixed signals. She says she's quite alone. She doesn't know exactly what to do. She may go to the Riviera; she might go back to Steepletop. "But what I'm really hoping is that things are not really over between George & me." If not, she better stand by. Then, in what appears to be a concluding paragraph, she virtually gives the game away:

> For whereas you and I are never really apart, no matter how far away from each other we may be, between myself and George the distance widens very rapidly when once we're separated. And this doesn't mean that he doesn't love me, because he does. But he just is like that.

But the next evening she added more pages to the letter, including the lines: "I wonder if you will understand why, when I'm simply crazy to see you, & when I really need you awfully, I say that you'd better not come just now." It would be "too easy" to return to him. "I mustn't forget. I mustn't be diverted. I must taste this thing & eat it & find out what it's made of. I must know whether I can get along without him or not, whether I can do it while I'm all alone." She will make no effort to contact George. "It's just in order to know myself a little better that I'm interested to know how I feel."

Closing at last, she begged Eugen not to think she was unhappy or desperate—she only had an ache "in the pit of my memory. . . . I have to stick it out a little while longer.—If I didn't need you so, I'd ask you to come. Can you beat it? Is de skoit crazy? Love from me," and she covered the page with snowflake-shaped kisses.

Eugen received this enormous epistle on June 30, and cabled his wife immediately that he would sail for France in a week if she did not wire to stop him. The letter he wrote her on July 1 is brilliant. "Forgive my emotional wires. But I cannot help going crazy when I think of you unhappy. If I did believe it, I'd go to New York and steal an airplane and fly over to you. . . . You'll see Skiddles soon, even if you have sent me a cable not to come. I'll hide myself somewhere in the country. And when you think you're unhappy I'll stand outside your window and pull funny faces and make funny noises and make you laugh."

Eugen's approach was thoughtful and consistent. He did not for a moment presume that she was done with her young lover. Rather he expressed alarm that she had sent Dillon packing. Eugen urged that they go back to the drawing board: "Let's try to be all three together. Let's make another heroic attempt. Maybe we can teach him not to be jealous of me. Maybe we can teach him to like me." If Eugen's stance was a ploy, a kind of "reverse psychology," his letters never show it, as they proffer a sincere (if strained) argument for free love. He told Edna she was dead wrong about how *he* felt about George. "I *do* like him. Under other circumstances I doubtless would love him. But although I don't rave and roar like a jealous man, and although I don't run around with a gun, don't think for a moment that I am not jealous. . . ."

He wanted Dillon to meet him on "neutral ground." That's why he was determined to go to Paris, and would not take no for an answer. "I don't want you to be unhappy. There is a way and we'll find it. I will do anything. And I can do anything. It is preposterous that three intelligent and courageous people should have to decide that the only way out would be to be resigned to be unhappy. It is preposterous. It is against nature." Dillon probably disagreed.

On July 3, Edna cabled him saying that everything was all right and that he must telephone her on July 5. "I wonder what you mean by all right and I wonder why you want me to telephone you?" he wrote. He thought she wanted to prevent his coming to Paris, and feared he would go anyway:

> But then I am always stronger than I think I will be. And I do want you to be happy. . . . But God is putting me through my paces. Sometimes I think I am going crazy. But then one does not go crazy so easily. By this time my guts must be made out of thick rubber, ribbed and cross-ribbed, like a new Cadillac tire. . . . I can stand anything and I will. Am I not going normally through life, while waiting till tomorrow to telephone you and hear your voice and what you have to say? I do not know how I am going to stand it. I am as nervous as a rat.

Eugen had made arrangements to telephone Paris from Pittsfield, as the connection could not be made from the farm. He packed a bottle of wine and a bottle of gin in the Cadillac, and took Norma Ellis with him for comfort. He left Norma in the car, sworn to secrecy in case he should decide later that he wanted no one else to know he had spoken to his wife. What he had written in a letter he would say on the phone:

"You poor kid, having two such nice boys crazy about you. If only one of us was less nice or loved you a little less. Poor kid, I'll help you as much as I can. But in a way it must be grand. . . . You know you are alive and beautiful and terribly desirable, and that is something worth suffering for."

But she had made her choice. She was coming home.

*M*illay gratefully returned to her bittersweet reunion with Eugen, the spectacular beauty of Steepletop in summer and autumn, and renewed inspiration for poetry.

> Earth does not understand her child,
>   Who from the loud gregarious town
> Returns, depleted and defiled,
>   To the still woods, to fling him down.
>   (from "The Return")

Her fame and her income increased, as, on Christmas 1932, she began a series of radio broadcasts over the WJZ Blue network. She was the first American poet ever to command a medium usually reserved for show business personalities, statesmen, and broadcasters.

Still, despite the comforts of her home and the thrill of the poetry pouring from her pen, Millay needed distraction. She felt landlocked at Steepletop, so in July of 1933, she and Eugen purchased Ragged Island, one of the outermost islands in Casco Bay, near Brunswick, Maine, for $750. The rocky island had just enough room for the small fisherman's cottage that stood on it. They often stayed there for a few weeks in the spring and summer, so Edna could hear the sound of the sea again. She and Eugen would swim and float naked in the ocean for hours. As she wrote to "Lulu" Powys, they would "gather driftwood, haul our lobster-traps, make fish chowders, and sail and read, and sit on the rocks."

> There you row with tranquil oars, and the ocean
> Shows no scar from the cutting of your placid keel;
> Care becomes senseless there; pride and promotion
> Remote; you only look; you scarcely feel.
>   (from "Ragged Island")

George Dillon remained in Paris for two years, studying at the Sorbonne, and perfecting his French so that he could become a serviceable translator of Baudelaire and Racine. His love affair with Millay was not yet over. In

1934, when she and Eugen were wintering on the Riviera at Cap d'Antibes, Edna slipped away to spend the weekend of March 9 with Dillon in Paris just before he sailed on the *City of Havre*, bound for Baltimore. He was going to live with his parents in Richmond. That summer Dillon visited Steepletop where the poets agreed to collaborate on a translation of Baudelaire's *Les Fleurs du Mal*. For eight months they worked on the poems, he in Virginia, she in New York and Florida. What had been the most passionate affair of Millay's life was winding down into a working relationship, a friendship, and although his side of the story will never be known, her inconsolable grief over the loss of her young lover suggests that it was against her will—despite what she told Eugen.

> Well, I have lost you; and I lost you fairly;
> In my own way, and with my full consent.
>
> . . . .
>
> Some nights of apprehension and hot weeping
> I will confess; but that's permitted me;
> Day dried my eyes; I was not one for keeping
> Rubbed in a cage a wing that would be free.
> (from Sonnet XLVII, *Fatal Interview*)

She grieved for Dillon even as she mourned for her mother and her own fading beauty. Returning from Europe a month after seeing Dillon in Paris in 1934, she wrote in her diary: "I wish I could be kept under morphine the whole way until we dock," and she is not speaking figuratively. Instead of taking morphine as an anodyne, she stayed drunk. Her drinking in 1933 and 1934 was constant, gargantuan, from breakfast champagne to gin fizzes with lunch, afternoon martinis, wine with dinner, and brandy nightcaps (except for April 30–July 23, 1933, when a Dr. Beebe ordered her to quit on pain of death).

In November 1934 she published *Wine from These Grapes*, the best of her later works, and it is naturally a book of elegies—for the loss of Dillon, for her mother, for the demise of youth. It includes one strong sonnet, which concludes a six-part elegy for Cora.

> Time, that renews the tissues of this frame,
> That built the child and hardened the soft bone,
>
> . . . .
>
> Attends no less the boy to manhood grown,
> Brings him new raiment, strips him of his own.
>
> . . . .

Such hope is mine, if this indeed be true,
I dread no more the first white in my hair,
Or even age itself, the easy shoe,
The cane, the wrinkled hands, the special chair.
Time, doing this to me, may alter too
My anguish, into something I can bear.

The sonnet may as well have been written to George Dillon, and the conditional "may" in the next to last line is crucial. She dreaded old age as only a woman who has been very beautiful can. And Time let her down, failing to alter her anguish into something she *could* bear. It may have been the gradual loss of Millay's beauty that finally put off her young lover, and she would never get over the shock of it, the horror, and the disappointment. Before that she may truly have believed she was immortal.

There are no love poems in *Wine from These Grapes*. During her time in Paris with Dillon she wrote only one poem, which she mentioned in a letter to Eugen as a sad one. She did not name it, but the piece is probably the posthumously published "Armenonville," a free verse narrative that prophesies the end of the affair. The lovers are seated at a table near the lake in the Bois de Boulogne. She describes the beautiful scene, the small pink and red begonias in profusion covering the embankment. Suddenly, turning aside in shyness from her lover's too intense gaze, she spies a water rat emerging from the begonias. And when she turns back to her lover, "I was aghast at my absence, for truly I did not know / Whether you had been asking or telling." There had been a time when she hung on George's every word, as he did hers, but now that he had grown demanding, she was tuning him out.

The affair would end, dying piecemeal over a period of several years in which the older woman continued to be teased by hope. The love affair ended, but the pain for Millay would not. She had lost the erotic power to hold Dillon, and he could not let her down gently enough. His young blood was the last taste she would ever have of that elixir that had inspired her for twenty years, the heady wine of eros. She loved Eugen more than anyone in the world, and he would have given her anything. But her husband could not give her that, any more than he could restore her lost youth or his own.

The next ten years of the poet's life would be spent in search of an effective anodyne, some substance or pastime besides poetry to ease her pain. Millay's fame and earning power stood at their peak, honorary degrees and laurels showered upon her, but neither money nor fame could ease "the ache in the pit of my memory." Of course, the first line of defense was writing poetry, but even the greatest poet cannot write poetry more than a few hours a day; sometimes Millay would go for months without writing a single verse. The second line of defense was alcohol. But booze is a notoriously treacherous friend, and by 1935 Fleischmann's gin had become one of Millay's worst enemies without her seeming to realize it.

She swam whenever she could, and she played tennis daily, doubles, in good weather, five or more sets a day. Travel was always a welcome distraction, when her health permitted it. Beginning with the winter of 1934–1935, the Boissevains became snowbirds, leaving Steepletop during the winter for the Virgin Islands, Cuba, and Delray Beach, Florida. There they rented a house near their friend William L. Brann, who had a horse farm nearby at Boynton Beach. With Brann, Millay could pursue her education in Thoroughbred horse racing and breeding, which had become a new obsession.

She was a loyal, in many ways an exemplary friend, even when chronic illness disabled her in her mid-forties. She sent money to the ailing Edgar Lee Masters. She kept in touch with Floyd Dell, advising him in the writing of his memoirs. She and Eugen visited her old lover Llewelyn Powys and his wife, Alyse, in England in April 1934. When Millay learned that Lulu was not only unwell but in financial trouble due to a bogus libel action against him, she gave the Powyses two thousand dollars in March 1935, insisting: "If you wish to hurt me beyond healing, refuse my gift."

And she could refuse no family member who was in need. On September 28, 1935, she heard from her long-lost father.

> Dear Vincent,
> You will be surprised to hear from me and under such conditions; matters have gone badly with me for the last few years and I have gotten where I must do something. I have been sick much of the time for some years and especially the past year. I had a partial stroke last summer which affected my head. . . . I really have no income at all. . . .

His friends had helped him all they could, and Henry Millay was in debt. "Some seven or eight dollars will take care of me weekly after my immediate needs are taken care of. . . . Unless you can see your way clear to help me there is nothing for me but to apply to the state for aid which I am loathe to do."

She immediately sent her father the money he needed, and she continued to support him until he died four years later. During those years, Edna and Eugen would also be the sole financial support of her sister Kathleen, who was descending into paranoid schizophrenia, a bizarre drama that would become a constant torment to Edna before reaching its tragic end.

But friendship continued to console her. The most fascinating, and perhaps the most affecting of Millay's friendships—apart from Eugen—was the long and dynamic relationship with Arthur Ficke. Starting with their flirtation by mail, he had known her since she was a girl. He had been her "spiritual advisor," her literary critic and editor, her lover, then her friend. Arthur built his home near Steepletop to be near Vincent. Abundant evidence in Millay's journals and letters, as well as in interviews that Anne Cheney conducted in 1971 with Gladys Ficke, shows that the tension between Edna and Gladys became nearly unendurable over the years. Notwithstanding the women's lifelong devotion to each other, Millay's proximity created a ceaseless low-level dissonance in the Fickes' marriage. Yet there was never any serious talk of the Fickes moving away from the Boissevains.

Ficke's lungs were frail from tuberculosis, and his discomfort at times undermined his usual good humor. This, and possibly Millay's affair with George Dillon, for a while opened a gulf between Arthur and Vincent. In her diary of May 22, 1934, she wrote: "Arthur is very embarrassed now when he is with me. We both think of the evening shortly before I sailed last winter when he told me he doesn't like my poetry any more, and held up to scorn specifically the phrase 'cool and aimless beauty' [from "My Spirit, Sore from Marching"] finding it execrable. 'That's not Beauty's massive sandal,' he said," referring to her great Euclid sonnet. She began to explain to him, "It's a different kind of thing entirely," but then she gave up.

Ficke disliked the poetry she was writing, and the poems were not altogether to blame. That summer of 1934, while Edna was working so hard on the Baudelaire translations, Arthur was rushed to the hospital for surgery. Edna and Eugen visited him there and found him so weak he could hardly speak. Near death, he heard Eugen's voice, "as if directly inside his ear." Eugen said, "You see now that there are many modes of being, and that all you have to do is choose which level you prefer and stay there." Arthur decided to live. A few years later he would undergo psychoanalysis with Dr. Karl Menninger, and this helped him to cope with his feelings for Millay. Remnants of unresolved anger and remorse still smoldered beneath the unending love between Millay and Ficke, as the following incident shows.

The stockbroker George La Branche, a wealthy neighbor, invited both the Boissevains and the Fickes to a cocktail party in 1937. Edna, as usual, had been drinking heavily: she was "at least six cocktails off my guard" when she joined Arthur by the fire in the gun room of the stockbroker's house. Soon they were deep in conversation. Arthur, who had a lawyer's way of springing questions on people, asked Edna out of the blue: "To whom did you write that sonnet, Vincie? *And you as well must die, beloved dust, / And all your beauty stand you in no stead.*"

Millay, her eyes misting, confessed that she had written it to him.

Two days later, September 23, in a letter eventually published, she scolded him and issued a categorical retraction. "This will be one of the most unpleasant letters you ever received, and I'm sorry. But it's time I got this matter off my chest and onto yours, where it belongs,—for it's all your fault my dear, for persisting in asking such shockingly indiscreet questions. The sonnet was not written to you." This was an out-and-out lie that she would not admit to Arthur until he was about to die years later. She would read the sonnet at his funeral.

Three days later, he wrote a gentleman's apology, promising he would "never again bother you with a kind of conversation that is so distasteful." But he insisted she eventually would find him "not quite so much to blame. . . . I asked my question respectfully, not snickeringly, as you seem to think." He asked her why she did not simply refuse to answer. Then he confessed: "I cannot assume the responsibility for the fact that the answer you chose to give was the one, of all conceivable ones, that would eventually cause me the most pain." It pained Arthur to realize that she had loved him that much.

Her reason for the lie was simple, and as he lay dying she told him, "I didn't want you to know, for sure, how terribly, how sickeningly in love with you I had been. And perhaps, also, I was still in love with you, or I shouldn't have cared."

Rich and poor, in sickness and health, Millay and Ficke remained devoted to each other—and to the poetry that had brought them together—until the day he died.

❧

Neither work nor friendship, nor the natural beauty of Steepletop and Ragged Island that she records so lyrically in her diary could dull the pain she felt in remembering her young lover. She wrote to Witter Bynner on May 2, 1935, "I am at present under the influence of hashish, gin, bad poetry, love, morphine and hunger. . . ."—a poisonous mix for sure, the medicine more dangerous than the disease. It is hard to say when Millay began using morphine habitually. But certainly by this time, when she had no physical complaints more serious than hangover headaches, menstrual cramps, and eye pain, she must have been taking the drug at her own discretion. Even then morphine was a controlled substance, but Eugen was able to obtain whatever she wanted from a pharmacy in Great Barrington.

Still she worked: "I never worked so hard on anything in my life," she said of the Baudelaire translations, in a letter to Powys after *The Flowers of Evil* was published in April 1936. No sooner did she finish the translations, in the little furnished house at Delray Beach, than she began writing the philosophical closet drama *Conversation at Midnight*, composing much of a first draft of the play before returning to Steepletop. On May 2, she and Eugen stopped for a night at the Palms Hotel at Sanibel Island, on their way north. While Eugen engaged the room and saw to their luggage, Edna walked on the beach gathering shells at sunset. She turned back a few minutes later and saw that the hotel was in flames.

Eugen was fine, but her clothing, books, and the manuscript for *Conversation at Midnight* went up in smoke. Her memory was excellent, so that summer she was able to recall most of the verses she had completed, though, she wrote to a friend on October 6, "with those on which I was still at work, I have been having an exhausting and nerve-wracking time."

In early November 1936, she and Eugen were driving up the hill to the farm in their Cadillac when her door flew open. She fell out and rolled down into a rocky gully, injuring her right shoulder. Later she wrote of the strange sensation of being "hurled out into the pitch-darkness," and how for long afterward she was in constant pain from an injury to nerves in her back. The doctors prescribed painkillers—Dilaudid and morphine.

In December she went to New York to buy new clothing because so many of her best things had been burned up in the hotel at Sanibel Island. In May she wrote to the poet Rolfe Humphries: "And in December, I came down with the flu. And in January something else happened, and I am still here. I have been working all winter and all spring on my new book—not like a dog, not like a slave; dogs and slaves must be relieved and rested from time to time, otherwise they crack up."

"Something else happened . . ."—the phrase in Millay's published letter to Humphries (May 17, 1937) has troubled biographers for half a century, the mystery of what kept Millay at the St. Regis Hotel for six months, much of it without Eugen. An unsigned letter from George Dillon, written on January 18, may illuminate what happened. He notes that she telephoned him in Richmond upon "an atavistic impulse": she wanted him to come to her. He found it "somehow quite in line with this strange and unseasonable January—the forsythia blossoms, etc." And he came. It was George Dillon who kept her in New York that winter: her "physician minus physic, minus robe," she had called him in *Fatal Interview*, the "one mortal on the teeming globe / Could minister to my soul's or body's needs."

But once again the medicine proved worse than the ailment, as the poems that arose from this eleventh-hour liaison—the love poems in *Huntsman, What Quarry?*—so sadly demonstrate. What had been a raging fire of passion between them had dwindled to a few embers they could not fan to flame again, and the age difference between the lovers caused Millay a new anguish. They met in a shabby cubicle on Eighth Street that Dillon had tried to brighten with fresh flowers. She wrote, in her poem "Rendezvous," that "Indeed I could have loved you better in the dark. . . ." She would have preferred rooms more casual, less aware of history.

> Yet here I am, having told you of my quarrel with the taxi driver over
>   a line of Milton, and you laugh; and you are you, none other.
>
> Your laughter pelts my skin with small delicious blows.
> But I am perverse: I wish you had not scrubbed—with pumice, I
>   suppose—
> The tobacco stains from your beautiful fingers. And I wish I did not
>   feel like your mother.

The love poems she wrote then are sad, when they are not remorseful. In "What Savage Blossom," she struggles to find words for her experience with Dillon, "the onslaught of a little time with you," and cannot call it love, and cannot call it hate, either. "Call it by name, / Now that it's over, now that it is gone and cannot hear us. / It was an honest thing. Not noble. Yet no shame."

The longest poem in *Huntsman*, the eight-part "Theme and Variations," is a reflection upon her last encounter with Dillon. "Not even my pride will suffer much," she bravely begins, "If this ill-timed, intemperate clutch / Be loosed by you and not by me. . . ." But she was wounded. "What can you mix for me to drink / That shall deflect me? What you do / Is either malice, crude defense / Of ego, or indifference. . . . Some love, and some simplicity, / Might well have been the death of me."

> V
>
> I had not thought so tame a thing
> Could deal me this bold suffering.
>
> I have loved badly, loved the great
> Too soon, withdrawn my words too late . . .
>
> . . . .

You only, being unworthy quite
And specious,—never as I think
Having noticed how the gentry drink
Their poison, how administer
Silence to those they would inter—
Have brought me to dementia's brink.

On February 25, 1937, she was so depressed that she wrote to a Dr. Cassel asking if her blood pressure (which was normal) might be the reason that getting out of bed, bathing, dressing, even rising from a chair, not to mention housework or writing, took such effort.

Might not this low blood pressure all by itself account for the fact that I must exert so great an amount of will-power and of stern discipline of the quick, anxious, angry and determined mind over inert and uninterested matter, in order to force myself to do anything at all? Is benzedrine [an amphetamine stimulant] the *only* thing which can for a few hours give me a feeling of energy & the power to do the things I so much desire to do, but am kept from doing by physical, not mental inertia?

CHALLEDON

Jockey Seabo has done damned well on Challedon so far; he knows the horse, and believes in him; he doesn't tease him and he doesn't make him nervous; he doesn't shake him awake until he's had his regular four-furlongs' sleep; and when he does wake him up he whispers something in his ear that makes the whole thing plain, and the horse goes thundering past the stand and wins the trophy.

(from Millay's 1939 letter to W. L. Brann)

Millay loved the races. Bill Brann liked to drive the Boissevains to the track in his Rolls-Royce. The poet and her husband found excitement handicapping and betting on the Thoroughbreds. It got her mind off her heartache for hours at a time, and set her pulse drumming more safely than did the

Benzedrine inhaler. At Belmont and Saratoga she stole moments of ecstasy. Almost no one knew how serious a fan of the turf Millay had become.

During the 1930s she reached the height of her fame and earning power, netting between $17,500 and $21,000 annually from 1934 to 1939, according to her income tax returns. Much of her gross income, as well as revenue from the farm (which usually showed a loss), was offset by tax deductions—her travel and work expenses, plus Steepletop's upkeep—so that her net income was almost wholly discretionary; $20,000 in 1935 had the purchasing power of more than $300,000 today. In Europe the dollar was even stronger. (On June 6, 1932, Eugen had informed Edna that $1,000 would be plenty of money for her to stay in Paris until November and sail home first class.) Living at Steepletop for the Boissevains, their maids, farmhands, and livestock cost about $2,000 per year.

So one of the mysteries in Millay's life is this: What did she do with all that money? Certainly she purchased fantastic clothing, but not much after 1936. After they disposed of the $42,000 Cartier emerald ("much too valuable for me to wear . . ."), Millay did not own expensive jewelry. They drank good wine, but made a lot of it themselves. Opiates were remarkably inexpensive. Her bill at the St. Regis in May of 1936 prompted this trenchant letter to her editor at Harper's:

> I have no time to soften this blow: I've got to have a thousand dollars right away. . . . I know that my royalties will be transparent from erosion for the next thousand years, but I can't help it. I want also, if it is acrobatically possible, to have my June advance doubled to one thousand. . . .

She wanted her June and July advances doubled, and for her August, September, and October payments of $500 to continue, although they were due to expire in July. "It will take almost a thousand dollars to buy my way out of this hotel," she wrote, but she had demanded $3,500 of advance monies over and above what the company owed her.

Why was she so desperate for money? The answer lies in her voluminous unpublished correspondence with Bill Brann. It may take an FBI agent, one of those operatives armed with an accounting degree, to examine the Boissevains' financial records and uncover the final proof of the following hypothesis. But it will someday be proven.

Millay was a major shareholder in a horse farm in Maryland that stabled twenty Thoroughbreds. It is probable that she was at one time the sole owner of the farm and horses, and nearly certain that she was a silent partner with controlling interest during the late 1930s, when she was pleading with her publishers for more money.

Here is how it came about. Before the stock market crash in 1929, two advertising executives, William L. Brann and Robert Castle, decided they had seen enough of the business world. As Bill Brann told the story, they were "two tired and retired businessmen who turned to racing and breeding for recreation." They purchased land near Frederick, Maryland, and engaged C. J. Fitzgerald, an expert breeder, to purchase a top racing prospect.

This was the same Bill Brann who owned a farm near Steepletop, the man who was one of Eugen's best friends. Under Brann's tutelage the Boissevains became racing enthusiasts. Edna, who did nothing halfway, became a fanatic, devouring books on horses and turf history. Her secretary, Helen Bruce, who accompanied Millay on reading tours, recalled the mnemonic device the poet used to warm up her voice and memory before her recitals: Pacing up and down backstage Millay would recite all the Kentucky Derby winners, from 1875 forward: Aristides, Vagrant, Baden-Baden, Day Star, Lord Murphy, Fonso, Hindoo, Apollo, etc. The horses' names made a beautiful music. The poet once wrote to her friend Autti James, "If I wasn't so busy finding out what horses won the races in Maryland today, I might have time to write."

In 1931 Brann and Castle purchased Challenger II, an expensive top-class colt from England. Right away the colt was injured in a freak accident in Maryland, running into a barbed-wire fence, so he never raced. That was a bad start for Brann-Castle Farm, as it was then called. As a stallion, Challenger II sired only fifty-one foals through 1935, and the farm was not prospering. In 1936 Brann bought out Castle, and in 1937 he changed the name of the farm to Glade Valley.

During the mid- to late-1930s, when Millay was "ill" and reclusive and complaining to her literary friends of "epistophobia" (the absolute incapacity to write letters), she was typing hundreds of pages of remarkable letters to William L. Brann in the utmost secrecy. She signed her letters W. L. Millay, Owner; he signed his W. L. Brann, Manager, from farms in Florida, Maryland, and Arizona.

There can be no question as to the authorship of these letters. The literary style alone would prove these were Millay's; but there are also hundreds of corrections, postscripts, and marginalia in Millay's hand. Brann was also an elegant writer. Their secret correspondence concerning the breeding, purchasing, training, and racing of Millay's Thoroughbreds—which would make a hefty book—will be of incalculable value to sportsmen and historians of the turf.

It is inconceivable that it was only a charade they were playing, as she instructed him in purchasing, training, and naming the horses, and hiring and firing personnel on the farm—as well as premier jockeys—and deciding when and where to race the horses. Inconceivable, because there were enormous amounts of money involved and prices discussed. Brann did what Millay told him to do, her humble and obedient servant, because it was her money—most if not all of it.

In an eight-page typed letter to Brann of November 19, 1937, she tells him, "I am far from satisfied with the way things are going at that farm of mine in Maryland." Then she mentions several significant changes in the personnel she made there last spring, when she was dunning Harper's for the $3,500.

> Another, and here I refer to my changing of trainers, was something, as you know, which I had wanted to do for at least seven years and which you have dissuaded me from doing by one argument after another of your own. I think you can't deny that I've lost a great deal of money and considerable prestige [in stud fees] by following your advice so long in this matter.

So, she had been investing in the farm since 1930. It was her money that enabled Brann to buy out Castle in 1937—nobody had that kind of cash during the Depression except gangsters and best-selling poets. By the time Brann-Castle Farm was renamed Glade Valley in November 1937, W. L. Millay was calling the shots from Steepletop and watching her horses run whenever the track was within hailing distance.

By 1936 she had twenty horses at Glade Valley, including Harp Weaver, Ugin, Savage Beauty, Journey On, The Schemer, Challenger, and Challephen. She and Brann soon reduced the number to twelve so that they might afford better broodmares. Also, Brann wrote, "the money you will have to put up for the farm will be one-third less."

Her knowledge of horses and racing, particularly of her own horses, was formidable, astounding. It could only have been gained by hundreds of hours at the track, in stables and paddocks, and many, many more hours in study.

> Why was not Challephen scratched last week in the Bowie Handicap? Why was he permitted to run against Seabiscuit [sic] and Esposa over a fast track? Everybody knew, except apparently you and [Louis, the trainer] Schaefer, that this horse had no chance against horses of that class unless they were all running in black bean soup. Everybody expected him to be scratched—him and Chanceview. And Chanceview

was scratched; and Chanceview, two days later, came home in the Prince George's Handicap *in the mud.*

There are hundreds of pages of such detailed analysis, all of it well informed, and much of it hilarious, vintage Millay humor. Here she addresses the subject of a talented but shady jockey she wants for an important race:

> You want, as you never wanted a woman in your life, [jockey] Don Meade. Well, he can be had. He seems to be riding for Tom, Dick and Lucky Teter. . . . I know if Meade rides in New York again it'll be over the dead bodies of a lot of sports-column writers. He can ride in California, I suppose; anybody could ride in California. They'd let Al Capone ride in California, if he could get his weight down. They'd probably give him a silk ladder out of Alcatraz, if he could ride, and if he could get his weight down. But about Kentucky, I don't know.

She upbraids Brann for passing up a sale in which she might have purchased a superb broodmare:

> Peplum is by Chicle out of Frilette by Man O'War and she is a full sister of Jabot. What would have been the harm of getting a little of that blood into Walkersville? Peplum went for $6200. What do you expect me to pick up in a claiming race or in any other smart way as good as that for much less than that? I was willing to pay that price; in fact I would have gone higher.

She is furious at her manager because his attention is divided—he is overseeing farms in Arizona and Florida in addition to hers.

She needs a great broodmare for Challenger. "We've got to aim high, and we've got to be prepared to pay a price that will hurt. . . . Good God, the horse has got to have *some* cooperation! He can't be sire and dam both!"

Her goal is clear: "What I would rather do than anything else on God's good Tan-bark is to breed one great horse." In this same letter of November 19, 1937, she notes that she has been "confined to the house for a month with nothing to do but read detective stories which are all bad, and worry about the state of my horses and their management, which is even worse." There is nothing the matter with her—that the doctor can find, anyway—but a head cold. "But you and I know there is plenty more the matter. . . ." Brann did not know exactly, but she was grieving over George Dillon, and the demise of her erotic power and beauty, and she was increasingly dependent upon opiates to calm her nerves and lift her spirits.

For the next two years, until the spring of 1939—years that have always drawn a blank in Millay's biographies, apart from her writing *Huntsman, What Quarry?*—her secret passion, her obsession, waking and sleeping, was horse racing. In fact it was one horse in particular. She fell in love with a colt that Challenger had sired in 1936 out of a broodmare that Brann had bought for the poet for a mere two thousand dollars. She would name it Challedon.

※

Why did Millay keep her passion a secret? Her mother had divorced her husband for his compulsive gambling, among other offenses. This might have been reason enough for Vincent to keep her Thoroughbreds a secret, at least while Cora was still living. Owning racehorses is no more than a glamorous form of high-stakes gambling, with odds for the owners about as fair as what a sporting man gets at the betting window.

After Cora's death there were more compelling reasons for keeping the stable a secret. The poet, ever protective of her public image in every detail, did not want America to know that the money folks paid for her books was pouring into a gambling enterprise. Millay was known as beauty's disciple, the handmaiden of the Muses, the American Joan of Arc. She would not allow the name of Edna St. Vincent Millay to appear on the humorous stories she wrote for *Vanity Fair*, using instead the pseudonym Nancy Boyd. She did not want to see her name published daily in the various racing papers. It would be the death of her reputation as a serious poet.

Brann, of course, was only too happy to have Millay's financial backing as well as her uncanny expertise in matters of breeding and racing horses, for which he took all the credit. In December 1937 Millay wrote to him:

> I have every hope for a real success with my horses. . . . The get of Challenger which is an English horse, whose whole style and stamina were built up by English procedure, would do much better in my opinion, to take their time in growing and forming their bones without the strain of coming to race as two-year-olds, fully prepared by daily long gallops to run easily over a long track without tiring.

This would turn out to be the crucial advice in the making of a champion, Challedon. That colt from Glade Valley made Brann famous in his lifetime and guaranteed his place in the history of Thoroughbred horse racing.

The questions now left for historians and CPAs are how the partners handled the huge amounts of money; how they got the dollars to Brann without the government knowing about it (and therefore, inevitably, the public); and how, if ever, the Boissevains got a return on their investment. Let it be said that the horse-racing business in the days of Al Capone was subject to less stringent supervision than it is today, and more open to cash infusions from criminal and other anonymous sources.

On December 18, Brann wrote Millay "the heart-breaking news" that "this year you have only four yearlings by Challenger," two colts and two fillies. He asked her to name them. She had recently written a poem called "The Ballad of Chaldon Down," so Millay named the colt by Challenger out of Laura Gal "Challedon."

Millay's life was rich with ironies and fabulous reversals of fortune. While she and Brann were still angling for the ideal mare for Challenger, throwing tens of thousands of dollars at the game, the humble Laura Gal foaled Challedon, who became "one of the greatest thoroughbreds ever seen in this country," according to the eyewitness authority John "Salvatore" Hervey.

Challedon was a bay with black points, without a spot of white on him except for a fleck between his eyes. He stood 16.1 hands. In 1938 Salvatore described him as "all muscle, sinew and whipcord. . . . His head clean, blood-like, eager and of a fine expression. . . . His neck is rather thin, he has depth through the heart . . . hindquarters of a stayer, lean and rakish. . . . He stands well off the ground upon long legs and this gives him a grand, reaching stride which is at the same time very high. . . ." In full flight the horse was a thrill to behold.

Millay fell in love with the colt and became involved with every detail of his training. The poet had hired Louis J. Schaefer, a thirty-year-old former Maryland jockey, to oversee Challedon's daily regimen. Schaefer's colleagues, as well as the press, often questioned him for his unorthodox handling of the colt, charging him with inexperience. But Schaefer was merely following Millay's orders regarding two-year-olds: to let him "take his time growing." Described as a "late-blooming colt at two," Challedon began to burn up the turf in the autumn of 1938 when he won the New England Futurity, the Pimlico Futurity, and the Maryland Futurity for a total of sixty-seven thousand dollars in purses. As often happens in this business, the money was not coming in quite as fast as it was going out—on expenses, on travel, jockeys, new broodmares and racing prospects, and on paying off a mountain of debt. Although there is no record of it, Eugen and Edna were probably betting heavily on their horses to increase the excitement, hoping to parlay their inside information— and this, too, becomes a losing proposition over the long term.

In May of 1939, Challedon placed second in the Kentucky Derby, finishing far behind the winner and heavy favorite, Johnstown. It was a terrible blow to Millay. Being a perfectionist, she had hoped for a Triple Crown winner. A month later Challedon lost again to Johnstown in the Dwyer Stakes—and the poet was beside herself with fury. Challedon would not be eligible for the Belmont Stakes. Although Millay's colt did manage to defeat Johnstown in the Preakness on May 13, and went on to become Horse of the Year in both 1939 and 1940, Millay must have sold out to Brann before Challedon's purses mounted into the six digits. Incredibly, on the verge of rare fortune, she walked away from it. Two years later the poet had lost interest in horse racing, and she and Eugen were in debt. Challedon's lifetime earnings were $326,485.

LITTLE NANCY

❧

At forty-seven years of age, the image she saw in the mirror was disturbing. Alcohol and drugs had taken a fateful, undeniable toll. Her body sagged, her lips shriveled, her teeth were discolored, and pain had engraved her face. Writing poetry had been her first line of defense against pain, the anguish of growing old, of losing her erotic power and George Dillon's love. Then there was a steady stream of alcohol. And for two years the beautiful colt Challedon had been a constant source of excitement, a distraction from her heartaches. Now she had let go of the horses, and every month brought new agonies.

Now sometimes she addressed her alter ego, Nancy Boyd—which both was and was not really Edna—as "Little Nancy." Concerned that her dependence on drugs was getting out of hand, Millay began to write memos such as "Advice to Little Nancy":

> Exercize Will-Power in *all* things, big or little. Don't become self-indulgent. Don't become sloppy in *anything*, in your thinking, in your dress, in *anything*.
>
> Don't fool yourself. If you feel nervous, don't purposely (half-subconsciously) make yourself *more* nervous. Instead, turn your attention at once to something that interests you.

Have a drink, instead, sometimes.

Never let the other person see you using the hypodermic, or know that you are about to do so, or have just done so. *Never* leave the syringe about where you see it.

But the pressures on her seemed unbearable. World War II began in September 1939, and Eugen feared for his family in Holland. His assets there were frozen (he would lose them altogether when Germany invaded the Low Countries in 1940). And all the while Millay was training Challedon, sister Kathleen had been sinking deeper and deeper into a depression that was verging on paranoia. By 1939 the Boissevains were completely supporting Kathleen as she wandered aimlessly from coast to coast, in and out of psychiatric wards. They claimed her as a dependent on their tax returns. Yet her letters became ever more importunate, desperate, and finally threatening.

Kathleen Millay's tragic descent into madness darkly coincides with Edna's slide into morphine addiction. Kathleen's letters during the early 1940s ranged from long mournful requests for money—pathetic chronicles of hard luck and illness—to brief and sardonic thank-you notes, and finally to harangues and jeremiads against Edna and her husband. Kathleen threatened legal action over "reneged promises" of financial support, and over property jointly owned by the sisters that she claimed Edna and Norma had stolen from her. At length Edna handed the correspondence over to Eugen, who, under his wife's supervision, treated the poor madwoman with enormous kindness and tact. Whatever money he could send her he sent; whatever property Kathleen demanded—chiefly the cottage in Camden their mother had owned, plus some furniture—he simply signed over to her.

Kathleen believed that Edna's fame and fortune had all come at her expense. As her doctor S. Bernard Wortis wrote on September 7, 1939, Kathleen felt "that many of the ideas her sister has incorporated in her works were ideas that she [Edna] has stolen from the patient." Her rage culminated in a letter to an autograph dealer named J. Duane Upton, which she wrote for an undisclosed sum, accusing Edna of letting her little sister starve. The scoundrel Upton mailed a copy to Boissevain, threatening to release the letter to the newspapers if Miss Millay did not comply with his requests for "longhand copies of any two of the following poems of hers: 'God's World,' 'Recuerdo,' 'Travel,' or 'Afternoon on a Hill.' Each copy to be signed by her of course." Eugen contacted the State's Attorney, filing charges for blackmail.

On September 19, 1939, Eugen wrote to Norma: "We go every week now to New York where Edna sees an eye doctor and an osteopath." In letters, published and unpublished, Millay referred to the continual shoulder and back pain that had been caused by her tumbling out of the automobile in 1936. Sometimes she complained she was too sore to hold a pen, sometimes too sore to type (while, in fact, she was typing weekly to Brann). Sometimes visitors to Steepletop saw her wearing a sling. But on November 22, 1939, Millay was so ill that a Dr. Connie Guion was summoned to Steepletop from Manhattan.

The poet was driven to New York Hospital, where she remained for twelve days. Neither the resultant bills nor the letters between Dr. Guion and the Boissevains points to a diagnosis. The doctors could not find any underlying cause for Millay's nervous panic and pain. The pain itself seemed to be the problem, and nothing but morphine could alleviate it. Dr. Guion was both extremely accommodating to her famous patient and protective of her privacy. "I did not wish to have any discussion by the house officers of the amount of morphine she was taking. To avoid this I signed for it daily and personally ordered the drug." In January and February 1940, at Eugen's request, the doctor provided prescriptions for the drugs that Millay needed.

※

The poet's intimate friend and former lover Llewelyn Powys died of tuberculosis on December 2, 1939. Then Millay's father passed away on December 19. Nowhere does she mention her father's death, although her checks supported him until the end. Arthur Ficke, like Lulu Powys, was slowly suffocating from TB. But Arthur would soldier on for a few more years, until his last breath, as her most devoted friend—the one with the greatest influence over her. He helped to save her life when drugs had carried her beyond the reach of reason.

Very rapidly during 1940, and in pain, Millay wrote the verses that appeared in the final book of poems she published in her lifetime, *Make Bright the Arrows*. From April 16–27, and then from May 25–30 of that year, Edna St. Vincent Millay was a patient at New Haven Hospital in Connecticut. Although in letters she and Eugen explained to everyone that she underwent surgery on the "nerves of the dorsal spine," the medical records and bills do not support this. It is unlikely that Millay ever had such surgery. No doubt she was in pain, and the physicians drugged her accordingly. She wrote to her editor Eugene Saxton begging for an advance. "The outrage of unalleviated pain has been coupled with the infuriating obligation of laying one sweet luscious grand ($1000) after another between the self-complacent and condescending teeth of one officious and inefficient hospital after another." During all that time she continued to write.

Make Bright the Arrows was published in November of that year. She knew the work was not her best. In a letter to George Dillon she called the verses "not poems, posters; there are a few good poems, but it is mostly plain propaganda. If some bright boy reviews it for *Poetry, please* remind him that I know bad poetry as well as the next one." Dillon was then *Poetry*'s editor, and William L. Brann was one of the magazine's major benefactors, so she had every reason to expect fair treatment in its influential pages.

She subtitled the book *1940 Notebook* so that critics might regard this as something other than poetry and thereby relax their standards. But they would not. Ficke tried to warn her not to publish such lines as: "I have gone to war, I am at war, I am at grips / With that which threatens more than a cold summer; / I am at war with the shadow, at war with the sun's eclipse, / Total, and not for a minute, but for all my days" (from "An Eclipse of the Sun Is Predicted"). It was not just that this was propaganda, Ficke said, but "it was *bad* propaganda." He persuaded her to omit half a dozen of the worst poems, but he could not stop her from publishing the book, which opens with a "Joan of Arc" poem. Like Joan, Millay wanted to lead her country to war—in her case before America was ready. In February Millay had sent the British American Ambulance Corps a check for two thousand dollars to purchase a "Canteen Ambulance" for the Allies. And in June the Boissevains donated one thousand dollars to Pearl Buck's China Relief Fund.

But the reviewers were merciless, condemning the few good poems in *Make Bright the Arrows* along with the bad. She took it hard, shocked and disappointed that the poetry world did not allow her some dispensation—they failed to appreciate the sacrifice she had made, how painful it had been to write these "acres of bad poetry," even in such a noble cause. She would feel vindicated somewhat after Pearl Harbor.

※

In the Millay collection at the Library of Congress are the fully itemized monthly statements from two pharmacies in Great Barrington, Massachusetts: John M. Cassidy at 274 Main Street, and John T. Harper on the other side of the street at 311. The accounts from May 1940 to September 1945 show that Eugen Boissevain was purchasing staggering quantities of Dilaudid, paregoric, Nembutal tablets, codeine, Progynon, phenobarbital, Benzedrine, hypodermic syringes, needles, and numbered prescriptions for ampules of morphine solution and Demerol. Also he bought quarter-grain tablets of morphine one hundred at a time, sometimes two hundred or more per month. This was in addition to cases of Fleischmann's gin, Taylor's vermouth, Teacher's scotch, and Berry's rum procured at the same stores.

In 1941 Millay was well on her way to a three-grain-per-day morphine habit, which she usually supplemented with three or four grains of codeine and countless Nembutal tablets. (A grain equals sixty-four milligrams; ten milligrams of morphine is a standard dose for acute pain.) Alcoholism had already compromised her liver, making her more sensitive to the opiates; she was a small woman taking a dangerous quantity of drugs. One of the frightening aspects of the addiction is that she seemed to be in denial about it (as she was *not* about her alcoholism) until 1943, when she first tried to reduce her dependence. She pleaded headaches, backaches, shoulder aches, eye pain, menstrual cramps, and a broken ankle (in February 1942) as reasons for taking more and more opiates, while her health and spirits deteriorated, and her tolerance for morphine increased. The chain-smoking and the double martinis were not doing her much good, either.

On March 10 she wrote to her editor Saxton, "Seldom has the morphine seemed so slow in getting to me; although poor Ugin, who naturally hates like hell to have to give it to me, is quicker with it than the doctor by now." By then both of them were quick with the needle.

Somehow, through it all, she continued to work. Millay's final public reading was on January 18, 1941, when she read the poem "Invocation to the Muses" in New York. The National Institute of Arts and Letters (she had been elected to membership in 1940) had commissioned the poem for its Public Ceremonial in Carnegie Hall.

> O Muses, O immortal Nine!—
> Or do ye languish? Can ye die?
> How shall we heal without your help a world
> By these wild horses torn asunder?
> How shall we build anew?—how start again?
> How cure, how even moderate this pain
> Without you, and you strong?
>
> . . . .
>
> Oh come! Renew in us the ancient wonder,
> The grace of life, its courage, and its joy!

The sound of Millay's voice, as always, was electrifying as she read the hundred-line poem. Her audience of fellow poets and writers might have valued the performance even more had they realized they would never see her again.

After the Nazis razed the village of Lidice, Czechoslovakia, in the summer of 1942, killing all the men and sending the women and children to work camps, Millay wrote the ballad "Murder at Lidice." While this was not a good poem, it spoke to the mood of the times, and Millay still had the prestige to attract the interest of a major radio network. The dignified movie star Paul Muni (famous for portraying Louis Pasteur and Émile Zola) read the ballad over NBC's microphone on October 19, 1942, and all of America listened. It was an American version of Picasso's *Guernica*.

> And one, who was dying, opened his eyes,
> For he smelled smoke, and stared at the skies
> Cloudy and lurid with smoke and flame;
> From every building it billowed; it came
> From every roof, and out it burst. . . .
> From every window about him burst
> The terrible shape of flame,
> And clawed at the sky, and leapt to the ground,
> And ran through the village with a crackling sound
> And a sudden roar where a roof fell in;
> And he thought of his mother, left alone
> In the house, not able to rise from her chair. . . .

Norma was sitting by the radio at 10:30 when Alexander Woollcott excitedly introduced the poem. She wrote to Edna: "It just wasn't radio at all— it was alive. One could tell that Muni had hold of something that mattered to him." Norma said it was the best thing she had ever heard on the radio. Her friends called her afterward. "Bessie Poor called—they had all read it [in *Look* magazine] and had waited eagerly too. She was very moved, as she said, were they all."

Hundreds of letters poured in to NBC headquarters, from people moved to tears by the sentiment and the plight of the poor Czechs. At the end of October, Millay donated one thousand dollars to Czechoslovak Relief, more than NBC had paid her. The poet for whom World War I had been little more than a disruption of her love life was truly wracked by the insane cruelty of World War II—because of her husband's relatives' suffering in Holland, and because the war rushed into a vacuum left in her by the flight of Eros. Her pain matched the world's; she was dying, and it appeared the world was dying, too.

That spring, in order to avoid an overdose, she began keeping a log of her hourly dosages of morphine, Dilaudid, codeine, and Seconal. And she was studying to be a better wife—she even made lists for her alter ego Little Nancy about how to interact with Eugen more pleasantly. "1. Care for *Nothing* so much, (after your poetry) as to make You-Know-Whom happy. Put everything from your mind but this. . . . 2. *Never* mention yourself. . . . Never bring the conversation round to yourself to show that you understand what You-Know-Who is saying. . . . 3. Go out of doors EVERY DAY, no matter *what* you are working on, for at least a short walk."

She had become a recluse, tethered to Steepletop, her source of drugs. For six years she and Eugen would not even travel to Ragged Island; her agoraphobia grew so extreme that he would have to force her to get up out of her chair, move about, change out of her nightgown and into regular clothing. Her hair would go unwashed until Eugen shampooed it. She had been a proud beauty. Now she was ashamed to be seen. Somewhere she had enemies. Along with two hundred fan letters after "Murder at Lidice" was broadcast came a chilling card from New York, unsigned:

A Rag and a Bone and a Hank of Hair! You and Mahatma Gandhi would make a first-class team. You could give him some of your hair and some of your rags. Come down to earth. Be yourself. After all you are not a Second Messiah—really. The Lord have mercy on your husband.

Kathleen halted her ranting letters to Eugen after the blackmail incident. This was a relief for a few months, but then Edna began to worry. By October, when efforts to locate her sister failed, Edna was in a panic. Eugen wrote to Norma in late October asking if she and Charlie could make one last attempt to find Kathleen. If they had no luck he was going to put the case into the hands of a detective agency.

On Thanksgiving 1942 Norma and her husband visited Steepletop and found Vincent in a dreadful nervous state. Norma wrote to Ann Eckert, Kathleen's friend: "At any mention of Kathleen, Vincent couldn't get beyond her heartbreak that no matter what she did she couldn't make Kathleen love her. She called it the great tragedy of her life."

Kathleen was living in Manhattan, on Bedford Street, working a little in a war plant in New Jersey, and drinking heavily. In the summer of 1943 (just after the sudden death of Eugene Saxton, Millay's beloved editor) Kathleen became ill with stomach trouble. She grew so weak her friends begged her to go to the hospital, and finally her close friend Geraldine Morner, who had been taking care of her, took the sick woman to St. Vincent's Hospital on September 21. Coming out of the X-ray room, Kathleen lost consciousness and died almost immediately. She was conveyed to Bellevue for the autopsy, which revealed that the cause of death was "acute alcoholism."

Norma attended the funeral. Edna could not leave Steepletop.

Millay's increasing addiction to morphine after Kathleen's death so deeply troubled Arthur Ficke that he confronted her in a letter on October 15, 1943. By this time Millay's drug logs indicate that she was taking, by mouth and by injection, every hour on the hour (and sometimes all night), a total of between two and three grains of morphine every twenty-four hours. Ficke wrote:

> Now, Vincie darling—you are so much loved, so deeply loved, by so many people. . . . You would be quite wrong if you felt that you were lost in some private well of loneliness. It is not so.
>
> But darling, you are *sick*—you are just as sick as if you had been poisoned by the wrong mushroom. *You know that*, don't you?
>
> Dear Vincie, please do the thing which those who love you most want you to do. Try, with honest effort—with complete relinquishment of your personal will, for a few days—to be physical clay in the hands of those specialists whom Voorhuis suggests.

She and Arthur had discussed all of this before. She was afraid that the doctors would tamper with the spirit that made her poems, and even more terrified that they would use physical force on her—straitjackets or other restraints. "That is *utterly impossible*," Ficke assured her. "These are not State Troopers, but people who know who and what spirits such as yours are like. . . . They will undoubtedly expect from you a strict discipline, for a few days. . . . But what of it? . . . But, darling, *do it*! Please!!!!!!"

But she refused to enter the clinic then, thinking that she could go off the drugs without help, in her own way. By October 20 she had reduced her morphine intake by 25 percent, and by November 5 she had cut it in half. On November 6 her notebook records: "Misery, loss of courage," even though she was taking up to 4.5 grains of codeine and three tablets of Nembutal per day to compensate for the morphine reduction.

On Friday, November 12, 1943, she wrote:

> Awake all night with a sore throat: no *fair*!—Last week it was a burned finger: the week before a sprained knee! How am I to give up taking morphine when I need it all the time for one darned thing after another? It must be hard enough *when it's just a habit*!

So as of that date she was still in denial. But the truth had begun to dawn on her. "Everybody says it's impossible unless you go to a hospital and have nurses injecting insulin and Lyoscine into you all day long." She was already injecting herself with insulin twice daily, a drug then used to treat depression.

By the end of that month she was back to taking three grains of morphine per day. There is a photograph of Millay and her husband dining outdoors under the trees one summer afternoon with an unidentified gentleman whose back is to the camera. Eugen, center, in an unbuttoned white shirt, is listening intently to the young man; although Millay is sitting on the right, the focus is upon her, in three-quarter profile. The fifty-one-year-old poet is wearing a loose, short-sleeved flower-print dress. She is leaning forward slightly, her right arm at rest on the table in reach of a full glass of wine and an empty plate. The classic profile is sharp and lovely, but the eyes are gone: She is nodding out—the nod of a junkie, neither alive nor dead but in an eternal twilight. Her body is shapeless in the dress, and the flabby, mottled left arm that falls from her sleeve is the arm of an old woman.

Eugen, in contrast, looks as youthful as he did at forty, despite the receding hairline. As he had written to her years before: "I will do anything. And I *can* do anything." He had asked Inez Milholland on her deathbed if he should follow her out of life. Now Eugen would make the same gesture toward his second wife. He would help her out of this drug habit if it killed him. He would join her in it. He would follow her into hell to be with her and to lead her out—if that was what it took—or they would both die there together.

His name begins to appear in the drug logs in 1943 and 1944, and although he outweighed her by sixty pounds, he never was able to take more than two grains per day, and he usually took less. In a green notebook she titled "From Misery to Victory" Ugin kept score. He increased his dosage, which he greatly enjoyed, and then, with steely discipline, he would reduce it to nothing. He had to admit this hurt like hell, but he did prove to her it could be done. She tried to follow his lead but she did not fare so well.

Meanwhile Millay was writing no poetry. She was doing not much of anything but sitting in her favorite armchair under the window in the parlor, in her cloth robe, waiting from hour to hour for her next dose of morphine, codeine, or Nembutal. On St. Patrick's Day 1944, she consumed five grains of morphine in various forms in a twenty-four-hour period, not including a pellet of Dilaudid, two of codeine, and many Nembutals.

In May 1944 the Writer's War Board asked her to write a poem for a special twenty-four-hour NBC broadcast that the company had secretly scheduled in anticipation of D day. Somehow she managed to compose a "Poem and Prayer for an Invading Army." On June 6, 1944, while America listened, the actor Ronald Colman read the poem over the airwaves:

> You who have stood behind them to this hour,
> move strong behind them now: let still
> the weary bones encase the indefatigable Will
>
> . . . .
>
> Oh Lord, all through the night, all through the day,
> keep watch over our brave and dear, so far away.
> Make us more worthy of their valor; and thy love.
>
> "Let them come home! Oh, let the battle, Lord, be brief,
> and let our boys come home!"

Colman's dramatic voice gave shape to the long, rambling prayer, which in terms of sheer poetic technique was little better than the "acres of bad poetry" that had been published in her last book. But the poem expressed the simple sentiments of millions of Americans whose sons, brothers, and husbands were facing death in the cause of freedom.

❧

In letters to friends written much later (including Edmund Wilson, in her published *Letters*, August 1946), Millay explained that her nervous breakdown in 1944 was the result of the war and five years of writing nothing but propaganda. "I can tell you from my own experience," she wrote to Wilson, "there is nothing on this earth which can so much get on the nerves of a good poet, as the writing of bad poetry. Anyway, finally, I cracked up under it." There was some truth to this. But the main reason for Millay's entering the hospital in 1944 is that her drug addiction had become a matter of life and death, and she finally realized it. Eugen, Arthur, and Millay's old friend Witter Bynner worked together to lead her into treatment. The eminent specialist Foster Kennedy had treated a family member of Bynner's, who put the Boissevains in touch with Dr. Kennedy.

She entered Doctors Hospital in Manhattan at the end of July. Ficke wrote to her on August 4 to say how deeply he felt for her and the misery she must be going through, "Yet I am happy about the situation as a whole. Foster Kennedy would not take your case unless he felt confident of the exact elements of the situation. . . . He simply has no time to waste on sinking ships."

Then on August 22, 1944, Ficke wrote: "From all I have ever heard and read, what you are going through right at this stage of the performance is, quite literally, the most excruciating misery that it is possible for the human consciousness to experience. . . . Well, don't you forget that everybody is aware of the intensity of your suffering, and of the deep fortitude of concentrated will that enables you to go on." The doctors told Eugen that she was doing superbly, and that they had no doubt that "her courage would be repaid by the complete wiping out of this nightmare condition."

She must have made for an inspiring figure as she rocked in her hospital room or walked the floors, flogging her memory, memorizing and declaiming page after page of poetry—Shelley's "Ode to the West Wind," Keats's "Eve of St. Agnes," poem after poem of Gerard Manley Hopkins:

> Love I was shewn upon the mountain-side
> And bid to catch Him ere the drop of day.
> See, Love, I creep and thou on wings dost ride:
> Love, it is evening now and thou away;
> Love, it grows darker here and thou art above;
> Love, come down to me if thy name be Love.
> (from "The Half-way House")

When Dr. Kennedy felt that she was physically out of danger at the end of September 1944, he discharged her from the hospital. Millay was still shaky and weak. Her orders were to get as much rest as possible and avoid all drugs and alcohol.

She did not realize until she got home that Arthur was dying—strangling from edema (closure of the throat from swelling of the surrounding tissue). He went into the hospital just as she was leaving. Ficke would stay there until after Christmas; then he was told he might live a year at best.

The trees at Steepletop put on their autumn colors; the leaves fell and the wind whirled them on the terrace. October and November dragged on, and the thing she feared even more than the drugs had befallen her. She could not write. She was afraid the drugs or the doctors had stolen her spirit, and that she would never write again. Arthur tried to reassure her, but the winter and spring passed by without her writing a line.

In the summer of 1945, she and Eugen drove to Ragged Island for the first time in many years. The writer Vincent Sheean came to visit. In his book about Millay, *The Indigo Bunting*, Sheean described her then as "a frightening apparition to many of us. Her temperament was so variable that it was impossible to tell what mood might overwhelm her next; and she was so painfully sensitive that any untoward phrase or sudden noise could thrust her into a private hell."

The poet was terrified that the Muses had abandoned her. Her critical standing had sunk so low that her royalties had dwindled and her books were going out of print. She and Eugen had taken out a second mortgage on Steepletop, they were selling some of Edna's holograph manuscripts, and, to her great dismay, they had to sell a Walt Kuhn painting of a clown that hung over the mantel—her favorite painting—for which she had paid "a king's ransom" in the 1930s. She feared she would succumb to alcohol and morphine. And she was horrified over Arthur Ficke's suffering.

Ficke's agony during the last months of his life was beyond imagining: "A hundred times a day and night you are driven into the extremes of panic as you choke and strangle in the effort to draw your next breath. Why I did not simply kill myself I do not really understand," he wrote to Edna. Eugen instructed him in the use of morphine, and saw to it that Ficke got what he needed.

Millay could not endure any sound as loud as the ringing of the telephone, so she had Eugen rip out the lines. On September 30, 1945, she wrote a one-page will in longhand, leaving everything to her husband unless he were to die first, in which case Norma was to be sole heir. The handwriting looks drunken—down-sloping, crabbed, suicidal—unlike any other existing specimen of Millay's penmanship. Norma was worried. She kept writing letters proposing various treatments for her sister, but Edna would not even allow her to visit. On a blue scrap of paper in her bedroom at Ragged Island Millay wrote: "I'm through. I'm not going to live just in order to be one day older tomorrow."

On October 27 Ficke wrote to Millay from Hudson City Hospital, thanking her for at last admitting that the sonnet "And you as well must die, beloved dust" had been written to him. "I like to think that your and my very strange, very fluctuant, profound love for each other has, in all these many years, been evocative of the very finest things in each of us, many a time."

And in a tiny script he wrote her one more letter, on November 8, 1945, thanking Vincent and Eugen for their kind care of his wife, Gladys.

> I myself am completely and utterly lost now, down a road where all I hope for is a *quick* turning. I do not repine about that: I have had a wonderful life: all I ask now is that life not torture me *too* long, before it lets me sleep.

Arthur Ficke died on November 30, 1945.

COURAGE

❧

On February 5, 1946, Millay reentered Doctors Hospital to undergo another round of detoxification treatments under Dr. Kennedy's care. This time her situation was even more serious than it had been before. A year later, she wrote of the experience in an unpublished letter to Kennedy.

In the doctor's office, she said to Eugen and Dr. Kennedy: "You see, I don't want to live." There was a long silence. Later she would write that she had meant to finish the sentence with "unless I can be cured"; she did not really want to die, but "out of regard for simple human dignity, unless I might again be a reasonable and decent person, it seemed preferable to be nothing." At the time, she was too tired to explain.

Kennedy asked her, "How much do you want to get well?"

"More than anything in the world," she replied, tearfully. And she was thinking, "How silly this all sounds. Not only melodramatic, but illogical. Obviously, if I do not want to live, then there is nothing in the world that I greatly want, not even to get well. How overwrought, how hysterical, how stupid I do sound."

Then she said to herself: "Well, old thing, you *are* overwrought, and probably you *are* hysterical. So, don't be any stupider than you have to be—since you can't talk sense, shut up."

Kennedy looked her in the eye and promised he would make her well.

"And the next thing I remember is falling out of bed. Which was reasonable. Because the bed was too high, and not broad enough, and I disliked it. So I fell out of it, and that was refreshing. From that moment I began to get well."

She stayed at Doctors Hospital until March 7. Millay was treated with large doses of scopolamine, which, according to her eye doctor, caused her to see double for months afterward. But when the time came to discharge the patient, Kennedy would not let her go home. He insisted that she go to the Hartford Retreat. She entered the psychiatric clinic against her will. She hated it, and after two months there she begged Eugen and the doctors to let her out so she could go home. Kennedy wrote to her saying she was still in grave danger but she did not answer him until long after she had left Hartford.

Your kind and anxious letter disconcerted me, even frightened me, but it could not persuade me. For I reflected "Dr. Kennedy himself has never been confined here against his will, as I am. His address has never been, as mine is, The Looney Bin Beautiful, care of The Alienist Eminent. He does not know how closer every minute I am being led to a nervous breakdown compared to which the one I had at Doctor's Hospital last summer would seem to be but a girlish giggling fit."

She went back to Steepletop, weary, nervous, but determined not to touch drugs or alcohol. The poet had promised Kennedy she would write him a report of her progress, on the anniversary of her discharge from Doctors Hospital. And on March 7, 1947, she honored her promise and wrote him a twenty-page letter, which is the source of this account. "A year ago today [I left]," she wrote, "and if it had not been for that terrible experience in Hartford, I should be quite well now." Her only explanation was a lengthy comic narrative about how she was denied sleep at Hartford: A nurse awakened her at every hour of the night to ask if she were sleeping, and to offer her Ovaltine. But it was obviously the affront to Millay's dignity, the vigilant concern of others that she might kill herself, that she could not tolerate. And she missed Eugen.

In 1947, after months at Ragged Island and Steepletop, she proudly reported to Kennedy, "I am strong and muscular and brown from months of swimming in the sea and working in the hot sun about the shore of our island. . . . I am clean of drugs now, and clean of alcohol; eight months without a drink, six months without even a drop of wine. . . ."

Her only bad habit now, she confessed, was her constant cigarette smoking. "But after all," she argued, "a person who has been as wicked as I have been, would feel a bit too naked perhaps, without at least one little vice to cover her."

❧

Somehow she had summoned the courage to vanquish her morphine habit. And in that same year of triumph the poet rediscovered the courage to create. She was writing poetry again, poetry of the first magnitude. Out of her battle with addiction and depression she wrote this sonnet:

> I will put Chaos into fourteen lines
> And keep him there; and let him thence escape
> If he be lucky; let him twist and ape
> Flood, fire and demon—his adroit designs

Will strain to nothing in the strict confines
Of this secret Order. Where in pious rape,
I hold his essence and amorphous shape,
Till he with Order mingles and confines.
Past are the hours, the years, of our duress,
His arrogance, our awful servitude:
I have him. He is nothing more or less
Than something simple not yet understood;
I shall not even force him to confess;
Or answer. I will only make him good.

She wrote poem after poem in 1946 and 1947, many of the finest verses that would appear in the posthumous book *Mine the Harvest*:

The courage that my mother had
Went with her, and is with her still:
Rock from New England quarried;
Now granite in a granite hill.

Cora had left Vincent a golden brooch, which she treasured; but she coveted "That courage, like a rock, which she / Has no more need of, and I have." Vincent claimed it, during these brief years when she lived for her poetry and for Eugen, who was overjoyed to have his wife back again, whole and healthy. And at last she was sure he was indeed the love of her life.

She wrote memos to herself: "Things I *must* do for Eugen, if I truly love him,—and I *do*, more than anybody ever loved anybody." The list includes "Even if I am suffering *TORMENT*, speak in the strong, gay, rich voice he loves, the voice of a person vitally interested in things. . . . Cry as little as possible, but *Never* whine!!!" She advises herself to go outdoors often. "Let Ugin *find* you outdoors, instead of *Still in Bed*, or in your SPECIAL CHAIR (Pah!—Old Woman!) in the drawing room." The list goes on, everything from washing her hair at least twice a week ("keep young, keep pretty, FOR UGIN!") to never bringing up an unpleasant subject while her husband "is feeling a little bit gay."

On February 2, 1948, Eugen kissed her good-bye, and drove off in his Buick to do errands. She wrote him a letter:

You've gone away and I'm lonesome. You've been gone a long time. It is at least one minute and a half. . . . I suppose I could write something. . . . I suppose I could just sit with my eyes closed and remember some of the beautiful poems I know by heart. But the minute I start remembering, I start remembering you, and you've been gone forever, and it will be at least two hours before you get back, and what do *I* care about the 'Ode to a Nightingale?'

She rarely saw anyone other than her husband. She had not seen Edmund Wilson in nineteen years. In August 1948, he and his wife Elena found themselves near Austerlitz, on the way to the Berkshire Music Festival. Wilson telephoned, and then he and his wife drove up the hill to Steepletop.

Eugen greeted them, shuffling in his moccasins, "graying and stooped," according to Wilson in his memoir "Epilogue, 1952." In the Boissevains' living room Wilson found the same furnishings he had seen in 1929, the frightening "Ethiopian Sappho," on its heavy marble pedestal, her black irises making the whites of Sappho's eyes glow, and an Indian tapestry of golden birds on a green background. But the birds had faded. He found the furniture badly worn, and "the whole place seemed shabby and dim."

Outside the parlor window stood three oil drums on which the poet had set out seeds to attract the birds she studied and catalogued in her notebook.

When Millay entered, wearing slacks and a white working shirt, open at the neck, Wilson hardly recognized her.

> She had become somewhat heavy and dumpy, and her cheeks were a little florid. Her eyes had a bird-lidded look that I recognized as typically Irish. . . . She was terribly nervous; her hands shook; there was a look of fright in her bright green eyes.

Eugen made martinis for everyone. So, although Millay had given up drugs, she had resumed social drinking. Wilson observed that Eugen "would baby her in a way that I had not seen him use before but that had evidently become habitual." She talked about the war poetry she had written. "She knew she had deserved the reviews she got, but had been hurt by them nevertheless." Edna showed her old friend some new, unfinished poems, all "of an almost unrelieved blackness," and she discussed her efforts to translate Catullus. With the martini, her nervousness wore off, as did Wilson's feeling of strangeness. He asked Edna to read aloud so that Elena could hear her. After some coaxing, Millay began to recite "The Poet and His Book":

> Stranger, pause and look;
> From the dust of ages
> Lift this little book,

Turn the tattered pages,
Read me, do not let me die!

Wilson recalled that the room became so charged with pathos that he could hardly endure it. Although Elena believed they should have stayed a little longer, Edmund, with regrets, insisted on bidding the Boissevains adieu. Later he understood that he had felt the presence of death in the house.

In the summer of 1949, an unthinkable thing happened—Eugen got sick, very suddenly. After undergoing X-ray exams in Albany, he drove with Edna to Boston where doctors at Deaconess Hospital confirmed a diagnosis of cancer in his right lung. On Friday, August 26, surgeons removed the diseased lung, and the prognosis was hopeful, but just when it appeared he was recovering satisfactorily, he had a stroke. Eugen died of a cerebral hemorrhage on August 29. Three days later he was cremated at Forest Hills Cemetery, Jamaica Plains, Massachusetts. He was sixty-nine years old.

Millay fell apart, and had to return to Doctor's Hospital. After staying more than a month there, she insisted on going home, alone. Norma Millay Ellis and Cass Canfield (Millay's last editor at Harper's) were loathe to allow the widow to return to Steepletop all by herself, but there was really nothing anyone could do to make her change her mind. She promised everyone that she was not going to commit suicide.

❧

She had the telephone service reinstalled, so she could keep in touch with family and friends that way if she wished. Watching her diet carefully, she took vitamin supplements, and drank lots of orange juice. She saw to it the shabby furniture in the parlor was reupholstered, the floors were refinished, and the kitchen was rebuilt. But she declined to receive visitors.

The poet continued to work, daily, on her new book of verse and revising William Rose Benét's introductions to new editions of *The Buck in the Snow* and *Second April*. She translated Latin and kept up her correspondence. She saw almost no one but the postmistress, Mary Herron, and John Pinnie, the old family retainer, who brought her mail and firewood and groceries. For a while Herron wrote Millay's checks for her, and answered the hundreds of letters of condolence that arrived after Eugen's death.

Holidays were difficult. Millay wrote to Cass Canfield that she wasn't sure how she could get through "the first Thanksgiving Day I had ever spent all alone." She dealt with the holidays "by simply by-passing them. . . . The only thing I did by way of observance, was to sit at the piano on Christmas Eve, and play and sing some Christmas Carols." On New Year's Eve, 1949, she telephoned Eugen's family in Holland.

On March 29, 1950, she wrote in her journal, in a firm, strong hand, that washing dishes, and keeping her new kitchen spotless, and "trying to wangle enough heat into my bathroom to be able to take a bath without having to break the ice to get out of it. . . . & much business to attend to of which I know nothing at all—all added up together makes a full-time job." But she was proud she had managed so well. "I have done it. So far, it is seven months ago today that Eugen died. How I have lived through these seven months without cracking up or going all to pieces, I don't know. It is more terrible than anything I could ever possibly have imagined."

Millay was terrified of the spring, "shrinking from being hurt too much," she wrote to Herron. "I have already encountered the first dandelion. I stood and stared at it with a kind of horror. And then I felt ashamed of myself, and sorry for the dandelion. And suddenly, without my doing anything about it at all, my face just crumpled up and cried. How excited he always was when he saw the first dandelion!"

"Alas, alas, and alas," she continued. Admiring the budding trees at Steepletop, she wrote in her notebook the fragment: "I will control myself, or go inside. / I will not flaw perfection with my grief. / Handsome, this day: no matter who has died."

Millay maintained her correspondence with Norma, Cass, Tess Root, and many others, usually assuming a brave, lighthearted tone. In August 1950, she informed Tess that Ragged Island was not for sale because "as soon as I can bear it, I shall go back there. Possibly next summer." She told Cass proudly that summer that she had received a handsome commission to write a Thanksgiving poem for the *Saturday Evening Post*, and she was working diligently on it.

> Hard, hard it is, this anxious autumn,
> To lift the heavy mind from its dark forebodings,
> To sit at the bright feast, and with ruddy cheer
> Give thanks for the harvest of a troubled year.

She was thinking not only of her own trouble, but also of the war in Korea.

> God bless the harvest of this haggard year;
> Pity our hearts, that did so long for Peace. . . .
> Let us give thanks for the courage that was always ours
> And pray for the wisdom which we never had.

She took tablets of Seconal. And when the leaves turned red and gold after the summer she drank wine or gin whenever the heartache was more than she could endure. On October 18, she worked all day and into the night making editorial comments and corrections upon some new translations of Catullus that Rolfe Humphries had done. Before retiring for the night she left a note on the kitchen table for the housekeeper, to please not heat the iron too hot or it will scorch the bedsheets.

The next afternoon, John Pinnie was hauling in wood for the parlor fireplace when he saw Millay on the landing at the bottom of the stairs, collapsed like a marionette, her head at an impossible angle, her eyes staring. Pinnie said, "There was blood everywhere." She smelled heavily of alcohol. Evidently she had fallen from the top of the stairs and broken her neck. The fifty-eight-year-old woman had probably been lying there since the night before.

For Eugen's first wife, Millay had written the line that marks her own stone in Poets' Corner at the Cathedral of St. John the Divine: *Take up the song; forget the epitaph.*

EPILOGUE

Norma and Charles Ellis held a modest funeral service for the poet in her parlor at Steepletop on October 21, 1950. Mostly neighbors attended, making a group of twenty-seven in all, including Mary Herron, John Pinnie, the LaBranches, and the McKees. The only other family member present was Edna's "Auntie Clem" from Maine, Cora's sister. There were no poets, or clergy, present.

Norma read several of her sister's poems, and Allan Ross Macdougall read others. At the end of the ceremony, Tess sat down at Edna's ebony Steinway and played Beethoven's "Appassionata" sonata.

Millay was cremated at the Gardner Earl Memorial Chapel and Crematorium in Troy, New York, on October 23, 1950, and her ashes were interred with her husband's in the mountain laurel grove at Steepletop, a few yards away from Cora's grave under the pines and hemlocks.

Norma and Charles moved to Steepletop. There she managed the farm and the literary estate, preserving and arranging her sister's papers with an eye to writing the definitive biography, and authorizing rights and permissions for the poems and plays. Requests for permissions came in a flood, but Norma, an indifferent businesswoman, often ignored them. With Allan Macdougall she edited the *Letters* (1952), and in 1954 she edited the volume of poems *Mine the Harvest* that Millay had been preparing when she died.

Although Norma lived in the farmhouse until her death in 1986, she preserved her sister's residence much as it had been on the night she died in 1950. Norma occupied the poet's bedroom, while Charlie inherited Eugen's in the adjacent wing. But she never so much as cleared Edna's clothing and shoes out of her closet or from the chest of drawers next to the bed. She did not move a brush, or a mirror, or a picture on the wall. According to friends, Norma "camped" there, using the adjacent bathroom as her clothes closet, hanging her own garments on the shower curtain rod over the tub.

Charles Ellis retired from the stage, but continued to enjoy painting in oils in his studio at Steepletop until his death in 1976.

Witter Bynner regretted that he could not attend the funeral. Despite his failing eyesight, the venerable poet continued to write and publish several distinguished volumes of prose and verse before his death in 1968. These included a memoir of D. H. Lawrence and his wife, whom Bynner had known in New Mexico, called *Journey with Genius* (1951), and a collection of *New Poems* (1960).

George Dillon served as editor of *Poetry: A Magazine of Verse* (Chicago) until 1949. He still lived with his parents in Richmond; when his father retired from business in 1953, Dillon followed his mother and father to Charleston, South Carolina. He worked on translations of poetry and drama from the French, publishing *Three Plays of Racine* in 1961. He never married. When the bachelor died in Charleston in 1968, the local *News and Courier* reported that he had lived in such seclusion that "not many of his neighbors knew of him." The last existing photo of him, on his driver's license, shows a withered, long-faced, owlish man, completely bald, who looks as if he has seen precious little daylight. After his Pulitzer Prize–winning collection of 1931, Dillon never published another book of verse.

Challedon, "Pride of Maryland," entered stud in 1943 in Kentucky, was syndicated for $250,000 in 1948, and remained in the Bluegrass State until he died in 1958. He was inducted into the Thoroughbred Racing Hall of Fame in 1977, with Brann as sole owner.

Edmund Wilson went on to publish many more books of essays, plays, memoirs, and diaries, including *The Scrolls from the Dead Sea* (1955), *Patriotic Gore: Studies in the Literature of the American Civil War* (1962), and *Upstate: Records and Recollections of Northern New York* (1971). He died in 1972.

Millay's poems, in many editions, are still in print, and her play *Aria da Capo* continues to be produced all over the world. *Mine the Harvest*, the book she was working on when she died, received respectful, if not enthusiastic, reviews when it came out in 1954, during the heyday of the New Criticism. The publication of *Collected Poems* two years later sparked a Millay revival, inspiring tributes in *The New Republic* and the *New York Times*.

The Edna St. Vincent Millay Society, founded in 1978 as a nonprofit educational organization, is dedicated to preserving the literary work, personal belongings, and real property of Millay for the enjoyment of present and future generations. Steepletop is today a National Historic Landmark. Under the stewardship of the society, Millay's house and gardens at the site are in the process of being restored.

NOTES

❧

Sources clearly cited in the text are not listed below. Except where otherwise indicated, quotes from unpublished letters, journals, diaries, and poems come from the unprocessed Millay papers at the Library of Congress. Sources named below also include the Berg Collection at the New York Public Library, the Millay Collection at the White Hall Inn in Camden, Maine, and the *Letters of Edna St. Vincent Millay* edited by Allan Ross Macdougall. Until now those edited letters have been the chief source of information on Millay's life. The initials ESVM refer to Edna St. Vincent Millay.

Love o' Dreams

3–5   Diaries of ESVM, April 3–October 3, 1911.

Cora

6   Certificate of Divorce, Supreme Judicial Court Knox County, Maine, no. 5264, January term, 1904.

6–10   From Cora Millay's unpublished memoir *Millay Country*.

10   ESVM, "To live alone like that . . ." Undated memoir "Copied from Notebook in Cabin."

11   *Millay Country*.

11–12   ESVM, diary, July 19, 1908.

School Days and Stage Lights

14–15   The story of Frank Wilbur, *Downeast Magazine* p. 48, n.d. circa 1970, clipping in White Hall Inn Collection.

15   *Millay Country*. Tibbetts quote comes from *Downeast*, July 1962.

17   "My soul is too big . . ." Diary, July 20, 1910.

18–19   Source is contemporary playbills and diary entries.

21   Stella Derry and Eleanor Gould as interviewed for *Downeast Magazine*, clipping in White Hall Inn Collection.

22   Diary, April 26, 1909.

24–35   *Millay Country*.

29–32   ESVM, Diary of 1910.

Little Girl Grown Up

33   ESVM, Diary of 1910.

41   Diary, May 3, 1911.

42   Allan Ross Macdougall, *Letters of Edna St. Vincent Millay* (New York: Harper & Brothers, 1952), p. 10.

44   ESVM, Diary, October 10, 1911.

45   "I will send out my love . . ." Diary, October 3, 1911.

46   *Letters*, p. 42. The poem was first published in *The Vassar Miscellany* in July 1914 with the stage directions. In subsequent printings these were eliminated.

Renascence

49   "I am frightened." Diary, January 24, 1912.

53   Re: divorce, letter from Cora Millay to Sister Sue, January 10, 1929.

54   ESVM, Diary, March 1 and 2, 1912.

56–58   ESVM to "Dear Children" (mother and sisters) March 17, 1912.

59   "A dear place . . ." Diary, April 1, 1912.

60   "Essay on Faith," from Notebook of 1911.

61   ESVM, Diary, May 27, 1912; "My love for you . . ." Diary, February 11, 1912.

62   "to reach just such budding geniuses . . ." Ferdinand Earle to ESVM, August 14, 1912; "Second Letter" of Earle's is quoted in ESVM's letter to Gladys Niles, August 12, 1912, White Hall Inn Collection.

62   ESVM to Gladys Niles, October 1912, White Hall Inn Collection; "It doesn't matter in the least . . ." Undated letter, ESVM to Earle, in the Library of Congress Collection.

63   *the end of his marriage* . . . Letter from Ferdinand Earle to Eugen Boissevain, June 18, 1940.

64   ESVM, Diary, August 29–September 3, 1912.

65   "It was the most wonderful thing." Diary, September 3, 1912; "The Lyric Year is to come out . . ." Diary, October 25, 1912.

67   "I realized it was . . ." *Letters*, p. 18; "Renaissance is the best thing," Diary, November 14, 1912.

The Whirlpool of Eros

71–75   Except where indicated, all quotes are from ESVM, Diary of 1913.

74–75   Conversation with Bynner is taken from *Letters*, p. 36.

76–77   Information on Arthur Hooley comes from *Who's Who in America*, vol. 9, 1916–1917, edited by Albert Nelson Marquis (Chicago: A. N. Marquis), p. 1199.

77   "hunted up the page . . ." Diary, January 6, 1913; data on Kennerley comes from Christine Stansell, *American Moderns* (New York: Metropolitan Books, 2000), pp. 157–59; and from Matthew J. Bruccoli, *The Fortunes of Mitchell Kennerley, Boookman* (New York: Harcourt Brace, 1986).

79   Description of Hooley comes from a photo enclosed in a letter from him to ESVM, March 1, 1916.

80   "told Fritz . . ." Diary, August 10, 1913.

81   Henry Noble MacCracken, *The Hickory Limb* (New York: Charles Scribner & Sons, 1950), quoted by Jean Gould in *The Poet and Her Work* (New York: Dodd, Mead, 1969), p. 53.

82   "I hate this pink-and-gray college . . ." *Letters*, pp. 48–49.

83   ESVM to Norma Millay, n.d., autumn 1913.

87   ESVM to Arthur Hooley (a.k.a. Charles Vale).

87–88   "In you there are so many beautiful possibilities," ESVM to Hooley, October 6, 1915; "Don't sit there, Edna," ESVM to Hooley, February 3, 1916; "saturated," ESVM to Hooley, January 1, 1916; "One can get on . . ." Ibid.

89   "Don't do that, Edna . . ." Ibid.

90–91   ESVM to "Dear Family," September 17, 1914.

The Sappho of North Hall

92　　"I felt *perfectly* at home . . ." ESVM to family, March 8, 1915.

94　　Vincent and Katharine Tilt's tea, Diary, December 6, 7, 1913.

95　　"Reunion dance." Diary, December 12, 13, 1913.

97　　"I recline there . . ." ESVM, letter to sisters.

97　　"Hello Princess," Ibid.; "And I have more dinner dates . . ." Ibid.; Her room looked like a florist's shop, Letter ESVM to family March 8, 1915.

98　　"Bad Vincent . . ." ESVM to family, October 29, 1914.

101　　"I think of you . . ." Isobel Simpson to ESVM, August 9, 1917.

102　　"Tired to death . . ." ESVM to Arthur Hooley, February 3, 1916.

102–3　　"I am *cursed* . . ." Diary, March 3, 1913; "*ravishing* to behold . . ." ESVM to Arthur Hooley, February 3, 1916; "It really isn't necessary . . ." ESVM to Arthur Hooley, February 28, 1916.

103　　"This is a strange place . . ." Ibid.

105　　"It was very real to me . . ." ESVM to Arthur Hooley, March 13, 1916.

105　　"Edna, Edna, even if you *had* cared . . ." Arthur Hooley to ESVM, March 1916; "My time and thoughts . . ." ESVM to Arthur Hooley, July 25, 1916.

110　　*She and Arthur had worked out* . . . Ibid.

The Goddess

112　　Biographical data on Salomón de la Selva comes from the *Oxford Companion to Spanish Literature.*

113　　"You must be beautiful . . ." Salomón de la Selva to ESVM, September 7, 1915.

114　　"Love, why do you build . . ." Ibid.

115　　"I wish, once and for all . . ." Salomón to ESVM, November 11, 1916; "I have received from England . . ." Ibid.

116　　"One might take her . . ." Ibid, March 2, 1918.

116　　"I was thinking . . ." Ibid, December 6, 1917. *"Linda!"* Ibid, n.d., winter 1917.

117　　"I have a scheme . . ." ESVM to Cora, June 25, 1917. "Don't you suppose Mother . . ." *Letters*, p. 68.

119　　"followed her back to the Inn . . ." Eberhart in *Selected Poems*, "Forward," p. xii, edited by Colin Flack (New York: HarperCollins, 1991).

120　　"I flopped in a faint . . ." ESVM to Cora, September 22, 1917.

120　　"Oh, you're a wonder . . ." *Letters*, p. 80.

The Village

123　　"a serious affair . . ." Floyd Dell, *Homecoming* (New York: Farrar & Rinehart, 1933), p. 243.

123–27　　All quotes from Dell about his life and thought, and data about his career, comes from *Homecoming*, pp. 243–309.

124　　"He took her to the theater and to dinner . . ." Norma Millay to Cora, December 1, 1917.

125　　"Three days after . . ." Ibid.; "Unpublished interview" Anne Cheney, *Millay in Greenwich Village* (The University of Alabama Press, 1975), p. 64.

127　　"We always quarrel . . ." Dell to ESVM, n.d.

131　　"The most extraordinary," Edmund Wilson, *Shores of Light* (New York: Random House, 1952), p. 760; "even more than Edna . . ." Ibid.

132　　"A poet with the profile . . ." Britten, p. 43.

132　　Description of the apartment comes from ESVM letter to Kathleen Millay, February 25, 1918, in the Berg Collection of the New York Public Library.

133   "No less a person . . ." Ibid.

134   "I did not know . . ." Arthur Ficke to ESVM, n.d. The letter was preserved in an unpostmarked envelope addressed to 156 Waverly Place. This leads to an intriguing question about the date of composition.

135   "A large mouth . . ." *Letters*, pp. 99–100.

138   "The whole show . . ." Ficke to ESVM, October 28, 1918.

139–40   "Her landlord . . ." Maurice Hale to ESVM, December 12, 1918; information about Millay's schedule and income comes from Cora's diary; "You know the one . . ." *Letters*, p. 90.

141   "the most beautiful . . ." Alexander Woollcott, *New York Times*, December 14, 1919, sec. 8, p. 2.

142   "Through all the trial . . ." Jim Lawyer to ESVM, January 6, 1920.

143   "Edna, don't ever doubt . . ." Ibid., January 9, 1920.

144   "I am telling everyone . . ." Ibid., n.d.

144   "that poor fish . . ." ESVM to Dearest Family, February 26, 1920.

Ménage à Trois

146   "I have never made . . ." ESVM to Dearest Family, February 26, 1920.

146   "I am becoming very famous . . ." *Letters*, p. 101.

147   Details of Nevins's party, Edmund Wilson, *The Shores of Light*, p. 748; "he was still . . ." Jeffrey Meyers, *Edmund Wilson* (Boston: Houghton Mifflin, 1995), p. 60.

147–48   All quotes from Wilson are from *The Shores of Light*, pp. 746–57.

149   "With a polite exchange . . ." Edmund Wilson, *The Twenties* (New York: Farrar, Straus & Giroux, 1975), pp. 64–65.

149   "Choir Boys of Hell," Ibid, p. 65; "Edna ignited," Ibid, p. 64; "She did not reject," *Shores of Light*, p. 764.

150   "I don't know what to write . . ." *Letters*, pp. 98–99; "My subsequent chagrin" and following Wilson quotes from *Shores of Light*.

150   John Peale Bishop to ESVM, June 5, 1920.

151   "For God's sake . . ." Bishop to ESVM, November 1920; "The Great Queen," Wilson, *The Twenties*, p. 65.

152   "& another small nervous breakdown . . ." *Letters*, p. 105; "We were both afraid . . ." *Shores of Light*, p. 769; "such a lovely book . . ." *Letters*, p. 113.

154   Llewelyn Powys to ESVM, December 16, 1920 and December 20(?), 1920.

155   "If I live to be eighty . . ." Powys to ESVM, December 31, 1920.

Europe

158   Edmund Wilson, *Letters on Literature and Politics 1912–1972* (New York: Farrar, Straus & Giroux, 1977), p. 67.

160   "I knew she was not . . ." *The Twenties*, p. 92; "It is wicked and useless . . ." *Letters*, p. 133; "It is true I love . . ." *Letters*, p. 142; "We should make . . ." *Letters*, p. 144.

163   "A long time . . ." *Letters*, p. 118; "Your letter put things . . ." Ibid. p. 146.

164   *Norma Millay Ellis told her friend Elizabeth Barnett* . . . Author's Interview with Elizabeth Barnett, Steepletop, October 12, 2000.

Marriage

168 Information about Eugen Boissevain comes from his obituaries, *New York Times*, August 31, 1949, p. 23; Max Eastman's *The Enjoyment of Living* (New York: Harper & Row, 1948); and *Love and Revolution* (New York: Random House, 1964).

169 Information about Inez Milholland comes from "To Inez Milholland," Memorial Service Notes, 1917, Library of Congress Collection.

170 "No, you go ahead . . ." Max Eastman, *Enjoyment of Living*, p. 572.

171 Boissevain's book collection is in the library at Steepletop; "a strain of something feminine . . ." Eastman, Ibid., p. 164.

172 "high bright gaiety . . ." Miriam Gurko quoting F.P.A. in *Restless Spirit* (New York: Thomas Y. Crowell, 1962), p. 152.

172 "The book is . . ." ESVM, "Elinor Wylie's Poems," *New York Evening Post Literary Review*, January 28, 1922; "I did not know . . ." *vide* note on page 134 re: Arthur Ficke to ESVM, n.d.

173 From Floyd Dell's *Homecoming*.

174 "Eugen and Edna," Ibid., p. 308.

175 "What were once mountains . . ." Norma Millay quoted in news clipping "Edna St. V. Millay Is Wed," n.d., Library of Congress Collection.

175 "I ain't going to bust," *Letters*, p. 174.

177 Accounts of the wedding and operation include *New York Times*, July 19, 1923; *New York Evening Journal, Daily News*, n.d.; *New York Evening Telegram*, July 19, 1923.

177 "Well, if I die now . . ." Gurko, *Restless Spirit*, p. 155.

179 Boissevain letter is undated.

180 "I suppose it is a mean pride . . ." *Letters*, p. 177.

181 "Somehow, ever since . . ." *Letters*, p. 178; "Hers is the naked . . ." *Times Literary Supplement*, June 26, 1924.

182 Allan Ross Macdougall, an old friend of Millay's, wrote the much-quoted article "Husband of a Genius" for *Delineator*, October 1934.

183 Information on Millay's tour comes from the *New York World*, February 18, 1924; "This is a desolate place . . ." ESVM to Boissevain, Jan 20 (?), 1924.

183 "Oh Jesus, if ever . . ." ESVM to Boissevain, January 30, 1924; "My hands are so dirty . . ." *Letters* p. 180; "wistful, appealing . . ." *Rochester Democrat & Chronicle*, February 15, 1924.

185 "At times the reading . . ." *Rochester Democrat & Chronicle*, February 15, 1924.

185 "Marriage, if not abused . . ." Ibid.

Steepletop

187 Details about Steepletop come from direct observation and from Form 10–300, U.S. Dept. of Interior National Park Service National Register of Historic Places Inventory Nomination Form, "Steepletop."

189 "She must not . . ." Macdougall, "Husband of a Genius."

190 Joan Dash, *A Life of One's Own* (New York: Harper & Row, 1973), p. 169.

191 Harper's Royalty Statement, May 1, 1929.

191 *That winter she wrote to her mother,* ESVM to Cora, January 6, 1927; "There will be at least four . . ." Ibid.; "It is almost incontestable . . ." *The New Yorker*, February 26, 1927, p. 61; *vide* March 5, 1927, pp. 68–69.

192 ESVM, Diary, March 11, and 12, 1927.

195   "great flat-footed..." ESVM, Diary, April 11, 1927; "she is the foulest..."
       August 18, 1927; "The only people..." October 3, 1927.

Fatal Interview

199   "We never quarrel..." ESVM, Diary, March 26, 1934; "a vow of..." Max East-
       man *The Enjoyment of Living*, pp. 521–22.

201   Hardy's comment comes from Gurko, *Restless Spirit*, p. 216; Housman's comes
       from his letter to Sir Sidney Cockerell of January 15, 1932, as quoted in a letter
       from Carl Weber to ESVM, March 14, 1941.

201   Information on George Dillon comes from "Reflection by unnamed friend of
       family," n.d. (circa 1935) in the George Dillon Collection, Syracuse University
       Library; *Chicago Sunday Times*, May 8, 1932; *Twentieth-Century Authors* (Bronx:
       H. W. Wilson, 1942), pp. 381–82; "A Poet of the Wind and Stars," by Robert
       Hazlemere, (British Columbia) *Colonist* (newspaper), November 5, 1928, in Dillon
       Collection; "Here and There with Home Folks," by Francele Armstrong in (Hen-
       derson, KY), *Gleaner and Journal*, April 28, 1940; and obituaries in *New York
       Times*, May 12, 1968; (Charleston) *News and Courier*, May 27, 1968; "quite the
       thrill of discovery..." quoted by Armstrong, in *Gleaner and Journal*.

201   "There is a story," n.d., unsigned clipping in Library of Congress; "Tenderly,
       wistfully..." clipping from a Los Angeles newspaper, 1928, "Edna Millay Reads."

202   "The sonnet form..." Ibid.; "Already her voice..." Ibid.; squeezed the wrist,
       Gladys Campell paraphrased by Mary Oliver, *Blue Pastures* (San Diego: Harcourt
       Brace, 1995), p. 80.

210   "I want to sit..." ESVM to George Dillon, December 29, 1928.

211   "My darling, forget..." Ibid., February 21, 1929.

212   "Everybody wants to give..." Ibid., April 25, 1929; "and I was trembling..."
       Ibid.

213   "Miss Millay wants..." Boissevain to Eugene Saxton, May 15, 1930, Berg Col-
       lection, New York Public Library.

214   *Vide* John Crowe Ransom's "The Poet as Woman" in *The World's Body* (New
       York: Charles Scribner Sons, 1938), pp. 76–110.

215   "Two were written..." ESVM to George Dillon, n.d. (end of 1929).

215   "I shall never kiss..." Ibid., n.d., (August?) 1929.

218   "You should have known..." Ibid. November 15, 1930.

218   "Poor child..." Ibid., November 19, 1930.

The Mountain Laurels

219   *Cora had visited*... ESVM to Norma Ellis, June 15, 1929.

219   "If I get anywhere near you..." ESVM to Cora, n.d.; "Things all around..."
       Boissevain to Cora, n.d.

220   The story of Cora's death comes mostly from ESVM letter to Kathleen, February
       18, 1931, the Berg Collection.

221   "Baby, my typewriter..." ESVM to Kathleen, February 6, 1931, Berg Collection.

221–22 The story of Cora's burial comes from Boissevain's letter to Powys, n.d., but just
       after burial.

225   Robinson Jeffers to ESVM, October 31, 1931.

226   O'Keeffe to ESVM, August 17, 1931.

Paris or Steepletop

229　Details of Eugen's departure: from his letter of May 10, 1932, to ESVM.

229–31　The story of Eugen's rescue of Venys is from *L'Intransigeant*, March 14, 1932, and Floyd Dell's account of the incident in the *New York Herald Tribune*, March 19, 1933. Dell split his $500 fee with Eugen.

232　"Rainbows on the starboard . . ." Boissevain to ESVM, May 10, 1932.

233　"Here is Dr. Lambert's . . ." Ibid., May 25, 1932.

236　"The daisies and heliotropes . . ." Ibid., June 28, 1932; "Edna, darling . . ." Ibid., July 1, 1932.

236　"I lost 12 pounds . . ." Ibid., June 11, 1932.

238　"Let's try to be . . ." Ibid., July 1, 1932; "I wonder what you mean . . ." Ibid., July 4, 1932.

239　"You poor kid . . ." Ibid.

The Last Love Poems

240　"Gather driftwood . . ." ESVM to Powys, *Letters*, p. 237.

241　Millay's weekend with Dillon: Diary, March of 1934; "I wish I could be kept under morphine . . ." Ibid., April 22, 1934.

243　"If you wish to hurt . . ." ESVM to Powys, *Letters*, p. 256.

244　"as if directly inside his ear . . . you see now . . ." Ficke's poem "Hospital," quoted by Gould, p. 236; "at least six cocktails . . ." ESVM to Ficke, *Letters*, p. 292.

245　"never again bother you . . ." Ficke to ESVM, September 26, 1937.

246　"I never worked so hard. . . ." ESVM to Powys, *Letters*, p. 279; "but with those . . ." ESVM to Herbert C. Lipscomb, Ibid., p. 284; "hurled out . . ." ESVM to "friend," *Letters*, p. 282.

Challedon

249　"I have no time . . ." ESVM to Eugene Saxton, May 20, 1937.

249–55　All data concerning Challedon and William L. Brann, other than what comes from the quoted correspondence between ESVM and Brann, is from Cindy Deubler, "Challedon, Pride of Maryland," *The Maryland Horse*, April 1989.

251　"the money you will have . . ." W. L. Brann to ESVM, November 29, 1937; "Why was not Challephen . . ." ESVM to Brann, November 19, 1937.

252　"You want, as you never . . ." ESVM to Brann, February 2, 1939. "Peplum is by . . ." Ibid.; "We've got to aim high . . ." Ibid.

253　"I have every hope . . ." ESVM to Brann, December 8, 1937.

Little Nancy

255　"Exercize Will-Power . . ." ESVM memo, n.d., July 1942(?).

256　Letters from Kathleen in the Library of Congress, on which this account is based include: January 5, April 28, August 10, December 1, 1939; April 8, 1940; June 20, 1941; and others undated. They cannot be quoted.

257　"I did not wish to have . . ." Guion letter to Boissevain, September 24, 1940; a patient at New Haven Hospital, invoices from New Haven (Connecticut) Hospital, and receipts, paid April 27, 1940, and June 27, 1940; "The outrage of unalleviated pain . . ." *Letters*, p. 312.

258　"not poems, posters . . ." ESVM to Dillon, *Letters*, p. 309; "acres of bad poetry . . ." ESVM to Sister Ste. Helene, *Letters*, p. 310.

258   Pharmacological information provided by Dr. Robert Liner; "Seldom has the morphine . . ." *Letters*, 314; Millay's exact drug dosages are recorded in a red notebook marked "Agrico Drug Log" (May and June 1942); green notebook, "From Misery to Victory" (April 4–May 11, 1944); and unnamed brown Parallex spiral binders referring to May to August 1944, September to November 1943.

260   "It just wasn't radio . . ." Norma Ellis to ESVM, October 28, 1942; "Care for nothing . . ." ESVM memo, n.d.

261   Eugen wrote to Norma, October 25 (?), 1942; "at any mention . . ." Norma Ellis to Ann Eckert, October, 1943; information about Kathleen's death comes from an undated (and unmailed) letter from Norma to ESVM, written circa October 1943, also *New York Times* obituary, September 23, 1943.

265   "a frightening apparition . . ." Vincent Sheean, *The Indigo Bunting*, p. 35.

266   "a hundred times a day . . ." Ficke to ESVM, June 18, 1945; Eugen instructed him, memo from Ficke to Boissevain, n.d.

Courage

268   ESVM to Foster Kennedy, March 7, 1947.

269   "Things I *must* do . . ." ESVM memo, n.d.

271   Information about Eugen's death comes from *New York Times* obituary, August 31, 1949, and Forest Hills Cemetery Burial Certificate, September 1, 1949, no. 26302.

271   "the first Thanksgiving Day . . ." ESVM to Canfield, *Letters*, p. 365.

272   "shrinking from being hurt . . ." ESVM to Herron, *Letters*, p. 368; "as soon as I . . ." Ibid., p. 373; she took tablets of Seconal—*vide* invoices from the John T. Harper Drug Store, 1949–1950.

273   The details of Pinnie's discovery of Millay come from an interview with Elizabeth Barnett.

Epilogue

273   Details of Millay's funeral come from Norma's notes and guest list, October 21, 1950, and the *New York Herald Tribune*, October 23, 1950; Certificate of Cremation, Troy, New York, October 23, 1950, no. 45609.

274   Information on Norma and Charles Ellis comes from Elizabeth Barnett and Holly Peppe.

274   Information on George Dillon, *New York Times* obituary, May 12, 1968.

274   Challedon: Deubler, "Challedon, Pride of Maryland."

SELECTED BIBLIOGRAPHY

Books by Edna St. Vincent Millay

Renascence and Other Poems (New York: Mitchell Kennerley, 1917).
A Few Figs from Thistles: Poems and Four Sonnets, Salvo One (New York: Frank Shay, 1920. Enlarged editions, 1921, 1922).
Second April (New York: Mitchell Kennerley, 1921).
The Harp-Weaver and Other Poems (New York: Harper & Brothers, 1923).
The Buck in the Snow (New York: Harper & Brothers, 1928).
Edna St. Vincent Millay's Poems Selected for Young People (New York: Harper & Brothers, 1929).
Fatal Interview (New York: Harper & Brothers, 1931).
Wine from These Grapes (New York: Harper & Brothers, 1934).
Conversation at Midnight (New York: Harper & Brothers, 1937).
Huntsman, What Quarry? (New York: Harper & Brothers, 1939).
Make Bright the Arrows: 1940 Notebook (New York: Harper & Brothers, 1940).
The Murder of Lidice (New York: Harper & Brothers, 1942).
Mine the Harvest (New York: Harper & Brothers, 1954).
Collected Poems (New York: Harper & Brothers, 1956).
Translation, with George Dillon: *The Flowers of Evil* (New York: Harper & Brothers, 1936).

Plays by Edna St. Vincent Millay

Aria da Capo (Premiered in New York 1919, published by Mitchell Kennerley, 1921).
The Lamp and the Bell (New York: Frank Shay, 1921).
Two Slatterns and a King: A Moral Interlude (Cincinnati: Stewart Kidd, 1921).
The King's Henchman (New York: Harper & Brothers, 1927).
The Princess Marries the Page (New York: Harper & Brothers, 1932).

Books about Edna St. Vincent Millay

Atkins, Elizabeth. *Edna St. Vincent Millay and Her Times* (Chicago: University of Chicago Press, 1936).
Britten, Norman A. *Edna St. Vincent Millay* (New York: Twayne Publishers, 1967).
Cheney, Anne. *Millay in Greenwich Village* (University of Alabama Press, 1975).
Dash, Joan. *A Life of One's Own* (New York, Harper & Row, 1973).
Gould, Jean. *The Poet and Her Book* (New York: Dodd, Mead, 1969).
Gurko, Miriam. *Restless Spirit: The Life of Edna St. Vincent Millay* (New York: T. Y. Crowell, 1962).
Shafter, Toby. *Edna St. Vincent Millay, America's Best-Loved Poet* (New York: Julian Messner, 1957).

Sheean, Vincent. *The Indigo Bunting: A Memoir of Edna St. Vincent Millay* (New York: Harper & Brothers, 1951).

Yost, Karl. *A Bibliography of the Works of Edna St. Vincent Millay* (New York: Harper & Brothers, 1937).

ACKNOWLEDGMENTS

The author gratefully acknowledges the following individuals and institutions for their kindness and generosity.

First and foremost I would like to thank Elizabeth Barnett, literary executor of the Estate of Edna St. Vincent Millay, for her immediate and constant encouragement, and for granting me permission to study the unprocessed Millay papers at the Library of Congress. Ms. Barnett also was instrumental in securing permission to quote from those papers, as well as from Millay's published writings, without which this book would be a poor shadow of the poet's life and thought. I also want to thank Ms. Barnett for her hospitality at home in Cambridge, Massachusetts, and at Steepletop, where I was given the run of the place for as long as I needed to investigate the house, the grounds, the poet's library, her clothing and effects.

Next I would like to thank Dr. Alice Birney, the literary manuscript historian at the Library of Congress, for her swift and tireless efforts in making available to me the 20,000 uncatalogued, "unprocessed" items of the Millay Collection in Washington, D.C. I will never forget the patience of Dr. Birney and her staff, including Fred W. Bauman Jr., Jeffrey M. Flannery, Bruce Kirby, and Bradley E. Gernand. Not only did they help me to find boxes of documents when I required them, but Mr. Bauman and Mr. Flannery also solved knotty research problems. The Library's Millay Collection, acquired under Dr. Birney's direction, is the chief source of information for my book.

I am grateful to my agent Neil Olson, to my editor Jack Macrae, and his assistant Katy Hope for their bold support of this project from its inception.

I am also indebted to the New York Public Library, where I studied letters and manuscripts in the Berg Collection, which houses the papers left by Kathleen Millay. There Philip Milito and Diana Burnham were helpful to me in locating and copying letters and documents.

In Camden, Maine, librarian Ellen Dyer opened up the public library's Millay collection and was helpful in advising me about houses where the Millays had lived. William Hitchcock's diorama of Camden Harbor, circa

1920, enabled me to reconstruct the view from the tenement where Millay began "Renascence." Maggie and Chris Martin were moving into 82 Washington Street, where the poet finished "Renascence," on the day I stopped to inspect the house. They kindly let me in. Janet Dudson showed me the interior of the Camden Opera House. The Millay collection of the White Hall Inn contains significant Millay letters not to be found elsewhere. Preserved by the Dewing family, the Inn looks much as it did when Millay performed there in 1912. I am grateful to Wendy, Chip, Edward, and J. C. Dewing for their gracious hospitality during my stay in Camden.

Thanks to my friends and research assistants: Ann Marshall, for her excellent work with the George Dillon papers at Syracuse University Library; Neil Grauer and David Bergman for countless historical details; Michael Cataneo and Joseph Kelly for the history of Challedon; Dr. Robert Liner for medical and pharmaceutical history; biographer Jeffrey Meyers for much good advice; and the librarians at the research desk of the Enoch Pratt Library for miscellaneous facts. Scholar Holly Peppe, president of the Millay Society, was helpful in providing texts of fugitive poems and in answering questions about Millay's later poetry.

I want to thank Jonathon Bishop for permission to quote from his father's unpublished letters, Nan Sussmann for permission to quote George Dillon, and Peter Miller for help with photographs. Once again, I appreciate the many suggestions of Michael Yockel regarding prose style. Thanks are due to Rosemary Knower, the first reader of this book. Without her constantly pointing to ideas, facts, and feelings that lay outside my field of vision, my point of view would be a narrow chink in a colossal wall.

And finally, to my wife, Jennifer Bishop, I owe the strength that allowed me to finish this book during a difficult time.

INDEX

ABOUT THE AUTHOR

❧

*D*aniel Mark Epstein is an award-winning poet, essayist, playwright, translator, and biographer. He has won the Prix de Rome and a Guggenheim Fellowship and has been anthologized in many collections of essays and poetry. His books include biographies of Aimee Semple McPherson and Nat King Cole and seven volumes of poetry. He lives in Baltimore, Maryland.